Technology Literacy Applications in Learning Environments

David D. Carbonara
Duquesne University, USA

Information Science Publishing

Hershey • London • Melbourne • Singapore

Acquisitions Editor:	Renée Davies
Development Editor:	Kristin Roth
Senior Managing Editor:	Amanda Appicello
Managing Editor:	Jennifer Neidig
Copy Editor:	Maria Boyer
Typesetter:	Cindy L. Consonery
Cover Design:	Lisa Tosheff
Printed at:	Yurchak Printing Inc.

Published in the United States of America by
Information Science Publishing (an imprint of Idea Group Inc.)
701 E. Chocolate Avenue
Hershey PA 17033
Tel: 717-533-8845
Fax: 717-533-8661
E-mail: cust@idea-group.com
Web site: http://www.idea-group.com

and in the United Kingdom by
Information Science Publishing (an imprint of Idea Group Inc.)
3 Henrietta Street
Covent Garden
London WC2E 8LU
Tel: 44 20 7240 0856
Fax: 44 20 7379 3313
Web site: http://www.eurospan.co.uk

Library of Congress Cataloging-in-Publication Data

Technology literacy applications in learning environments / David Carbonara, editor.
p. cm.
Summary: "This book discusses the efficacy of instructional technology in various, global learning environments"--Provided by publisher.
Includes bibliographical references and index.
ISBN 1-59140-479-7 (hard) -- ISBN 1-59140-480-0 (softcover) -- ISBN 1-59140-481-9 (ebook)
1. Educational technology--Cross-cultural studies. 2. Education--Effect of technological innovations on--Cross-cultural studies. I. Carbonara, David, 1952-
LB1028.3.T39734 2005
371.33--dc22

2004029769

British Cataloguing in Publication Data
A Cataloguing in Publication record for this book is available from the British Library.

All work contributed to this book is new, previously-unpublished material. The views expressed in this book are those of the authors, but not necessarily of the publisher.

Technology Literacy Applications in Learning Environments

Table of Contents

Preface

This book is designed to present the reader with a view of technology literacy in a learning environment. As technologies evolve, it is postulated that technology literacy will also evolve. While word processing skills are important, the development of technology skills covers the areas of presentation software, storage, human interaction, and virtual reality. Further, the field of instructional technology is not merely concerned with point-and-click skills. Rather, instructional technology is dedicated to discovering and developing the pedagogical skills of teaching and learning in a technology-enhanced learning environment.

The book is divided into four sections. The first section discusses the defining aspects of instructional technology skills. The disciplines of sociology, psychology, and leadership form the foundation of the first chapter and create a framework to build a curriculum that evolves from knowledge to application to research skills.

The second section discusses the use of technology literacy in higher education. Students in higher education not only prepare for specific job classes, but also develop problem-solving skills and human interaction skills. The chapters in this section investigate the personality or *soft* skills necessary in the 21st century, but also how to change the university culture in order to enhance student learning and faculty teaching in these learning environments.

The third section begins a look at the problems that technology created for society. The rift between those with computer access and those without grows to create the digital divide. This section begins to look at this rift and how to bridge the gap.

The final section presents a series of examples and guides that promote instructional technology literacy. As the use of technology evolves, new literacies will develop. Multimedia and virtual reality are presented for the reader to examine the role these technologies play in the learning process. Further, the reader is encouraged to reflect on the these technologies as the "basic literacies" of the 21st century.

The book begins with a chapter by Lawrence A. Tomei, titled *The Pillars of Instructional Technology*. This chapter discusses the foundation of teaching and learning as it describes the pillars of psychology, sociology, history, and leadership. The chapter also describes the K-A-RPE model of Instructional Technology as it explains the Knowledge, Application, and Research categories of an IT program.

Klarissa Ting-Ting Chang and John Lim provide a meta-analysis of —how information technology is used in learning in the chapter titled, *The Role of Information Technology in Learning: A Meta-Analysis*. Sixty-eight experimental studies were conducted on the application of IT in the classroom. The authors calculated effect sizes and found effects that were moderated by several factors. Implications for further research are discussed.

Antonio Cartelli discusses the need for a widespread ICT literacy in mankind in his first work, titled *Computing and ICT Literacy: From Students' Misconceptions and Mental Schemes to the Monitoring of the Teaching-Learning Process*. Professor Cartelli discusses the development of ICT literacy and the problems that led to the digital divide.

In the next chapter, *Technology-Infused Instruction: A New Paradigm for Literacy,* Rose Mary Mautino and Stefan L. Biancaniello introduce a model of technology-infused literacy instruction. The model is based on the constructivist approach to teaching and learning. A paradigm shift is necessary to change our curriculum, ask new questions, and design new methods of teaching and learning.

Next, Professors Jennifer Sharkey and D. Scott Brandt discuss the integration of two diverse disciplines of technology literacy and information literacy in their chapter, titled *Integrating Technology Literacy and Information Literacy*. They argue that both issues must be addressed in order for students to be truly literate in the technology areas.

The next chapter contributes the work of Pamela M. Frampton, Michael S. Mott, Anastasia M. Trekles, Robert J. Colon, and Jerry P. Galloway from Purdue and Indiana University Northwest in a work titled, *Design, Management, and Evaluation of Online Portfolios: Matching Supply and Demand for Building-Level Educational Administrators.* This work discusses the practical issues of implementing electronic portfolios.

Ann Monday and Sandra Barker contributed their chapter, *Developing Graduate Qualities Through Information Systems and Information Technology Literacy Skills*, from the University of South Australia. This study discusses the role-play and case study practices to develop graduate qualities in information systems and information technology literacy skills.

Professors Karen S. Nantz and Barbara E. Kemmerer from Eastern Illinois University examine the relationship between learning preferences and technological literacy in their chapter, titled *Understanding the Role of Type Preferences in Fostering Technological Literacy.* The chapter argues for using a framework of personality differences based on the work of Carl Jung and Myers-Briggs.

Maureen Diana Sasso presents a case for different departments working together in her chapter, titled *Evolution of a Collaborative Undergraduate Information Literacy Education Program.* She discusses a program that incorporates critical thinking, research, and communication skills into a freshman-level course. The skills, competencies, and content are based on the Association of College and Research Libraries' (ACRL) information literacy research agenda.

Katia Passerini and Kemal Cakici provide a collaborative work, titled *Achieving University-Wide Instructional Technology Literacy: Examples of Development Programs and Their Effectiveness.* They discuss a thematic approach to faculty workshops that begin with computer productivity skills and end with statistical analysis using SAS system software. Their efforts are presented as evidence of a support program that is a mix of technology skills and instructional design seminars.

The development of new teachers is an important endeavor. Professors Silvia L. Sapone and Kim Johnson Hyatt discuss the infusion of technology into preservice teacher education programs with their chapter, titled *Technology for Management, Communication, and Instruction: Supporting Teacher Development.* The chapter argues that technology changes the way teachers interact with the curriculum, their students, families, peers, and administrators.

Junko Yamamoto, Mara Linaberger, and Leighann S. Forbes discuss how to support teachers as they learn and practice new instructional technology literacy skills. Their chapter, titled *Mentoring and Technology Integration for Teachers,* presents a case for using a mentoring model in a suburban K-12 school, in an urban K-12 school, and in a college. They discuss the mentoring process as part of a professional development model.

Glenn Lowry from United Arab Emirates University and Rodney Turner from Victoria University of Technology discuss *Information Systems Education for the 21st Century: Aligning Curriculum Content and Delivery with the Professional Workplace.* The authors present an argument on what to study and how to study in student-centered learning environments. The chapter also reviews information system reform issues and strategies to meet the needs of students.

Sandra Barker uses 'real-life' scenarios with undergraduate business students to enhance their understanding of end-user development of database applications. Her chapter is titled, *Business Graduates as End-User Developers: Understanding Information Literacy Skills Required.* The process is intended to identify real-world problems and solution paths that the students will encounter after graduation.

The next chapter is presented by June K. Hilton from Jurupa Valley High School in Mira Loma, California. She begins the discussion of the lack of resources available to provide a technology literacy program in her chapter, titled *Narrowing the Digital Divide: Technology Integration in a High-Poverty School.* This discussion is based on empirical data from a secondary school that wanted to increase technology integration in the classroom. This chapter looks at the data to support the concept of the effective use of technology in elementary and secondary classrooms.

Ellen Whybrow, from the University of Alberta, continues the discussion of access in her chapter, titled *Digital Access, ICT Fluency, and the Economically Disadvantaged: Approaches to Minimize the Digital Divide.* She offers guidance to schools faced with addressing the digital divide issue.

Professors George Stonehouse and Jonathan D. Pemberton from the University of Northumbria, UK, look at the system in their chapter, titled *Learning to Become a Knowledge-Centric Organization.* They begin with an understanding of the importance of knowledge to an organization's performance and identify the primary characteristics of knowledge-centric organizations.

The next chapter is titled, *Fundamentals of Multimedia.* This chapter is included in the book because it presents a review of the basic skills of multimedia. These skills are part of a rapidly changing discipline. Palmer W. Agnew and Anne S. Kellerman describe these skills, as they exist in 2004, and how the future trends may evolve.

Jaroslav Král and Michal Žemlička, from Charles University in Prague, Czech Republic, discuss the literacy skills for software developers in their chapter, titled *What Literacy for Software Developers?*. They review the evolution of software development and the skill needed by developers in 2004.

Antonio Cartelli and Marco Palma, of the University of Cassino, Italy, present a view of research and didactic applications in the next chapter, titled *Computing and Information Systems in Latin Paleography Between Research and Didactic Application.* The authors review the connections between research and teaching, and the technology skills needed to conduct a research/teaching endeavor.

Daniel Brandon's chapter is titled, *The Role of Project Management in Technology Literacy.* This professor from Christian Brothers University in Memphis, Tennessee, discusses the management of technology resources. Professor Brandon reviews the technology skills to manage projects.

Another chapter on Project Management is presented by Earl Chrysler and is titled, *Developing Technology Applications: Effective Project Management.*

This chapter discusses the methodology for teaching a software project management course.

Gerard L. Hanley and Sorel Reismann from California State University examine how to create and support learning communities with their chapter, titled *Enabling Electronic Teaching and Learning Communities with MERLOT*. They discuss the progress in enabling student success in distance learning by delivering academic courses with a course management system.

Franco Orsucci, from the Institute for Complexity Studies, Rome, Italy, and Nicoletta Sala, from Università della Svizzera Italiana, Mendrisio, Switzerland, present a series of examples from the realm of virtual reality in their chapter, titled *Virtual Reality, Telemedicine, and Beyond: Some Examples*. Here they discuss the area of virtual reality and how it may become the new basic literacy of the present and the future.

The final chapter is from Nicoletta Sala and Massimo Sala from the Università della Svizzera Italiana, Mendrisio, Switzerland, and is titled, *Virtual Reality in Education*. The authors argue for the technological literacy of virtual reality in a learning environment. They introduce the technology as an educational tool to support different learning styles.

Acknowledgments

The editor thanks all of the members of the Department of Instruction and Leadership at Duquesne University. They provided moral support and guidance during the production of this scholarly work. Conversations, e-mails, and Faculty Scholarly Luncheons contributed to the ideas that led to this book. Dr. Tomei, the Program Coordinator, and Dr. Barone, the Department Chair, encourage the production of research and scholarly endeavors. They provided the resources needed to undergo this project.

The editor acknowledges the contribution of all of the authors of this book. The intent of the book began with the notion to define instructional technology literacy. The global authors followed that theme and produced scholarly works that explain this changing field. It is hoped that a revised book will be produced, in a few years, to articulate the changes in technology literacy.

With this peer-reviewed, scholarly book, the reviewers provided an immeasurable service. Content and style issues were discussed to improve this book. The editor thanks them for the suggestions they offered to improve each chapter.

Special thanks also go to the publishing team at Idea Group, Inc. In particular, Jan Travers and Jennifer Sundstrom provided technical and moral support during this project. Their expertise, diligence, and understanding of delays provided the editor with the ample time to see this project to completion.

I also thank my wife, Janice, and my children, Matt, Gia, and Brian. They provided countless support and encouragement during this process. Janice's critique of the final readability and form was greatly appreciated.

David D. Carbonara, Duquesne University, USA

Section I

Defining Instructional Technology Literacy

Chapter I

The Pillars of Instructional Technology

Lawrence A. Tomei
Robert Morris University, USA

Abstract

This chapter provides an overview of the foundational components of teaching and learning with technology. The pillars of instructional technology include the philosophy of technology (What are we teaching about IT?), the psychology of technology (How are we teaching with IT?), the sociology of technology (Who are we teaching with IT?), the history of technology, and technology leadership. Each "pillar" offers a venue for creating a program of instructional technology at the higher education level. In addition, a new model for implementing an instructional technology program is introduced: the K-A-RPE Model of Instructional Technology provides the infrastructure for any institution of higher learning to infuse technology into its undergraduate, graduate, and post-graduate teacher curriculum.

Introduction

Philosophy, psychology, sociology, history, and leadership are the pillars of teaching and learning—whether in the classroom or by way of distance-based tools. As such, instructional technology is supported by the following five foundations:

1. **Philosophy,** that answers the question "**What** are we teaching about instructional technology?"
2. **Psychology,** that addresses "**How** do we teach with instructional technology?"
3. **Sociology,** involving the "**Who** are we teaching with instructional technology?"
4. **History,** encompassing the "**When** (in the history of education) are we teaching with technology?"
5. And, **Leadership,** focusing on "**Whom** (sic) is responsible for using technology to teach?"

The Philosophy of Instructional Technology

What Are We Teaching about Instructional Technology?

Technology has played a significant role in education and in most successful educational reform movements of the past four decades: charter schools and home schooling; standards, testing, and accountability; best practice; outcome-based learning; professional teacher qualifications, and so forth. It remains a catalyst for changing what we teach—the essence of a personal philosophy of technology.

The International Society for Technology in Education (ISTE) provides technology standards for students and divides them into six broad categories. Standards are meant to be integrated into K-12 curriculum at the introduction, reinforcement, or mastery levels. At the state level, 49 of the 51 states have adopted, adapted, aligned with, or otherwise referenced at least one set of standards in their state technology plans, certification, licensure, curriculum plans, assessment plans, or other official state documents (ISTE, 2004).

With respect to the philosophy of instructional technology, teachers have these standards and profiles as guidelines for planning technology-based activities in which lesson-based learning outcomes are focused. Table 1 displays the current technology standards for students. For technologists, NETS*S represents much of "What are we teaching about technology?"

Technology fosters better communication, removing barriers that, in the past, have stymied learning. Yet, technology is not a magic potion for resolving all the woes of education. Technology, in and of itself, does not create better teachers, learners, or administrators. However, when technology is used side by side with other school improvement efforts, it can be a very effective vehicle for progress.

*Table 1. Technology foundation standards for students (NETS*S, 2004)*

1. Basic operations and concepts
   - Students demonstrate a sound understanding of the nature and operation of technology systems.
   - Students are proficient in the use of technology.
2. Social, ethical, and human issues
   - Students understand the ethical, cultural, and societal issues related to technology.
   - Students practice responsible use of technology systems, information, and software.
   - Students develop positive attitudes toward technology uses that support lifelong learning, collaboration, personal pursuits, and productivity.
3. Technology productivity tools
   - Students use technology tools to enhance learning, increase productivity, and promote creativity.
   - Students use productivity tools to collaborate in constructing technology-enhanced models, prepare publications, and produce other creative works.
4. Technology communications tools
   - Students use telecommunications to collaborate, publish, and interact with peers, experts, and other audiences.
   - Students use a variety of media and formats to communicate information and ideas effectively to multiple audiences.
5. Technology research tools
   - Students use technology to locate, evaluate, and collect information from a variety of sources.
   - Students use technology tools to process data and report results.
   - Students evaluate and select new information resources and technological innovations based on the appropriateness for specific tasks.
6. Technology problem-solving and decision-making tools
   - Students use technology resources for solving problems and making informed decisions
   - Students employ technology in the development of strategies for solving problems in the real world.

Learning is a process that happens when teacher and student share a common experience. When students gather and process information (and as a result, form new knowledge, attitudes, or change their behavior), learning occurs. One popular philosophy of teaching and learning offers that "the teacher does not deliver education, the student constructs it." Technology plays a significant role in changing the instructional environment by promoting the role of the teacher as a guide in educational discovery, serving as a resource to the student-as-information-gatherer. In other words, the effective teacher serves "not as the sage-on-the-stage but rather as the guide-by-the-side."

Barriers to learning that once prevented students from participating fully in the educational experience are being methodically erased with the integration of technology. The "what are we teaching" question now includes assistive technologies that help special needs students experience opportunities heretofore unavailable in the traditional classroom. Computers and other technologies are powerful tools supporting students with disabilities. Auditory output devices, print magnification equipment, graphic organizing software, and voice recognition systems all offer students with disabilities equal opportunities to more fully participate in the teaching-learning process (Lengyel, 2003).

Technology has become an increasingly integral part of the educational process. But, what is its true value as a teaching-learning strategy? Is technology just a tool for improving how we teach and learn? Or, is it also a content area equal in importance to science, mathematics, social studies, and languages? The Philosophy of Instructional Technology answers the question, "What are we teaching about instructional technology?"

The Psychology of Instructional Technology

How Do We Teach with Instructional Technology?

The literature is replete with historically accepted schools of educational psychology. Behaviorists believe that the best way to learn is through repetition, a principle of learning that has dominated educational thinking since the time of Ivan Pavlov and his experiments with animals. The environment is the key to teaching and learning, viewed in terms of stimuli and response and the reinforcement that links them to changed behavior. Technology is appreciated as an instructional strategy because it offers a media for organization and presentation of information in a designed sequence.

Cognitive psychologists focus on the learner as an active participant in the teaching-learning process. Those who adhere to this psychology of learning believe that instructional technology is more effective when tied to prior student knowledge, and linked to information processed and stored in an individual's memory. Technology offers the schemata for presenting knowledge as a series of building blocks that the teacher places one on top of the other to build upon a student's understanding. It was actually the information processing model, the principle upon which instructional technology is grounded, that first contributed the archetype of input, process, and retrieval of information used by today's cognitivists supporting technology for the classroom.

Humanism as a psychology is the relative newcomer on the educational scene. Technological applications of humanistic thought are even more recent. The affective elements (feelings, emotions, etc.) of learning have expressed themselves in the latest innovation for teaching and learning—the Internet. For the humanistic teacher, technology creates an educational environment that fosters self-development, cooperation, positive communications, and personalization of information (Tomei, 1998).

Taxonomy for the Technology Domain, introduced in 2001, offers a view for using technology to enhance student learning (Tomei, 2001). Research shows that teachers who use a classification scheme when teaching with instructional technology prepare instructional learning objectives that tend to produce more successful student learning outcomes (Kibler, Barker, & Miles, 1970; Krathwohl & Bloom, 1984). The classification system proposed for the Technology Domain includes Literacy, Collaboration, Decision Making, Infusion, Integration, and Tech-ology (see Table 2 for more detailed definitions). Each classification offers a progressive level of complexity, and success at each level depends on mastery of the previous step. Many educators accept teaching with technology as perhaps the most important instructional strategy to impact the classroom since the textbook.

The pillar of psychology examines the key foundations of teaching and learning as applied to instructional technology. Included are issues such as faculty and student attitudes towards instructional technology, professional portfolios for educators, learning theories, instructional technology learning theories (pedagogy and androgogy), and the taxonomy for the technology domain.

The Sociology of Instructional Technology

Who Are We Teaching with Instructional Technology?

Sociology addresses issues affecting the developers of educational systems and the educators who implement, administrators who manage, and learners who take delivery of such systems. This pillar of instructional technology examines the perspectives of each community and its relation to one another.

Educators use technology to enhance individual learning as well as to disseminate knowledge within a society. They expect technology to blend with their individual approach to instruction. However, most are not fully aware of the potential applications of technology in the classroom or corporate training room, or how these technologies might mitigate (or perhaps eliminate entirely) the various barriers to learning from a rapidly expanding, vastly heterogeneous body of learners.

Table 2. The taxonomy for the technology domain (Tomei, 2001)

Taxonomy Classification	**Defining the Level of the Technology Taxonomy**
Literacy  **Understanding Technology**	**Level 1.0**—The minimum degree of competency expected of teachers and students with respect to technology, computers, educational programs, office productivity software, the Internet, and their synergistic effectiveness as a learning strategy.
Collaboration  **Sharing Ideas**	**Level 2.0**—The ability to employ technology for effective interpersonal interaction.
Decision Making  **Solving Problems**	**Level 3.0**—Ability to use technology in new and concrete situations to analyze, assess, and judge.
Infusion  **Learning with Technology**	**Level 4.0**—Identification, harvesting, and application of existing technology to unique learning situations.
Integration  **Teaching with Technology**	**Level 5.0**—The creation of new technology-based materials, combining otherwise disparate technologies to teach.
Tech-ology  **The Study of Technology**	**Level 6.0**—The ability to judge the universal impact, shared values, and social implications of technology use and its influence on teaching and learning.

Administrators experience a widening continuum of challenges with respect to instructional technology. For example, evaluating educational technology programs can be a formidable endeavor, particularly if the administrator has opted to remain unschooled in the applications of technology for learning. As more and more states, districts, schools, and training companies develop technology plans to ensure its effective use to benefit learning and achievement, the need to understand technology's impact on improving that achievement has become even greater. Furthermore, funding issues necessary to implement components of technology plans often require sound fiscal, as well as pedagogical, evaluation. The question thus becomes, how do you evaluate educational technology programs that impact the types of learners served, the curriculum areas in which technology is used, and the type of technology itself?

Learners are demanding more technology—a simple, but understated reality of education in the twenty-first century. Just a few of the technologies found in classrooms and corporate training rooms include: computer-mediated communications, distance-based learning environments, distributed learning environments, educational multimedia, human-computer interface, hypermedia applications, intelligent learning/tutoring environments, interactive learning environments, network-based learning environments, online education, simulations for learning, and Web-based instruction/training. The sociology of contemporary technology-based learning involves an understanding of organizations, groups and classes, and even social movements in an effort to address the question, "Who are we teaching with instructional technology?"

The History of Instructional Technology

When (in the History of Education) Are We Teaching with Technology?

More than any of the pillars of instructional technology, history plays an integral role in the successful introduction, implementation, and evaluation of technology for teaching and learning. The historical perspective epitomizes how technology matured by succumbing to the well-known adage, "Necessity is the mother of invention."

A short timeline of key historical instructional technology events is provided in Figure 1.

Since the advent of text-based programmed instruction in the 1940s, historical events have impacted the development of the field of instructional technology. WWII surfaced the need for mass training and caused educators to seek more scientific methods and research to provide effective training materials and systematic training efforts. In 1954, Russia launched the Sputnik satellite, and the space race was on. The United States began to take seriously the effectiveness (or lack thereof) of academic curriculum and pursue with vigor the steps necessary to address learning shortfalls.

Figure 1. Timeline of critical events in the history of instructional technology

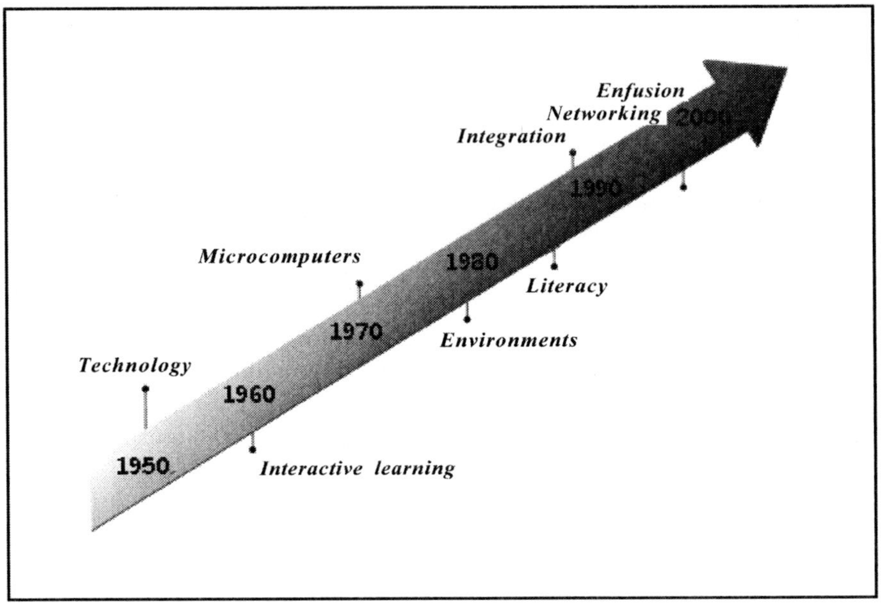

Another historical event of importance to instructional technology occurred in 1958 when B.F. Skinner built his now infamous drill and practice teaching machine that permanently established the potential of technology in the classroom.

The Information Age began in 1978 with the marketing of the first personal microcomputer. Further development of communications schemata grew to a shared resource environment and eventually produced the Internet and the World Wide Web.

By all accounts, technology has matured past its first-generation tubes and circuit boards, beyond the second-generation transistors and programming languages, onwards past third-generation integrated circuits and desktop applications, to globalization in which the world communicates, shares information, and learns digitally. Lifelong learners travel and telecommute quickly and effectively without regard to national boundaries, literally changing forever the rules of how education serves its learner client and answering the question, "When (in the history of education) are we teaching with technology?"

Leadership in Instructional Technology

Whom (sic) is Responsible for Using Technology to Teach?

Leaders in technology, whether academic or corporate, face an "information revolution." The Aspen Institute Communications and Society Program (NSBA, 2003) offered the following ways new information technologies are spurring complex patterns of change. They include dichotomies of centralization versus fragmentation, holistic perspective versus specialized knowledge, too much information versus too little information, leadership versus fellowship, worker isolation and alienation versus community connections, sharing versus withholding access to information, and public intervention versus private decision making.

Learning in the 21st century demands a greater dependence on new communication and computing technologies supporting greater learner activity and investigation. It advances the role of educators as mentors, researchers, publishers, technology users, knowledge producers, risk takers, and lifelong learners. Technology will open doors for participation by adult learners and parents to play a more interactive role in their own education and that of their children. Leadership in technology demands a partnership with local businesses and community organizations that have such a deep interdependency on the human yield of education.

Think about how future leadership roles will change as we build the schools of the future. Just a few of the consequences future schools must necessarily consider involve how they intend to become more open and flexible to the scheduling demands of their clients; how communications will promote collaboration and higher level learning; how educators will be supported in their use of technologies for learning, professional development, and their own collaboration; how future learners will use technology to achieve new levels of success and better prepare for academic or vocational future; how educational managers will use technology as a tool to direct their learning communities; and how technology will remove barriers caused by geographic separation, a variety of learning styles, and inequitable access to technology.

From a non-technical leadership perspective, some of the key issues facing school and corporate leaders with respect to technology include: authentic assessment tasks supported by technology; project-based, cooperative learning skills; available access to technical assistance; support for innovations from the district, state, and federal levels (or the local, regional, or national/international corporate levels); and implementation of technology in a safe (and professionally non-threatening) environment. Together, these issues guide the implementation of technology for educators so they can once again become learners and share their ideas about teaching and learning and address the question, "Whom (sic) is responsible for using technology to teach?"

Grasping each of the pillars already defined will not ensure success without considering the necessary distinction among instructional technology programs at the undergraduate, graduate, and post-graduate levels, and the degree of mastery and technical competency required at each level. Enter the *K-A-RPE Model.*

The K-A-RPE Model

Bringing the Pillars to Life

The K-A-RPE (Knowledge, Application, and Research, Practice, and Evaluation) Model offers the necessary distinction among instructional technology programs.

Assumed at each level of the model is mastery and competency at previous levels. At the *Knowledge Level* of the model, candidates are introduced to technologies as personal learning tools. Examine the following learning objective found in an undergraduate IT course:

> *"Given a lecture/demonstration on the basic features of electronic spreadsheets, the (undergraduate) teacher-candidate will be able to create a 10 cell x 10 cell worksheet to capture semester quiz grades and correctly compute an average (mean) score."*

Graduate candidates, on the other hand, seek to master technology for the advancement of their students. As practicing classroom teachers, instructional technology is presented to foster infusion into the classroom curriculum. At the *Application Level*, candidates seek to master technology-based skills that are immediately functional in everyday classroom instruction. An example of such a graduate-level IT learning objective follows:

Figure 2. The K-A-RPE moel

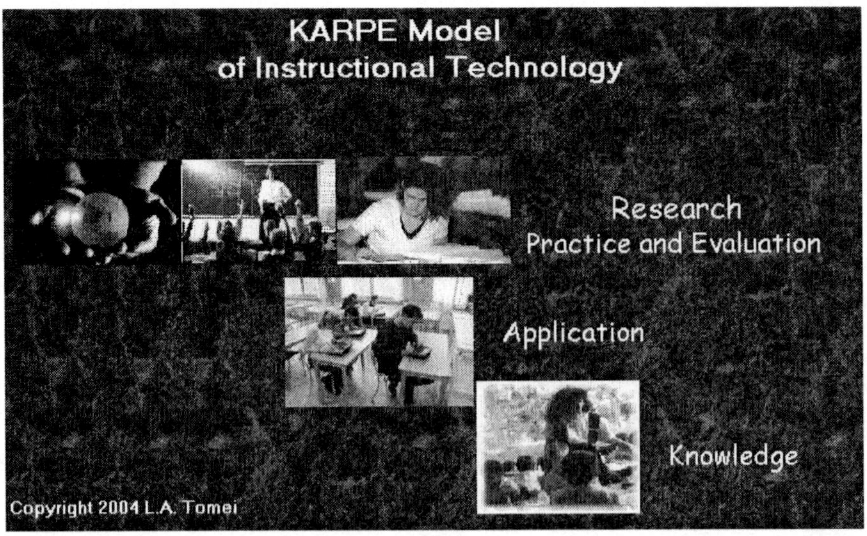

> *"Using an instructional system design model of their choosing, candidates will design, develop, and publish a minimum eight-page, text-based, student workbook containing all the essential elements of a workbook appropriate for their selected classroom lesson."*

At the highest level of the K-A-RPE Model lie Research, Practice, and Evaluation. Doctoral candidates, too, must learn new technologies. But they do so with a rich research base to support their implementations of technology as a teaching and learning tool. They are charged with changing the way technology is experienced (i.e., practiced) in the classroom. And they do so with an eye on achievement—"technology for technology's sake" is an empty philosophy.

With a focus on the *Research Level* of the model, the doctoral candidate is asked to conduct the necessary investigation to determine whether the number of computers located in a particular school affects student achievement scores as evidenced in standardized tests. Here is an example:

> *"Using Internet-based data from the state department of education, candidates will seek to determine a correlation between student achievement scores received by a selected school district and the ratio of students-to-computers found in those schools. Research focus."*

Instructional technology changes at this highest level of the model by improving the *Practice Level* of teaching and learning wherever and whenever possible. Examine this doctoral program learning objective:

> *"Candidates will develop a visual presentation suitable for school directors and technology coordinators that provides an overview of instructional technology and its potential impact on district decision making to include: administration (planning and budgets); faculty (professional development, curriculum, and teaching load); and staffing. Practice focus."*

Finally, at the *Evaluation Level,* using technology implies assessment of student achievement; an examination of how technology succeeds (or fails) as a tool for learning. In every respect, it presupposes a firm grasp of the pillars of instructional technology education and merits co-equal status in the K-A-RPE Model. A learning objective evidencing evaluation follows:

> *"Candidates will assess at least three educational software packages in each of the core academic areas of mathematics, social studies, language arts, and science. The assessment must include an appraisal*

of content coverage, effective use of technology, and impact on student learning outcomes. Evaluation focus."

The K-A-RPE Model distinguishes among instructional technology programs throughout higher education. With little argument, technology has become an increasingly integral component of the educational process. It is a catalyst for changing what we teach—the essence of the pillars of instructional technology.

Conclusion

This chapter focuses on the five Pillars of Instructional Technology; specifically, the what, how, who, when, and whom of technology for teaching and learning. Philosophy aids in understanding the elements of instructional technology important enough to be worthy of our attention. Psychology considers the applications of technology for teaching and learning, and involves an examination of all aspects of faculty and students as well as instructional strategies and learning theories.

Sociology defines the target population of our technology efforts and specifically characterizes learners who will participate in our programs. History sets technology-based instruction within the context of time and space, and reminds us that instructional technology, while not a new educational reform, remains to be mastered. Leadership places technology in the milieu of budgets, attitudes, standards, and expectations all playing an integral role in any successful technology program.

The chapter concludes by introducing the K-A-RPE Model for implementing the pillars in instructional technology education. Knowledge, application, and research, practice, and evaluation focus curriculum for pre-service, in-service, and professional teacher development, and establish varying levels of technical competency expected by educators throughout their academic careers.

References

Lengyel, L. (2003). Technologies for students with disabilities. Chapter 10 in *Challenges of teaching with technology across the curriculum: Issues and solutions.* Hershey PA: Idea Group, Inc.

National School Board Association. (2002). *Education leadership toolkit.* Retrieved from *www.nsba.org/sbot/toolkit/*

Tomei, L.A. (1998). *Learning theories—A primer exercise: An examination of behaviorism, cognitivism, and humanism.* Retrieved from *www.duq.edu/~tomei/ed711psy/11ngtheo.htm*

Tomei, L.A. (2001). *Teaching digitally: A guide for integrating technology into the classroom.* Norwood MA: Christopher-Gordon Publishers.

Chapter II

The Role of Information Technology in Learning: A Meta-Analysis

Klarissa Ting-Ting Chang
Carnegie Mellon University, USA

John Lim
National University of Singapore, Singapore

Abstract

This study provides an updated meta-analysis on the effects of information technology (IT) in education. Sixty-eight experimental studies conducted on the application of IT in the classrooms were integrated and analyzed. Positive effect sizes were found for learning outcomes, including academic achievement, knowledge retention, task performance, self-reported learning, and self-efficacy. Further analysis revealed the primary effects to be significantly moderated by several factors, categorized under learner and course characteristics. These findings have important implications for both research and practice.

Introduction

Emerging as a precious asset in pedagogy, technology is viewed as a potential element that can influence traditional education. Learning effectiveness has been a major issue in recent research, and the growing knowledge repository has implications on all levels of education with the advent of new technologies. The goals of using information technology (IT) in education are to enhance teaching and learning, and to increase the efficiency and effectiveness of the educational organization (Windschitl, 1998). This is readily reflected in the large amount of resources invested in IT spending (Volery & Lord, 2000). Concomitantly, calls for greater depth and breadth in the studies for technology-mediated learning (Alavi & Leidner, 2001; Owston, 1997) indicate growing interest in the pedagogical impacts of IT on education.

Since the first computer was introduced in education, many studies have been conducted to investigate the effects of educational technology. IT is increasingly used to complement or replace conventional teaching methods (Leidner & Jarvenpaa, 1995). Many researchers believe that the use of technology is inherently 'good' for learning (Niemiec, Sikorski, & Walberg, 1996). Yet, the application of old solutions to new problems in online learning usually leads to the 'no significant difference' phenomenon (Russell, 2002), in which IT applications tend to produce results similar to those in traditional pedagogy. Therefore, there is a need to understand the strengths and weaknesses, as well as the appropriateness of implementing IT in schools. Correspondingly, a number of studies were carried out to determine whether IT, in fact, has produced beneficial effects. In a typical study, learners are divided into experimental and control groups. Learners in the experimental group are taught educational content using some forms of technology, while those in the control group receive their instruction by traditional methods. But no individual study can conclude whether IT is generally effective. Conflicts in research findings (Kulik & Kulik, 1991; Niemiec et al., 1996) show that the conditions under which the use of IT is beneficial have ramifications not completely understood despite the plethora of research commentaries.

To reach general conclusions, reviewers must consider results from studies carried out in varied settings and under different conditions. Research syntheses are usually classified into narrative reviews, box score tabulations, and meta-analyses. Narrative reviewers give concise summaries of major studies and draw conclusions about overall impacts based on these studies reviewed. However, the early traditional reviews are inexplicit about their search procedures, inclusion criteria, and analytical procedures for synthesizing the studies. Box score reviews often report the proportion of studies favorable and unfavorable to an experimental treatment, and provide narrative comments about the studies (Kulik & Kulik, 1990). Meta-analyses, on the other hand, take a quantitative approach and have made increasing appearance in IS research (e.g., Benbasat & Lim, 1993). Hunter and Schmidt (1990) defined meta-analysis as a set of statistical procedures for accumulating experimental results across independent studies that address a related set of research questions. Meta-analysis is an integrative analysis that combines the findings from individual studies for the purpose of research synthesis. By aggregating results across studies, researchers can gain a more accurate representation of the population relationship than that provided by individual study estimators (Glass, 1981).

The current study used a meta-analytic approach to integrate the inconsistent results on the use of IT in education. The focus here is on the use of technological tools for instructional purposes, although management functions may be aided to increase educational productivity (Kosakowski, 1998). Two important research questions this study aims to address are: *What are the effects of the use of IT on commonly researched educational outcomes? Under which conditions does the use of IT appear to be most effective?* The second question differentiates the current study from the earlier meta-analyses (Kulik & Kulik, 1991), which focused principally on the main effects (i.e., whether or not IT can help to learn or teach). As importantly, the current study analyzes the most up-to-date sample (1990-2003).

Background

Dependent Variables: Learning Outcomes

The increasing repository of information and the escalation of skill requirements for working environments create the need for more effective learning (Alavi, 1994). The introduction of IT allows both synchronous and asynchronous learning for individual and group endeavors, whether in the same place or under distance education conditions. Studies involving synchronous learning include the use of Group Decision Support Systems for collaborative learning activities. Studies involving asynchronous learning are often based on the use of other computer-mediated communication systems, such as computer conferencing (Benbunan-Fich & Hiltz, 1999). In some studies, the term computer-assisted instruction (CAI) is used collectively to refer to drill and practice, tutorial, and dialogue systems, whereby the computer is used to reinforce concepts introduced in classrooms, as well as to present lessons or practice exercises. Research on CAI has rapidly evolved, and ubiquitous use of Internet technologies has led to an increase in studies investigating the impacts of Web-based learning. Previous empirical studies examined IT effects on outcome variables that are well-established in education and psychology literature. The learning outcomes examined by these studies focused mainly on actual learning and perceived learning.

Actual Learning

Cognitive and affective dimensions constitute two important aspects of learning (Bloom, 1956). Affective dimension refers to the internal state of influence on the learner's choice of personal action (Bloom, 1956). Enhanced learning effectiveness includes heightened affective responses and better attitudes.

Identified as particularly salient to learning effectiveness, cognitive aspect is the focus of this chapter (Kulik & Kulik, 1991; Susman, 1998). Cognitive dimension includes verbal knowledge, knowledge organization, and cognitive strategies. Verbal knowledge refers to the declarative (information about *what*), procedural (information about *how*), and tactic knowledge (information about *which*, *why*, and *when*). Knowledge organization deals with internal organization of knowledge. Cognitive strategies deal with regulation of the learner's cognition.

Operationally, three learning outcomes typically studied are academic achievement, knowledge retention, and task performance. These variables are believed to be important outcome effects that can reflect the extent of success in learning (Mandler, 1989).

Academic achievement is broadly defined as any increase in learning (Susman, 1998). For most studies, effect on achievement is still measured by means of a final exam. This dependent variable is researched in almost all the studies visited. In the traditional model of teaching and learning, exams are still a preferred measure of the extent of knowledge and materials acquired or learned by the students. IT encourages academic achievement by increasing effective learning time, during which learners actively attend to important instructional tasks—with success (Mandler, 1989; Squires & Preece, 1996). In other words, the use of IT can improve achievement by focusing a learner's attention on the relevant areas of concern.

Knowledge retention refers to the performance on a follow-up exam, usually the same exam as the first one, given some time after the completion of the instructional program (Dees, 1991). This dimension seeks to find out how much of the course content is being assimilated into individual learners. It is interesting to note that the idea of knowledge retention aligns with the traditional mindset whereby knowing and understanding is memorizing. The treatment condition is generally effective, as knowledge is retained longer and skills attained decay less rapidly than in the traditional instruction.

Task performance is another measure that is believed to represent the amount of learning (Leidner & Jarvenpaa, 1995; Sankaran, Sankaran, & Bui, 2000). In the educational domain, task performance is indicated by individuals producing higher quality and quantity of solutions in computer-mediated environments than those in traditional face-to-face conditions.

Perceived Learning

Experimental evidence obtained from past studies indicated that instruction using technological tools was efficacious in terms of perceived learning. The main hypotheses were that IT enhances learning effectiveness defined by self-reported learning and self-efficacy. *Self-reported learning* refers to students' perceptions of their learning process. Technology-supported groups generally expressed higher levels of perceived learning and self-reported learning (Alavi, Marakas, & Yoo, 2002); this has possibly to do with the increase in learning process gains and reduction in process losses, which help to enhance learning effectiveness (Alavi, 1994). *Self-efficacy* refers to the degree to which learners feel capable of learning from a given method (Leidner & Jarvenpaa, 1995).

Figure 1. Research model

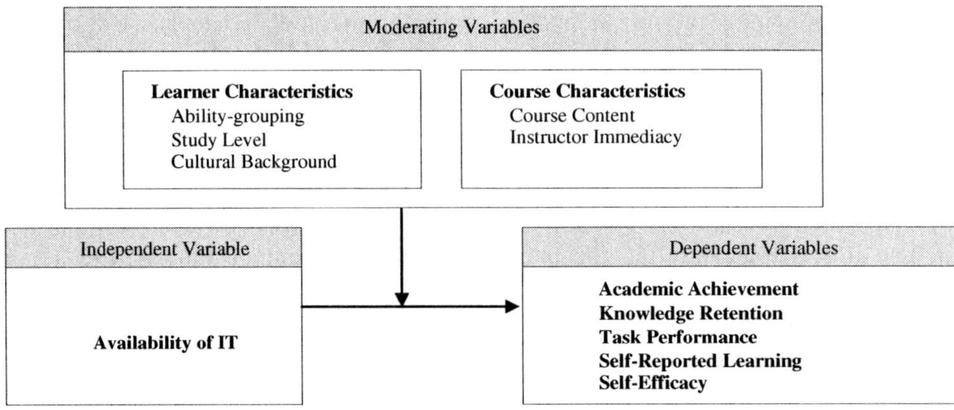

When learning is supported by technology, it is expected that self-efficacy will be high. Students may consider IT as a procedural convenience, rather than as a cognitive advantage.

How IT influences the learning outcomes depends on the *context*. Review of the literature highlights characteristics of learner and course as potential moderators. Figure 1 depicts the moderating relationships that are to be deliberated in the next sections.

Moderating Effects of Learner Characteristics

Many dimensions are associated with the inherent characteristics of the learners. The more commonly researched features can be categorized as cognitive (ability level) and descriptive (study level and cultural background) characteristics. *Ability-grouping* refers to the combination of learners with different capacities to comprehend learning concepts and control learning. Heterogeneous groups consist of learners with different levels of ability. Homogeneous groups consist of learners with similar levels of ability. Learners with higher ability are typically identified through their superior achievements in tests (Lefrancois, 1991). Studies have reported that IT tools are more effective for learners who have lower prior knowledge and less ability in the domain learned (Cathcart, 1990). Low-achieving learners tend to require more structure, which can be provided by software packages with step-by-step instructions. The system can provide instantaneous and non-judgmental feedback, a characteristic that is especially beneficial to learners with lower self-esteem and ability. The boosted confidence can help to achieve better results (Susman, 1998). This suggests that learners with lower aptitude tend to perform better when using technologically based learning packages than those with higher aptitude, although some studies indicate that high achievers benefit more in IT settings (Hooper, Temiyakarn, & Williams, 1993). By understanding how and when to group learners according to their cognitive ability, the comparison of heterogeneous and homogeneous ability-grouped classes can bring insight into conditions of the effective use of IT. In a heterogeneous group, the high-ability learners may act as motivational models to help their low-ability counterparts in the learning process. While the academic benefit of the latter may not be enormous in some situations, there is little evidence to suggest negative impacts of heterogeneous groups.

> *Proposition 1: The effect size of the use of IT on actual learning (academic achievement, knowledge retention) will be larger for ability heterogeneously grouped learners than for ability homogeneously grouped learners.*

On the other hand, differential effects of IT on high- and low-achieving learners may be manifested not only in cognitive outcomes, but also in task-related variables. Despite an *individualistic* technological setting (technology employed such that one learned via interaction with a computer), learners are seldom isolated from others, as they still work side-by-side on similar tasks. Although low achievers may receive instant help from peers who serve as substitute instructors, the presence of others introduces an element of competition that induces social comparisons. These comparisons may depress the social acceptance of low achievers as their slow pace can be noticed by other learners, and may increase the social acceptance of high achievers as their higher gains are continuously publicized by the computer. Task performance, being a surrogate measure of the amount of learning, is believed to be better for higher achievers. At the group level, task performance is contingent upon learners who are of similar ability levels.

> *Proposition 2: The effect size of the use of IT on actual learning (task performance) will be larger for ability homogeneously grouped learners than for ability heterogeneously grouped learners.*

As far as *study level* is concerned, most studies reasonably assumed that school or pre-college learners (grades 1 to 12) are younger than the college or university learners. According to Lefrancois (1991), young children, between four and 12 years old, are interested in the essence of IT (what IT is), and in what way it is similar to or different from other things such as their toys. Older learners, between 13 and 18 years old, are interested in the control (how to use IT). Relatively speaking, younger learners are able to adapt to a variety of uses of IT more easily, and are less resistant to accept the use of IT in the course curriculum (Kulik & Kulik, 1991). To add to these contrasts is the premise that technology is not as effective in teaching more subtle ideas and concepts (Windschitl, 1998). Accordingly, effects on learning would be more visible when IT is used in schools than in colleges. Further, school children may need a higher level of guidance from and interaction with instructors, as compared to college learners who are expected to learn more independently, with instructors acting as facilitators rather than instructors (Owston, 1997). Insofar as promoting interaction, IT should play a greater role in schools than in colleges.

Proposition 3: The effect size of the use of IT on actual learning (academic achievement, knowledge retention, task performance) will be larger with school students than with college students.

Cultural background is believed to be influential in learning achievement (Chen, Mashhadi, Ang, & Harkrider, 1999). The culture of the institution and the beliefs of individuals determine how and when IT is to be used and implemented (Earley, 1994). Experience and conceptions of learning differ in various cultural contexts. To date, culture has not been studied to any significant extent in the area of educational technology. Only experiments conducted on collaborative environments have a longer tradition in researching the element of culture (Jonassen, 1993). Yet, this variable is increasingly important with the growth of the Internet and distance education. Culture is viewed broadly here as the beliefs, values, and patterns of action by individuals and groups (Chen et al., 1999). While differences between the western and eastern cultures form a major topic of study in and of itself, for the purposes here it suffices to highlight the following. Sleeter and Grant (1993) have discussed differential cultural perspectives, indicating a general tendency of western culture to value individualism, personal achievement, and human interactions that are functionally based. In contrast, people with non-western culture orientations are portrayed as emphasizing group cooperation and affective expression. Self-reported learning and self-efficacy are expected to be more congruent to learners in the western culture.

Proposition 4: The effect size of the use of IT on perceived learning (self-reported learning, self-efficacy) will be larger for learners in a western culture than for learners in an eastern culture.

Moderating Effects of Course Characteristics

The effectiveness of IT is conceivably also a function of the course content and the degree of the instructor's presence in the course. *Course content* can be differentiated into hard and soft disciplines (Biglan, 1973). Examples of hard disciplines include science, engineering, and medicine. Examples of soft disciplines include social sciences, humanities, and languages. Finding out how different types of course content are related to the use of IT is still in the research repertoire of many contemporary researchers. However, hard disciplines have been the preferred subject matter in most experimental studies. It is possible that learners benefit more from IT in hard disciplines by invoking feedback and individualized-pacing features (Dees, 1991). The effect of computer-based instruction on learning was rather low for soft disciplines (Susman, 1998). General conclusions that hard disciplines have a greater moderating effect on learning have been made (e.g., Niemiec et al., 1996).

Proposition 5: The effect size of the use of IT on actual learning (academic achievement, knowledge retention, task performance) will be larger for hard disciplines than for soft disciplines.

Proposition 6: The effect size of the use of IT on perceived learning (self-reported learning, self-efficacy) will be larger for hard disciplines than for soft disciplines.

Instructor immediacy has to do with whether the course is to be "taught" using IT totally (where IT becomes a substitute for instructor) or partially (where IT supplements the instructor); obviously, instructor immediacy is higher in the latter than in the former. Computer-assisted instruction, for example, is generally considered a form of substitute for instructors, whereas networked learning is supplementary, as instructor presence is still distinctive. Substitution usually means learning *from* technology, where computers are tutors that direct the activities of the learner toward knowledge acquisition (Jonassen, 1993). Supplementation, on the other hand, usually means learning *with* technology (Yalcinap, Geban, & Ozkan, 1995); computers are used as cognitive tools to extend human minds and help learners to construct their own knowledge (Jonassen, 1993). Most researchers are interested in whether the use of IT can replace instructors completely. Underlying this notion is that as IT becomes more pervasive in educational institutions, there is the possibility of eliminating all human instructors and substituting them with machines. Nonetheless, research on instructor immediacy has found it related to measures of achievement (Richmond, Gorham, & McCroskey, 1987). IT is consistently shown to be an effective supplement to instruction.

Proposition 7: The effect size of the use of IT on actual learning (academic achievement, retention, task performance) will be larger for high instructor immediacy (IT being supplementary) than for low instructor immediacy (IT being substitute).

Proposition 8: The effect size of the use of IT on perceived learning (self-reported learning, self-efficacy) will be larger for high instructor immediacy (IT being supplementary) than for low instructor immediacy (IT being substitute).

The propositions are summarized by dependent variables in Table 1.

Table 1. Summary of propositions

Primary Causal Relationship	Potential Moderating Variables and Effects on Primary Relationship	
Availability of IT and Academic Achievement	Study Level	School > College*
	Ability-Grouping	Heterogeneous > Homogeneous
	Course Content	Hard > Soft
	Instructor Immediacy	High > Low
Availability of IT and Knowledge Retention	Ability-Grouping	Heterogeneous > Homogeneous
	Study Level	School > College
	Course Content	Hard > Soft
	Instructor Immediacy	High > Low
Availability of IT and Task Performance	Ability-Grouping	Homogeneous > Heterogeneous
	Study Level	School > College
	Course Content	Hard > Soft
	Instructor Immediacy	High > Low
Availability of IT and Self-Reported Learning	Cultural Background	Western > Eastern
	Course Content	Hard > Soft
	Instructor Immediacy	High > Low
Availability of IT and Self-Efficacy	Cultural Background	Western > Eastern
	Course Content	Hard > Soft
	Instructor Immediacy	High > Low

**This should be read as "The relationship between availability of IT and academic achievement is stronger (or more evident) in school settings than in college settings."*

Summary of Meta-Analysis

Data Sources

The meta-analytic approach used in this review is similar to that described by Hunter and Schmidt (1990). In addition, Glass' (1981) classic approach to meta-analysis was followed by: 1) locating studies through unbiased and replicable data searches, 2) coding the studies for prominent features, 3) describing each study's outcomes and creating a common scale, and 4) using statistical methods for combining a mixed set of results into a quantified conclusion. The search for related articles took four months, followed by regular monthly updates for the next three months. The primary studies located for this meta-analysis came from several sources. A computerized search of online databases resulted in over 100 studies that used words such as *technology, computer, communications, distance learning, Internet, achievement, academic skills, knowledge, retention, performance, satisfaction, school, college,* and *university* in their titles or abstracts. Additional studies were identified when study levels—for example, *fifth grade*—were used. A total of 204 studies with abstracts were generated in the computer search, and only 106 studies were available in full text from online journals.

Physical journals containing research and articles related to technology and computers in education were also identified, and these sources were reviewed from 1990 to the most recent issue available to check for additional references. Secondary sources for searching the studies were bibliographies from documents located through computer searches and journal articles. Finally, dissertation abstracts were searched for any doctoral thesis research not found in the previous efforts. Among other criteria for inclusion in this meta-analysis, a study had to include quantitative results in which educational outcome variables were the dependent variables for both experimental and control groups, and content of the course had to be part of regular curriculum in the implementation of technology.

Units of Statistical Analysis

Additional guidelines helped ensure the set of primary studies was as representative as possible. Some studies reported more than one finding for an outcome area because of: (1) the use of more than one experimental group, or (2) the use of several subscales and subgroups to measure a single outcome. Using several effect sizes to represent results from one outcome area seemed to be inappropriate as the effect sizes were usually non-independent. Hence, the procedure adopted in this meta-analysis was to calculate one effect size for each outcome area of each study. The rule of thumb used was to code total score and total group results, rather than sub-score and subgroup results in all other cases.

When several papers reported same comparison, the single, most complete report/update was used for this analysis. When the same comparison was carried out several times in the same course in the same institution for one or more semesters, data from the most recent semester was used. When two distinct studies were described in the same article (e.g., one study comparing results in secondary classes and one comparing results in tertiary classes), findings from the two studies were treated as separate results.

The inclusion criteria had to be stringent in order not to overlap with previous meta-analytic reviews. Majority of rejected studies that did not meet the criteria for integration into this study either did not statistically analyze the data, or had inadequate statistics (which were needed for calculations) reported. Attempts through e-mails were made to contact authors of the latter studies to request additional statistics, but these efforts were unsuccessful (either responses were negative or e-mails were not replied to). Out of more than 300 articles located and perused, 68 sets of results met the predetermined criteria for inclusion in this meta-analysis.

Variables Coded from Studies

To describe the main features of the various studies, the following variables were coded from each study: three variables that define learner characteristics are ability-grouping, study level, and cultural background; two variables defining course characteristics include course content and instructor immediacy. A reliability check was conducted on these variables coded. A research assistant helped to code all the study characteristics in the 68 primary studies accumulated. The rate of agreement on the coding of the variables was 96%. Conflicts were largely attributed to the values coded for instructor immediacy. Some studies involved instructors who behaved as facilitators and did not intervene in the experiments. The inconsistency was addressed by agreeing upon the operational definition of instructor immediacy: presence of the instructor playing a major role to assist and advise learners on learning content.

Data Analysis

The main effects of the use of technology across the different studies are shown in Table 2. There is an overall effect when the mean effect size differs significantly from zero. Confidence interval for each effect size is also computed to determine the rejection of the null hypothesis that the population effect size equals zero. All main effects were significant and positive. Homogeneity statistic (e.g., Benbasat & Lim, 1993) showed that the effect sizes were heterogeneous for all dependent variables. Moderating variables were used to account for the variation in technology and no-technology differences. The

Table 2. Summary of statistics for IT vs. no-IT differences

Dependent Variable	N	Mean–Weighted ES[a] ($\bar{d}$)	95% CI L	95% CI U	Homogeneity Statistic (Q_T)[b]
Academic Achievement	58	.507**	.431	.582	1688.86**
Knowledge Retention	39	.912**	.930	1.094	520.67**
Task Performance	42	.879**	.776	.981	1354.78**
Self-Reported Learning	40	.595**	.515	.674	332.01**
Self-Efficacy	34	.892**	.794	.991	1249.81**

Note: N = number of studies; ES = effect size; CI = confidence interval for mean weighted ES; L = lower limit; U = upper limit

* $p < .05$; ** $p < .01$

[a] *Effect size (ES) refers to the strength of a relationship between the use of IT and the dependent variable. It measures the difference of outcomes between the use of IT and the non-use of IT in education.*

[b] *Significance indicates rejection of the hypothesis of homogeneity.*

regression model was used to test the effect of the moderating variables. The categorical variables (ability-grouping, study level, cultural background, course content, and instructor immediacy) were coded as dummy variables.

Table 3 shows the regression analyses. In general, the R^2 values indicated that the predictors could explain the variability of the effect sizes. The small values of Q_E (error sum of squares) compared to the critical value also showed a good fit of each model.

Table 3. Multiple regression analysis for effect sizes

Dependent Variable	Moderating Variable	Regression Coefficient	R^2	Q_E	N	Fail-Safe N, N_{fs}	Proposition Supported?
Academic Achievement			.724	22.42	52	98	
	Ability-Grouping[i]	.542**					Yes
	Study Level[ii]	.061					No
	Course Content[iii]	.458**					Yes
	Instructor Immediacy[iv]	.114					No
Knowledge Retention			.732	24.31	36	99	
	Ability-Grouping	-.552**					No
	Study Level	-.254					No
	Course Content	.295*					Yes
	Instructor Immediacy	.045					No
Task Performance			.717	21.35	32	78	
	Ability-Grouping	.032					No
	Study Level	.539**					Yes
	Course Content	-.021					No
	Instructor Immediacy	.016					No
Self-Reported Learning			.731	24.04	32	87	
	Cultural Background[v]	.499**					Yes
	Course Content	-.109					No
	Instructor Immediacy	.474**					Yes
Self-Efficacy			.698	20.10	28	73	
	Cultural Background	.501**					Yes
	Course Content	.304*					Yes
	Instructor Immediacy	-.010					No

* $p < .05$; ** $p < .01$

i. *0: Homogeneous; 1: Heterogeneous*

ii. *0: College; 1: School;*

iii. *0: Soft; 1:Hard;*

iv. *0: Low (Substitute); 1: High (Supplement);*

v. *0: Eastern; 1: Western;*

Note: Effect sizes documented are positive for differences in the use of IT direction and negative for differences in the non-use of IT direction. Each model is weighted least square regression, with weights calculated as the reciprocal of the variance for each effect size.

Discussion

Learner Characteristics and IT

Ability-grouping was found to moderate IT's effect on academic achievement and knowledge retention. First, heterogeneous groups are found to achieve better academic results than homogeneous groups. This finding is consistent with previous work investigating behavior on the use of IT in cooperative learning (Susman, 1998). The IT experience might have made classroom activities more meaningful, reflected in the low achievers' increased interest in the subject matter. With this argument, IT must be credited, even if indirectly, for its role in helping to increase interest and motivation that could account for higher scores. The results also suggest that IT can reduce the differences in learning achievement among learners with different cognitive abilities.

On the other hand, the analysis indicated surprisingly that the homogeneously grouped learners had the tendency to do better in a re-test two to eight weeks later. They retained information longer when IT was being used to teach pedagogical content. Interestingly, learners in heterogeneous groups had done well in the first examination, but did not perform as well in the retention tests. Several factors, such as experience, time, and attitude, appear to be related to this finding. It is plausible that the lower-ability learners, with the experience of the first test, and given a longer time to assimilate what they learned, would be able to outperform the higher-ability learners in the same test a few weeks after the first test. Low-ability learners in heterogeneous groups might also have better achievement in the first exam due to influences of their higher-ability counterparts, but this benefit was not retained over time. A further correlation test between academic achievement and knowledge retention found the correlational coefficient to be -.88 ($p<.01$). This implied that decreasing results for retention tests were strongly observed for higher scores of achievement. Academic achievement, in this case, may act as an intervening variable in mediating the effects of the use of IT. Learners who performed better in the first test deteriorated in their performance for the retention test. Several studies tried to account for this conflict by suggesting that attention for the heterogeneous groups may be lower after performing well in the first test. The scores of higher achievers tend to reach the ceiling, hence making knowledge acquisition and improvement difficult over time. This set of findings is revealing, as it is contradictory to earlier work suggesting heterogeneous groups do equally well in the re-test (Escalada & Zollman, 1997).

Study level was found to moderate the impact of IT on task performance. The effect of IT in fostering learning was more pronounced among school learners in evaluations of task conducted. Manifested experience of learners may influence the ability of IT to communicate information effectively for increasing task performance. Learners may be more flexible in adapting to the use of IT for complex tasks at young ages. Bloom (1956) asserted that the environment would have the most profound effect on a trait during its period of rapid growth, in the case of school learners. With increasing age, these learners may become less susceptible to forces (IT applications) that might initially serve to aid them in carrying out their tasks. The use of IT, as a tool itself, may also be acting to enhance the ability of younger learners to question conventional wisdom by communicating frequently with instructors, instead of passively accepting that wisdom.

The cultural background of the learners was found to significantly moderate the effects of the use of IT on self-reported learning and self-efficacy. Learners in the western countries were found to perceive learning to be better when IT was used to teach the course. However, the literature also showed exceptional cases. For instance, the highly meritocratic and technologically biased system of Singapore might produce learners who perceived learning to be satisfactory (Ho, 1995). The findings also suggest that caution has to be taken when IT is being implemented in an eastern culture.

Course Characteristics and IT

Course content was found to moderate the effects of IT on academic achievement, knowledge retention, and self-efficacy. Academic achievement of learners was higher when IT was used to teach hard disciplines. A plausible explanation is that the structure of hard disciplines is commensurate with the discrete and objective steps that are inherent in technological instruction (Kwok & Khalifa, 1998). For instance, drill-and-practice software can help young learners develop competence in counting and sorting (Swan, 1991). On the contrary, a soft subject involves a more holistic approach to learning that may be incongruent with the use of IT (Davidson, Elcock, & Noyes, 1996). As predicted, the effect on knowledge retention for hard disciplines was higher than that for soft subjects. This trend is in contrary to earlier meta-analyses, where findings on soft disciplines were stronger. These studies argued that instruction in the hard disciplines was more difficult to improve, as learners are already achieving near their maximum. Hence, it was not clear whether the trend was favorable toward hard courses for learners to perform well academically and toward soft courses for achieving higher retention level.

Instructor immediacy was found to moderate IT's effect on self-reported learning. Human instructors can provide various types of advisement to assist learners in making informed decisions. The instructors can also help temper comments on learners' individual characteristics, especially in settings devoid of psycho-social cues available in a traditional classroom (Kitchen & McGougall, 1999). Learning is likely to be perceived better if instruction and information are provided via the presence of the instructor. One point to note is that although IT produced modest effects in a typical evaluation study, some individual studies reported large effects. Included among the studies that reported unusually strong, positive effects are several in psychology and music education. Researchers may want to scrutinize results of these atypical studies to point the way for better uses of technology in the years ahead.

Limitations

In undertaking this research, several limitations were encountered. Firstly, the findings for this meta-analysis faced similar limitations as the primary studies collected. For example, traditional methods of evaluating the effectiveness of educational technology presented a number of problematic issues for these experiments. Most available tests did not reliably measure the outcomes being sought as they are usually based on traditional instruments. New measures need to be developed to access higher-level skills and other effects often affected by technology, but it is difficult to measure students' progress when the tasks are so organic. Moreover, by the time long-term studies are completed, the technology being evaluated is often outdated. Secondly, Hunter and Schmidt's (1990) approach to meta-analysis should, ideally, estimate true effect sizes under conditions typical of those represented in the studies and predict treatment effects under conditions determined by the reviewer. This technique requires substantial information such as means and standard deviations from individual studies for accurate estimation of effect sizes. Unfortunately, this information is not always available in research reports.

Thirdly, the file drawer problem may exist since it is unlikely to include every possible study in this meta-analysis. Moreover, it is purported that many research journals publish studies that report only statistically significant and positive effects of technology. Such publication biases may have increased the effect sizes found in this meta-analysis and make journals an unreliable source for information about the effectiveness of experimental treatments. Hence, the fail-safe N was calculated to investigate whether this file drawer problem was significant. The large values of the fail-safe N calculated indicated that the small number of studies included in the meta-analysis did not pose a serious limitation on the results.

Finally, this study is subject to criticisms of the technique of meta-analysis. The reproach has been made that meta-analysis mixes "apples" and "oranges" (Hunter & Schmidt, 1990). In a sense this is true because the review has to cover a variety of studies that necessarily differ in a number of characteristics. This is to have an adequate scope to arrive at meaningful conclusions about a research domain. On the other hand, meta-analysis is valuable because it allows researchers to cumulate the findings of multiple studies (particularly those that are small in size) into a single measure of outcome. It estimates a specific magnitude for an independent variable's impact.

Other methods that aggregate diverse studies, such as box score reviews, indicate overall patterns and trends in research findings, but do not estimate the degree of influence of one variable on another. Meta-analysis allows the integration of the studies statistically and objectively to add strength to the narrative reviews currently available. Thus, there is no longer a serious criticism today that rejects meta-analysis methodology per se.

Future Trends

Teaching and learning are more complex than most research studies suggest. This study, undoubtedly, is no exception. While technology can make a difference, learning effectiveness ultimately depends on the learner, the course characteristics, instructional design, and the myriad of variables that interact as a function of learning effectiveness (Lefrancois, 1991). Technological instruction that optimizes the combination of effective variables will probably be the most effective. This induces several implications on research and practical issues.

This study focused on a comparison between the outcome effects of the use of IT and traditional methods of instruction. One important point to note is that there was no singularly influential moderating variable on most of the dependent variables. The absence of a strong moderating factor leads to some research implications. First, it is not sufficient to investigate only a single variable since the objectives of learning are too diverse (Kulik & Kulik, 1991). It is important to study how each powerful factor influences the pedagogical process, and how the specific features of these variables are appropriate with IT usage. Researchers have to explore the interacting effect of these potential variables instead of studying one particular factor in future work. Further, after overly exclusive, and probably inevitable, focus on technical development, educational technologists should attach increasing importance to the contributions of learner and course characteristics in their research agenda. In the long term, the use of IT should aim at the improvement of present education by giving learners more autonomy and possibilities to be creative. Moreover, by getting learners to work with technology, they gain familiarity with the future environment and the variety of tools that they will have at their disposal. Of importance is the change introduced in the relationship between instructor and learners, where the instructor is the one encouraging creative thinking of learners. However, inherent characteristics of learners should not be taken for granted. It is necessary for researchers to further study important characteristics such as ability level of learners and their cultural background.

On the practical side, in order to maximize the potential of technology, it is necessary for educators to match the use of IT with educational goals. Educators have to differentiate the needs of the learners and the outcomes that they want to achieve, and complement IT usage with the related moderating factor. Designers of IT applications need to appreciate that it is difficult to develop a system that will satisfy all the requirements of different schools. They have to identify the optimum combinations of attributes and treatments to be incorporated into their IT design. Our results also hold implication on another practical issue—the use of IT may be helpful in improving knowledge retention of learners with homogeneous ability levels, but less significant for those in heterogeneous settings. It shows the potential in improving learners' academic achievement and knowledge retention in hard disciplines. New curricula for teaching will have to be developed in light of the new horizons being opened up by the information technologies.

Concluding Remarks

Advanced technologies can be used to help instructors identify the conceptual frameworks of their learners, and help learners reconcile their prepositional knowledge with knowledge-in-action. The classroom of the information age will have to integrate learner-learner and learner-instructor dialogue with learner-computer dialogue in a way that treats the learners' own ideas not as errors or misconceptions, but as emergent theories with bugs (Susman, 1998). Studies of learning effectiveness should be augmented to encompass influences such as technical (e.g., type of media used) and instructor characteristics (e.g., past training with technology). Most studies have treated the use of IT as a black box with its products defined on pedagogical outcomes. Future studies should open up the black box to analyze the processes involving IT usage. Only then will the understanding of advantages and disadvantages help educators in deciding the use of IT applications that are more suitable in the unique milieu of the educational environment.

References

(The references marked with an * are studies included in the meta-analysis.)

Alavi, M. & Leidner, D.E. (2001). Research commentary: Technology-mediated learning—A call for greater depth and breadth of research. *Information Systems Research, 12*(1), 1-10.

Alavi, M. (1994). Computer-mediated collaborative learning: An empirical evaluation. *MIS Quarterly, 18*(2), 159-174.

Alavi, M., Marakas, G.M., & Yoo, Y. (2002). A comparative study of distributed learning environments on learning outcomes. *Information Systems Research, 13*(4), 404-415.

*Anderson, D.K. & Reed, W.M. (1998). Effects of Internet instruction and prior computer experience on Internet attitudes and knowledge. *Journal of Educational Computational Research, 19,* 37-44.

*Anthony, G. (2000). Technological factor influencing first-year students' success in mathematics. *International Journal of Mathematical Education in Science and Technology, 31*(1), 23-31.

*Bacon, S.F. & Jakovich, J.A. (2001). Instructional television versus traditional teaching of an introductory psychology course. *Teaching of Psychology, 28*(2), 88-91.

*Baron, L.J. & Abrami, P.C. (1992). The effects of group size and exposure time on microcomputer learning. *Computers in Human Behavior, 8,* 353-365.

Benbasat, I. & Lim, L.H. (1993). The effects of group, task, context, and technology variables on the usefulness of group support systems: A meta-analysis of experimental studies. *Small Group Research, 24*(4), 430-462.

Benbunan-Fich, R. & Hiltz, S.R. (1999). Effects of asynchronous learning networks: A field experiment. *Group Decision and Negotiation, 8*, 409-426.

Biglan, A. (1973). Relationships between subject matter characteristics and the structure and output of university departments. *Journal of Applied Psychology, 57*(3), 204-213.

Bloom, B.S. (1956). *Taxonomy of educational objectives: Handbook I: Cognitive domain.* New York: Longman, Green.

*Briggs, R., Ramesh, V., Romano, M.C., & Latimer, J. (1995). The Exemplar Project: Using group support systems to improve the learning environment. *Journal of Educational Technology Systems, 23*(3), 90-93.

*Brothen, T. & Wambach, C. (1998). An evaluation of lecture in a computer-based psychology course. *Journal of Educational Technology Systems, 26*(1), 12-17.

*Carrell, L.J. & Menzel, K.E. (2001). Variations in learning, motivation, and perceived immediacy between live and distance education classrooms. *Communication Education, 50*(3), 230-240.

*Carswell, L., Thomas, P., Petre, M., Price, B., & Richards, M. (2000). Distance education via the Internet: The student experience. *British Journal of Educational Technology, 31*(1), 29-46.

*Cathcart, G. (1990). Effects of logo instruction on cognitive style. *Journal of Educational Computing Research, 6*(2), 231-242.

Chen, A.Y., Mashhadi, A., Ang, D., & Harkrider, N. (1999). Cultural issues in the design of technology-enhanced learning systems. *British Journal of Educational Technology, 30,* 217-230.

*Clark, B.C. & Donohue, C. (1999). Comparing changes in attitude in 3 different introductory computing courses. *Journal of Educational Technology Systems, 27*(4), 211-216.

*Collins, M. (2000). Comparing Web correspondence and lecture versions of a second-year nonmajor biology course. *British Journal of Educational Technology, 31*(1), 21-27.

*Dalal, N.P., Haworth, D.A., Davis, M.A., Fowler, D.G., & Randolph, J.T. (1992). Educational software—it isn't always. *Journal of Educational Technology Systems, 20*(3), 169-178.

*Davidson, J., Elcock, J., & Noyes, P. (1996). A preliminary study of the effect of computer-assisted practice on reading attainment. *Journal of Research in Reading, 19*(2), 102-110.

*Dees, R.L. (1991). The role of cooperative learning in increasing problem-solving ability in a college remedial course. *Journal for Research in Mathematics Education, 22*(5), 409-421.

*Dietz-Uhler, B. & Bishop-Clark, C. (2001). The use of computer-mediated communication to enhance subsequent face-to-face discussions. *Computers in Human Behavior, 17,* 269-283.

Earley, P.C. (1994). Self or groups? Cultural effects of training on self-efficacy and performance. *Administrative Science Quarterly, 39*(1), 89-117.

*Erdner, R.A., Guy, R.F., & Bush, A. (1998). The impact of a year of CAI on development of first grade learning skills. *Journal of Educational Computational Research, 18,* 68-77.

*Escalada, L.T. & Zollman, D.A. (1997). An investigation of the effects of using interactive digital video in a physics classroom on student learning and attitudes. *Journal of Research in Science Teaching, 34*(5), 467-489.

*Fallah, M.H., How, W.J., & Ubell, R. (2000). Blind scores in a graduate test: Conventional compared with Web-based outcomes. *ALN Magazine*, *4*(2).

*Feldman, S.C. & Fish, M.C. (1991). Use of computer-mediated reading supports to enhance reading comprehension of high school students. *Journal of Educational Computing Research, 7*(1), 25-36.

*Fillion, G., Limayem, M., & Bouchard, L. (1999). Videoconferencing in distance education: A study of student perceptions in the lecture context. *Innovations in Education and Training Instructions, 36*(4), 302-315.

*Fletcher, C.P. (1992). Evaluation of the Stanford CAI program. *Journal of Educational Psychology, 83,* 333-343.

*Galbraith, P. & Haines, C. (1998). Disentangling the nexus: Attitudes to mathematics and technology in a computer learning environment. *Educational Studies in Mathematics, 36,* 275-290.

*Gershman, J. (1992). Computer-assisted remediation and evaluation: A CAI project for Ontario secondary schools. *Educational Technology*, *33*, 40-43.

Glass, G.V. (1981). *Meta-analysis in social research.* Beverly Hills, CA: Sage Publications.

*Gonzalez, G.M. & Birch, M.A. (2000). Evaluating the instructional efficacy of computer-mediated interactive multimedia: Comparing three elementary statistics tutorial modules. *Journal of Educational Computing Research, 22*(4), 411-436.

*Hiltz, S.R., Coppola, N., Rotter, N., & Turoff, M. (2000). Measuring the importance of collaborative learning for the effectiveness of ALN: A multi-measure, multi-method approach. *JALN*, *4*(2).

*Ho, M.S. (1995). *Learning and teaching in cyberspace: An empirical investigation of computer-assisted instruction for geography.* Academic Exercise, Department of Geography, FASS, National University of Singapore.

*Hooper, S., Temiyakarn, C., & Williams, M.D. (1993). The effects of cooperative learning and learner control on high and average ability students. *Educational Technology R&D, 41*(2), 5-18.

*Horton, S. & Lovitt, T. (1994). A comparison of two methods of administering group reading inventories to diverse learners. *Remedial and Special Education, 15*(6), 378-390.

*Hounshell, P. (1992). The microcomputer and achievement and attitudes in high school biology. *Journal of Research in Science Teaching, 31,* 543-549.

*Huang, H.C. & Eskey, D.E. (1999). The effects of technology on the listening comprehension of Intermediate English as a Second Language students. *Journal of Educational Technology Systems, 28*(1), 22-25.

*Hunter, M. & Chen, A. (1992). A microcomputer-networked information system for daily academic activity by low achieving students. *Journal of Special Education, 11*(4), 108-114.

Hunter, J.E. & Schmidt, F.L. (1990). *Methods of meta-analysis.* Newbury Park, CA: Sage Publications.

*Hurlburt, R.T. (2001). "Lectlets" delivery content at a distance: Introductory statistics as a case study. *Teaching of Psychology, 28*(1), 15-20.

*Jackson, A.C., Fletcher, B.C., & Messler, D.J. (1992). When talking doesn't help: An investigation of microcomputer-based group problem solving. *Learning and Instruction, 2,* 185-197.

Jonassen, D.H. (1993). Thinking technology. *Educational Technology, 33*(1), 35-37.

*Justen, J.E., Waldrop, P.B., & Adams, T.M. (1991). Effects of paired versus individual user computer-assisted instruction and type of feedback on student achievement. *Educational Technology, 30*(7), 51-53.

Kosakowski, J. (1998). *The benefits of information technology.* Retrieved March 2002 from *www.ericae.net.*

*Kwok, R.C.W. & Khalifa, M. (1998). Effect of GSS on knowledge acquisition. *Information and Management, 34,* 307-315.

Kulik, C.C. & Kulik, J. (1991). Effectiveness of computer-based instruction: An updated analysis. *Computers in Human Behavior, 7*(12), 75-94.

Lefrancois, A. (1991). *Psychology of teaching.* New York: Holt, Rinehart and Winston.

Leidner, D.E. & Jarvenpaa, S.L. (1995). The use of information technology to enhance management school education: A theoretical view. *MIS Quarterly, 19,* 265-291.

*Lewis, E.L., Stern, J.L., & Linn, M.C. (1993). The effect of computer simulations on introductory thermodynamics understanding. *Educational Technology, 34,* 45-58.

*Lieber, J. & Semmel, M. (1997). The relationship between group size and performance on a microcomputer problem-solving task. *Journal of Educational Computational Research, 16,* 24-31.

*Litchfields, R.E., Oakland, M.J., & Anderson, J.A. (2002). Relationships between intern characteristics, computer attitudes, and use of online instruction in a dietetic training program. *American Journal of Distance Education, 16*(1), 23-36.

*Liu, M. (1998). The effect of hypermedia authoring on elementary school students' creative thinking. *Journal of Educational Computational Research, 19,* 112-116.

*Lyons-Smith, C.L. (1991). Impact of graphic CBI on English mechanics for written communication. *Journal of Educational Technology Systems, 19*(3), 215-227.

*Maki, R.H., Maki, W.S., Patterson, M., & Whittaker, P.D. (2000). Evaluation of a Web-based introductory psychology course: I. Learning and satisfaction in on-line versus lecture courses. *Behaviour Research Methods, Instruments, & Computers, 32,* 230-239.

*Maki, W.S. & Maki, R.H. (2002). Multimedia comprehension skill predicts differential outcomes of Web-based and lecture courses. *Journal of Experimental Psychology: Applied, 8*(2), 85-98.

Mandler, G. (1989). Affect and learning: Causes and consequences of emotional interactions. In D.B. McLeod & V.M. Adams (Eds.), *Affect and mathematical problem solving: A new perspective* (pp. 3-19). New York: Springer-Verlag.

*Mevarech, Z.R. (1993). Who benefits from cooperative computer-assisted instruction? *Journal of Educational Computing Research, 9*(4), 451-464.

Niemiec, R.P., Sikorski, C., & Walberg, H.J. (1996). Learner-control effects: A review of reviews and a meta-analysis. *Journal of Educational Computing Research, 15*(2), 157-174.

*Ocker, R.J. & Yaverbaum, G.J. (1999). Asynchronous computer-mediated communication versus face-to-face collaboration: Results on student learning, quality and satisfaction. *Group Decision and Negotiation, 8,* 427-440.

*Ortiz, E. & MacGregor, S.K. (1991). Effects of logo programming on understanding variables. *Journal of Educational Computing Research, 7*(1), 37-50.

Owston, R.D. (1997). The World Wide Web: A technology to enhance teaching and learning? *Educational Researcher, 26*(2), 27-33.

*Piccoli, G., Ahmad, R., & Ives, B. (2001). Web-based virtual learning environments: A research framework and a preliminary assessment of effectiveness in basic IT skills training. *MIS Quarterly, 25*(4), 401-426.

*Postthast, M.J. (1995). Cooperative learning experiences in introductory statistics. *Proceedings of the Annual Meeting of the American Educational Research Association,* San Francisco, California.

*Reeder, L.K. & Leming, J.S. (1994). The effect of logo on the nonverbal reasoning ability of rural and disadvantaged third graders. *Journal of Research on Computing in Education, 26*(4), 558-564.

*Reimer, G. (1995). The effects of LOGO computer programming on readiness of first grade, creativity, and self concept. *AEDS Monitor, 31,* 8-12.

Richman, W., Kiesler, S., Weisband, S., & Drasgow, F. (1999). A meta-analytic study of social desirability distortion in computer-administered questionnaires, traditional questionnaires, and interviews. *Journal of Applied Psychology, 84*(5), 754-775.

Richmond, V.P., Gorham, J.S., & McCroskey, J.C. (1987). The relationship between selected immediacy behaviors and cognitive learning. In M. McLaughlin (Ed.), *Communication yearbook 10* (pp. 574-590). Newbury Park, CA: Sage Publications.

*Rosser, J.C., Herman, B., Risucci, D.A., Murayama, M., Rosser, L.E., & Merrell, R.C. (2000). Effectiveness of a CD-Rom multimedia tutorial in transferring cognitive knowledge essential for laparoscopic skill training. *The American Journal of Surgery, 179*(4), 320-324.

*Russell, M. (1999). Testing on computers: A study comparing performance on the use of computers. *Educational Policy Analysis, 7*(20).

Russell, T.L. (2002). The "no significant difference" phenomenon. Retrieved from *teleeducation.nb.ca/nosignificantdifference/*

*Sankaran, S.R., Sankaran, D., & Bui, T.X. (2000). Effect of student attitude to course format on learning performance: An empirical study in Web vs. lecture instruction. *Journal of Instructional Psychology, 27*(1), 66-73.

*Schoenfeld Tacher, R., McConnell, S., & Graham, M. (2001). Do no harm—a comparison of the effects of on-line vs. traditional delivery media on a science course. *Journal of Science Education and Technology, 10*(3), 257-265.

*Schutte, J.G. (1997, March). Virtual teaching in higher education: The new intellectual superhighway or just another traffic jam? *Proceedings of the All University Conference on Teaching and Learning Technologies.*

*Schware, R. & Jaramillo, A. (1993). Technology in education: The Turkish experiment. *Educational Technology Research and Development, 41*(2), 42-47.

*Shaw, G.D. (1992). Effects of LOGO on problem-solving abilities. *AEDS Journal, 27,* 176-189.

*Shin, E.C., Schallert, D.L., & Savenye, W.C. (1994). Effects of learner control, advisement, and prior knowledge on young students' learning in a hypertext environment. *Educational Technology Research and Development, 42*(1), 33-46.

Sleeter, C. & Grant, C. (1993). *Making choices for multicultural education.* New York: Macmillan.

Squires, D. & Preece, J. (1996). Usability and learning: Evaluating the potential of educational software. *Computers and Education, 27*(1), 15-22.

*Stephens, L.J. & Konvalina, J. (1999). The use of computer algebra in teaching intermediate and college algebra. *International Journal of Mathematical Education in Science and Technology, 30*(4), 483-488.

*Summers, J.A. (1991). Effect of interactivity upon student achievement, completion intervals and affective perceptions. *Journal of Educational Technology Systems, 19*(1), 53-55.

Susman, E.B. (1998). Cooperative learning: A review of factors that increase the effectiveness of computer-based instruction. *Journal of Educational Computing Research, 18,* 303-322.

*Swan, K. (1991). Programming objects to think with: Logo and the teaching and learning of problem solving. *Journal of Educational Computing Research, 7*(1), 89-112.

*Teh, B. (1995). Gender differences in achievement and attitudes among students using computer-assisted instruction. *International Journal of Instructional Media, 22,* 27-30.

*Vogler, C., O'Quin, K., & Paterson, W. (1991). Grade and knowledge improvement as a result of computer-assisted instruction. *Journal of Educational Technology Systems, 19*(3), 201-212.

Volery, T. & Lord, D. (2000). Critical success factors in online education. *The International Journal of Educational Management, 14*(5), 216-223.

*Wang, A.Y. & Newlin, M.H. (2000). Characteristics of students who enroll and succeed in psychology Web-based classes. *Journal of Educational Psychology, 92*(1), 137-143.

*Waschull, S.B. (2001). The online delivery of psychology courses: Attrition, performance, and evaluation. *Teaching of Psychology, 28*(2), 143-146.

*Wegner, S.B., Holloway, K.C., & Garton, E.M. (1999). The effects of Internet-based instruction on student learning. *Journal of Asynchronous Learning Networks, 3*(2).

Windschitl, M. (1998). The WWW and classroom research: What path should we take? *Educational Researcher, 27,* 28-33.

*Wishner, R.A., Curnow, C.K., & Seidel, R.J. (2001). Knowledge retention as a latent outcome measure in distance learning. *American Journal of Distance Education, 15*(3), 20-35.

*Yalcinap, S., Geban, O., & Ozkan, I. (1995). Effectiveness of using computer-assisted supplementary instruction for teaching the mole concept. *Journal of Research in Science Teaching, 32*(10), 1083-1095.

*Yu, F. & Yu, H.J. (2002). Incorporating e-mail into the learning process: Its impact on student academic achievement and attitudes. *Computers and Education, 38*(1), 117-126.

Chapter III

Computing and ICT Literacy: From Students' Misconceptions and Mental Schemes to the Monitoring of the Teaching-Learning Process

Antonio Cartelli
University of Cassino, Italy

Abstract

Three main questions guided the author in the writing of this chapter: Is there the need for a widespread and in-depth ICT literacy in mankind? What has to be meant for ICT literacy? And are there special problems in students' learning of ICT topics? And last but not least: How can ICTs themselves improve teachers' work and students' learning on ICTs? The introduction answers the first question and shows how difficult the search can be for solutions to the problem of the digital divide. The answer to the second question comes from a short survey of the experiences that some institutions made for the introduction of basic computing skills and ICT literacy in school curricula. In the meantime the problems that the students usually meet while attending computer programming and ICT literacy courses are described. Finally the author reports the results of some experiences involving the use of ICTs in teaching and describes how he arrived to hypothesize the adoption of action research strategies, of Web technologies and data mining techniques for the monitoring of the teaching-learning process and its improvement.

Introduction

In today's society, often defined the knowledge society, the mastery of ICTs (information and communication technologies) is considered very important for future citizens. It is well known, in fact, that computers and communication are everyday more and more present in human life, and that mankind has to be skillful in its use to win the challenge of contemporary and future complexity. As an example of the above remark, lifelong learning and the number of rights everyday needing the basic ICT skills can be considered: in the former case the continuous update of personal knowledge and skills is more and more, depending on the cleverness in ICT use; in the latter case e-government, e-commerce, e-learning, and so forth are good examples of the relevance that ICTs will have in the exercise of the citizens' rights, both today and in the future.

The importance of ICT influence on mankind has already been analyzed in various contexts, and the term *digital divide* has been adopted to describe the gap existing between developed and underdeveloped countries. As an example, the words of Malloch Brown (2001), of the UNDP (United Nations Development Program), are reported here:

> *"...Now, the Internet has become both the fuel and the vehicle for a dramatic spread in democracy, intensifying demand for and supporting the spread of genuinely transparent and participatory and more efficient systems of government at both the national and global levels. The number of democracies worldwide has doubled in little more than a decade. But in too many countries, institutions remain fragile, services are weak, officials unaccountable. And the lack of a democratic dividend—in terms of jobs and better services—has been undermining public faith in these new systems, particularly among the poor. ICT offers real hope in all these areas, offering greater citizen input into decision making and better social services for all...."*

Alternatively, it must be noted that digital divide was recently evidenced at different extents in developed countries. Warschauer (2003), for example, stated that digital divide is a social problem marking the differences among social classes (80% of high-income families in the U.S. connect to the Internet, while only 25% of low-income families do) and ethnic groups (55% of the White population in the U.S. uses ICTs, but only 31% of the African-American population and 32% of the Hispanic population do the same). He also stated that there isn't a unique digital divide marking the difference between "people who can" and "people who cannot" access computing and ICTs. What is more, he argued that there isn't a unique factor responsible for the separation among the different social groups and their ICT use. In other words ICTs alone cannot be identified only with the equipment to be inserted in the poorest contexts or with the people training; there are in fact many examples of failing experiences based on the above assumptions.

From what has been said to this point, it can be deduced that the digital divide is one of the contemporary pedagogical emergencies (Cartelli, 2004), and great efforts have to be made in everyday teaching to guarantee the diffusion of an effective ICT culture. The author's experience with the use of ICTs for the monitoring of the didactic process will show how the same ICTs can be turned into powerful instruments for improving the efficacy of teaching-learning processes and will help people in overcoming the problems they meet when they attend computing or computer programming courses.

Background

During the last two decades, all disciplines made progress in analyzing phenomena and developed new paradigms for interpreting reality. As a consequence the traditional procedure of transferring disciplinary knowledge into teaching practice led to a continuous revision of school programs and curricula.

On the other hand many psycho-pedagogical hypotheses were developed to explain the ways people build new knowledge when starting from previous knowledge, and experimental techniques were applied to individuals and communities to find new strategies and instruments for improving teaching.

One of the results of the above experiments was the discovery of misconceptions and mental schemes in students' minds and more in general in people's minds.

A good survey of the research on misconceptions and mental schemes can be found at the MLRG (Meaningful Learning Research Group, 2004) Web site (www.mlrg.org), where the proceedings of some conferences on misconceptions, wrong ideas, and meaningful learning are partially reported. Those studies collect research carried out all over the world and concern differently aged people, from pupils, to middle school, high school, and university students (sometimes they also include workers, professionals, and teachers).

Two main aspects clearly emerge from the above experiences (Cartelli, 2002b):

a. Preconceptions, misconceptions, and mental schemes can be found in all domains of human knowledge; most parts of the investigated fields concern scientific knowledge such as mathematics, physics, statistics, computer science, chemistry, biology, natural sciences, cosmology, and so forth, but there is a relevant number of studies (and that number is still growing) investigating the wrong ideas that students show with language, literature, history, and other human sciences,

b. Two main approaches can be adopted in such studies: a former one, labeled by Driver and Erickson (1983) as ideographic or naturalistic, analyzes the pupils' reasoning and more generally the ideas that people show when they explain phenomena with no reference to scientific paradigms—that is, they only evaluate the internal coherence of the people's concepts and ideas; the latter one, defined by the same authors, concerns people who already approached scientific topics (or were beginners), and evaluates the correctness of their ideas with respect to the scientifically accepted ones.

Regarding ICTs and especially computer science, the following events intervened in making more complex the situation: (1) the exponential growth with the time of the discipline topics (i.e., during the last three decades), (2) the spreading of personal computing, (3) the revolution in human-computer interaction induced by graphics interfaces, and (4) the Internet.

The main results of the studies carried out during last two decades concern the presence of wrong ideas and misconceptions in students attending computer programming courses (du Boulay, 1986; Soloway & Spohrer, 1988). More recently it looked as if the introduction of special GUI (graphic user interfaces) and WYSIWYG (what you see is what you get) strategies could help novices in overcoming the above difficulties, but the results of other studies did not agree with this hypothesis, and showed the presence of preconceptions and misconceptions, even with the new human-computer interaction (Ben-Ari, 1998; Christozov & Mateev, 2003).

Computer Science Teaching and Computing Literacy: A Survey

It must be noted that before digital divide evidence, many scholars (mostly computer scientists) already assigned great importance to the introduction of computer science elements in the curricula of high schools or junior high schools (at least in Western countries). On the other hand, it must be said that there has never been a general agreement on the computing topics to be taught in the schools; nevertheless, professional associations (ACM and Computer IEEE, first of all) produced syllabi or suggested different solutions in this respect.

The most important consequence of the above uncertainties was the lack of a unique proposal for the planning of the introduction of computing teaching in education. As an example the analysis of the Italian situation will be reported in the following section (Cartelli, 2002c), and the results of some experiences the author led with his students will be discussed.

The Italian Experience in Computing Teaching

In 1985 the Italian Ministry of Education collected the results of many research projects on computer use in education which were carried out all over the country and which stated that computer science could be used in high school education in the following ways: (a) as an instrument to automate the school administration, (b) as an instrument to help teachers in their work or a resource for students, and c) as a knowledge amplifier to develop reasoning and problem-solving skills in the students.

Among other things it was supposed that computer science could help students in: (a) problem analysis and formalization of its solutions (algorithmic), (b) use of data structures, (c) coding of procedures in computer instructions, and 4) use of CAI (computer-assisted instruction) and CAL (computer-assisted learning) tools. In other words the adoption of all Taylor's (1980) metaphors—tutor, tool, and tutee—in everyday teaching was suggested.

To make concrete the above proposals, the National Plan for Computer Science (PNI—*Piano Nazionale di Informatica*) was started. This plan was devoted to a revision of the mathematics and physics curricula in the first two years of high school, with the main aim of developing computing knowledge and skills in the more general context of the above disciplines. The same plan had two phases: a former one for the training of a task force (mostly teachers already involved in computing teaching experiences), and a latter one that used the above staff members in training courses for the other teachers.

A few years later a new document of the Ministry of Education analyzed the results of the PNI application and suggested the reconsideration of the introduction of new technologies in education. (It must be noted that the ministry now adopted the term *new technologies* in place of the previous *computer science*). The different terminology has its roots in a paper of V. Midoro, G. Olimpo, and D. Persico (1996) at the ITD-CNR (Institute for Technologies in Education–National Research Council); they proposed the term *didactic technologies* to describe computer use as a special case of technology introduction in education, and focused on the use of special tools for supporting class work more than on computer programming and related skills. Because of the above change, the Ministry of Education in 1997 began a new project called PSTD (a triennial plan for the development of didactic technologies). This project mainly involved primary and junior high schools, and gave to these schools the funds needed to create multimedia computing laboratories for teachers and students.

Recently, mostly yearly, statistical analyses on the evolution of the ICT presence and use in the schools were carried out. The most relevant results can be summarized as follows: (a) all the schools have at least a PC (if not a computer room) and Internet access, (b) a relevant number of teachers (more than 50%) attended or are attending computing literacy courses (mostly online), (c) only a few teachers (less than 10%) systematically use the Internet in their teaching work, and (d) a very little number of students (less than 15%) systematically use ICTs and especially the Internet at school.

Misconceptions and Mental Schemes in Computer Programming

If computer programming is considered very useful in the development of problem-solving and planning skills, the author's experience as a computing teacher in a high school (the Italian Technical High School, with a specific computer science curriculum) shows how difficult the teaching of the above topics can be.

It is well known, in fact, that computer programming is a complex task for students and that it requires great effort from them (Lemut, 1993), but it is less known that the students' difficulties can persist notwithstanding the change in methods and techniques the teachers can adopt in their work, and that many students also manifest the same incorrect ideas after attending specific make-up courses.

Some computer programming topics (related to imperative languages like Pascal and C) for which students evidenced wrong ideas are reported below (Cartelli, 1994, 1996):

1. *The range of the numerical data types:* The students almost never verify the correctness of a variable data type if the result of an automatic calculus differs from the handmade one.
2. *The use of the cyclic structures (for...to...loop, etc.):* Many students cannot write the correct statements for an iterated sum containing a total variable (often they put a specific assignment for that variable after the end of the loop), or would like to use the for...to... structure much more than the other ones (and also when it is impossible to use it).
3. *The use of conditional statements:* While composing these statements the students always write the relationships among the variables and dislike the use of Boolean variables, when explicitly asked to use these variables they tend to relate them with the values true and false (for example they write: if A = true then ... with A Boolean variable),
4. *The use of the structured data types (arrays):* Many students cannot manage the single elements of an array (they use the whole array in input, output, or calculus operations) and almost never succeed in writing the correct statements for finding the least or the greatest values in an array.
5. *The subprograms*: The students often insert in a function or a procedure many statements better belonging to the main program.
6. *The recursion*: This is one of the most difficult topics to be taught and learned, and often the students confuse iteration with recursion.
7. *The abstract data types (stack, list, queue, tree, etc.):* The students have a few problems in understanding the theory and the application principles for these topics, but have great difficulties in the use of the pointer variables for the management of the same data types.

Other problems can be found in logic programming, OOP (object oriented programming), and data file management, so it clearly appears that almost all computer programming fields evidence teaching-learning problems, requiring a great attention from professors and students.

A good aid in the improvement of the teaching-learning process is represented from the individual and group strategies a teacher can adopt in the class (it should be noted that the author's classes, like most nationwide, had no more than 28 students). In the former case the tools making transparent the execution of an algorithm by means of the visualization of the variables' values and the evolution of the system's states are very useful in helping students to overcome some difficulties; in the latter case the individual and social constructivist strategies usually adopted in communities of learners (Brown & Campione, 1994) can lead students to the meaningful learning of the proposed topics (Greening, 2000) (participated lessons, class discussion of problem finding and solving, group discussion of case analysis, individual and group discussion and evaluation of the procedures to be used, individual and group adoption of metacognitive strategies, cognitive apprenticeship strategies, construction of distributed expertises).

It must be also noted that when both of the above strategies are applied in a class with great success (the measure of such a success is usually taken from the results of the periodic and ending tests the students are submitted to), there is no guarantee for the students' overcoming the problems reported above. The students can in fact show difficulties and make errors, after having attended the above courses, when asked to answer special or misleading questions (Cartelli, 2002a).

ICT Literacy Misconceptions

If there is common agreement on the difficulties the students meet in computer programming study, it is important to note that computing literacy is not seen in the same perspective. Instead, it is commonly seen as a vocational training involving the following topics: computer structure and computer use for data management (use of an operating system), communication (the Internet use), and office automation (word processing, calculus, presentation tools, database management systems).

The author does not agree at all with the above point of view (he is persuaded there is no computing literacy without a computing culture), but his opinion has no relevant influence on the knowledge, the abilities, and the skills people must obtain at the end of a basic computer science course. On another hand, the computing associations joining the CEPIS (the European computing professionals association) greatly supported proposal of a definition of a unique syllabus for basic computing skills; the ECDL (European computer driving license) is now the standard de facto for computing literacy in Europe.

Nevertheless, no syllabus can delete the following question: Are there wrong ideas, misconceptions, and mental schemes in computing literacy or basic computing courses? In the author's opinion this situation is very similar to the computer programming one, and there are many topics needing a great deal of attention from teachers and trainers (Christozov & Mateev, 2003). In fact, the experience the author had in vocational and basic university courses (with first-year students of the educational and social courses at the Faculty of Humanities) evidenced the presence of wrong ideas on the following topics (Cartelli, 2002a):

- *Input/output, memory, and processing units:* Very often the students do not recognize the category of a given device when they are asked to specify it.

- *Operating systems:* When asked to specify what this is, most of the students chose the wrong answer, "It is an integrated hardware/software system that makes the PC active," instead of right one, "It is the set of the programs letting [the] user manage the computer resources."
- *Icons and pointers*: When asked to specify what these are, many students selected the less right answers, "Images letting the user access the computer parts" and "Instruments for the displacement of the objects on the desktop or in a window," instead of the right answer for both questions: "They are the instruments of the computer-human interaction."
- *The Internet:* Many students state "It is a communication system based on the use of the telephone" rather than "It is a communication system based on computer networks."
- *The Web:* When asked to explain what it means to browse the Web, many students state "to connect to the Internet" rather than "to use a special program like the MS Explorer or the Netscape browsers to see Web pages."

With respect to computer programming experience, some differences can be noticed: (a) the wrong ideas reported above were obtained from the students' answers to written tests, (b) the number of the students attending the lessons was now higher than in a computer programming situation, and (c) individual and social constructivist experiences were planned and carried out with the help of an e-learning platform and with the cooperation of tutors (who managed online and presence work), but very little ameliorations in the students' ideas could be observed at the final examinations.

E-Learning and Computing Literacy

What has been reported in the above section needs further explanation for its implications. It should be noted, in fact, that the misconceptions were detected during long-term teaching and the results of former experiences led to the development of a special information system for the monitoring of the didactic process (it is a dynamic Web site interfaced with a relational database storing all information coming from the students' browsing of the site). The didactic materials of previous basic computing courses (Cartelli & Ruggiero, 2000, 2001) were integrated into the information system, which was planned taking into serious consideration the results of the research on students' misconceptions and mental schemes.

The system, very similar by its features to an e-learning platform, offered—together with a well-structured knowledge tree of the topics to be taught/learned—the following functions: (a) various communication areas implementing virtual environments for teachers/professors, tutors, and students; (b) a careful management of the students' evaluation and assessment tests; and (c) two functions for the analysis of the students' access to the course materials and their use of the communication services.

The management of all information in the site was guaranteed from five user levels or selected accesses: (a) the system administrator, (b) the professors, (c) the tutors, (d) the students, and (e) the researchers and scholars (who could only retrieve the information on the students' access to the course materials).

The two information retrieval functions to be used for students' monitoring had the following features:

1. The former one reported the number of times that a single student or a group of students accessed the site's pages until the query date (the numerical data were reported in the tree structure of the site).
2. The latter one gave the sequence of each student's access to the Web site, ordered by date and hour of access. It could also report the messages the student left in the electronic blackboard, in the chat, in the forum, and in the case study areas, and let the teachers compare all the data stored in the same time interval.

After a first positive test of the system on a limited number of students (66), the study was extended to the students attending two first-year courses. The high number of students (more than 350) now made the continuous monitoring of the didactic process impossible and didn't allow an instantaneous control of students' incorrect ideas if the data stored in the system were available for further elaborations (they were analyzed after the end of the courses).

Strictly speaking the experiment was positive for the students—there was only a 20% loss of students at final examinations, and more than 65% of them had positive if not excellent scores.

Alternatively, the subsequent analysis of the students' access to the course's Web pages confirmed the presence of a relevant number of persons still showing misconceptions and wrong ideas. Other results emerging from that analysis were: (a) there is always a good correlation between the highest scores at the assessment test, and the systematic and repeated browsing of the online materials; and (b) little score increments from the entry to the last test are always related to successful browsing of the online materials.

Conclusion and Further Hints

The results of the above experiences clearly show: a) the implications ICTs have on the meaning of knowledge both to an individual and a disciplinary extent, b) the computer science topics that should be taught in school, and c) the innovations that must be introduced in everyday class work for the improvement of the teaching-learning process.

Regarding the first point, it must be noted in the author's opinion that psycho-pedagogical hypotheses looking at learning as a static and definitive process need a deep revision. It has been shown that individual knowledge, also when well settled and consistent with discipline knowledge, can be neglected by individuals and can lead to misconception.

As a consequence, teaching and didactic research have to evolve together, and the question on the topics to be taught must be replaced with the following question: Do we have to accept the risk of misconceptions and mental schemes in students' minds and hypothesize a cyclical teaching process leading to a continuous amelioration of the proposed topics, or do we have to carefully plan a deeper analysis of the discipline themes soon leading to a right disciplinary knowledge? In both cases new instruments for a more efficient monitoring of the teaching-learning process are needed.

In the author's opinion a good move in this direction comes from the systematic adoption of Web technologies interfaced with information systems. These systems could store all students' operations, and produce descriptive and inferential statistical analyses on the data stored. An indirect evidence for this need comes from the results of the experience reported in the last section where the continuous monitoring of the didactic process was impossible because of the lack of statistical analysis features in the two available functions (which only reported the data stored in the system, without making any elaboration on them).

Furthermore the use of the above information system will make possible the systematic adoption of the action-research strategies by the teachers. It will revert the usual strategies until now adopted in the management of the teaching-learning process because, with respect to well-established methods, it will be event driven; that is, the students' learning styles, profits, and scores will be the phenomena to be observed and translated in indices describing the environment within which the teaching-learning process will be continuously re-planned. The statistical analysis of the data stored in the information system will give:

1. the change in the time of the features of a single student (by means of indices describing well-defined behaviors and learning styles);
2. the change in the time of the features of the students' groups, such as the classes and the whole schools; and
3. the change in the space of the features of the students' groups, that is how different environments can influence the evolution of the students' learning models.

In other words data mining strategies could be applied to the analysis of the teaching-learning process, and great improvements will follow for the management of that process and for the students' results.

References

Ben-Ari, M. (1998). Constructivism in computer science education. *Proceedings of the 29th SIGCSE Technical Symposium on Computer Science Education* (pp. 257-261). New York: ACM Press.

Brown, A.L. & Campione, J.C. (1994). Guided discovery in a community of learners. In K. McGilly (Ed.), *Classroom lessons: Integrating cognitive theory and classroom practice* (pp. 229-270). Cambridge, MA: MIT Press.

Cartelli, A. (1994). Misconcetti e schemi alternativi in informatica. In A. Andronico, G. Casadei, & G. Sacerdoti (Eds.), *Proceedings of DIDAMATICA 1994—Informatica per la Didattica* (pp. 87-102). Cesena, Italy: Il Ponte Vecchio.

Cartelli, A. (1996). Analisi di alcuni schemi mentali in studenti di informatica. In A. Andronico, G. Casadei, & G. Sacerdoti (Eds.), *Proceedings of DIDAMATICA 1994—Informatica per la Didattica* (pp. 64-78). Cesena, Italy: Il Ponte Vecchio.

Cartelli, A. (2002a). Didattica, tecnologie Web e apprendimento: Analisi e prospettive. In A. Andronico, A. Chianese, & B. Fadini (Eds.), *Proceedings of DIDAMATICA 2002—Informatica per la Didattica* (pp. 169-176). Naples, Italy: Liguori.

Cartelli, A. (2002b, June 18-22). Web technologies and sciences epistemologies. In E. Cohen & E. Boyd (Eds.), *Proceedings of the IS 2002 Conference* (pp. 225-238), Cork, Ireland. Retrieved December 21, 2004 from *ecommerce.lebow.drexel.edu/eli/2002Proceedings/papers/Carte203Webte.pdf*

Cartelli, A. (2002c). Computer science education in Italy: A survey. *inroads SIGCSE Bulletin (ACM Quarterly), 34*(4), 36-39.

Cartelli, A. (2003). Didactics and Web technologies: A proposal for the monitoring of the didactic process. In F. Malpica, A. Tremante, & N. Sala (Eds.), *Proceedings of the EISTA 2003 Conference—Education and Information Systems: Technologies and Applications* (pp. 225-238), Orlando, Florida: IIIS.

Cartelli, A. (2004). Pedagogia, didattica e nuove tecnologie: Tre saggi per una rivoluzione annunciata. *Quaderni del Centro di Facoltà per le TIC e la didattica on line 1.* Cassino, Italy: U. Sambucci.

Cartelli, A. & Ruggiero, S. (2000). Misconcetti e Web: Un sito dedicato all'autovalutazione ed all'autoapprendimento. In A. Andronico, G. Casadei, & G. Sacerdoti (Eds.), *Proceedings of DIDAMATICA 2000—Informatica per la Didattica, Sezione Lavori Scientifici* (pp. 123-133). Cesena, Italy: Il Ponte Vecchio.

Cartelli, A. & Ruggiero, S. (2001). Un'esperienza di formazione a distanza: Il progetto icaro. In A. Andronico, A.M. Fanelli, G. Piscitelli, & T. Roselli (Eds.), *Proceedings of DIDAMATICA 2001—Informatica per la Didattica, Sezione Lavori Scientifici* (pp. 121-129). Bari, Italy: G. Laterza.

Christozov, D. & Mateev, P. (2003). Warranty as a factor for e-learning success. In E. Cohen & E. Boyd (Eds.), *Proceedings of IS + IT Education 2003 Conference* (pp. 491-495). Retrieved December 21, 2004 from *ecommerce.lebow.drexel.edu/eli/2002Proceedings/papers/Carte2003Webte.pdf*

Driver, R. & Erickson, G. (1983). Theories in action: Some theoretical and empirical issues in the study of students' conceptual frameworks in science. *Studies in Scientific Education, 10*(37).

du Boulay, B. (1986). Some difficulties of learning to program. *Journal of Educational Computing Research, 2*(1), 57-73.

Greening, T. (2000). *Computer science education in 21st century.* New York: Springer-Verlag.

Lemut, E., du Boulay, B., & Dettori, G. (1993). Cognitive models and intelligent environments in learning programming. *NATO ASI Series 111.* New York: Springer-Verlag.

Malloch Brown, M. (2001). *Democracy and the information revolution.* Retrieved October 9, 2001, from *www.digitaldividenetwork.org/content/stories/index.cfm?key=192*

MLRG (Meaningful Learning Research Group). This Web site reports the titles of the papers presented at four different international meetings on misconceptions and meaningful learning: *Proceedings of the Misconceptions in Science and Mathematics, Second Misconceptions Proceedings, Third Misconceptions Proceedings,* and *Proceedings of "From Misconceptions to Constructed Understanding" Conference.* Retrieved April 19, 2004, from *www.mlrg.org*

Midoro, V., Olimpo, G., & Persico, D. (1996). *Tecnologie didattiche. Metodi e strumenti innovativi per la didattica.* Ancona, Italy: Menabò.

Soloway, E. & Spohrer, J.C. (1988). *Studying the novice programmer.* Mahwah, NJ: Lawrence Erlbaum.

Taylor, R. (1980). *The computer in the school: Tutor, tool and tutee.* New York: Teachers College Press.

Warschauer, M. (2003). Verso l'uguaglianza informatica. *Le Scienze (Italian Edition of Scientific American), 421*(September), 62-67.

Chapter IV

Technology-Infused Instruction: A New Paradigm for Literacy

Rose Mary Mautino
Duquesne University, USA

Stefan L. Biancaniello
Duquesne University, USA

Abstract

This chapter introduces a model of technology-infused literacy instruction that implements a constructivist approach to teaching and learning that defines a new paradigm for the classroom of the twenty-first century. It argues that in the face of the constant change process that is redefining literacy instruction today, it will be necessary to rethink our curriculum and redesign our instruction to infuse new technologies. In this new paradigm it will be necessary to not only ask different questions, but also to redefine the context in which the questions are posed. Students learning must focus on exploration, investigation, paradoxes, and inquiries. We must teach students to start their inquiries with "essential questions" in mind, and to seek not answers but rather new questions, new theories, and new ideas. The technologies of literacy in the future will need to function as cognitive tools that guide students in the generation of the concentric circles of lifelong learning.

Deictic Change

As the twenty-first century begins to unfold, it is becoming increasingly evident that change is defining the nature of literacy. The impact of the information age has produced enormous impetus for rapid and continuous change in literacy, driven predominately by the appearance of new technologies designed to address the ever-changing needs for information and communication. These new technologies produce new kinds of literacy that in turn produce new applications of the technology. The mutual initiatives generate continuous cycles of innovation that accelerate the process of change. Today continuous rapid change regularly redefines the nature of literacy and increases the challenges educators face as they consider how best to prepare students for literacy in the future.

Perhaps for the first time in history, we are attempting to prepare students for a literacy future that we cannot define nor predict. Literacy and being literate are routinely redefined through the innovation of new technologies, and the constant demand for increased speed and scope of communication in what many have called an "informational revolution." In an attempt to understand this phenomenon, Donald Leu has identified three distinct relationships between literacy and technology: (1) transformative change, in which technology regularly and systemically changes literacy through the evolution of literacy-based technological advances; (2) transactional change, where technology and literacy interact and change each other as new technologies generate new potential and implementation initiates variations to the technology; and (3) deictic change, which is a constant state of change of both technology and literacy demonstrated through human impact with new technologies. This is manifested in most cases by immediate human adjustment to the implementation vision of these new technologies. The result is a continuous change process that impacts planning, potential, and performance.

In both transformative and transactional change, there is some delay time in the impact between the arrival of new technology and the implementation literacy needed to make the technology useful for teaching and learning. This delay can provide time for analysis, practice, and infusion into the learning experience. The reality, however, is that this delay produces significant variations in interpretations of the technology, its application, and implementation in the teaching and learning process. This diversity can and does erode the effectiveness and impact of technology in classroom instruction. Recent research has shown that the results of this time delay may have many root causes, but at the center, two situations have demonstrated significant impact: (1) a lack of opportunity to develop an understanding of the potential presented by the innovation, and (2) a lack of teacher experience with new technologies, exploring, experimenting, and learning how these tools can enrich the learning experience. Further study is needed in this area to identify why education is experiencing confusion and less focus on how new technology and subsequent new literacy can enrich the learning opportunity. Perhaps it is the lack of expertise in schools and school districts to provide professional development for teachers on the use and application of emerging technologies in the instructional environment. Perhaps it is the lack of time to deliver professional development and practice with the new technologies and new concepts for instruction, or a combination of both. Regardless, these delays in the face of deictic change have been problematic.

As the delay time between technology and implementation decreases, questions of equity in opportunity, relativity of curriculum, and professional preparedness have raised concerns within the educational community.

Coping with Change

Eisenberg and Johnson (1996) found that in many schools, most teachers and students were using computers more or less as expensive flash cards, electronic worksheets, or word processors. Over the past several years, there has been a slow and steady influx of classroom applications that include the online resources of the Internet and presentation software that engage students in Web site review and publication of student work. In addition, new interactive software with decision modules can engage students in problem analysis, solution generation, and evaluation of their strategies. There is much evidence that technology has produced the potential to dramatically impact instruction and literacy, but little evidence that it has reached that level of practice. One bright spot in this research was the fact that Eisenberg and Johnson also identified some encouraging signs in new curriculum thinking design that were seeking to integrate technology into a wide range of content areas. What they found was new technologies were creating tension (a creative pressure if you will) to find applications for these new tools that present so much promise in the challenge to engage students in rigorous thinking experiences and motivate students to produce rich student work. At present, there remains much work in formalizing the cycle of technological impact on instruction. Time issues, budget issues, curriculum issues, and instructional methodologies all have been identified as genuine roadblocks to creative technology interfaces to support literacy.

In 1991 Sandholtz, Ringstaff, and Dwyer conducted research that identified three important insights with respect to technology integration: (1) high access by both teachers and students was critical, (2) increased time for sharing iterations between educators increased the speed and depth of innovative implementations, and (3) any successful implementation of these innovations requires change at multiple levels. School readiness for these changes was a critical indicator for success in the infusion of creative technologies into instruction. As evolving technologies become more sophisticated, literacy demands more diverse, and pressure from society more intense, our schools, classrooms, and teachers struggle with the challenge of infusing technology and new literacy into curriculum and instruction. The deictic process produces a rush of continuous new thought and new potential that generates constant pressure on the education community to learn, adapt, and implement new literacy simultaneously and continuously. Today, even though we may see more visible use of technology in literacy instruction, we are also experiencing dramatic shortfalls in realizing the full potential of this interface. Extending the work of Sandholtz, Ringstaff, and Dwyer, Moersch (1995) identified several levels of instructional practice that produced a continuum of skill and application with respect to the implementation of technology in the learning environment. His research produced categories or phases of implementation and integration of technology in the learning environment.

At Level I, learning materials, activities, and teaching methodologies were all tied directly to specific content and specific objectives. Instruction was strictly sequenced emphasizing explicit skill development with an expository delivery model. Whole-group instruction and teacher-centered lessons were used. Evaluation was traditional with technology utilized for drill and practice instruction and computer-based content software programs used to remediate students who were achieving below grade level. In some instances, technology was also being used as a management system to track student progress through the content presented by the software. Many of these iterations of technology presented information, but did not link to the curriculum or the content standards. Technology was employed, but functioned more as a parallel instructional process than one integrated into the curriculum.

Level II implementations demonstrated more problem-solving activities, with multiple performance assessments and technology functioning within the curriculum through isolated experiences. Once again, these experiences may or may not tie to the curriculum. They were however problem based and engaged the students in some higher-order thinking activities. It is only at Level III where he identified technology as an integral piece of the learning experience. Instruction was delivered with and through technology. Learning objectives were directly addressed through the technology. Students interacted in small groups, and independently in performance tasks and inquiry-based learning environments.

As you might expect, many more classrooms were functioning at Levels I and II. Reaching Level III required knowledge and skill for teachers and students, and the presence of all three of the indicators identified by the earlier research of Sandholtz, Ringstaff, and Dwyer. Today, almost 10 years after this research, we still see many more classrooms and schools functioning at Levels I and II. It is the small number of adventurous and risk-taking teachers who have pushed their thinking to more effectively use technology. It is the innovative school community that is stimulating the potential of teachers and technology. Both seem to be the exception rather than the rule.

New Challenges

To address the current deictic change process, new challenges exist to generate learning environments in which technology interacts with curriculum and instruction seamlessly. The technological interface will need to be invisible as the innovations are used as tools for gathering information, coordinating concepts, testing hypotheses, and producing student work. Teachers and students will need to be engaged in a learning community and construct knowledge through innovative infusions of technology into the teaching and learning process. There is compelling evidence that a disconnect exists in the potential and realization of the impact of technology as a true extension of student learning. What we know is that the deictic change process of literacy and technology has produced additional pressure in the face of standards and new accountability. How do we cope?

The Disconnect between Potential and Reality

The drive to compete in the marketplace of the twenty-first century and the demand for information and communication is spearheading the rise of new technologies in both industry and education. A quick survey of most classrooms would produce evidence that technology is indeed visible and accessible to students. However, the evidence from recent research points to the realities that training, professional development, and practice with the emerging technologies in the education forum is lagging far behind and subsequently producing gaps as educators try to catch their breath in the face of rapid change.

Recent reviews (e.g., Ayersman, 1996; Reinking, McKenna, Labbo, & Keiffer, 1998) provide a number of observations depicting technology use supporting literacy. Educators have responded to this push from the marketplace. School communities have made technology available to students and teachers. At question is evidence of the impact of these innovations on student learning. Important to note here is the fact that results of any study must be viewed within the context of this deictic change process. As new technologies arise the variables that exist impacting the infusion of technology into the teaching and learning process change, making correlation study results vulnerable. It is difficult to separate the student learning effects that are due to the technology innovation from those of "best practice" instructional methodology. In fact, Finkelman and McMunn (1995) and Tierney et al. (1997) suggest that the success or failure of technology implementation designs may reside more with the use of creative instructional methods rather than the introduction of a new technology interface. Limited technology skills demand more creative instructional strategies to melt technology into instruction. As we attempt to imbed new technology into the current paradigm of curricula, this interference of processes will continue to disguise impact. The disconnect between availability and implementation of technology will persist without creatively addressing the needs to bring professional staff to a level of expertise that supports technology as a creative instructional tool and the production of curricula that infuses technology into instruction. Unless we rethink our curriculum to provide the time and opportunity to genuinely engage the students in student-centered, standards-based meaningful investigation with technology, measuring the impact of these technologies will remain questionable.

Current Interventions of Technology in Literacy

Given this disconnect, schools and teachers have continued to address technology and implement its application into existing curricula. What have these efforts produced? The proliferation of technology in the classroom experience, especially language arts, has been significant over the past decade. Creative and innovative software has been incorporated into instruction and assessment in both lesson delivery and management.

In many districts and classrooms today, technology does interact with students and the curricula. There are countless types of content-based software applications and online programs that provide access to reading material, problems, experiments, and so forth. The local area networks functioning in most schools now provide creative communication venues for learning and sharing. Electronic portfolios, e-mail, and the explosion of resources of the Internet have generated a whole new world of opportunity. Data tracking software and online assessment have opened new doors for the analysis of student achievement data. A partial answer to the question "What did the effort produce?" is evidenced by the diversity of applications of technology in many classrooms. The impact on student learning is much more elusive. How is this powerful tool for human thinking really being used to enrich, augment, and extend the learning process especially in the area of literacy and comprehension?

Cognition and Social Learning

To address this question, it is important that we have some understanding of how the human brain processes information and uses that information to think, reason, and make meaning. The diverse research on human cognition has demonstrated that our brain is not a formal logic machine. Indeed, it is much better at making sense of life by finding patterns and order. Our intrinsic motivation and need to know are two of our greatest gifts. Our brain was designed as a meaning maker. Each of us comes into the world ready to explore, make meaning from our environment, and learn through what we experience. As educators, our role is to engage the human mind in a process that provides the opportunity and resources for this knowledge to grow. The deep and comprehensive research of Lauren Resnick focuses on the cultural and developmental theories of Vygotsky, and the constructivist lines of epistemological theories of Piaget have identified what Dr. Resnick calls "intelligence as social practice." Simply translated, this means that people can learn to be smart; they learn through communication. It is this communal process of education that enriches the learning potential and experience. The almost limitless potential for communicating using new technologies presents a powerful springboard for student learning if we can harness its potential. This fact is crucial for all educators in the twenty-first century. The standards movement has emphasized that all children must reach high levels of achievement. The accountability for student learning has driven legislative efforts at the state and national levels to establish benchmarks for student achievement and consequences for schools that fail to reach those benchmarks. The importance of knowing each learner, using student work to monitor student progress, and engaging students in inquiry to develop the metacognitive skills necessary to achieve at high levels are critical for success. Research has shown that children learn differently, at different rates, and through different processes. This can present enormous issues in the high accountability world in which we currently exist. Can technology, especially new technologies, provide assistance and increased potential for more children to succeed? How can these new technologies engage in this learning? What do we as educators need to do in the face of the deictic changes process and the accountability for student learning?

Central to the challenge of all children learning at high levels is a fundamental belief that all students can learn. This learning potential is diverse, multidimensional, and challenging, therefore educators must construct learning experiences that address individual student needs. Rothman (1996) speaks to a growing concern of educators on these issues. All students must be able to learn at high levels. However, the differentiated instruction in today's increasingly crowded classrooms is not producing the results to meet these high achievement goals. Socio-economic conditions and deficiencies in prior knowledge and learning environments produce inequities that become significant hurdles for many students to achieve at high levels. The paradoxical position he addresses identifies two distinct definitions of learning. To some, "high levels of learning" refers to the ability to think and reason through processes that use information to make meaning, while to others, "high levels of learning" refers to comprehensive content knowledge that is demonstrated by the ability to apply the knowledge. In fact, E.D. Hirsch Jr., the author of "*Cultural Literacy,*" argues that students cannot reason without facts, and the purpose of schooling is to provide those facts, especially to those students who lack the development of rich stores of prior knowledge and experience. As cognitive research has shown, knowledge and reasoning are essential, and through inquiry and social interaction, students can create experiences that fill in the prior knowledge gaps that may exist. There is no thinking without knowledge and there is no knowledge without thinking. We construct knowledge based on what we already know. For Rothman and Resnick the issue is clear. If all students are to achieve at high levels, it will be necessary for schools and indeed classrooms to provide each student with instruction that engages them in rigorous content and social inquiry that socializes the knowledge and supports individual meaning making. This will require teachers to generate learning environments that tap the individual student prior knowledge base and lead them through the process of constructing meaning, through the integration of prior learning, with new information infused with diverse perspectives and ideas.

Becoming literate in the twenty-first century demands that we construct a repertoire of skills, knowledge sets, and communication techniques that contribute to the culture and the knowledge base of our society. Herein lies the challenge to educators in the twenty-first century literacy classroom. As we have seen, current research identifies a deictic change process, pushing teachers and schools to keep pace with new technologies and redefined literacy. At the same time, collateral research is identifying gaps between the knowledge base, comfort zone, competency levels, and learning impact of all these new technologies and continuously evolving literacy. It is becoming increasingly more evident that to succeed we must engage these issues as learning communities constructing meaning and solutions through exploration, inquiry, and the socialization of our knowledge. To succeed in the classroom of the twenty-first century, it will be imperative that we construct learning environments that embrace the diversity of thought and reasoning—environments that engage the change process as a reality that provides continuous opportunity to explore and challenge the collective reasoning of all engaged in the experience.

Technology in the Constructivist Learning Environment

Integral to this constructivist approach is the imperative to engage students in the learning environment. If the human brain seeks meaning and connections, then we must begin to emphasize within our instructional paradigm tools that will help students seek new information, uncover new sources of knowledge, and construct new wisdom from the vast array of information available. New technology can become an exciting vehicle for this process. As an extension of the human brain, these powerful tools can become portals for investigation, exploration, communication, and meaning making. Imagine cognitive tools seamlessly woven into student investigations of concepts in content. Envision students using technology to probe not for answers, but for new questions and new frontiers in an ever-expanding universe of unknowns. To accomplish this we must reinvent how we as educators frame instruction. We must recast the tools that have driven the education process for centuries. We must transform our curriculum into a questioning arena where students develop the skills to identify, discriminate, synthesize, evaluate, and apply specific information. We must replace simple topical questions, activities, and research with projects requiring original thought. Questions are the tools required for us to "make up our minds" and develop meaning (McKenzie, 1998). It is time that we seek innovative applications of these tools, stretching thinking and making new connections through instructional technologies.

With respect to technology and literacy, if we are to succeed in the process of infusing technology into the learning experience, it will be necessary to not only ask different kinds of questions, but also to redefine the context in which the questions are posed. Students' preparation must focus on exploring essential issues, paradoxes, and inquiries. We must teach students to start their explorations with these "essential questions" in mind, seeking not answers but rather new questions that in turn generate the concentric circles of lifelong learning. The potential for this kind of constructivist inquiry through the medium of technology is enormous. Before we get too excited about this potential, it is important to realize that this process will accelerate the deictic change process. The individual nature of constructivist inquiry and the social interaction evolving from that environment will produce a continuous pool of ideas, questions, and challenges that will emerge from a curriculum that encourages this kind of diverse thought and expression.

If that is the vision for tomorrow, what do we know about the present? How close are we to realizing that vision? According to Ronald Hyman, for every 38 teacher questions in a typical classroom, there is only one student question. Schoolhouse research has too often fallen into the "go find out about" category. Such topical research requires little more than information gathering. We must move past projects that are searching for answers to simple questions. We must stop asking for the educational equivalent to fast food. No more trivial pursuit (McKenzie, 1998). If we pose questions that require fresh thought, our students must make answers, not gather them. Whether they are engaged in individual or social inquiry, student work products, or classroom dialogue, accountability to standards of reasoning and standards of evidence must guide the learning. In classroom dialogue, participants must be accountable to the learning community, listening, elaborating on ideas, and using questions to clarify, expand, and defend thinking. Evidence supporting hypotheses and arguments must be invoked to make meaning.

We do have some research and convergent thought to guide us along this path. The American Library Association's definition of information literacy asserts that by itself, information is not knowledge; it is bits of data that we gather by reading, observation, or hearsay. To become knowledge, information must be filtered through our experiences and applied to our lives.

Toffler (1990a) defines data as unconnected facts; information as data that has been fitted into categories, classifications, schemes, or other patterns; and finally, knowledge as information that has been further refined into more general statements.

There have been some scholars who have observed that as information doubles, knowledge halves and wisdom quarters. Increasing the information to which students are subjected does not necessarily ensure an increase in their knowledge. Thus, just having the potential to access information and the knowledge to use the technology to massage and present the information is not enough to reach the deep processing and meaning-making levels of the learning that the human brain seeks. We must integrate the dynamic information-seeking process in a learner-based, or information seeker-based, curriculum (Lennox & Walker, 1993). If we are to survive and thrive in the deictic change of literacy instruction in the future, we will need to redefine curricula to provide the opportunities to focus learning around enduring concepts, or "big ideas" of content and process. We must also guide individual student inquiry and expression, allowing the emerging technologies and redefinitions of literacy to fold into the learning experience. To summarize, we will need to be conscious of the context of our learning environment as much as we are cognizant of the content and process of learning experiences. With respect to technology, we will need to imbed technological interfaces into experiences that reinforce the accountability indicators of the evaluative and affective elements of literacy comprehension. We will need to reinforce the communal process of learning (lest we forget, education is a human process). The genuine power of socializing knowledge must be accentuated. The push for standards of reasoning and evidence to sculpt and guide classroom learning is a major imperative for the future. Technology, with its diverse potential, can and needs to be a vehicle to support, enrich, and drive this social inquiry.

For this to occur and for new curricula to be developed that engages students in the investigation of enduring concepts, it is implicit that several conditions be simultaneously present. First students must desire to know, use analytical skills to formulate questions, identify research methodologies, and utilize critical skills to evaluate results. Second, students must posses the skills to search for answers to those questions in increasingly diverse and complex ways. Third, once a student has identified what is sought, he or she must be able to access it (Lennox & Walker, 1993). For new technologies to successfully extend learning in these conditions, they must motivate students to learn, be user friendly, and be accessible to all students and teachers.

The vision projected in this model of technology-infused instruction addresses pieces of the comprehension continuum that speak to the deep, rich, and interactive segments of that skill. Currently in literacy classrooms at most grade levels, explicit concepts of comprehension are routinely taught and assessed. Students seek the main ideas, sequence information, find details, and engage in retelling. Even the more implicit learning objectives are integral pieces of most literacy curricula. A visit to any literacy classroom will provide insight into how students are taught to predict, infer, interpret, and so forth. In some of those classrooms, technology may even be implemented to drive that instruction using content-based software, word processing, and/or Internet sites and sources. For the future, however, more emphasis must be placed on the evaluative and affective pieces of comprehension. Classroom instruction, student work products, and inquiries must be accountable to standards of evidence and reasoning. The work of teaching and learning must be focused on answering new questions about student learning. What do students know? How do they know what they know? What is the evidence for this knowledge? Why is this evidence for student learning? What must be done next to move each student's learning forward? It is in these arenas, the places where judgments are constructed and value placed on information, that the human learning brain is truly engaged. It is in these places that the drive to make meaning takes over the learning process and generates the self-actualizing precepts that motivate, challenge, and support student exploration and risk taking. If you have not already guessed, this format will require a regeneration of curricula to focus not only on this deeper learning experience, but on the implementation of new technologies to support those broad-based inquiries.

A Model for Implementation

Up to this point, we have identified many of the crucial issues facing technology and literacy instruction for the twenty-first century. The deictic change process confronting education encompasses curriculum, instruction, thinking, and learning. We have also posed several questions that issue a challenge for literacy educators. Can technology, especially new technologies, provide assistance and increased potential for more children to succeed? How can these new technologies engage in this learning? What do we as educators need to do in the face of the deictic change process and the accountability for student learning?

To address the issues, we project an instructional model that outlines new curriculum dynamics that infuse technology as a cognitive tool—a tool that engages the individual student in inquiry-based instruction, embedded in an environment that encourages and supports the human meaning-making brain. This model outlines new thinking in the challenges to find time and opportunity for teacher skill development. It engages new ideas in the construction of curriculum around "big ideas" and enduring concepts to address the way the human brain makes meaning. It demonstrates new strategies in the infusion of technology into an invisible interface and a vehicle to extend student inquiry. Although the activities with technology may seem familiar, the implementation is quite different.

An example of a model designed to address these issues is demonstrated by Figure 1. Several key concepts are visible in the graphic. Student constructivist inquiries mature as students move through the process. Meta-cognitive strategies are fluid, providing opportunities for diverse student learning. Benchmark performance standards guide the process. The teacher role changes as students become more proficient in developing questions and inquiries. Technology plays a vital role in how students make meaning.

To focus our discussion further, a model of this technological curriculum can be applied to a secondary literacy classroom. We need only to identify an enduring concept in literature, a questioning protocol to guide student investigations and instructional experiences that engage each student in a search for personal meaning within the concept and a venue to share those meanings in the public forum of classroom dialogue, discussion, analysis, and synthesis. To be more specific, let us look at a tenth-grade literature course designed around five "big ideas": (1) The Short Story, (2) The Novel, (3) Non-Fiction, (4) Drama, and (5) Poetry. These five focus areas are deep concepts rich in content and provide solid core knowledge for tenth-grade English. Students will explore these concepts through instruction that is designed to lead them to construct knowledge in each of the five core concepts and then link this new knowledge through their own inquiry, analysis, synthesis, and performance.

For the sake of providing a model of how this new curriculum might function, let us look at just one of the "big ideas": constructing a learning experience that allows for individual student inquiry and creative uses of new technologies to extend and challenge their thinking, and then sharing those thoughts and ideas with others in the room, in the school, or perhaps across the globe.

Using content standards to identify what students should know and be able to do, and performance standards to determine just how good is good enough for student work, instruction will provide a forum for students to demonstrate the knowledge and skills acquired in each of the "big ideas." Student work produced will demonstrate knowledge and guide the teachers' instructional decisions and interventions with individuals and groups of students. For each of the core knowledge "big ideas," students will produce written narrative accounts and procedures, along with persuasive pieces to demonstrate depth of understanding. Students will participate in conferences (personal and electronic) with teachers and peers using their knowledge in a social learning experience to test ideas, assess positions, construct new questions, and produce opinions and judgments. Embedded in each of these deep comprehensive pieces of work are the requirements for proper use of literacy conventions and proper protocol for research and knowledge generation. Technology will be alive in this process, used with ease and fluency, and integrated as fundamental vehicles for learning. It will provide opportunities to access information on a global scale. Through the interaction with online writing rubric software, students will be able to write responses to research and have their work scored electronically with immediate feedback and suggestions. Students' work will include captured resources from online research, streaming video, and computer designed decision modules that infer and predict new ideas, projections, or explain student thinking and positions.

For our tenth-grade English model, one iteration of this process focused on the enduring concept of drama and could include some or all of the following processes. The teacher establishes expectations for the performance inquiry by assessing student prior knowledge of the concept of a paradox. The student dialogue that follows is focused on the construction of "essential questions" that guide student inquiry implemented through technology. Emerging from this rich investigation are new questions. At this stage, the teacher helps focus student work through a reading performance task. Students will choose two books from a list demonstrating a paradox in the genre. Each book will require a review including developmental drafts. Students reading similar book paradoxes will share learning through "Book Talks," where they will have the opportunity to extend and enrich learning personally or through technology. To attain the first benchmark, students will produce a reflective piece of work that compares and contrasts the sides of the paradox they have confronted. Each student will then work with the teacher to design a protocol for research using technology, and formulate a series of guiding questions (discriminating inquiries) that will focus and shape the cyber-search and the investigative synthesis produced through that process. In this model, the technology will become an extension of the essential questions in their protocol, and will become the vehicle that transports them through the broad and diverse resources literally at their fingertips. A research report capturing the synthesis process is required to meet benchmark two. At this stage of the learning, the analysis of the evidence and synthesis of those data produces an investigative focus. One focus might be on the variations between character developments for the stage versus character development for the screen. With technology leading the way, students can explore video clips and interviews with authors, actors, writers, and editors or accumulate information across a broad spectrum of American literature. At each stage of each student inquiry, new questions will produce new avenues to explore. The purpose of the research report is to crystallize student thinking and prepare them to project meaning they have constructed through the process. Finally, the students will produce an original piece of work using technology. Perhaps this would take the form of an electronic literary analysis of the differences between the characters of two distinguished authors, Stephen King and Alfred Hitchcock. This original creative piece of student work completes benchmark three and establishes the context for students to demonstrate what they know, how they know, why they know, and the evidence to support their learning. An important format structure is evident in this model. Through the benchmarks, student thinking is taken deep into the learning task. Progressively, they take students through convergent thinking supported by evidentiary analysis of their inquiries, both of these producing the foundation for creative meaning making.

This is just one example of the kind of thinking potential and thinking process that will be necessary to meet the demands of deictic change. Curricula must be redesigned to respond to the change process by narrowing the width and extending the depth of content subject, and focusing more deeply on connections between concepts. This type of design will more directly address the way the human brain thinks. It will also restructure how teachers will work in and out of the classroom. By design, the new curricula will provide time for teachers and students to explore the potential of new technologies within the constructs of the performance tasks and benchmark objectives. Teachers and students will learn together, forming learning communities. Students will spend more time posing questions to focus inquiry, while teachers monitor student work products and performance procedures. The restructured questioning formats guide students to think and work differently. Technology will become a vehicle that extends the search for meaning, produces new venues to develop questions and the search for new meaning.

Figure 1. Technology-infused investigative instruction model

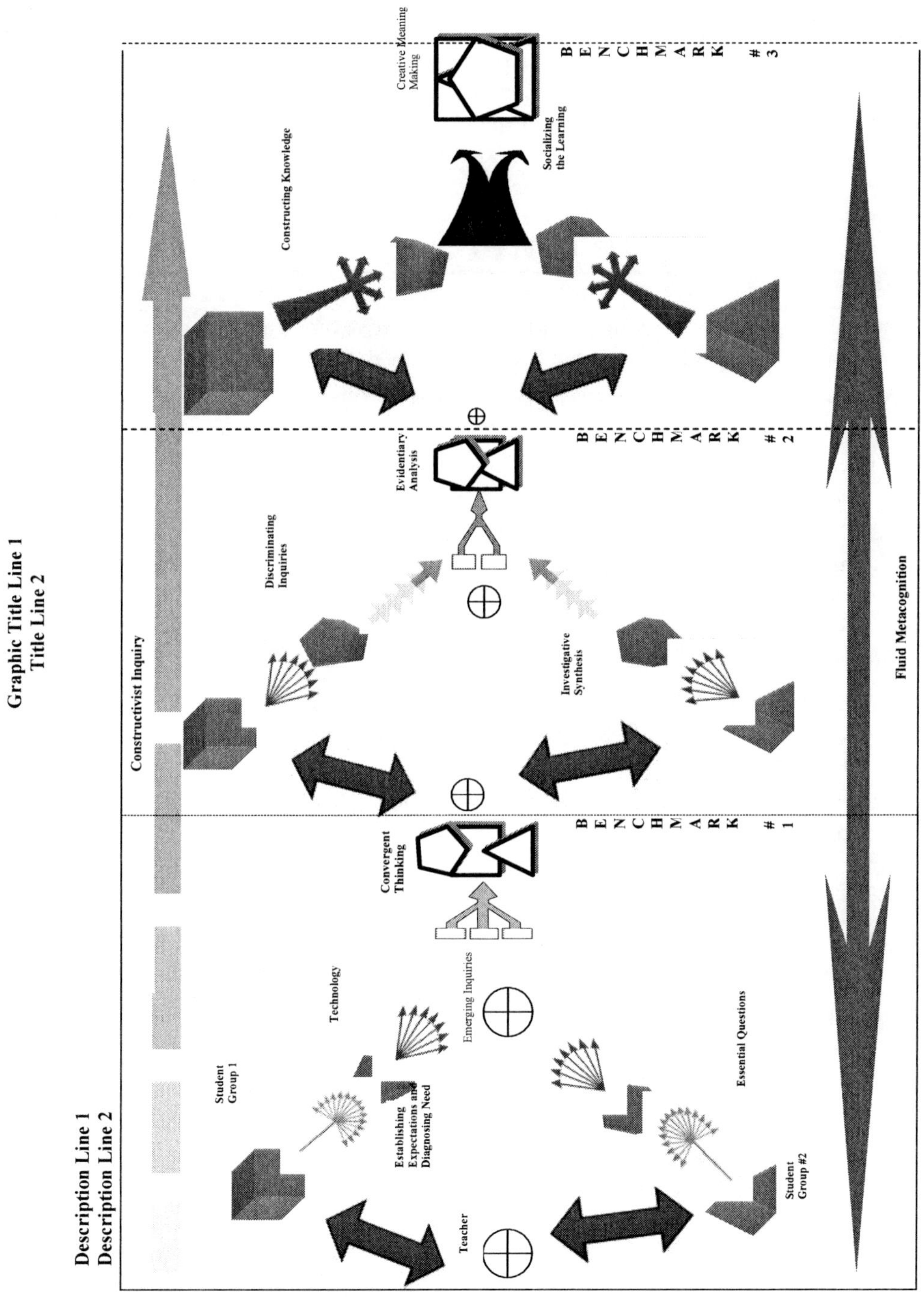

What is important to glean from all of the issues presented here is that if educators are to succeed with the challenges facing them on the journey through the twenty-first century, education must respond, indeed embrace change and use it to their advantage. Curriculum, instruction, and technology integration must reach beyond the current paradigm and reconfigure to address the learning potential of all students. This will necessitate creative strategies and the time and opportunity to focus effort. There is a desperate need for more research. What we have now is a clearer vision of the challenge—still ahead is the hard work and commitment to realize that vision.

References

American Library Association Presidential Committee on Information Literacy. (1989, January). Chicago: American Library Association.

Ayersman, D.J. (1996). Reviewing the research on hypermedia-based learning. *The Journal of Research on Computing in Education, 28,* 500-525.

Eisenberg, M.B. & Johnson, D. (1996). Computer skills for problem solving: Learning and teaching technology in context. *Clearinghouse on Information Technology,* (March).

Finkelman, K. & McMunn, C. (1995). *Micorworlds as a publishing tool for cooperative groups: An effective study.* Report No. 143, Curry School of Education, University of Virginia, Charlottesville, Virginia, USA.

Lennox, M.F. & Walker, M.L. (1993). Information literacy in the educational process. *The Educational Forum, 57*(Spring).

Leu, D.J. & Kinzer, C.K. (1998). *Effective literacy instruction* (4th edition). Englewood, NJ: Merrill.

McKenzie, J. (1998, September 26-31). Grazing the Net: Raising a generation of free-range students. *Phi Delta Kappan.*

Means, B., Olson, K., & Singh, R. (1995). Beyond the classroom: Restructuring the classroom with technology. *Phi Delta Kappan, 77*(1), 69-72.

Moersch, C. (1995). Levels of technology implementation: A framework for measuring classroom technology use. *Learning and Leading with Technology, 23*(3), 40-42.

Reinking, D., McKenna, M., Labbo, L., & Keiffer, R. (1998). *Handbook of literacy and technology: Transformations in the post typographic world.* Mahwah, NJ: Lawrence Erlbaum Associates.

Resnick, R. (1995). From aptitude to effort: A new foundation for our schools. *Daedalus, 124*(4), 55-62.

Rothman, R. (1995). *Organizing so all children can learn: Applying the principles of learning.*

Sandholtz, J., Ringstaff, C., & Dwyer, D. (1991). *Research findings, technology innovations and collegial interaction.* ACOT Report #13. Cupertino, CA: Apple Computer Inc.

Tierney, R.J., Keiffer, R., Whaling, K., Kesai, L., Moss, A.G., Harris, J.E., & Hopper, J. (1997). *Assessing the impact of hypertext on learners' architecture of literacy learning space in different disciplines.* Follow-Up Study, Reading Online.

Toffler, A. (1990). *Powershift: Knowledge wealth and violence at the edge of the 21st century.* New York: Bantam Books.

Chapter V

Integrating Technology Literacy and Information Literacy

Jennifer Sharkey
Purdue University, USA

D. Scott Brandt
Purdue University, USA

Abstract

Information technology literacy can be seen as an integration of what are commonly two separate literacies—technology literacy and information literacy. This chapter defines them, reviews issues related to both, and argues that both must be acquired and functionally utilized for students and workers to achieve success in our heavily technology-oriented society and workplace. The authors address learning outcomes and design components that should be considered in training and instructional settings, and give examples of instructional strategies for achieving them.

Introduction

To succeed in today's higher education and workforce environments, one cannot rely solely on either technological or information literacy skills. The two are complementary, and they must be interlocked to provide a complete inventory of needed skills and knowledge. In some places the phrase "information technology literacy" is used to address both; here they are addressed separately before describing why they are complementary. Integrating and utilizing standards and competencies for both through an instructional systems design (ISD) approach strengthens curriculum and program development in the digital age. Building skills upon skills allows for continued proficiency acquisition and adaptation to changing environments, and infuses the concept of continued lifelong learning.

The need for technology skills and knowledge in schools, the workforce, and society is an obvious extension and consequence of living in the digital environment of what Alvin Toffler coined as "the Information Age." Computers and computing have become a way of life and the primary means for doing work in today's world. Governments, schools, and business have attempted to address issues in acquiring specific technical skills for some time. Often missing from discussions about technology literacy is technology's interdependent relationship with information. There is a reason, after all, why it is not called the Technology Age—technology is tools or the use of tools, but it is the result of using them that is important. Computers have not only made creating, acquiring, tracking, storing, retrieving, and analyzing data and information easier; they have made it more accessible than their original creators could have ever imagined. The skill sets needed at the very center of this vortex where technology interfaces with information are both technology literacy and information literacy.

Background

Traditionally, technology skills have been thought to be the responsibility of employers. Duemestre (1999) argues that while arts and technology should be balanced in education, the latter is more likely best addressed by employers in a work setting. However, the Deputy Director of the National Science Foundation noted in his October 24, 2002, address to participants of the Advanced Technology Education program that this was a challenge—the skills students need for the workplace is an issue that should be reviewed in the context of the traditional college curriculum. Bordogna (2002) avers that technical skills are increasingly the purview of community colleges. Others have suggested that in particular, information technology skills should be incorporated into a minor as part of college programs (Bailey & Stefaniak, 1999).

Early on, information literacy was taught primarily in undergraduate environments, where the need for honing research skills was seen to be the greatest. Information literacy, as it is now known, began in the '70s when computers were first used in publishing, and the amount of information began to grow. In the '80s, computers began to be used as tools to organize and retrieve published information, and accessing information became even more complicated for end users. The '90s, of course, saw the proliferation of both published and unpublished information via ubiquitous networked computers and the World Wide Web (Murray, 2003). A recent review of trends in librarianship noted that information literacy research has progressed from codifying a doctrine for librarians, to proving its effect in supporting both general education and lifelong learning for students, to integration into specific curricula through collaboration (Arp & Woodard, 2002).

The two literacies have taken parallel, if not mutual paths. Each was once considered the responsibility of a specific constituency—employers or librarians. Each became more complex as computers became a driving force in both the workplace and education. And each has begun to be seen as set of skills and knowledges which underlies larger needs and outcomes in both areas. The two paths have, at this point, crossed.

Defining the Literacies

What comprises technology literacy, knowledge, and skills? Often it depends who you ask. People in a higher education setting tend to view technology literacy as either the ability to work with technology within a given discipline, such as biology, or as a generalized set of IT skills necessary to perform perfunctory work in a computer-rich environment (Kock, Aiken, & Sandas, 2002). Educators in K-12 settings view more narrowly the skills of "computer literacy" as being able to use the computer for keyboarding, basic programming, and so forth (Murray, 2003). Government and industry view things in very applied and outcome-oriented terms; technology literacy can be described as mastery over technological tools, usually specific to a company and the products it produces (Bailey & Stefaniak, 1999).

The National Academy of Engineering's (NAE) (2001) Council on Technological Literacy notes that in addition to specific skills (including, for instance, the ability to change a fuse), people who are technically literate also have "a sense of the risks, benefits, and trade-offs" in using technology in various situations. Many technology inventories of competencies are available on the Internet and show a wide range of skill sets. The CPSI Technical Skills Inventory (1999) identifies hundreds of specific industry skills by categories, such as software and hardware engineering, operating systems, data bases, Web/Internet, desktop publishing, and so forth. For schools, the Carl D. Perkins Vocational and Applied Technology Education Act of 1990 has had a major impact. Many schools now address a variety of technology competencies at both K-6 and 7-12 levels, including such specifics as demonstrating "knowledge and use of appropriate connectivity methods, basic networking, and communication hardware and software" (Conroe Independent School District, 1999, Section 1, Paragraph 2).

Information literacy encompasses a different domain of skills and knowledge, those involved in finding, retrieving, and using information. The context has been computer-based information, even as noted in the American Libraries Association (ALA) report of 1989 which predates the World Wide Web. Like the NAE, university librarians believe information literacy must include knowledge and understanding of the context of information in today's society, its composition and organization, as well as its use in lifelong learning (Dupuis, 1997). K-12 educators take a simple, though related view: information literacy includes skills for locating and using information, as well as knowledge for interpreting and evaluating it (Murray, 2003).

Specific information literacy approaches include identifying standards, goals, objectives, or outcomes. For instance, from the ALA, information standards include accessing, using, and evaluating information "critically and competently" (American Association of School Librarians, 2004). Examples of K-12 goals include abilities to define information problems, determine range of possible sources, and extract relevant information from a source (Eisenberg, 2003). University objectives tend to be more specific, such as: "Given an industry-related task, the user can identify and obtain critical information to support the decision-making process" (Purdue University Libraries Faculty, 1995, Goal 1, Paragraph 5).

Increasingly, the skills and knowledge used in information seeking and retrieval require sophistication using computers as tools of access, analysis, and formatting. The Association of College & Research Libraries' (ACRL) (2000) Information Literacy Competency Standards for Higher Education is an updated framework for information literacy in an academic setting. It notes: "Information technology skills enable an individual to use computers, software applications, databases, and other technologies to achieve a wide variety of academic, work-related, and personal goals" (Association of College & Research Libraries, 2000). Basic skills that support information literacy may include using e-mail, managing personal databases, and troubleshooting operating system problems. In many ways, it is impossible for anyone to work and survive in the Information Age without information technology skills (Latham, 2000). And at this point in time, it could go without saying that these skills and knowledge extend to networks, the Internet, and the World Wide Web.

Overall standards for literacies vary. As noted, the nomenclature used to describe them can be expressed as objectives, skills, expectations, competencies, or standards, depending on the context. Generally, standards are the highest conceptual level of expression, and objectives are concrete and detailed expression of outcomes designed for an instructional session, course, or program. A sampling here indicates the variability in scope and specificity of skills.

University Setting (Instructional Technology Committee of the Campus Computing and Communication Policy Board, 1998):

- Handle e-mail attachments (send, find, open, read, and store).
- Open a browser and find various sites.
- Download/save images and files.
- Find help and search university's Web page.

Public School Setting (North Carolina Department of Public Instruction, 2003):

- Select and use technological tools for class assignments, projects, and presentations.
- Practice and refine knowledge and skills in keyboarding/word processing/desktop publishing, spreadsheets, databases, multimedia, and telecommunications in preparing classroom assignments and projects.
- Use word processing and/or desktop publishing for a variety of writing assignments/projects.
- Select and use appropriate technology tools to efficiently collect, analyze, and display data.
- Use electronic resources for research.

Statewide Setting (Linberg, 2000):

- Manage large hierarchical file system, organize tools, re-order scattered files.
- Find, install, and use plug-ins; use secure space, manage advanced browser features.
- Import/export to/from text, tab, or other delimited formats.
- Devise solutions/workarounds when no help is available.

Designing Literacy Components

A closer look at designing literacy objectives gives further insight into how outcomes and skills can be facilitated. When developing any instructional sessions or courses, basic instructional systems design (ISD) principles can go a long way in helping develop effect activities and solid learning outcomes. One main benefit of using basic ISD principles is that learning outcomes can be tied directly to the types of activities and projects assigned to students. To use these principles, an appropriate model should first be identified to create the effective integration of skills. Gagné, Briggs, and Wager (1988) state that developers of instruction must pay close attention to internal and external influences on the learning environment and how this affects the learning process. A common instructional systems design model used is the ADDIE model. This model focuses on key components of the instructional design process, which can be easily applied by an individual or design group. The ADDIE model is an acronym for Analysis, Design, Development, Implementation, and Evaluation.

The model used isn't as important as keeping in mind what is to be accomplished by the instruction. "All stages in any instructional systems model can be categorized into one of three functions: (1) identifying the outcomes of the instruction, (2) developing the instruction, and (3) evaluating the effectiveness of the instruction" (Gagné et al., 1988, p. 14). Prior to instruction the first three steps of the ADDIE model help with the creation of the instruction. The *Analysis* step determines the need for instruction and what learners should gain overall from the instruction. *Design* and *Development* is the process of creating the structure of the instruction. This includes determining outcomes and objectives, developing assignments and activities, and creating methods of assessment. How the structure is built directly influences the level of success when conducting or implementing your instruction. Morrison, Ross, and Kemp (2001) recommend using the following questions to address the components of designing instruction.

- For whom is the program developed? (characteristics of learners or trainees)
- What do you want the learners or trainees to learn or demonstrate? (objectives)
- How is the subject content or skill best learned? (instructional strategies)
- How do you determine the extent to which learning is achieved? (evaluation procedures) (p. 5)

As with Gagné, Briggs, and Wager's recommendations for instructional design, these points focus on key components of the overall process of developing instruction.

When incorporating technology, it should not overwhelm or supplant content to be taught or substitute class time that is typically spent on content. Just using technology will not bring benefit to the overall outcomes of the instruction or the students. Using an ISD model can help one avoid this trap. A design model, called eTIPS (educational technology integration and implementation principles), was developed specifically to help teachers design instruction with effective incorporation of technology. This model helps anyone using technology to avoid the trap of using technology for technology's sake. Specifically, this model encourages "a teacher-designer to consider what they are teaching, what added value the technology might bring to the learning environment, and how technology can help to assess student learning" (Dexter, 2002, p. 57).

Writing quality objectives will help determine the rest of the instruction's structure. In the context of most classes, creating objectives that just focus on the use of a particular technology can take time away from the content of the class and the overall learning outcome. When writing objectives, focus on the use of a technology as it supports the established learning objectives and desired behavior of the student either in assignments or assessment (Dexter, 2002). Examples of these types of objectives can be as follows: 'Students will conduct a half-hour interview of a local historian using a digital camcorder.' or 'Students will present to the class a critical analysis of fresh-water ecosystems literature through an electronic presentation.' These objectives demonstrate that the focus of the assignment is on the content of the class, but use technology to support the achievement of the objective and therefore the overall learning outcomes.

Figure 1. ABCD model applied to an objective

Audience	Students
Behavior	will present to the class
Condition	a critical analysis of fresh-water ecosystems literature
Degree	through an electronic presentation.

Developing concrete outcomes can be a challenge if someone is not used to creating curriculum from an ISD standpoint. Using the ABCD model to create solid objectives can make the development of them much easier. The acronym stands for Audience, Behavior, Condition(s), Degree (of success). Each component of the model has a specific function in the creation of an objective. Essentially, this type of objective guides the learner (Audience) to perform (Behavior) in a certain situation (Condition) to a specified level of success (Degree) (Schuman & Ritchie, 1996). See Figure 1 for an example of this model and its application to a learning objective.

Projects or assignments developed for instruction need to be in direct support of the objectives of the course. When developing a project, some basic questions should be asked: How does this project support the overall goal of the course? What main objectives are directly supported by this project? Is the project focused on the course content and not directly on the tool? One pitfall professors and instructors tend to fall into is creating an assignment for using a tool which does not support the curriculum. If it is important for students to know how to develop a Web site, a Web development assignment should not arbitrarily be created; the Web development assignment should be put into the context of the course. Students can create a Web site that demonstrates their knowledge of main concepts of the course or shows their research and critical thinking skills through an examination of the course content.

When integrating technology and information literacy, students can acquire skills in multiple ways. While there are many studies and models discussing how these skills should be gained, more recent discussions show that the point-and-click demos in particular are no longer the best way for skills to be transferred. A report produced by the Panel on Educational Technology (1997) recommends that projects, assignments, and instruction overall should not just focus on the technology or hardware, but use these as a complement to support the instruction. A research project, for instance, contains the traditional aspects of information literacy such as using scholarly journal articles and providing critical analysis. However, the container in which the project is handed in to the professor can vary in format. Some examples of containers can be a Web site, video presentation, documentary short, or e-portfolio. The appropriateness of the container greatly depends on the course content as well as overall learning outcomes.

> *Another key to the successful use of technology for learning is to encourage the interactivity of learners with curricular material and one another. Multimedia learning materials are well designed if they encourage learners to be active, engaged, and purposeful about their learning. Computer conferencing tools and applications are well designed if they also foster constructive dialogue among learners around critical concepts (Abrami, 2001, p. 118).*

Specific Literacy Outcomes

Information and technology literacy skills can be acquired in several ways, as well as on multiple levels. The basic research paper requires fundamental technology skills such as word processing to write the paper and a Web browser to access online sources. The same research paper may require higher-level information literacy skills such as finding multiple types of sources, evaluating the validity of the sources, and critically analyzing the content of the sources as they support or refute the student's hypothesis or thesis statement. These higher-level information literacy skills don't need to be compromised for the technology component of the project to go to a higher level. If the traditional research paper is just one type of container for the research project, then other, more technology-based containers can be produced.

Some examples have been mentioned above on how to incorporate technology into instruction. Specific examples of instruction that can be used in academic courses are given below. All three examples have been used at Purdue University in association with the Digital Learning Collaboratory. These examples were used in English literature classes, a communications class for PR majors, and a Botany class.

Electronic presentations have become quite standard as a requirement for student projects. Many people use PowerPoint because of easy access and familiarity. However, people typically don't move beyond the basic functionality of PowerPoint, often creating dull and unimpressive presentations (Abram, 2004). PowerPoint's capability to apply custom animations, embed video and audio, and create voice-over narration can allow a student to create a presentation that pushes his or her creative envelope.

Since literature classes often require the critical analysis of text, a group presentation was created as a final project in three English literature courses. Each group of four to five students was to develop a 20- to 25-minute presentation that examined, developed, and expanded an idea, theme, or metaphor in literature, which embodied personal as well as cultural aspects. Students were required to include both personal views and scholarly documentation. Students could use photos (personal or commercial), newspapers, magazines, journals, books, music, DVDs, videos, personal narrative, and so forth to support their views and critical analysis. This assignment was created by Dr. Binnie Martin while a PhD student in the English department.

As students advance through their major, it is not uncommon for higher-level classes to require a semester-long project. The subject area greatly influences the container type of the final project, but it is not unusual for the project to be in the form of a 25-plus-page research paper. As universities focus on alternative learning experiences such as service learning, opportunities are provided to incorporate exploration of scholarly communication, various types of technology, and applied experience into semester-long projects.

Developing campaigns is a standard component of the Public Relations industry. To help students gain practical experience, a service learning assignment was created by Dr. Mohan Dutta-Bergman, Assistant Professor of Communication. Students working in groups of nine to ten were to create an advertising campaign for a local non-profit agency to help promote awareness, address an issue, or solve a problem in the contingency served by that agency. This project required the development of a campaign plan and materials in physical or electronic format. The campaign plan needed to be a strategic document that presented the different elements of communication strategy proposed by the students to help address the agency's need. The materials could be created using various hardware and software such as digital cameras, scanners, graphic editors, video editors, Web development, and so forth. The development of the plan and materials needed to be supported by scholarly research and published statistical data.

E-portfolios are becoming a more common way for students to showcase their skills, expertise, and accomplishments during their college career. The e-portfolio format provides a way for projects and products to be shown in a way paper cannot. A quality e-portfolio also demonstrates a student's skill and knowledge of technology. An e-portfolio is typically considered a tool for presenting specific work when seeking employment. However, it can be used in the classroom environment to effectively support learning and provide an assessment tool (Cole, Ryan, & Kick, 1995). In the classroom setting, the e-portfolio is often the container in which the final project is enveloped; the content of the final project greatly depends on the assignment and course subject. An effective research project utilizes the components of information literacy, which are then evident in the products included in the e-portfolio. Because the e-portfolio can easily incorporate multimedia, components of the e-portfolio can include audio files, video files, animations, digital images, 3D graphics, and electronic documentation.

In a class focusing on Plants and the Environment, students were required to examine how plants influence and are influenced by the environment. The students' research and findings of this semester-long project were to be encapsulated into an e-portfolio. The project required students to find scholarly research relating to plants and the environment, grow actual plants and capture this growth as digital images, interview a local scholar using a digital camcorder, and develop a field study report tying together their work over the course of the semester. The e-portfolio could be in the form of a Web site, DVD, or CD-ROM, but needed to include effective navigation to the various portions of the project requirements. This project was created by Dr. Carole Lambi, Associate Professor of Plant Pathology.

Conclusion

Technology and information will continue to influence academic, work, and personal environments. To function effectively in these environments, individuals will need to be both technology and information literate. It is no longer a viable option for employers or universities to expect the other to handle the development of these skill sets. It is argued here that a university setting affords a great opportunity to combine and integrate these literacies in a variety of learning situations. Inclusion of technology into curriculum, while it should not be arbitrary, does not have to be an overwhelming or complicated process. Utilization of an instructional systems design model can guide the development of instruction, creation of objectives, and application of technology. To be successful, instruction must be designed to balance the two literacies, and integrate them with course content and goals to create meaningful results for students' immediate outcomes, to prepare them for the workplace, and to position them for lifelong learning.

References

Abram, S. (2004). PowerPoint: Devil in a red dress. *Information Outlook, 8,* 27-28.

Abrami, P.C. (2001). Understanding and promoting complex learning using technology. *Educational Research and Evaluation, 7*(2-3), 113-136.

ALA Presidential Committee on Information Literacy. (1989). *Final report.* Chicago, IL: American Library Association.

American Association of School Librarians. (2004). *Information literacy standards for student learning.* Retrieved February 29, 2004, from *www.ala.org/ala/aasl/aaslproftools/informationpower/informationliteracy.htm*

Arp, L. & Woodard, B. (2002). Recent trends in information literacy and instruction. *Reference & User Services Quarterly, 42*(2), 124-132.

Association of College & Research Libraries. (2000). *Information literacy competency standards for higher education.* Retrieved February 18, 2004, from *www.ala.org/ala/acrl/acrlstandards/informationliteracycompetency.htm*

Bailey, J.L. & Stefaniak, G. (1999). Preparing the information technology workforce for the new millennium. *ACM SIGCPR Computer Personnel, 20*(4), 4-15.

Bordogna, J. (2002, October 24). From pipelines to pathways. *Proceedings of Assessing the Impact: ATE National Principal Investigators Conference.*

Cole, D.J., Ryan, C.W., & Kick, F. (1995). *Portfolios across the curriculum and beyond.* Thousand Oaks, CA: Corwin Press.

Conroe Independent School District. (1999). *Texas essential knowledge and skills.* Retrieved January 13, 2004, from *www.conroe.isd.tenet.edu/instructional/teks/bench7-12.htm*

Currier Professional Services, Inc. (1999). *Skills inventory menu*. Retrieved January 15, 2004, from *www.currierprof.com/ts_ol.htm*

Dexter, S. (2002). eTIPS—Educational technology integration and implementation principles. In P.L. Rogers (Ed.), *Designing instruction for technology-enhanced learning* (pp. 56-70). Hershey, PA: Idea Group Publishing.

Duemestre, M. (1999). The impact of technology on U.S. higher education: A philosophical approach. *Journal of Information Technology Impact, 1*(2), 63-72.

Dupuis, E. (1997). The information literacy challenge: Addressing the changing needs of our students. *Internet Reference Services Quarterly, 2*(2&3), 93-111.

Eisenberg, M. (2003). *A Big 6 skills overview*. Retrieved February 18, 2004, from *www.big6.com/showarticle.php?id=16*

Gagné, R.M., Briggs, L.J., & Wager, W.W. (1988). *Principles of instructional design* (3rd edition). New York: Holt, Rinehart and Winston.

Instructional Technology Committee of the Campus Computing and Communication Policy Board. (1998). *Information technology literacy for effective use of instructional technology*. Retrieved March 7, 2004, from *ist-socrates.berkeley.edu/~edtech/cccpb-it/itliteracy.html*

Kock, N., Aiken, R., & Sandas, C. (2002). Using complex IT in specific domains, developing and assessing a course for nonmajors. *IEEE Transactions on Education, 45*(1), 50-56.

Latham, J. (2000). The world online: IT skills for the practical professional. *American Libraries, 31*, 40-42.

Linberg, S. (2000). *Adult literacy and basic education teacher technology competencies v2.1*. Retrieved March 7, 2004, from *www2.wgbh.org/mbcweis/ltc/alri/abecomps.html*

Morrison, G.R., Ross, S.M., & Kemp, J.E. (2001). *Designing effective instruction* (3rd edition). New York: John Wiley & Sons.

Murray, J. (2003). Contemporary literacy: Essential skills for the 21st century. *MultiMedia Schools, 10*(2), 14-18.

National Academy of Engineering. (2001). *Characteristics of a technologically literate person*. Retrieved January 13, 2001, from *www.nae.edu/nae/techlithome.nsf/Weblinks/KGRG-55SQ37?OpenDocument*

North Carolina Department of Public Instruction. (2003). *Computer/technology skills curriculum: Grades 9-12*. Retrieved March 7, 2004, from *www.ncpublicschools.org/curriculum/computer.skills/9_12.html*

Panel on Educational Technology. (1997). *Report to the president on the use of technology to strengthen K-12 education in the United States*. Washington, DC: President's Committee of Advisors on Science and Technology.

Purdue University Libraries Faculty. (1995). *Information literacy curriculum (ILC) goals and objectives*. Retrieved January 15, 2004, from *www.lib.purdue.edu/rguides/instructionalservices/ilcgoals.html*

Schuman, L. & Ritchie, D.C. (1996). *Understanding objectives*. Retrieved March 3, 2004, from *edWeb.sdsu.edu/courses/EDTEC540/objectives/ObjectivesHome.html*

Chapter VI

Design, Management, and Evaluation of Online Portfolios: Matching Supply and Demand for Building-Level Educational Administrators

Pamela M. Frampton
Purdue University Calumet, USA

Michael S. Mott
Purdue University Calumet, USA

Anastasia M. Trekles
Purdue University Calumet, USA

Robert J. Colon
Purdue University Calumet, USA

Jerry P. Galloway
Indiana University Northwest, USA

Abstract

This chapter focuses on implementing electronic portfolio systems into institutions of learning. In particular, the chapter discusses a particular model of portfolio implementation used at Purdue University Calumet for candidates graduating from the education administration master's degree and licensure program. The chapter also presents current research and varying viewpoints surrounding the issue of putting professional and performance-based portfolios into electronic formats. Practical aspects of the technology and personnel resources needed to implement the model portfolio process, as well as caveats and alternative methods, are presented, as well as the outcomes and opinions expressed by both the candidates and by local superintendents who would consider hiring them as building administrators upon graduation. Additionally, the reader will find other models and resources for implementing electronic portfolios in his or her own institution and program where portfolios for evaluating candidate and student performance are being used or considered for the future.

Introduction

Increasingly, managers in the corporate sector are utilizing electronic employment profiles to effectively match potential employee skill to position. Likewise, superintendents, facing a glaring lack of building-level administrative candidates, need access to a broad array of candidates in order to appropriately match candidate skill with building-level administration requirements. To foster this communication, the Center for Educational Leadership (CEL) Online Portfolio Project was designed, applied, and evaluated by university researchers and a cadre of superintendents in Northwest Indiana.

This chapter looks at the process of designing and implementing a Web-based service rooted in the Interstate School Leaders Licensure Consortium (ISLLC) standards for building-level administrators, rather than a candidate-driven, automated system. However, there are various other methods that can be used to implement an online portfolio system, as well; this chapter will discuss these, and provide guidelines for preparing a portfolio and developing portfolio entries.

Background

The Center for Educational Leadership (CEL) at Purdue University Calumet was designed to help current and future school administrators develop their skills as leaders. In order to achieve this goal, CEL has hosted several workshops for community principals and superintendents focusing on professional development and the Standards for Building-Level Administrators. CEL has also developed a Web site (cel.calumet.purdue.edu) that contains information on CEL events, links to important sites for school leadership development, a listing of current administrative job openings in Indiana and Illinois, and a membership application. All future and current school administrators in the Northwest Indiana region are encouraged to become members of CEL at no cost, and once they join, they are given first priority for participation in CEL events. CEL members are also granted a password to access members-only parts of the Web site which include several questionnaires, a recommended reading list, video clips from sessions with current school principals discussing the standards, and the beginnings of the CEL administrative candidate portfolio project.

Project Description

Purdue Calumet has one of the leading administrative licensure programs in Northwest Indiana, but for recent graduates of this program, finding a position has not always been easy. School districts in the vicinity of Purdue Calumet have always received aid from the university in hiring new teachers, but not necessarily new principals and administrators. So, the CEL portfolio project evolved as a means by which hiring school districts could easily look at work produced by candidates from Purdue University Calumet's graduate program in school administration. With membership to CEL, superintendents and principals from throughout the Northwest Indiana region would have the ability to review résumés, coursework, educational philosophies, and video of teaching practices produced by candidates from Purdue Calumet looking for administrative positions. These electronic portfolios would be hosted on the CEL Web site using existing hardware and Web technologies to achieve small, easily accessed portfolio "pages" for each candidate.

The CEL Web site is hosted on an AppleShareIP 6.3-based Power Macintosh G4 Server, with pages constructed using Macromedia Dreamweaver (version MX). The particular server from which the CEL site is run also serves as a file storage center for undergraduate and graduate education courses at Purdue Calumet. Because of this fact, certain data security measures had to be considered when implementing the portfolio project. If the system were to be automated, in whole or in part, candidates would need direct access to the server. However, if candidates did not have the software or hardware requirements necessary to upload their work into the system, how would they achieve this task? Also, how would their work appear on the Web site?

Initially, a FileMaker Pro database was constructed as a remotely accessed database system that each candidate could log into at any time and upload his or her coursework as desired. However, candidates had artifacts in a variety of file formats, including Microsoft Word, Microsoft PowerPoint, and QuickTime, many of which were proving quite difficult to include within the framework of FileMaker Pro. As these coursework files were intended to be the heart of the students' portfolios; a new plan had to be constructed.

Due to the relatively small number of candidates who graduate each semester from the administrative program at Purdue Calumet, it was concluded that, using the Purdue Calumet School of Education's current technological and financial resources, it was possible to provide electronic portfolios as a service, rather than as an automated system. During the pilot semester of the portfolio project (Fall 2001), six students volunteered to begin electronic portfolios, each from varying backgrounds and with varying levels of responsibility beyond the licensure program. Most were already working as teachers in the public schools, some as far as several hours from Purdue Calumet's campus. For these candidates, who also possess varying levels of technical expertise and available technological resources, it would have been nearly impossible to coordinate an automated portfolio system without the use of new software and possibly new server hardware as well.

The Portfolio Construction Process

Using a simple HTML template constructed in Dreamweaver, one page for each candidate was created on the Web site containing contact information and the candidate's photo (if desired). Students were contacted via e-mail and encouraged to send their documents to the CEL Webmaster as file attachments, which were then processed into Adobe Acrobat (PDF) files and posted as links within each candidate's portfolio page. Due to the relatively small volume of files received and the simplistic nature of the template, the Webmaster's part of the work was not time consuming, even though it was still not a completely automated procedure.

CEL's project was intended to hold the students' own professional portfolios, meaning that the candidates used their own discretion as to which items were included. Since the electronic portfolios were intended for hiring school administrators and not for university faculty as a measure of graduation qualification, leaving the core contents of the portfolio to each student seemed the best method of approach. Some students sent only a résumé; others sent professional reports and memorandums created during previous teaching or administrative service. Still others submitted reports and PowerPoint presentations created for courses taken at Purdue Calumet, descriptions of his or her personal teaching philosophies and experiences, and one student brought in a videotape showing her teaching and classroom management skills at work in her classroom. However, all candidates did consult with the CEL director and their other administration professors on what they would and would not include in their electronic portfolios.

Review of Literature

According to the newest standards for teacher preparation programs, all future teachers must be computer literate with Internet and Web-based skills (National Council for Accreditation of Teacher Education, 1997; Provenzo, 2002), and all should have an electronic portfolio. While there is a distinction between the needs of teachers, pre-service teachers, and school principals, portfolios are of current interest for all educators.

Frequently, a lack of understanding or knowledge of computing keeps pre-service teachers and school administrators from developing an electronic portfolio that demonstrates sound technological achievement. In fact, without reliable or sound leadership from advisors and faculty, many of these inexperienced candidates are likely to never make an attempt at creating an electronic portfolio at all. However, Warner and Maureen (1999) suggest that by developing an electronic portfolio, teachers will learn important computing skills and knowledge that can directly impact technology integration into the classroom. They believe that through demonstration by the teacher, students will in turn be motivated to develop their own electronic portfolios for assessment of knowledge and performance.

While most educators are following the trend toward professional portfolios, whether or not they are developed or packaged in an electronic format is controversial and not always widely accepted. It is especially difficult to implement an electronic portfolio system into an institution that has not yet adopted a paper portfolio system or any way to require students to connect varying course content within their field of study. In this situation, "a significant cultural shift is required to introduce the concept of portfolios and build the critical mass of participation to achieve full benefits from a Web-based portfolio system" (Gathercoal, Love, Bryde, & McKean, 2002). Changes in the attitudes and expectations of both students and faculty are sometimes slow to happen, but the benefits of Web-based and other types of electronic portfolios are indeed great, and once faculty discover this, the payoffs in integration with curricular standards, course content, and student learning and understanding are great.

Organization

Bullock and Hawk (2001) describe four necessary aspects of a portfolio: (1) demonstrated purpose, (2) target audience, (3) evidentiary products, and 4) reflections. They point out the importance of addressing standards such as the National Board for Professional Teaching Standards (NBPTS) or the Interstate New Teacher Assessment and Support Consortium (INTASC). These national movements toward performance-based assessments of teachers have resulted from the lack of increase in student achievement. This lack of student performance and the national call for reform in education has resulted in a national trend to make educators more accountable. The portfolio is an obvious choice for documenting competencies and performances for assessment.

Bullock and Hawk (2001) detail three types of portfolios: *process*, *product*, and *showcase*. The process portfolio documents development over time. Used to assess changes for a period of time, a process portfolio shows the progression of integration into teaching. They describe this notion in terms of very specific examples, such as a reading program or in-teaching writing, as if such endeavors or initiatives would each have separate process portfolios.

The product portfolio seems directed toward a specific goal with established criteria. That is, a specific goal would drive the content and assessment of the portfolio. All such portfolios in a given setting or environment would be similarly structured and would be examined according to the same criteria for the same objective. This seems a rather restrictive definition of a portfolio, but it can serve as a model for portfolios in general, considering that one's portfolio is still used for a particular purpose, such as getting a job or promotion.

The showcase portfolio is clearly the most quality-driven of the three, showing one's best work. The evidentiary materials, general content, and focus of the portfolio are up to the developer rather than being fashioned around established criteria. This makes the showcase more personal and individualized. The fact that the showcase portfolio contains the so-called "best work" seems like a moot point, considering that any portfolio would presumably strive for the same content quality.

In searching for a job, Bullock and Hawk suggest the product and showcase portfolios (2001). This seems obvious, but still leaves a question as to whether to target the portfolio toward established, known criteria anticipating a specific type of assessment (product portfolio), or instead to show off one's best features, skills, and accomplishments that may be more general, individualized, and personal (showcase).

Portfolios might also be organized around a set of principles or standards. As an organizational system for portfolios, Norton and Wiburg (1998) report seven domains of learning: (1) effective expression and communication, (2) self-awareness and self-esteem, (3) taking responsibility and preparing for the future, (4) social interactions and effective citizenship, 5) critical thinking and problem solving, 6) cultural and historical involvement, and 7) valuing and ethical decision making (pp. 237-238). While different institutions each develop their own language, these notions are not unique and might serve well as a structure for the organization of portfolios.

Accepting Technology

For over a decade, technology-based electronic résumés have already been present and are taking over the hiring process (Kennedy & Morrow, 1994; Quible, 1995). Kennedy and Morrow have even confirmed that the technology had been around since the early 1970s. They described Applicant Tracking Systems, as there were no widespread uses of Internet and personal Web pages, and they provided a rather obvious list of pros and cons related to technology. Clearly, technology has long been recognized as changing the methods and materials of the job market.

Contrary to teachers in practice, there is little if any real opposition to creating electronic portfolios in the literature. While many educators themselves may be hesitant to come to the electronic world, and may be unskilled and apprehensive about using educational technology to develop and maintain a portfolio, literature is generally very supportive. The use of portfolios for principals is even discussed electronically (National Association of Elementary School Principals, 2002) in an online forum. Anyone from the public can go online and comment on portfolios and participate in the open forum.

One of the earliest documents addressing electronic portfolios in a relatively modern format details both pros and cons in their development and use (Purves, 1996). While the advantages are many, the limitations are typical of most articles and address methodological issues common to virtually any use of technology. They are captured in the simple issue of becoming computer literate. That is, if one does not know how to scan a document or manage computer files, or does not have access to the necessary equipment, then obviously there would be difficulties effectively developing and managing an electronic portfolio. This simple reality tends to drive the content of so-called cons or negative aspects of electronic portfolios.

Norton and Wiburg (1998), like most authors on electronic portfolios, describe the advantages of an electronic portfolio, such as including the ability to track alternative development paths with a single set of materials and easy editing, updating, and browsing. McNulty suggests that an "electronic portfolio is not just the digital version of the filing cabinet where [material] is collected and catalogued" (p. 21). Electronic portfolios are continually consulted for work revisions, to reference previous work, to evaluate progress, and more. The advantages of electronic portfolios are many (Galloway, 2001; McNulty, 2002) and are easily accepted by "techies," but apparently, as discussed above, not so for many who still resist technology in education.

Part of the problem is certainly the mastery of technology still lacking among most educators. Barrett (1999) details skills applicable to the development of electronic portfolios. They involve file conversions, digitizing, scanning, graphic editing, CD mastering—all highly technical competencies and beyond the range of most working educators. The standards for educators often include only a token mention of technology. Standards for school leaders (Interstate School Leaders Licensure Consortium, 2002) mention technology only vaguely without any detail (Standard 3, p. 5). Even where portfolios are specifically addressed for school principals (Ohio State University, 2002), the context ignores the need for electronic or technology-based content and presentation. On the other hand, this may be changing if new generations of educators follow the new and aggressive standards for all beginning teachers in Texas (Texas State Board of Educator Certification, 2002). Virtually all teachers will be expected to develop competencies with multimedia and technology, and this should directly impact the trends toward electronic portfolios.

Aschermann (1999) gathered data on the required development of electronic portfolios stating that, "The 'notebook' [traditional paper formats] portfolio no longer would be suitable for the new uses of the portfolio" (p. 3). Web-based formats were considered the most desirable, while some comparisons were made with CD-based portfolios as compared to online formats. CD-ROMs offer the ability to store portfolio information in a self-contained format with a great deal of longevity. Having a portfolio on the World Wide Web does make the portfolio easy to access, but accessible only to those with Internet access immediately available; if it is available on CD, the portfolio is fully self-contained and accessible to any viewer at almost any time. However, Web-based formats are superior in that they allow for "on-the-fly" changes and updates to any and all parts of the portfolio.

Brown and Irby (2001) also outline the benefits and advantages of electronic portfolios as being ideal for self-assessment, reflection, and external evaluation. They indicate that portfolios are ideal for providing feedback, for documentation, and as a tool of career advancement. They directly imply that electronic portfolios have all of the attributes and advantages of their paper alternatives with the obvious benefits of the electronic world. In an earlier publication, Beverly and Genevieve described electronic versions of portfolios in a variety of formats, including Web based, HyperStudio based, and PowerPoint based (Irby & Brown, 2000). Various advantages of electronic media are covered as well as security issues. A major point was that electronic versions are not only emerging as common and marketable, but that they can also offer a competitive edge over non-electronic versions.

Aschermann (1999) also cites a great deal of negativity across a number of issues and student concerns:

- Simple resistance to breaking traditional paper-based habits.
- Lacking access to and desiring technology at home versus attending a school-based lab.
- Privacy of portfolio openness in a public domain allowing plagiarism and lower security.
- Exceeding their school-based computer space allocation.
- Losing computer-site accounts upon graduation.
- Students fail to connect "technology" to anything but their technology class, thus failing to apply their technology training to other aspects of their professional development.

The last factor was the most alarming, and yet very believable given a general resistance to adopting a technology-based professional lifestyle. Gathercoal and his colleagues (2002) explain this issue as something of an irony. In 1994, when the World Wide Web was new and yet very static and bland:

> *"...university and college faculty...would logically expect Web-based student portfolios to become commonplace in a few years. We wonder how this will happen when few instructors will voluntarily put their syllabi and assignments online...literature regarding the use of electronic portfolios testifies to this paradox." (pp. 29-30)*

It would seem that this problem is not necessarily the students and their failure to connect technology on all levels, after all. It may in fact stem from the models presented to them in their non-technology classes, where the faculty may not be perpetuating a culture where technology and its role in creating professional portfolios has been embraced.

Systems

Bullock and Hawk (2001) describe electronic portfolios in terms of either software generated or Web based. This is rather a limited notion, but consistent with many views about electronic portfolios. While electronic portfolios are described as an essential element of the profession that could even effect getting a job, Provenzo (2002) also describes them in the limited context of Web-page formats. Electronic portfolios may be a product of multimedia authoring programs or presented as Web pages. Of course, Web pages may also be generated through composing software or by more technical means. However, Maddux, Johnson, and Willis (2001) indicate that "most teachers are not willing to expend the time and effort necessary to learn such programs [authoring systems] well enough to produce quality products" (p. 41).

While Barrett (1999) makes a good case justifying a Web-based platform for electronic portfolios, Galloway (2001) suggests additional formats and that electronic portfolios should not be limited to or viewed exclusively as Web pages. For a Microsoft Office user, where most if not all documents—products involving word processing, spreadsheets, PowerPoint, and so forth—can be hyperlinked for easy browsing in a point-and-click environment, the portfolio artifacts may be the original documents themselves, rather than regenerating materials into a Web-based presentation. Of course, an electronic portfolio can also be a composite of these various environments. A portfolio service or portfolio generation tool will more likely impose a template environment rather than allowing the creativity of a personal approach.

Much of the current literature on electronic portfolios is reminiscent of writing two decades ago on the early presence of computers in education. There are attempts to analyze and report the advantages and disadvantages, to justify or document the merits of this new feature. The advantages of electronic portfolios are not unique to portfolios and are, for the most part, the same advantages common to all domains of technology. This is also true of the disadvantages or limitations of technology. They are not necessarily unique to the development of portfolios.

Results and Analyses

Superintendent Feedback

The authors of the current study surveyed several superintendents in the Northwest Indiana region to review the online portfolios and send back their feedback in a short, informal questionnaire. The majority of responses were overwhelmingly positive. While some reported encountering problems accessing video clips, this was found to be an error within the Web page. After the error was corrected, no superintendent reported having trouble accessing the online materials, indicating that their available technology was sufficient to allow proper viewing of all portfolio artifacts.

Superintendents also indicated a great preference for the layout of each portfolio, finding it easy to use and conducive to quick navigation. Some would have preferred a smaller number of artifacts to peruse, since superintendents are notoriously "crunched for time" and would likely wish to view only the barest minimum material. As for content, some superintendents indicated that they would have liked artifacts pertaining specifically to elementary/secondary and administration experience and qualifications. Long academic papers and lengthy recounts of the candidates' educational philosophies were deemed as a little "too much" and that the student may have gotten "carried away." The importance of high-quality, professional photographs was also mentioned. Many superintendents felt that they were able to get to know the candidates very well through the electronic portfolios.

Thus, based on the electronic portfolios they had reviewed, all superintendents articulated that they would ask for interviews with the candidates, and that they would use this same service when looking for potential administrative employees in the future. The ability to see more than just a résumé from a candidate allowed the superintendents to

Table 1. Summary of feedback received

Survey Questions	Comments Received
Were you able to access all items in the portfolio? Did you have any problems downloading necessary plug-ins or viewing any of the files?	A few superintendents noted a problem with downloading QuickTime videos on the site.
What was your overall impression of the design and layout of the portfolio? Did the layout allow you to find the information you wanted easily? Please feel free to write your comments.	All felt that the design of the portfolios was excellent, easy to follow, and very "business-like" in tone. Some had concerns about the use of too many or too lengthy artifacts that may or may not have bearing on the candidates' qualifications for hire.
Would this portfolio lead you to offer an interview to this student? What other information could have been added to the portfolio to increase your desire to hire this student?	All agreed that viewing such a portfolio would likely lead to interview. The superintendents found that they were able to "get to know" the candidates better in advance. Some felt that a professional photograph of the candidate would help the overall impression received by looking at the candidate's portfolio for the first time. A number of superintendents indicated that a short description of what each artifact contained would be helpful and would minimize the time needed to look through the portfolio and its linked documents.
Would you use this system for finding potential employees in the future? Please feel free to write your comments on why you would or would not make use of electronic portfolios like this one.	All indicated that they would enjoy having such a system available to them when screening for new employees.
What other aspects of the portfolio could have been done better? Would you like to have seen more material, less material, something done differently, et cetera? Any feedback you can give would be greatly appreciated.	The majority of respondents indicated that they would like to see fewer lengthy artifacts and instead have the candidates focus on a "highlight reel" of accomplishments. Many superintendents indicated the desire to see academic transcripts for the candidate included within the portfolio.

learn more about him or her in advance, saving time in the interviewing process. Using this system, the superintendents saw the potential of being able to make early and educated decisions about which potential hires would work best within their respective school districts. If it is obvious that a candidate will not meet the district's needs at that time, the superintendent can simply move down the list to the next portfolio.

All superintendents commented that the current electronic portfolios offered by CEL very effectively fulfilled their needs and expectations, and that they would ask CEL to keep the service available for future use.

Candidate Feedback

While no formal survey or assessment was given to the candidates who participated in the pilot portfolio program, all were asked to briefly communicate their experiences and thoughts about the project to the CEL Director. All candidates indicated that putting together the electronic portfolios was a valuable use of their time, and that they would like to continue adding to it as they grew nearer to securing positions within school administration. To this day, many do submit updates to their portfolios periodically. It is important to note that four of the six participants have obtained positions; the other two have just completed their programs and already have positive prospects. A comparison of the success rates of pilot participants with non-participants will be the subject of future research.

The candidates also enjoyed the ease with which their portfolios came together. Occasionally, they ran into problems—such as when it became necessary to scan hard copies of important documents into the computer before submitting them by e-mail—but overall, they found the experience simple and very helpful. After submissions were posted to the Web, candidates were encouraged to review their portfolios and suggest changes where appropriate to the CEL Webmaster. Each candidate was allowed access to his or her portfolio page only by means of individual usernames and passwords.

Another problem came when a candidate did not necessarily know how much or what kinds of materials to add to his or her portfolio. Some of the candidates required more guidance from their professors as to the content of their portfolio, while others felt that only a résumé and a short list of academic artifacts were enough. For candidates early in their programs, it was admittedly harder for them to think about their portfolio in the context of the ISLLC standards. More guidance and more emphasis on the standards may need to be offered to ensure that each candidate produces a successful electronic portfolio that would be of interest to prospective district employers.

Suggestions for Electronic Portfolio Implementation and Management

To manage an electronic portfolio service as we have described, it is preferred to have one or two people on staff that are dedicated to the task, especially if you are managing large numbers of portfolios. The following software and hardware will also aid in hosting and maintaining your portfolios on the Internet:

- a Web server, preferably a school-owned server to which your portfolio management team has direct access, to minimize the time and effort spent in uploading portfolio files;
- a security feature where only designated users with the correct password may enter the portfolio site (most Web server software titles, such as AppleShareIP, Mac OS X Server, and Novell Netware, have this feature built-in);
- HTML editing software, such as Macromedia Dreamweaver, Microsoft FrontPage, or Adobe GoLive;
- conversion software to make universally accessible files from the students' artifacts (Adobe Acrobat for the creation of PDF files is recommended, but other universal formats like plain text, Rich-Text Format, and HTML may also be considered);
- a designated e-mail address or FTP server to which students may upload their artifacts.

Of course, the portfolio management team will need to have sufficient experience in Web design and site maintenance in order for the project to be successful. The team should be aware that they might be asked to make changes to students' artifacts frequently. Original copies of all files sent to the team should be archived in case of server failure or the need to edit is apparent. Also, security must always be maintained to ensure that students' personal information is not transmitted to anyone but registered users of the system. This is especially important if academic transcripts and licensure documents are made available within the portfolios.

Future Trends in Electronic Portfolio Implementation

Larger programs or universities may wish to employ a more automated system for electronic portfolios. Within the past few years, several large textbook publishers have developed software packages just for this purpose including McGraw-Hill's *FolioLive* (www.foliolive.com). There is a minimal cost to students, who purchase their access to this service along with a small textbook, but portfolios may be accessed by anyone granted access, for as long as the student wishes to have his or her portfolio available. Many school districts and universities are beginning to look to programs like *FolioLive* as student-managed electronic portfolio solutions.

Another electronic portfolio solution comes from the Chalk and Wire Professional Development Group, based in Ontario, Canada (www.chalkandwire.com). Their *e-Portfolio with RubricMarker* product allows students to create professional-looking portfolios utilizing any technology they wish, including HTML, Adobe PDF files, and Microsoft Office documents. *e-Portfolio*'s creation and publication interface is simple and easy to understand regardless of the student's level of proficiency with computers, and the portfolios they create can be easily evaluated by faculty using any set of standards, including institutional and state-mandated standards, through the *RubricMaker* assessment tool. Additionally, unlike *FolioLive*, which is hosted solely by the company's file servers, institutions have the option of hosting both the *e-Portfolio* and *RubricMaker* tools on their own servers, with free upgrades and support included. Pricing for students is on an annual or semi-annual subscription basis; alternately; institutions have the option of purchasing anywhere from 20 to 40 or more subscriptions for student usage which includes additional free storage space for faculty.

More and more companies are becoming interested in electronic portfolios, both for professional environments and for education. A list of resources offering a variety of portfolio services can be found in Appendix B.

Conclusion

As feedback from the candidates and superintendents in the CEL study indicates, students will benefit from having some guidelines when choosing artifacts for their portfolios. Even if the portfolios are not meant as an assessment tool for graduation, students should be advised not to include many excessively long documents, and to choose documents that best reflect their abilities as teachers and potential as leaders. This is especially true when dealing with electronic portfolios that will be accessed from many different locations. Download speed and accessibility should be carefully considered when choosing to design and implement any electronic portfolio system.

References

Aschermann, J.R. (1999). Electronic portfolios: Why? What? How? *Proceedings of the SITE 99: Society for Information Technology & Teacher Education International Conference,* San Antonio, TX. (ERIC Document Reproduction Service No. ED432305.)

Barrett, H. (1999). Electronic teaching portfolios. *Proceedings of the SITE 99: Society for Information Technology & Teacher Education International Conference,* San Antonio, TX. (ERIC Document Reproduction Service No. ED432265.)

Brown, G. & Irby, B.J. (2001). *The principal portfolio*. Thousand Oaks, CA: Corwin Press.

Bullock, A.A. & Hawk, P.P. (2001). *Developing a teaching portfolio: A guide for preservice and practicing teachers*. Upper Saddle River, NJ: Prentice-Hall.

Galloway, J.P. (2001). Electronic portfolios (EP): A "how to" guide. *Society for Information Technology and Teacher Education Annual Proceedings 2001,* (1), 582-587. Retrieved from *dl.aace.org/3574*

Gathercoal, P., Love, D., Bryde, B., & McKean, G. (2002). On implementing Web-based electronic portfolios. *Educause Quarterly, 25*(2), 29-37.

Interstate School Leaders Licensure Consortium. (1996). *Interstate school leaders licensure standards.* Retrieved May 10, 2004, from *www.mpa.cc/pdf/isllc.pdf*

Irby, B.J. & Brown, G. (2000). *The career advancement portfolio.* Thousand Oaks, CA: Corwin Press.

Kennedy, J.L. & Morrow, T.J. (1994). *Electronic resume revolution. Create a winning resume for the new world of job seeking.* New York: John Wiley & Sons.

Maddux, C.D., Johnson, D.L., & Willis, J.W. (2001). *Educational computing: Learning with tomorrow's technologies.* Needham Heights, MA: Allyn & Bacon.

McNulty, K.T. (2002). Fostering the student-centered classroom online. *Technological Horizons in Education Journal, 29*(7), 16-22.

National Association of Elementary School Principals. (2002). *Principal online forums.* Retrieved July 7, 2002, from www.naesp.org/cgi-bin/netforum/open2/a/3—393.

National Council for Accreditation of Teacher Education. (1997). *Technology and the new professional teacher: Preparing for the 21st century classroom.* Washington, DC: National Council for Accreditation of Teacher Education.

Norton, P. & Wiburg, K.M. (1998). *Teaching with technology.* Orlando, FL: Harcourt Brace and Co.

Ohio State University, School of Education. (2002). *Principal portfolios for leadership and learning.* Retrieved May 10, 2004, from *www.acs.ohio-state.edu/urbanschools/principl/schoolwork7.htm*

Provenzo, E.F. (2002). *The Internet and the World Wide Web for teachers* (2nd edition). Needham Heights, MA: Allyn & Bacon.

Purves, A.C. (1996). Electronic portfolios. *Computers and Composition, 13*(2), 135-46.

Quible, Z.K. (1995). Electronic resumes: Their time is coming. *Business Communication Quarterly, 58*(3), 5-9.

Texas State Board for Educator Certification. *New educator standards: Technology applications.* Retrieved August 8, 2002, from *www.sbec.state.tx.us/stand_framewrk/pdfs/stand_techappall.pdf*

Warner, M. & Maureen, A. (1999). Educational progressions: Electronic portfolios in a virtual classroom. *Technological Horizons in Education Journal, 27*(3), 86-89.

Appendix A: Portfolio Preparation Guidelines and Templates

Select and document a minimum of four representative internship activities for each area of competency listed below. For each entry specify which of the ISLLC standards and the NASSP skills are addressed.

Instructional Program Activity #1 - Title	
Summary/Description	
ISLLC Standard(s) #	
NASSP Skill (S) #	

Supervision of Staff Activity#1 - Title	
Summary/Description	
ISLLC Standard(s) #	
NASSP Skill (S) #	

General School Management Activity #1 - Title	
Summary/Description	
ISLLC Standard(s) #	
NASSP Skill (S) #	

Budget Preparation & Control Activity #1- Title	
Summary/Description	
ISLLC Standard(s) #	
NASSP Skill (S) #	

School Community & Relations Activity #1 - Title	
Summary/Description	
ISLLC Standard(s) #	
NASSP Skill (S) #	

Professional Reading

Summarize at least four articles from professional journals that you have read during your internship. Write a brief statement indicating what you have learned in the article that you can translate into administrative/supervisory practice. Indicate how each journal article relates to your proposal. Include the citation.

Classroom Observation

Evidence of at least four classroom observations must be included in your portfolio. Briefly summarize each lesson observed, indicate the strategy used for collecting data, and include a copy of the observation report for each lesson.

Observation #1
Summary of Lesson: **Data Collection Strategy:** **Observation Report:**

Written Communication

Examples of at least five written communications that you prepared as part of your internship experience are to be included in this section. Explain the purpose for which the document was developed. You have the option of including the actual document with a hyperlink. The documents may include but are not limited to: research projects, analyzing achievement test results, database development, evaluating/writing curriculum, conducting workshops, working with substitutes, handbooks, memos, letters to parents, schedules, agendas, planning documents, etc.

Document #1
Purpose: **Document:**

Using Technology for the Professional Development of Teachers

Visit the Board of Education Web site and explore any three additional Internet sites. You may select the sites from those listed below or any other site that is of interest to you. Comment on each site as follows. In your discussion, address the following questions regarding the utility of the site.

- What are the purposes of the site? Who are the desired users? Is the site aesthetically attractive? Is the information well written? Is it easy to move around and locate information on the site? Do the pages appear uncluttered? Do illustrations, video, or audio add value to the site? Is there a well-labeled contents area?
- Describe how selected features of each site could be used for the professional development of teachers or administrators. Be specific.

New York City Board of Education	http://www.nycenet.edu
Association for Supervision and Curriculum Development	http://www.ascd.org
Educational Resources Information Center (ERIC)	http://ericae.net
Exploring Middle School Reform	http://www.middleweb.com
Pathways to School Improvement	http://ncrel.org
United States Department of Education Homepage	http://www.ed.gov

Professional Development

Membership in Professional Organizations	
Workshops/Conferences Attended	
Workshops Conducted	

Appendix B: E-Portfolio Services on the Internet

The Open Source E-Portfolio Tool: *www.theospri.org*

EPortaro: *www.eportaro.com*

Agilix GoBinder: *www.gobinder.com/index.html*

Chalk and Wire with RubricMarker: *www.chalkandwire.com/eportfolio/*

Catalyst (University of Washington): *catalyst.washington.edu/tools/#overview*

Nuventive iWebfolio: *www.nuventive.com*

Eport: *eport2.cgc.maricopa.edu*

Digital Learning Commons: *depts.washington.edu/lcommons/students/tools/ePortfolio.php*

Catalyst Portfolio tool: *catalyst.washington.edu/catalyst/tools/portfolio.html*

efolio University of Minnesota: *efolio.project.mnscu.edu*

KEEP: *www.carnegiefoundation.org/kml/KEEP/index.htm*

ProfPort: *www.folioworld.com*

TaskStream: *www.taskstream.com/pub/default.asp*

eFolio: *www.efoliomn.com/index.asp*

Epsilen Portfolios: *www.iupui.edu/epsilendotcom/home.html*

Section II

Higher Education Instructional Technology Literacy

Chapter VII

Developing Graduate Qualities Through Information Systems and Information Technology Literacy Skills

Ann Monday
University of South Australia, Australia

Sandra Barker
University of South Australia, Australia

Abstract

This chapter introduces role play and case study as an approach to developing graduate qualities through information systems and information technology literacy skills. It argues that a case study and role play approach provides a good vehicle to develop a student's understanding of the graduate qualities valued by employers by developing their skills in the areas of lifelong learning, conflict resolution, problem solving, group communication, and time management. It adds to the understanding of why it is important for business students who will become end-user developers to understand the risks to an organization of poor-quality end-user-developed applications and the responsibilities that they have to their organization to adopt good working practices.

Introduction

For some time universities have endeavored to address the shortfall in skill requirements that have been identified by prospective employers of graduates. The University of South Australia (UniSA) includes itself among these universities and has identified a number of 'graduate qualities' that are required to be developed within the curriculum. The development of graduate qualities is aimed at facilitating the transition from university to graduate employment. DETYA (2000) examines employer satisfaction with graduate skills, and concludes that deficiencies perceived by graduates and employers are in the areas of creativity and flair, oral business communications and problem solving, interpersonal skills, and understanding of business practice. Steven and Fallows (1998) explore "[t]he strategic decision to embed employability skills into each level of the undergraduate curriculum [to ensure that] every student is fully equipped, at graduation, with the skills necessary for the very important transition into the world of employment."

After consultation with business, UniSA (2000a) identified that a graduate:

1. operates effectively with and upon a *body of knowledge* of sufficient depth to begin professional practice;
2. is prepared for *lifelong learning* in pursuit of personal development and excellence in professional practice;
3. is an *effective problem solver,* capable of applying logical, critical, and creative thinking to a range of problems;
4. can work both *autonomously and collaboratively* as a professional;
5. is committed to *ethical action and social responsibility* as a professional and as a citizen;
6. *communicates effectively* in professional practice and as a member of the community; and
7. demonstrates *international perspectives* as a professional and as a citizen.

Appropriate graduate qualities are identified for each course (subject) within any given program, together with suitable teaching and learning strategies to facilitate the development of these graduate qualities. UniSA has adopted the approach to embed the graduate qualities into its courses rather than teach them separately. Each program is required to demonstrate the inclusion of all graduate qualities, though each course will develop different graduate qualities to different depths.

This chapter evaluates a case study and role play approach to embedding graduate qualities into an undergraduate business information systems course. It is not intended to explore each of the graduate qualities separately. The case study and role play approach will be used as the focus for the discussion that follows, and will demonstrate how this approach facilitates the development of the graduate qualities.

The course explored in this chapter is one of eight core courses in a business major. The focus of this course is on business students (end-user developers)—not IT or IS professionals—who will go out into the workplace and develop small-scale database applications to help them and their employers in their business role. There is much literature that explores the issues of non-IT/IS staff building poor-quality applications in their workplace, and the potential risks and actual failures that have occurred. In many instances this has resulted in major setbacks for businesses, and at the very least a massive waste of time, energy, and resources on the part of the end-user developer. This chapter explores the information systems and information technology literacy skills that are critical to the development of small-scale database applications by end-user developers.

Developing End-User Applications

The opportunity for end-users to develop applications that were useful to their own business roles arose in the early 1980s with the introduction of desktop PCs and simple spreadsheet and word processing applications. Simple database applications were later added to the desktop suite of programs.

As the price of hardware and software decreased and the technology advanced in speed and complexity, end-user computing became "crucial for increasing productivity in many firms" (Govindarajulu, 2003). Alavi (1985) identified that "...by developing their own applications, end-users can obtain results faster and satisfy ad-hoc demands for information and analytical capabilities—thereby leading to an increase in end-user productivity" (p. 200). However, it was also pointed out in Alavi's research that end-user development of software applications may lead to applications of questionable quality. Batra, Hoffler, and Bostrom (1990) found that "[e]nd-user development of information systems represents a major departure from the development of systems by trained and experienced specialists" (p. 126). It has been widely noted that end-users have a variety of knowledge, abilities, and experiences (Govindarajulu, 2003; Rockart & Flannery, 1983; Cotterman & Kumar, 1989), and to this end applications that are developed can range from the simple spreadsheet to the more complex Web pages, including those with database connection (Govindarajulu, 2003).

Certainly, with the increasing number of PCs available in business and the proliferation of relatively inexpensive application software (4GLs), employers are increasingly requiring business graduates to have some knowledge of the concepts of application development (Barker & Monday, 2000; Monday, 2001). End-users who undertake development of software applications do so primarily for themselves or other colleagues within their immediate department. It is therefore understood that end-users tend to work closely with those who will be using the application in order to ensure that the requirements of the end-user are carefully considered and implemented.

Sumner and Klepper (1986) identified that in a study of 33 user-developed applications, less than 20% of the applications contained appropriate controls, backup and recovery systems, and secure data protocols. They also cited research by Davis (1984) and Alavi (1985) that identified major concerns with user-developed applications were caused by the "lack of documentation, data validation and testing, controls, audit trails, backup and recovery, and data security measures" (p. 103).

Govindarajulu (2003) reported that "since end-user applications pose potential threats to data integrity and security, end-user support is crucial to educate users on avoiding risks" (p. 154). Alavi (1985) concluded that end-users should undergo a comprehensive education program in the area of application development to improve the success of end-user application development within organizations. The students taking this course are introduced to good working practices through case study and role-playing strategies.

Teaching and Learning Approaches

Case Study Approach

Yuan (2001) identifies a significant shift to alternative methods of teaching including problem-based learning, student-centered learning, and the use of case studies. Case studies are used to describe problems or incidents based on real-life situations (Roselle, 1996). The problems to be analyzed are usually those that have occurred in the past or are likely to be encountered by the students in their professional lives (Kreber, 2001). It is essential that case studies contain sufficient data for analysis and observation to be made while being conducted in their natural context (Yuan, 2001).

The features of a good case study have been summarized by Gross Davis (1993, cited in Kreber, 2001). It was identified that a case study is one that tells a story, raises issues for discussion, contains elements of conflict, lacks a definitive answer, encourages students' thought processes, requires a decision to be made, and is reasonably concise. Each case study is written within these parameters. Students are supplied with the basic procedures adopted by the organization and are required to develop a small-scale database to solve the issues raised by the business.

Role-Play

Role-play, as defined by Ladousse in Cutler and Hay (2000), is "a short, low-input/high-output, interactive teaching and learning technique." Rather than a role being mapped out for students, students are required to engage with the parties to the role-play, and their role is shaped as they learn (Cutler & Hay, 2000). They also note that this enables students to tackle 'live' projects, and adopt a role and view a situation from the viewpoint of their role; it also requires them to present arguments and defend their viewpoints in verbal and written form, and to work in teams, thus developing their group skills. This approach is particularly suited to the development of a number of graduate qualities. It provides students with an opportunity to interact with each other, and members of a 'business', in a group project. It allows the students to apply theory learned to a 'live' case. It provides a platform for testing a range of communication media, and requires students to manage themselves and the groups they work in.

The characteristics of a good case study and role-play approach align well with the course content and the development of the graduate qualities of the UniSA. The graduate qualities are explored in the following discussion, using the characteristics of case study (tell a story, raise issues for discussion, include elements of conflict, lack a definitive answer, encourage thought processes and require decisions to be made, be concise) and role-play (tackle a 'live' project, adopt a particular role).

Tell a story and be reasonably concise

The case studies used in the course are either based on the industrial experience of the tutors or written in consultation with businesses. Because students on the business programs typically find employment in both the public and private sector, and in large and small organizations, scenarios change for each delivery of the course. The case study is used to tell a story about the business—to provide sufficient and concise background to the business and partial information needs, and to provide appropriate business documentation.

The case study is also used to tell the story of the problems caused by end-user development and to demonstrate the responsibilities of the students as end-user developers. The 'story' of end-user developers emerges throughout the semester.

Raise issues for discussion

You will note above that the case scenarios provide only partial requirements of the business. As with any business situation, there are not only software issues that need to be considered when developing quality software applications. The needs of the business are rarely completely clear. In some instances discussion and analysis of a business situation will provide the clarification that is required. In many instances clarification is not immediately available, and it is not until a problem situation has been explored in a number of ways over a period of time that issues start to become clearer.

It is important that students learn to interact with a business, learn how to talk to the business, and use appropriate language and tone in both written and oral communication. It is also important that students learn how to research and investigate a business problem, identify potential solutions to problems, and present these scenarios to the business for consideration.

Students are required to analyze the data provided and identify what is required by the business. They must operate upon a 'body of knowledge' to understand the problem that is presented to them, and to identify potential solutions to the problem and satisfactory approaches that might be used.

Students are required to 'communicate' orally and in writing, face-to-face, via e-mail or discussion board, with the business, with other students in their group, and with tutors to gather information, clarify the problem that has been set, and to make the most suitable choices from several possible solutions at various stages of the project.

In terms of software development, students must understand and apply good design practices. They must be able to design appropriate data structures, and recognize and identify appropriate software features so that they can build a database that is accurate and robust. As noted earlier, end-user developers must also consider the needs of the users, not only in terms of the information that the database will provide, but also in terms of its usability and user-friendliness.

Include elements of conflict

The case scenario itself is designed to raise elements of conflict. Students are required to analyze a business and design a database application that meets the needs of end-users. End-users generally have different viewpoints and different requirements, even for the small-scale databases that we are discussing here. The students interact with the members of the business (role-played by tutors) who have differing requirements from the system. Members of the business will disagree about the requirements of the application, and students are required to manage the process and handle the conflict that arises. Students also work in groups and are required to manage their group and any conflict that arises within their group.

Lack a definitive answer

A common theme that arises with students is their need for a definitive answer. In problem solving they want to know 'the' answer when there may be several. In software development the same demand arises time and time again. Data structures are determined by the data that is required to produce the outputs of the system. However, input, output, and interface design are more subjective. There are good design principles that can be applied to design of inputs, outputs, and the interface. However, there is a large range of software features available and still a higher level of subjectivity in these aspects of database design than in the design of data structures.

Encourage thought processes and require decisions to be made

As with any systems analysis, design, and implementation, as discussed earlier, students are required to explore problems, investigate potential solutions, and make informed choices. Students working in groups are encouraged to think creatively, to brainstorm in order to explore the problem situation, and to investigate a range of potential solutions. They are encouraged to question, analyze and criticize, and 'think outside the box'.

Tackle a 'live' project

Interaction with a live business would give the students the opportunity to handle a real-life situation. However, the large numbers of students, both onshore and offshore, make this prohibitive. The case study and role-play provide an alternative 'real' scenario and a project that is complex enough to represent many of the features of a 'live' situation, including issues of ambiguity, managing relationships, and managing time.

Work in teams (and with the business and tutors) and adopt a particular role

Students are required to adopt a role with the 'business' and within their group, to view a situation, seek information, request clarification, present arguments, and consider the viewpoint of others. They are required to operate ethically and accept social responsibility in their project—with the business, with their peers, and with tutors.

Initially students are required to form groups and establish a good working relationship within their group, typically through the forming, storming, norming, performing, and adjourning stages (Tuckman, 1965 and Tuckman & Jensen, 1977, cited in Napier & Gershenfeld, 1999) of a group project. They are required to manage their group, allocate tasks according to individual strengths within their groups, work autonomously on their allocated task, work as a member of a group, and manage their time to successful completion of their project.

Issues and Challenges

The above approaches used in the development of graduate qualities, information systems, and information technology literacy skills have provided some significant successes for staff and students.

The ability to introduce students to real-life business problems and allow them to experience a simulated business situation has proven quite popular with the students. Staff have noticed an improvement in the communication skills of the students since the introduction of a range of media, including asynchronous discussion boards and e-mail. Increased face-to-face meetings and simulated business discussions have also contributed to the development of the students' communication abilities.

Throughout the course, students are exposed to a number of logic problems, giving them the tools to improve their ability to analyze business problems; they are also encouraged to 'think outside the box' in order to find a possible solution to the problem at hand.

The case study approach allows students to experience the process of developing a small-scale database and thus identify end-user issues. Experience has shown that they can learn them from reading about the issues, but they don't fully appreciate them until they have faced them.

However, a number of issues and challenges have become evident since the introduction of the course and during the development of this approach.

Developing the Case

A major issue in this approach is the length of time it takes to develop the 'case' and the frequency that this happens. Each case takes considerable time to research and write up in a format that can be used by students and by tutors involved in the role-play. The case has to provide sufficient information to give students a reasonable starting point in their analysis, but not too much to ensure students are still required to investigate and clarify the requirements of the users of the database. The case material must also be sufficient to ensure the tutors understand the problem situation and can play their 'roles'.

Adopting 'Roles'

Some students find it difficult to adopt a 'role'. Other students find it difficult to separate the tutor in their business 'role' from the tutor in their normal role. Given the course runs with a very small team, it is not possible to provide students with 'players' that are not teaching them as well.

Conflict in the Business

It is sometimes hard for students to accept disagreement within the business as just that—two members of a business who have different viewpoints. When disagreement arises, students have a tendency to see it as conflict between tutors and not members of the business.

Changing Assignment Criteria

The changes made throughout the case study are part of normal business life. These tend to cause stress for students who see the situation as tutors changing scope of assignment, which is not allowed, rather than the business changing its mind as it begins to understand what the database software can and cannot provide for the business.

A 'Perfect' Solution

The course has been offered using two different approaches to the database construction. In the first group, students have been allowed to follow through with incorrect data structures, causing problems with the implementation of queries, forms, and reports. The second group of students was given basic data structures to allow them to develop working queries, forms, and reports without the stress of incorrect tables and relationships. It has been the experience of the authors that students learn more about the importance of accurate tables and relationships, and about end-user issues by allowing them to follow through with incorrect data structures, but the students prefer to see finished and perfect data.

Managing Time

Before students can tackle their project, they have to become familiar with the body of knowledge that underpins the project. The approach adopted is a developmental approach, which requires students to complete activities and tasks on a regular basis to ensure that they are fully equipped to tackle the project effectively and efficiently. Although the tasks are clearly identified, the timelines are established by the student group based on the assignment due date, commitments of each member of the group, and the activities. This is regularly a stumbling block for many student groups.

Needs of the End-User

When a systems development project commences, it is often the case that the management and/or the users do not totally know what they want to achieve (or what is possible to achieve) with the new system. Therefore it is extremely important that the end-user developer understands the needs of management and/or the needs of the ultimate end-users. This has been a concept that the students have found difficult to interpret and implement in the development of the case study database.

Conclusion and Future Trends

The problem of end-user-developed applications is not a new one. It was flagged in the early 1980s by Panko (1986) and is a problem that still exists today. While basic IT skills are taught in many business degrees, it is still generally little more than a basic introduction to 4GL software. It is clearly not sufficient to teach basic IT software skills for would-be end-user developers.

Graduates need to be aware of the problems they can cause an organization in the development of an information system that contains poor data structures, has limited or no documentation, lacks data validation and security, and has no back-up or recovery systems in place. They must also be good communicators, problem solvers, and team members.

Throughout this course students are introduced to the concept of lifelong learning and experience a number of situations that will improve their lifelong learning skills, for example: conflict resolution, dealing with ambiguity, and managing time. They also have to accept that there is not always one right answer or a perfect solution to a problem situation. As discussed earlier, these are the areas that students have particular problems with.

The business information systems course discussed above provides a useful vehicle for exploring IT skills, end-user issues, and the graduate qualities.

References

Alavi, M. (1985). Some thoughts on quality issues of end-user-developed systems. *Proceedings of the 21st Annual Conference on Computer Personnel Research* (pp. 200-207), Minneapolis, MN, USA.

Barker, S. & Monday, A. (2000, December). Business students in information systems: Wizards or apprentices? *Proceedings of the Australasian Computing Education Conference,* Melbourne, Australia.

Batra, D., Hoffler, J.A., & Bostrom, R.P. (1990). Comparing representations with relational and EER models. *Communications of the ACM, 33*(2), 126-139.

Candy, P.C., Crebert, G., & O'Leary, J. (1994). *Developing lifelong learners through undergraduate education.* Canberra: Australian Government Printing Service.

Cotterman, W.W. & Kumar, K. (1989). User cube: A taxonomy of end-users. *Communications of the ACM, 32*(11), 1313-1320.

Cutler, C. & Hay, I. (2000). 'Club Dread': Applying and refining an issue-based role-play on environment, economy, and culture. *Journal of Geography in Higher Education, 24*(2), 179-197.

DETYA. (2000). *Employer satisfaction with graduate skills: Research report.* ACNielsen Research Services 99/7.

Govindarajulu, C. (2003). End-users: Who are they?. *Communications of the ACM, 46*(9), 152-159.

Kreber, C. (2001). Learning experientially through case studies? A conceptual analysis. *Teaching in Higher Education, 6*(2), 217-228.

Monday, A. (2001, May). The reality of teaching large groups of local and international business students to develop end-user applications. *Proceedings of the IRMA Conference*, Toronto, Canada.

Napier, R.W. & Gershenfeld, M.K. (1999). *Groups: Theory and experience* (6th edition). Boston: Houghton Mifflin Company.

Panko, R. (1988). *End-user computing: Management, applications, and technology.* New York: John Wiley & Sons.

Rockart, J.F. & Flannery, L.S. (1983). The management of end-user computing. *Communications of the ACM, 26*(10), 776-784.

Roselle, A. (1996). The case study method: A learning tool for practicing librarians and information specialists. *Library Review, 45*(4), 30-38.

Steven, C. & Fallows, S. (1998). Enhancing employability skills within higher education: Impact on teaching, learning and assessment. *EducatiOn-Line.* Accessed September 23, 2001, from *www.leeds.ac.uk/educol/documents/000000700.htm*

Summer, M. & Klepper, R. (1986, October). End-user application development: Practices, policies and organizational impacts. *Proceedings of the 22nd Annual Computer Personnel Research Conference* (pp. 102-116), Calgary, Canada.

University of South Australia. (2000a). Graduate qualities—Overview. *Learning Connection Teaching Guide.* Accessed September 23, 2001, from *www.unisanet.unisa.edu.au/learningconnection/teachg/tggqo.doc*

University of South Australia. (2000b). Graduate qualities—A program design and development process. *Learning Connection Teaching Guide.* Accessed October 4, 2001, from *www.unisanet.unisa.edu.au/learningconnection/teachg/GQprogdesign.doc*

Yuan, L.L. (2001). Quality-of-life case studies for university teaching in sustainable development. *International Journal of Sustainability in Higher Education, 2*(2), 127-138.

Chapter VIII

Understanding the Role of Type Preferences in Fostering Technological Literacy

Karen S. Nantz
Eastern Illinois University, USA

Barbara E. Kemmerer
Eastern Illinois University, USA

Abstract

This chapter examines the relationship between learning preferences and technological literacy. Based upon the work of Carl Jung, Myers-Briggs proposed a framework for understanding personality differences. The chapter suggests that applying this framework to the study of technological and information literacy can increase organizational effectiveness, particularly with respect to training, delivery methods, and information and knowledge acquisition.

Background and Need

In today's knowledge economy, technology is the "lifeblood" of the organization (Paynich, 2003). No longer is technology confined to specific occupations or sections (Pont & Werguin, 2001). Organizations that wish to thrive in the knowledge economy must assure that all employees know how to process and understand information. Computer literacy is the second most sought after skill (Moody, Stewart, & Bolt-Lee, 2002) by recruiters, second only to written and oral communication skills. Core skills now include not only cognitive skills, but also the ability to handle information and use computer technology effectively (Pont & Werguin, 2001).

The use of computers has become so prevalent that many managers assume they have a technologically literate workforce that understands rudimentary operating system commands, basic word processing and spreadsheets, e-mail, and Internet software. Making this assumption without considering the nature of the workforce is misguided and counter-productive. Not only may the workforce not be computer literate, but it may not be inclined to become literate. Elliott and Tevavichulada (1999) report that 95% of public sector employees and 82% of private sector employees have had some computer training. Only 35% of employees indicate that they receive computer training on a regular basis.

As a consequence, organizations also need to examine the factors that affect knowledge acquisition and use, both of which may provide the means to sustain competitive advantage and which are heavily dependent upon the technologies that support them. The purpose of this chapter, therefore, is to provide additional insight into the relationship between type preferences, the learning environment including knowledge acquisition and use, and technological literacy within the context of the training and development of individuals within organizations.

Defining Technological Literacy

We define technological literacy in two parts: computer literacy and information literacy. An employee is not technologically savvy unless both components have been addressed (Stern, 2001).

Computer literacy is the ability to use applicable hardware and software efficiently and effectively. Normally, this means using a personal computer for word processing, spreadsheets, databases, and e-mail, and understanding operating system commands and interfaces.

Information literacy is much broader and includes the ability to recognize information needs and identify, evaluate, and use information effectively (Bruce, 1999). Kanter (1995, p. 3) says: "It implies an understanding of the general concepts of information processing, how information systems shape and support a person's job function, a department or operating unit, or an enterprise-wide application." Understanding the vocabulary of technology is critical—employees must speak computerese (Dahmer, 1994). Angel (1994) notes a difference between being a computer literate and being a computer utilitarian: someone who has the skills and knowledge to manipulate the technology for the organization's good. We further expand this definition to include the ability to get the right information, in the right format, at the right time, to the right person, in the right amount to meet the organization's needs.

One concept that is very pertinent to technological literacy and type preferences is the paradigm of the learning organization. Garvin (1998, p. 51) defines the learning organization as "an organization skilled at creating, acquiring, and transferring knowledge, and at modifying its behavior to reflect new knowledge and insights." Learning organizations need to incorporate five basic disciplines, including systems thinking, mental models, shared visions, team learning, and personal mastery (Senge, 1994). In learning organizations, the emphasis is on continual acquisition of new skills and ways to apply them. Guns (1995) notes that in order for organizations to remain competitive, they must learn at a more rapid rate. This is particularly important for knowledge-based organizations. One way of increasing the rate of learning is through the use of technologies to transfer information across the organization more efficiently (Guns, 1995). Guns (1995) indicates that organizations need to develop strategies for selecting and developing individuals who can learn at an accelerated rate and to identify the level of learning which includes an attention to the acquisition of knowledge.

Stern (2001) points out that each employee needs enough technology to do the job effectively. Childers (2003) advocates a four-level approach to computer literacy: mastering general concepts, understanding use and applications, being able to program, and understanding the science of computation. Bruce (1999) notes, however, that organizations have focused on computer literacy and not on information literacy. Computer literacy is of concern to managers directing staff development, IS managers training and supporting end-users, and trainers (Bruce, 1999). We believe that attaining both computer and information literacy is important for an organization to meet its missions and goals.

The Nature of Technology Learning

As computers have become more user friendly, the assumption is that they are easier to learn and easier to use. In reality, the complexity of computer hardware and software has made learning about computers and updating the knowledge more difficult. Think of the difference between creating a simple autoexec.bat file and modifying a Windows XP registry file. As a consequence, attention needs to be directed toward the designers of software and related fields to provide users with appropriate materials that facilitate the learning of the technologies or to promote innovative computer applications that help the user capitalize on the technology itself (Filipczak, 1994).

There are literally thousands of journal articles dealing with computer training. Angel (1994) notes that we should be educating computer users, not training them. Bagozzi, Davis, and Warshaw (1992) point out that learning must be productive; otherwise, systems put in place to make the organization more productive can actually curtail the adoption and use. Angel (1994) also says that computer use is dysfunctional if it interferes with the overall good of the organization.

Part of the problem of achieving computer literacy is understanding how an employee "learns" computer skills and how inadequate computer literacy can affect the organization. Angel (1994) notes that inadequate training results in dysfunctional computer users and an under-utilization of computer resources. While most managers do not question the need for technology training, it is more difficult to sustain the importance of technology training when the return on investment cannot be shown.

Myers-Briggs Type Indicator

An important part of the educational process is looking at the individual differences of learners. One part of the training equation must be an assessment of learning or cognitive style. Since the 1950s the Myers-Briggs Type Indicator (MBTI) has been used in a variety of educational and work settings to assess learning styles, cognitive styles, brain patterns, and information processing (Myers, McCaulley, Quenk, & Hammer, 1998)

The MBTI is based on the work of C.G. Jung (1923), who developed a theory to explain differences in human personality. Jung coined the phrase "psychological type" to explain four conscious mental functions: sensing, intuition, thinking, and feeling. Jung's model helps explain why people perceive information and make judgments differently. Jung noted that any of the functions could be present in an individual, but one is most dominant.

The Myers-Briggs Type Indicator was developed by Katherine Briggs and her daughter, Isabel Briggs Myers, in the early 1950s to expand Jung's work, to give more practical applications of his work, and to accurately identify an individual's preferences for the four dichotomies. The instrument has evolved over the years, with the current form M consisting of 93 questions with paired answers. An individual has a type preference made up of one each of the four dichotomies (e.g., ESTJ).

According to the *MBTI Manual*, each of the dichotomies represents a multifaceted domain of psychological functioning. The MBTI places individuals into categories and

Table 1. Four dichotomies of the MBTI (Myers et al., 1998, p. 6; Bishop-Clark & Wheeler, 1994)

Extraversion-Introversion (How and where you get your energy)	Extraversion (E) Directing energy mainly toward the outer world or people and objects	Introversion (I) Directing energy mainly toward the inner world of experiences and ideas
Sensing-Intuition (What you pay attention to in your information gathering)	Sensing (S) Focusing mainly on what can be perceived by the five senses	Intuition (N) Focusing mainly on perceiving patterns and interrelationships
Thinking-Feeling (How you make your decisions)	Thinking (T) Basing conclusions on logical analysis with a focus on objectivity and detachment	Feeling (F) Basing conclusions on personal or social values with a focus on understanding and harmony
Judging-Perceiving (What type of life you will adopt)	Judging (J) Preferring the decisiveness and closure that result from dealing with the outer world using one of the judging processes	Perceiving (P) Preferring the flexibility and spontaneity that results from dealing with the outer world using one of the perceiving processes

gives a preference clarity index (1-30) that "reflects the degree of confidence in the accuracy of placement of a respondent into a particular type category" (Myers et al., 1998, p. 5). Since the MBTI is a self-reporting indicator, individuals must verify the results with the test administrator to assess indicator accuracy.

To further understand the MBTI, Table 1 gives expanded definitions of the four dichotomies.

Uses of MBTI

The MBTI is the mostly widely used personality instrument in the world (Hirsch & Kummerow, 1989). There are over two million test administrations each year (Myers et al., 1998, p. 9). Some of the most common uses include counseling and psychotherapy, academic aptitude, characteristics of learners, career counseling, and job satisfaction.

In an organizational setting, some of the most common uses include improving communication, conflict resolution, problem solving and decision making, managing organizational change, stress management, team management, and leadership development and coaching (Myers et al., 1998). Many research studies have assessed the reliability, validity, and uses of the MBTI. For the most part, researchers agree on its usefulness. Keen and Bronsema, as early as 1981, suggested that the MBTI be used as the basis for cognitive style research and information systems.

Table 2. Characteristics of learners by type dichotomy

Extrovert Wants collaborative learning Likes active experimentation Wants concrete experiences Easily bored unless actively engaged in learning Instruction needs to be presented in several ways Wants specific goals	Introvert Wants reflective observation Learns better with visual and auditory components Wants time to reflect about what's been presented
Sensor Wants sequential learning Likes to learn collaboratively Wants facts and methodical study	Intuitive Wants holistic learning Likes to learn independently
Thinker Wants a systematic approach to learning Likes fact orientation	Feeler Wants to follow perceptions Likes to jump around among concepts and facts
Judger Wants clear structure Needs to be highly motivated Likes structured classes Wants to know end goals and how they will be achieved	Perceptor Wants random approach to learning Wants to follow natural curiosity

The MBTI and Characteristics of Learners

Table 2 gives a brief explanation of learner characteristics by type.

Lawrence (1993), in his book *People Types and Tiger Stripes*, notes that the S/N dichotomy has been the type preference that most reveals basic learning style differences. We would agree, although we believe that each type is a unique combination based on the interaction of the four dichotomies. The entire type preference must be used to create successful training programs.

Type Preferences and Organizational Training

Any successful organizational training program needs to focus on not only what needs to be taught, but also on how people take in the information, how they prioritize the information, how they share it, and how they fit that information into existing value structures. Personality facets underlie most work tasks and training. If type preferences can be identified, training can enhance preferred learning styles and give perspective as to how employees perceive and analyze their organizational cultures. Angel (1994) says that the essence of computer training is evolutionary because there is a high learning curve, learners must feel free to experiment and build their skill set, and knowledge must be maintained over time.

Analyzing a trainee's type preferences can help that individual and the instructor to devise better learning strategies (Felder, 1996). Felder reports the use of the MBTI to "type" engineering students who were subsequently counseled to improve their academic performance. McClure and Werther (1993) found that understanding the personality types as measured by the Myers-Briggs Type Indicator greatly increased the effectiveness of management development programs, particularly with respect to the consultant's role in improving interpersonal communication and team building. For individuals attempting to become technologically literate, particularly with respect to computer usage and software applications, Filipczak (1994) discusses the concept of "technical empowerment." Technological literacy may require the teaching of business skills and computer skills together in order to convey the idea that users need competencies in the technology, the applications, and the meaning of the data that are generated (Filipczak, 1994). The emphasis needs to shift from skill acquisition to education.

The Learning Environment

Just as type preferences can influence learning behavior, the total training environment can also affect learning. Key components are the type preferences of the trainer, training delivery methods, and processes for acquiring and sharing information.

Trainer Type Preferences

There is no agreement among the numerous research studies whether it is better to match trainers with learners based on type or whether it is more advantageous to mix up trainers and learners based on type. MBTI studies have shown that students may benefit from different teaching styles at different points in their development (Myers et al., 1998, p. 265).

An extroverted (E) trainer gives choices to the class and can handle a certain amount of chaos and noise. An introverted (I) trainer wants quiet, orderly classes. A sensing (S) trainer wants a centralized learning environment by presenting the "how to" of the topic. An intuitive (N) trainer wants to focus on concepts and relationships. A thinking (T) trainer wants to create objective class standards and focus on the class as a whole. A feeling (F) trainer wants to participate in more individualized learning. A judging (J) trainer wants to adhere to schedules and get through the material in an orderly way. A perceptive (P) trainer wants to focus more on independent work.

One of the issues that Kroeger and Thuesen (1992, p. 279) point out in their book, *Type Talk at Work,* is that many training programs are designed by intuitives (N), so training emphasizes strategies and vision over hands-on and practical experiences (p. 279). The problem is that most managers are not intuitives. In national norms, almost 50% of middle managers were ISTJs or ESTJs, that is, Sensors, not Intuitives. These managers have different information-gathering strategies than their corporate trainers. Sensors need to perceive that training is useful and practical. Theory is of no interest to them. Intuitives, on the other hand, want to give the "big picture" and explain the whys. To them, facts and step-by-step sequences are boring.

Delivery Methods

Davis and Henry (1997) found that judgers did better in satellite-delivered classes where goals and schedules were established and there was closure. Perceptors preferred instructor-led classes that were more flexible. Kern and Matta (1987) found that intuitives like learning new skills, but become impatient with routine. Self-paced instruction appeals to them. Sensors want to apply previously learned skills. NT types performed significantly better using self-paced instruction; SFs performed significantly below average using self-paced instruction. Since technology is being used more frequently to deliver training material (Teresko, 2003), understanding the relationship between type preferences and methods of delivery should be given increased attention.

Information and Knowledge Acquisition and Sharing

In addition to training, organizations must also consider the processes they use to share information (Pfeffer & Veiga, 1999). Pfeffer and Vegia (1999, p. 46) note:

> *"Even motivated and trained people cannot contribute to enhancing organizational performance if they don't have information on important dimensions of performance and training on how to use and interpret that information."*

In addition to this knowledge of internal operations, Anand, Glick, and Manz (2002) discuss the importance of capitalizing on social capital, that is, knowledge that is acquired through others primarily from external sources. Anand et al. (2002) suggest that social capital is particularly critical for organizations that can be considered high-technology companies. In such cases, organizations may not be sufficiently capable of accessing in a timely manner knowledge that is continually generated. Anand et al. (2002, p. 95) recommend that organizations need to offer "access to multiple communication technologies, train them in their use, and sensitize them to the fact that some technologies are more suited than others for acquiring specific types of knowledge." Technological literacy in such a working environment is therefore a critical job requirement.

Conclusion and Recommendations for Further Study

For organizations promoting technological literacy, type preferences can offer valuable insight into ways in which organizations can offer training programs. Specifically, preference types of trainees and trainers, along with the training environment, affect the way in which individuals acquire technological skills. In addition, the demands of knowledge management and the challenges of learning organizations would suggest that type preferences need to be considered for organizations to be effective.

We believe that there are several areas of future research. First, research needs to explore the interaction of type preference and other factors that may impact technology use and training. For example, Thatcher and Perrewe (2002) found a significant relationship between personal innovativeness in information technology (willingness to try technology), computer anxiety, and computer self-efficacy. Other research has found that women typed as "thinking" and "feeling" types preferred different types of classroom climates (Persuad & Salter, 2003). Ziegart (2000) studied the relationship between students typed as NT (intuitive-thinking) and students typed as SF (sensing-feeling) in principles of economics classes. It was hypothesized that given the technical nature of economics, NTs would perform better than SFs. Results seemed to confirm that individuals typed at thinking performed better than feeling types, when considering course grades and performance on the Test of Understanding of College Economics. Other factors that may interact with type preferences include the ways in which jobs are designed, cognitive ability, and personality differences, particularly conscientiousness and openness to experience which have been positively related to job performance and training performance respectively (Behling, 1998).

Another important area of research pertains to the way consumers acquire technological literacy. Bitner, Ostrom, and Meuter (2002) note that many organizations are developing self-service technologies (SSTs) for their customers. A significant roadblock to their use, however, is the consumers' willingness to use the new technologies, as well as what actions they may need to take should the technologies not perform as expected. Failures of SST to perform as expected have been found to be related to the design of the systems and to the technological sophistication of the users (Bitner et al., 2002). What might be the effect of varying the type preferences of the technical designers of these systems or to at least be certain that they understand that individuals prefer and process information differently? Consumers that are not technologically inclined need to be trained on these systems so that when failures occur, they have sufficient knowledge to correct the problems themselves.

One final area of future research that needs increased attention is the role of virtual teams in the workplace. Kirkman et al. (2002, p. 67) define such teams as "groups of people who work independently with shared purpose across space, time, and organizational boundaries using technology to communicate and collaborate." Based upon the study of 65 cross-functional teams at Sabre, Inc., Kirman et al. (2002) indicate that technical, interpersonal, and individual differences represent increased challenges for organizations adopting virtual teams. Individuals on these teams must be accomplished in both the technical aspects of the work and be able to adjust to a work environment that does not often include frequent interpersonal interactions. Understanding the type preferences of individuals in environments in which technological literacy is a requirement can lead to more effective training and development approaches to achieve a more appropriate person-job-work environment fit.

References

Anand, V., Glick, W.H., & Manz, C.C. (2002). Thriving on the knowledge of outsiders: Tapping organizational social capital. *The Academy of Management Executive, 16*(1), 87-99.

Angel, N.F. (1994). Dysfunctional versus utilitarian computer use. *SAM Advanced Management Journal, 59*(4), 4-9.

Bagozzi, R.P., Davis, F.D., & Warshaw, P.R. (1992). Development and test of a theory of technological learning and usage. *Human Relations, 45*(7), 659-686.

Behling, O. (1998). Employee selection: Will intelligence and conscientiousness do the job? *The Academy of Management Executive, 12*(1), 77-86.

Berens, L.V. (1998). *Dynamics of personality type*. Huntington Beach, CA: Telos Publications.

Bishop-Clark, C. & Wheeler, D.D. (1994). The Myers-Briggs personality type and its relationship to computer programming. *Journal of Research on Computing in Education, 26*(3).

Bitner, M.J., Ostrom, A.L., & Meuter, M.L. (2002). Implementing successful self-service technologies. *Academy of Management Executive, 16*(4), 96-109.

Briggs, K.C. & Myers, I.B. (1998). *Myers-Briggs Type Indicator, Form M.* Palo Alto, CA: Consulting Psychologists Press.

Bruce, C.S. (1999). Workplace experiences in information literacy. *International Journal of Information Management, 19*(1), 33-47.

Childers, S. (2003). Computer literacy: Necessity or buzzword? *Information Technology and Libraries, 22*(3), 100-105.

Dahmer, B. (1994). Technology literacy. *Training & Development, 48*(12), 43-44.

Davis, M.A. & Henry, M.J. (1997). *Cognitive capacity of non-traditional learners in two instructional settings.* ERIC ED404991.

Elliott, R.H. & Tevavichulada, S. (1999). Computer literacy and human resource management: A public/private sector comparison. *Public Personnel Management 28*(2), 259-274.

Felder, R. (1996). Matters of style. *ASEE Prism, 6*, 18-23.

Filipczak, B. (1994). Technoliteracy, technophobia, and programming your VCR. *Training, 31*(1), 48-52.

Garvin, D.A. (1998). Building a learning organization. *Harvard Business Review on knowledge management* (pp. 47-80). Boston: Harvard Business School Publishing.

Guns, B. (1995). The faster learning organization. In S. Chawla & J. Renesch (Eds.), *Learning organizations: Developing cultures for tomorrow's workplace* (pp. 337-349). Portland, OR: Productivity Press.

Hirsh, S. & Kimmerow, J. (1989). *Life types.* New York: Warner Communication.

Jung, C. (1923). *Psychological types.* New York: Harcourt Brace.

Kanter, J. (1995). Computer-information literacy for senior management. *Information Strategy: The Executive's Journal, 11*(3), 6-12.

Keen, P.G.W. & Bronsema, G.S. (1981). Cognitive style research: A perspective for integration. *Proceedings of the 2nd International Conference on Information Systems* (pp. 21-52).

Kern, G.M. & Matta, K.F. (1987). Learning style as an influence on the effectiveness of self-paced computer-assisted instruction: Preliminary results. *Computers & Industrial Engineering, 13*, 203-207.

Kirkman, B.L., Rosen, B., Gibson, C.B., Tesluk, P.E., & McPherson, S.O. (2002). Five challenges to virtual team success: Lessons from Sabre, Inc. *The Academy of Management Executive, 16*(3), 67-79.

Kroeger, O. & Thuesen, J.M. (1992). *Type talk at work.* New York: Dell.

Lawrence, G. (1993). *Descriptions of the sixteen types.* Palo Alto, CA: Consulting Psychologists Press.

Lawrence, G. (1993). *People types and tiger stripes.* Gainesville, FL: Center for Applications of Psychological Type.

MacDonald, J.A. (1995). Computer literacy: A two-way street. *CMA Magazine, 69*(1), 5.

McClure, L. & Werther, W.B. Jr. (1993). Personality variables in management development interventions. *Journal of Management Development, 12*(3), 39-47.

Moody, J., Stewart, B., & Bolt-Lee, C. (2002). Showing the skilled business graduate: Expanding the took kit. *Business Communication Quarterly, 65*(1), 21-36.

Myers, I.B., McCaulley, M.H., Quenk, N.L., & Hammer, A.L. (1998). *MBTI manual, a guide to the development and use of the Myers-Briggs Type Indicator* (3rd edition). Palo Alto, CA: Consulting Psychologists Press.

Paynich, V. (2003). Are no two learners alike? *E-Learning, 6* (January).

Persaud, A. & Salter, D.W. (2003). Understanding women's classroom "fit" and participation as interactions between psychological and environmental types. *Journal of Classroom Interaction, 38*(2), 1-10.

Pfeffer, J. & Veiga, J.F. (1999). Putting people first for organizational success. *The Academy of Management Executive, 13*(2), 37-48.

Pont, B. & Werguin, P. (2001). How old are new skills? *The OECD Observer*, 222(March), 15-17.

Senge, P.M. (1994). *The fifth discipline: The art & practice of the learning organization.* New York: Currency Doubleday.

Stern, M. (2001). Nerds need not apply. *Canadian Business, 74*(2), 70-74.

Teresko, J. (2003). A partnership of muda fighters. *IndustryWeek, 252*(10), 43-45.

Thatcher, J.B. & Perrewe, P.L. (2002). An empirical examination of individual traits as antecedents to computer anxiety and computer self-efficacy. *MIS Quarterly, 26*(4), 381-396.

Ziegart, A.L. (2000). The role of personality temperament and student learning in principles of economics: Further evidence. *The Journal of Economic Education, 31*(4), 307-322.

Chapter IX

Evolution of a Collaborative Undergraduate Information Literacy Education Program

Maureen Diana Sasso
Duquesne University, USA

Abstract

This chapter examines the evolution of information literacy as a distinct concept incorporating critical thinking, and research and communication skills. It describes Duquesne University's efforts to develop its current information literacy program during a period of rapid technological change and evolving accreditation standards, and briefly addresses the Association of College and Research Libraries' (ACRL) information literacy research agenda. Duquesne's librarians and disciplinary faculty have collaborated to introduce information literacy into the curriculum. All freshmen and transfer students receive instruction geared toward establishing baseline competency in computer and information literacy skills. Collaboration among faculty, librarians, and campus computing staff has resulted in improved instruction and adoption of course management software to facilitate management of over a thousand students per semester, as well as sharing of course texts and assignments among instructors in the Schools of Business, Education, and Music, the College of Liberal Arts, and the library.

Introduction

As libraries adopt technology for delivering information, library users are increasingly confronted with the need to use technology effectively to attain their research goals. Today's student researcher requires multiple skill sets that include both technological and evaluative components. The proliferation of technology in higher education for research and teaching highlights the need for training in basic computer skills. From the librarian's perspective, students' training needs also include skills in information retrieval, evaluating resources, the ethical use of both computers and information, and synthesis and manipulation of information to create new knowledge.

Together these skills comprise information literacy. According to ACRL (2000):

> *"Information literacy forms the basis for lifelong learning. It is common to all disciplines, to all learning environments, and to all levels of education. It enables learners to master content and extend their investigations, become more self-directed, and assume greater control over their own learning. An information literate individual is able to:*
>
> - *Determine the extent of information needed*
> - *Access the needed information effectively and efficiently*
> - *Evaluate information and its sources critically*
> - *Incorporate selected information into one's knowledge base*
> - *Use information effectively to accomplish a specific purpose*
> - *Understand the economic, legal, and social issues surrounding the use of information, and access and use information ethically and legally."*

ACRL (2000) also distinguishes between information literacy and information technology skills. Information technology skills are those that enable an individual to use computers, software applications, databases, and other technologies to achieve a wide variety of academic, work-related, and personal goals. Information literacy has broader implications for the individual, the educational system, and society.

Background

Library literature of the 1960s through the 1980s used terms such as library orientation, library instruction, user education, and bibliographic instruction (BI) to describe the activities and programs librarians developed to teach research methods and orient users to library services and facilities. The most common name for this activity, BI, is still used, although since the early 1990s BI has often been seen as addressing only a subset of information literacy skills. Traditional BI programs are very practical in focus and aimed at teaching specific content and/or tools such as searching the library's card catalog or using microfilm.

> *"Most recently, bibliographic instruction activities have been integrated into the broader objectives of creating learning environments that foster critical thinking skills and information literacy. It would not be an exaggeration to say that technology has validated BI as an essential library mission (Sager, 1995, p. 51)."*

Mission statements of academic libraries generally speak to support for teaching and learning. This support takes the form of providing scholarly resources: content, expertise in developing and interpreting collections, and collaborative instruction. The significance of the groundswell of interest in instruction within librarianship has been a shift in thinking about the role of library instruction and the roles of the academic library and librarians.

Knapp (1966, p. 39) examined ways in which students' library experience could be studied as part of their overall college experience. She assumed that students could attain library competence only by using the library and only when use was significantly related to coursework. She found that students' "need" to use the library derives from the value placed upon such work by the instructor. Boyer (1987, pp. 160-161) reported that one in four undergraduates spent no time in the library during a normal week and 65% used the library less than four hours per week. Most undergraduates reported that they viewed the library as simply a good place to study. In addition to recommending strong support for library collections and reading requirements for all students, Boyer (1987) recommended:

> *"The library staff should be considered as important to teaching as are classroom teachers...We further recommend that every undergraduate student be introduced carefully to the full range of resources on campus. Students should be given bibliographic instruction and be encouraged to spend as much time in the library using its wide range of resources as they spend in class." (pp. 164-165)*

Boyer envisioned the library as the central learning resource on campus and librarians as liberally educated professionals who "understand and are interested in undergraduate education" (p. 165) and who are involved in educational matters. While urging libraries to lead by using technology to link to remote resources and provide access to users at a distance, Boyer framed the key issue of electronic access with this warning:

> *"There is a danger that greater credibility will be given to data than to ideas and that scholars will mistake information for knowledge. The challenge is to not only teach students how to use the new technology but also to encourage them to ask when and why it should be used." (p. 173)*

Education reform reports such as *College,* which showed that students valued the library primarily for its ambience rather than for the value of its resources, inspired a passionate response among library leaders. They perceived the information explosion as a societal challenge, raising issues of privacy and equitable access to information and technology that required a shift in education to emphasize lifelong learning. The American Library Association Presidential Report on Information Literacy (1989) criticized the emphasis on rote learning—especially in higher education—and sought to influence accreditors and others to support resource-based learning over traditional lectures supplemented by textbooks and reserve room readings. Advocating for information literacy as an educational philosophy for the Information Age, Breivik and Gee (1989) contended that:

> *"Academic institutions routinely cite the importance of teaching students how to think effectively, and claim that their graduates will be able to analyze and synthesize well as part of effective problem solving, while neglecting to consider whether it is possible to analyze and synthesize well if one cannot determine the accuracy or adequacy of the information base." (p. 24)*

The Main Thrust of the Chapter

Throughout the 1980s and 1990s, a shift in emphasis from providing traditional library instruction to the broader concept of information literacy gained momentum among academic librarians. By the mid-1980s instructional librarianship had emerged as a specialization, and librarians began working to influence educators, accreditors, and business leaders to adopt their vision of information literacy.

The last five years have seen the development of numerous standards, guidelines, and research reports articulating the need for infusing information literacy and information technology fluency throughout the educational system (Arp & Woodward, 2002, p. 125; ACRL, 2003a, 2003b). The Commission on Higher Education of the Middle States Association of Colleges and Schools (CHE), the primary accrediting body for colleges and universities in the Mid-Atlantic and Puerto Rico, has been a leader in promoting information literacy. Middle States standards (Commission on Higher Education, 1982) used between 1982 and 1992 emphasized the centrality of the library's role in the educational mission, stating that it "deserves more than rhetoric and must be supported by more than lip service. An active and continuous program of bibliographic instruction is essential to realize this goal" (p. 35). By 1994 Middle States (Commission on Higher

Education, 1994) had adopted its own definition of information literacy and the expectation that each accredited institution demonstrate "an active and continuing program of library orientation and instruction in accessing information, developed collaboratively and supported actively by faculty, librarians, academic deans, and other academic providers" (p. 15). Middle States' latest standards and publications (Commission on Higher Education, 2002, 2003a, 2003b) emphasize the expectation that information literacy become part of institutional culture.

Simmons (1992) further articulated the importance of information literacy, pointing to the need for programs that reach all students at all stages of their academic careers. Ratteray (2002) described information literacy as a "meta-outcome in the learning process" which is invoked "any time a student attempts to learn anything in any discipline whether or not a library is involved in the information gathering process" (p. 370).

Duquesne University's librarians recognized the significance of information literacy and began working to reframe their instructional programming in the mid-1980s. They believed adopting information literacy as a framework would directly benefit students by bringing an innovative approach to instruction, incorporating critical thinking skills and the ethical use of information, along with traditional research skills. They saw the potential of technology to assist in delivering instruction to large numbers of students and as common ground for collaboration with faculty. Finally, they recognized an opportunity for leadership in the self-study and accreditation process.

Library funding had been a significant concern during Duquesne's two previous Middle States reviews. Developing an information literacy program would demonstrate that both library and university understood its relevance to student learning and were willing to invest the necessary resources. With the 1987 accreditation review and the transition to a new administration, Duquesne experienced a decade of unprecedented growth and revitalization. The university began to systematically address the library's financial needs, making it possible to begin the groundwork for information literacy instruction.

The Gumberg Library at Duquesne University is a medium-sized academic library serving graduate and undergraduate students and faculty in 10 schools, including liberal arts and sciences as well as professional schools. Prior to 1990, Gumberg provided BI on an ad hoc basis. Course instructors most frequently requested orientation sessions and database searching demonstrations. No statistics on the number and variety of these sessions were kept, nor were evaluation procedures in place. The lack of a coordinated approach to BI meant that some students received no basic library instruction, while others received multiple instruction sessions that frequently covered identical content.

By the mid-1990s the most common form of library research instruction had become the "one-shot" 50-minute presentation. Librarians struggled with the workload, negotiating with faculty to fulfill requests for numerous customized instruction sessions. They felt that faculty often requested they cover more content than was realistic for students to absorb in one session. Lack of content standards made it impossible to consistently focus on basic research skills applicable across the curriculum. Instead the focus had become satisfying the needs of specific instructors for specific assignments.

Challenges abounded as the library undertook planning for the information literacy program. Widespread introduction of information technology and reliance on electronic resources increasingly required students to learn technology skills as a prerequisite to research skills. Librarians frequently needed to teach technology skills within research instruction. Although students and faculty most often welcomed these efforts, time spent covering technology significantly decreased time available for other instructional objectives.

The library had no classroom, insufficient computers, and inadequate projection systems for demonstrations. Often faculty did not give appropriate assignments, provide the assignments in advance, or accompany students to scheduled BI sessions. Students tended to view themselves as more proficient researchers than did their instructors. Some students resented being required to attend the library instruction, particularly when required to attend multiple sessions because several instructors had scheduled them independently.

Librarians were not seen as partners and collaborators in spite of holding non-tenure track faculty status at Duquesne. There was a distance between the library and the academic departments in general. The library's collection was widely viewed as inadequate due to two decades of insufficient funding.

Before formally approaching disciplinary faculty and administrators, librarians worked internally develop a proposal for an information literacy program. In early 1990 they approached the university's Core Curriculum Committee seeking a slot for information literacy, but were turned down. In December 1990 the library's Bibliographic Instruction Committee presented a draft proposal for a user education program to the University Librarian. No action was taken, so the committee developed it further and produced additional proposals in 1991, 1993, and 1997. The proposals' titles changed over time as reflection of the ongoing debate over the definition of information literacy (McCrank, 1992; Shapiro & Hughes, 1996), and concern that the term would seem remedial and therefore be rejected. Each proposal was based on targeting identified needs, adopting emerging standards, following best practice, and collaboratively satisfying Middle States guidelines. All advocated adopting the teaching library model, requiring the library to become actively and directly involved in implementing the mission of higher education: teaching, research, and community service (Guskin, Stoffle, & Boisse 1979; Stoffle, Guskin, & Boisse, 1984).

When no administrative action was taken on the 1993 proposal, librarians decided to utilize the self-study process to promote information literacy. They conducted needs assessment surveys of students and faculty in 1995. The faculty survey assessed perceptions of students' need for library research instruction. It asked faculty which students needed instruction and how it should be provided. The confidential survey was distributed to 769 full- and part-time faculty. One-hundred-seventy valid surveys were returned, 103 from full-time faculty. As shown in Table 1, results indicated that faculty preferred to collaborate with librarians to provide instruction to students at all levels.

Sixty percent of the faculty respondents preferred that instruction take place in the library, and 54% preferred that it occur in the first month of the semester. Computer-assisted instruction received the most positive responses, followed by review of research techniques for faculty and user guides accessible over the campus network. Seventy-four of the 110 positive responses for the option of a required first year unit in the core curriculum listed it as essential.

Table 1. Faculty survey responses

Question: Who would you prefer to provide library research instruction for the following groups of students?			
	Valid % librarians	Valid % faculty	Valid % both
Freshmen	68.5	0.8	30.8
Sophomore	60.9	3.5	35.7
Junior	47.5	11.9	40.7
Senior	48.3	12.9	38.8
Fifth Year	50.5	8.4	40.0
Masters	47.9	10.7	39.7
PhD	42.7	14.6	39.6

Student survey responses also indicated preferences for computer-assisted instruction and user guides. In addition, 45% of the student respondents rated the option of a required unit in the core as either essential or important, with another 20% rating it somewhat important. The majority of students rated themselves as "good" at finding, evaluating, and effectively using information. Over half indicated that they participated in required library research instruction at Duquesne, with the majority of participants reporting moderate improvement in their performance as a result (Kaufman, 1995, p. 2).

Based on these survey results, literature review, and their understanding of Middle States' objectives, the librarians determined to propose a program that would be uniform, mandatory, given in the first semester, tied to the curriculum, and evaluated on outcomes. They concluded that using technology would be instrumental in tracking and teaching large numbers of students, and in attracting support for the program.

They lobbied deans seeking a place for information literacy in each school's curriculum. While the deans were supportive, the message was universal—the curriculum was already overcrowded. Because no course reached every student, the Dean of the College of Liberal Arts suggested transforming an optional freshman orientation course into a mandatory information literacy course. No funding was available and the course was ultimately dropped.

The Department of Mathematics and Computer Science offered to add an information literacy component to an established course, *Elements of Computer Science*. Librarians prepared four 70-minute presentations for each of nine sections in Spring 1997. Lacking a classroom, they agreed to teach in a computer lab; however, this arrangement proved unsatisfactory due to schedule conflicts and demand for the lab.

This pilot produced significant firsts for Gumberg's information literacy program: entire class sessions devoted to information literacy, Web-based instruction, and a graded information literacy course component. A similar successful pilot was conducted in 1996-1997 in both freshman seminars taught by the Dean of Health Sciences. Librarians planned, taught, and evaluated three sessions on research skills. The dean attended all sessions and stressed their importance to his students. Students worked in pairs at the library's public computers due to inadequate remote access in campus labs. Librarians designed an assignment to assist students in writing the course paper. The assignment was not graded in the fall, however in the spring it represented 10% of the course grade.

Librarians worked simultaneously with Continuing Education to include information literacy in *Adult Transition Seminar,* with the Business School to create presentations and assignments for *Global Economic Perspectives*, and with the Nursing School to provide online instruction via the Web and FirstClass software.

Implementing new instructional programming while responding effectively to increasing demand for ad hoc instruction strained the library's resources. The Core English instructors, who as a group requested as many 50 instruction sessions in a semester, were not well served. Librarians were generally limited to offering one 50-minute presentation and exercise per section of Core English. Recognizing the opportunity this situation presented, the librarians suggested creating a standard one-credit information literacy course as a recitation for Core English. The affiliated departments of English and Communications expressed cautious interest, but preferred a more traditional approach. They requested collaboration on writing a workbook to be required for all Core English students, but dropped the project soon after it was begun.

The library's most recent information literacy program proposal presented to the Academic Council in 1997 recommended a comprehensive information literacy program to consist of three components:

1) an information literacy competency requirement for freshmen and transfer students entering with less than 60 credits,
2) course-integrated instruction for sophomore through graduate-level classes, and
3) individual consultations with librarians at the graduate level.

The proposal emphasized practical information literacy skills, including the ability to:

- articulate an information need,
- decide what information is needed,
- identify and select appropriate resources,
- evaluate the results of the search process, and
- ethically manipulate and synthesize information.

It was envisioned as a series of Web tutorials covering:

- accessing services through the library homepage,
- using the online catalog and a periodical database within the library and remotely,
- basic keyword searching techniques,
- locating Gumberg Library books and journals,

- citing sources, and
- evaluating information sources.

Program goals included reaching all students, preparing students for advanced instruction, and accommodating different learning needs by offering opportunities for both Web-based and face-to-face classroom instruction. The proposal recommended course-integrated instruction for advanced and discipline-specific instruction. Librarians and faculty would facilitate opportunities for hands-on searching experience supplemented by Web tutorials. Models for this proposal included the University of Wisconsin-Parkside (oldWeb.uwp.edu/library/2003/intro/index.htm), where information literacy is a mandatory general education requirement, and the Teaching Library at the University of California Berkeley (www.lib.berkeley.edu/TeachingLib/).

Proposed program evaluation methods included pre-tests, post-tests, and learning unit competency exams for the freshman component; participant evaluation forms for course-integrated instruction; and eventual collection of student work samples (portfolios) and of syllabi to show integration of information literacy into the curriculum.

The proposal recommended using course management software to track students' progress and provide feedback, and working directly with the Registrar and Advisement Office to inform students of the requirement and track compliance, thus eliminating the need for a required course.

In seeking support for the proposal, librarians found that most deans preferred adopting a course. The provost directed the librarians to work with computing center staff to prepare a syllabus for a one-credit course to include both computing and information literacy.

While preparing the requested syllabus, the library was approached by the Director of the Learning Skills Center to create an information skills course for at-risk students in Spring 1998. Recognizing faculty concerns about computing center staff participating in course development and basing a course in a support unit, librarians jointly developed and taught the course with a Computer Science faculty member.

Duquesne's Middle States accreditation report (Evaluation Team, 1998) reinforced the library's efforts to promote its proposal. The report recommended a mandatory information literacy requirement for all freshmen and transfer students. It affirmed the library as the locus of information literacy efforts and recommended that the university work to remove any barriers that might impede implementation of an information literacy program.

The Academic Council approved a one-credit pass/fail course that was piloted in 1998. The course was overseen by the Core Curriculum Committee, though it did not become part of the Core and was not listed in the catalog. The course premise was that all freshmen needed similar basic skills that should be supplemented with discipline-specific instruction, and therefore it would be required in all schools. The Dean of the Music School lobbied to have Music students exempted because they were already required to take 12 credits more than other students, including a course called *Computers for Musicians,* which covered similar computer skills.

What could have become a contentious issue instead became a successful collaboration between librarians and faculty. The content of the course developed by librarians and Computer Science faculty was included in *Computers for Musicians*. Librarians mentored Music faculty teaching the information literacy topics and provided the readings, assignments, and grading rubrics. Music faculty adapted the course text and assignments written for PCs to use with Macintosh computers used in the Music School.

Computer and Information Literacy was formally piloted with five sections in Fall 1998. It became mandatory in Fall 1999. Initially it was offered both in the classroom and online, however few students registered for the online version. One student expressed general concern saying she believed she would learn more from a "live" teacher.

In 2004 freshmen are more willing to learn online, but still may lack the necessary self-discipline. Many freshmen change schedules or experience adjustment issues, causing them to fall behind in their work. Once behind they often become discouraged and fail to complete assignments. Class attendance has proved the best predictor of success, though it was a problem initially. The academic advisors have suggested that students are less motivated because the course is pass/fail and meets only once a week. Changing from pass/fail to letter grades would require approval of the Academic Council; however, librarians have begun offering selected sections twice a week.

The course, now called *Research and Information Skills Lab,* is Web enhanced rather than online. All readings and some assignments are done online, but class attendance and in-class labs are mandatory. Instructors stress class participation to actively engage students. Many assignments are done in groups.

Pre-class surveys show that students often rate themselves proficient or expert in many of the skills taught, therefore they are offered a two-part challenge exam. Students use Thompson Course Technology's SAM assessment software to test their skills in Microsoft Office applications and Windows file management. SAM records and shows their scores immediately. Those who pass the computer literacy challenge exam are encouraged to take the information literacy challenge exam in the Blackboard course management system, which is used throughout the course. Students who pass both challenge exams are exempted from further attendance. Those who pass only the computer literacy challenge exam complete the course in nine weeks.

In Fall 2003, librarians taught 25 sections of the course and a Computer Science faculty member taught two. Of 913 students enrolled, only 113 tested out of the course, while 499 passed the computer literacy challenge exam, significantly reducing the class size for the computer literacy section taught as the second part of the course. To help manage large classes, the provost funded six students who had already passed the course to assist instructors in the classroom. Peer assistance has proven popular with current students. Instructors find it helpful to have student assistants troubleshoot computer problems, allowing them to continue teaching while individual problems are addressed.

Students have responded positively to course modifications. In Fall 2002 librarian instructors' mean scores on Duquesne's Teaching Effectiveness Questionnaire (TEQ) exceeded overall university scores and those for the Core in eight of 10 categories. Predictably, given student high self-ratings in the pre-class survey, the two lowest rated categories were the instructors' ability to make the course content interesting and to significantly increase the students' understanding of the subject. Aggregate TEQ scores for 2003 are not yet available.

The university recently received its mid-term review report from Middle States which cited the significance of the development of the *Research and Information Skills Lab*. The successful collaboration with Music faculty has been extended to the Schools of Business and Education, where faculty have adopted the content of *Research and Information Skills Lab* into a mandatory course in each school.

The provost has appointed a steering committee, co-chaired by a faculty member and a librarian, to serve as a forum for development of additional initiatives for information literacy across the curriculum. Its charge is to promote and document the infusion of information literacy skills into the curriculum, and make assessment recommendations to prepare for the next self-study. Librarians have been appointed to Duquesne's Outcomes Assessment Committee and Core Curriculum Committee. The Core is under review, and information literacy is expected to officially become part of Duquesne's general education requirements.

Future Trends

ACRL's Bibliographic Instruction Section Research Committee proposed a research agenda in 1980 which was revised in 2002 by the renamed Instruction Section's Research and Scholarship Committee. As the name change suggests, the research agenda has been expanded. The first listed three areas for potential research centered on defining needs and measuring library skills, designing and implementing bibliographic instruction programs—and the management aspect of those programs—while the current research agenda lists four potential areas for research with specific suggestions for each: learners, teaching, organizational context, and assessment. Given the current accreditation emphasis on outcomes assessment, Duquesne University's information literacy research agenda will be directed at outcomes assessment to prepare for the 2007 accreditation process. Student learning outcomes have not yet been documented for *Research and Information Skills Lab*. Librarians are being trained in outcomes assessment and are receiving Institutional Review Board training for assessment planning. The library hopes to pilot assessment software to facilitate tracking goals and objectives, and measures that support accreditation requirements.

Conclusion

All freshmen and most undergraduate transfer students at Duquesne University receive instruction geared toward establishing baseline competency in computer and information literacy skills, including: articulating information needs; finding, retrieving, evaluating, and ethically using information; and communicating research results using word processing, spreadsheet, and presentation software. Significant collaboration among faculty, librarians, and campus computing staff has resulted in improved instruction and adoption of course management software to facilitate instructors' sharing a single online course text and assignments, and to manage more than 1,000 students.

Key factors in the successful integration of information literacy into Duquesne's curriculum include faculty and librarian collaboration and technological, instructional, and administrative support. Focusing on meeting students' needs and accreditation standards provides the common ground needed to identify essential competencies and create course content within a workable structure. Using technology to support large-group instruction facilitates the goal to provide a common experience in addition to effectively tracking students and grades. Duquesne is well positioned to build on current efforts to move to the next level of integrating information literacy into the curriculum.

References

ACRL. (1980). *Research agenda for bibliographic instruction.* Retrieved November 24, 2003, from *www.ala.org/ala/acrlbucket/is/iscommittees/Webpages/research/researchagendabibliographic.htm*

ACRL. (2000). *Information literacy competency standards for higher education.* Retrieved March 31, 2003, from *http://www.ala.org/acrl/ilcomstan.html*

ACRL. (2001). *Objectives for information literacy instruction: A model statement for academic librarians.* Retrieved November 24, 2003, from *http://www.ala.org/ala/acrl/acrlstandards/objectivesinformation.htm*

ACRL. (2003a). *Characteristics of programs of information literacy that illustrate best practices: A guideline.* Retrieved November 24, 2003, from *http://www.ala.org/ala/acrl/acrlstandards/characteristics.htm*

ACRL. (2003b). *Guidelines for instruction programs in academic libraries.* Retrieved November 5, 2003, from *http://www.ala.org/ala/acrl/acrlstandards/guidelines instruction.htm*

ACRL. (2003c). *Research agenda for library instruction and information literacy.* Retrieved November 24, 2003, from *www.ala.org/ala/acrlbucket/is/iscommittees/webpages/research/researchagendalibrary.htm*

American Library Association Presidential Committee on Information Literacy. (1989). *Final report.* Chicago: American Library Association.

Arp, L. & Woodward, B.S. (2002). Recent trends in information literacy and instruction. *Reference & User Services Quarterly, 42*, 124-132.

Boyer, E.L. (1987). *College: The undergraduate experience in America: The Carnegie Foundation for the Advancement of Teaching.* New York: Harper & Row.

Breivik, P.S. & Gee, E.G. (1989). *Information literacy: Revolution in the library.* New York: Collier Macmillan.

Commission on Higher Education: Middle States Association of Colleges and Schools. (1982). *Characteristics of excellence in higher education: Standards for accreditation*. Philadelphia: Commission on Higher Education: Middle States Association of Colleges and Schools.

Commission on Higher Education: Middle States Association of Colleges and Schools. (1994). *Characteristics of excellence in higher education: Standards for accreditation*. Philadelphia: Commission on Higher Education: Middle States Association of Colleges and Schools.

Commission on Higher Education: Middle States Association of Colleges and Schools. (2002). *Characteristics of excellence in higher education: Eligibility requirements and standards for accreditation*. Philadelphia: Commission on Higher Education: Middle States Association of Colleges and Schools.

Commission on Higher Education: Middle States Association of Colleges and Schools. (2003a). *Developing research and communication skills: Guidelines for information literacy in the curriculum*. Philadelphia: Commission on Higher Education: Middle States Association of Colleges and Schools.

Commission on Higher Education: Middle States Association of Colleges and Schools. (2003b). *Student learning assessment: Options and resources*. Philadelphia: Commission on Higher Education: Middle States Association of Colleges and Schools.

Evaluation Team Representing the Commission on Higher Education of the Middle States Association of Colleges and Schools. (1998). Middle States update: A report to the faculty, administration, trustees, students of Duquesne University. *Duquesne University Times, 7*(23), 1-2.

Guskin, A.E., Stoffle, C.J., & Boisse, J.A. (1979). The academic library as a teaching library: A role for the 1980s. *Library Trends, 28*(2), 281-296.

Kaufman, T. (1995). Gumberg Library compiles library instruction survey results. *Duquesne University Times, 5*(12), 2.

Knapp, P.B. (1966). *The Monteith College library experiment*. New York: Scarecrow Press.

McCrank, L.J. (1992). Academic programs for information literacy: Theory and structure. *RQ, 31*, 485-497.

Ratteray, O.M.T. (2002). Information literacy in self-study and accreditation. *The Journal of Academic Librarianship, 28*, 368-375.

Sager, H. (1995). Implications for bibliographic instruction. In G.M. Pitkin (Ed.), *The impact of emerging technologies on reference service and bibliographic instruction* (pp. 49-62). Westport, CT: Greenwood Press.

Shapiro, J.J. & Hughes, S.K. (1996). Information literacy as a liberal art: Enlightenment proposals for a new curriculum. *Educom Review, 31*(2), 1-5.

Simmons, H.L. (1992). Information literacy and accreditation: A Middle States Association perspective. *New Directions for Higher Education, 78*(Summer), 15-25.

Stoffle, C.J., Guskin, A.E., & Boisse, J.A. (1984). Teaching, research and service: The academic library's role. In T. Kirk (Ed.), *Increasing the teaching role of academic libraries, new directions for teaching and learning* (pp. 4-14). San Francisco: Jossey-Bass.

Chapter X

Achieving University-Wide Instructional Technology Literacy: Examples of Development Programs and Their Effectiveness

Katia Passerini
New Jersey Insititute of Technology, USA

Kemal Cakici
George Washington University, USA

Abstract

This chapter reviews the efforts of a large university located in the East Coast of the United States to support faculty technology literacy through participation in development programs featuring a mix of technology skills and instructional design seminars. The success of these programs is evaluated on a series of criteria: faculty needs and satisfaction, ability to meet faculty learning objectives, and short-term and long-term benefits in terms of new initiatives implementation. Survey protocols and instruments used to evaluate program effectiveness are included to support future implementations by other institutions. The authors intend to encourage the development of similar programs, and the understanding of current obstacles that hinder a full deployment of technology in the classroom.

Introduction

For universities to effectively educate students in technology management, faculty development, and integration of instructional technology within the traditional curriculum is of primary importance. Faculty development is the key enabling strategy for the successful introduction of technology in the classroom and at a distance (Summers & Vlosky, 2001). There are many drivers that can support this development, and they span from providing instructors with opportunities to learn new technologies, facilities to develop the new skills, skilled professionals to support curriculum innovation, incentive systems that reward these efforts, and involvement in the change management process for the development of technology-rich curricula (White & Myers, 2001). Several universities are investing substantial resources to offer intensive development programs for faculty (Morales & Roig, 2002). Instructors participating in these programs often undertake new projects, and receive incentives and rewards (release time, student assistance, monetary, and resource support).

This chapter presents an example of the efforts of George Washington University—a large university located in Washington, DC—to support faculty development through educational technology seminars offered through winter and summer institutes (three- to five-day workshops). The programs results, evaluated on faculty needs and satisfaction, outcomes, and program benefits, are presented as a learning experiences to evaluate future implementations and as a tool for understanding lasting issues and concerns.

The Faculty Development Program

The instructional technologies development institutes offered at George Washington University (hereon referred to as 'Institutes') are part of a program designed to significantly increase proficiency in teaching with advanced technologies, particularly Web-based tools. The Institutes provide faculty with both pedagogical and technical training and development. They also provide yearlong staff support to assist faculty during design and implementation of instructional technology projects. The program was launched in the summer of 1999, and to date, several Institutes have been successfully offered each year reaching over 400 participants.

The Institutes are set up and funded by multiple units within the university, in a partnership model that leverages resources from different media and library services departments. The partners include university teaching centers, libraries, instructional technology labs, and computer resource centers. This model brings increased success due to synergistic efforts, and serves the diverse need of instructors in different fields. The partnership model also brings opportunities for program cost sharing across different cost centers, while achieving a satisfactory level of content variety and *ad hoc* support for each participant.

The Institutes accomplish the goal of increased faculty proficiency and use of instructional technologies through a series of three-day long workshops. The workshops provide faculty with occasions to experiment with new technology, assist in demonstrations, discuss curriculum impact, and submit grant proposals for technology-based projects in the classroom. Each summer, at least three of these Institutes are offered to faculty in the form of learning tracks or themes. The tracks are designed to provide a progressive series of experiences ranging from basic computer skills, to computer-based research skills (including productivity and classroom presentation tools), progressing to elaborate pedagogically sound multimedia and mediated learning projects. Over the years, the number of tracks increased to include additional learning opportunities in the area of video creation in a professional studio (for distance learning), as well as opportunities for statistical analysis review and practice with software programs such as the SAS systems. A sample list of theme areas and workshops offered in the Summer 2003 edition is presented in Table 1. The list shows how the workshops offering strived to reach the different disciplines and academic areas throughout the university to facilitate the introduction of technology across the curriculum.

Implementing an effective faculty development program is a complex endeavor. A significant program should first provide rationale and motivation for technology use in the classroom. It should offer a mix of technical skills, as well as the background for understanding how instructional technologies change traditional teaching environments. In addition to offering content-specific workshops, such as those listed in Table 1, a set of different learning experiences are provided as part of the Institutes. These experiences embrace:

- showcases from other faculty/colleagues to encourage the sharing of research findings among participants;
- guest speakers and key players (and vendors) in technology-based instruction that provide overview of possible applications;
- awards and grants for experimentations with new technologies;
- hands-on experience, assisted projects, and demonstrations that focus on both curriculum issues and software skills; and
- extensive training, particularly for managing increased workload and synchronous and asynchronous communication.

Offering a variety of experiences and framing the hands-on practice within a broader effort that reviews both theoretical and practical examples of classroom technology potential is a key element of continued technology adoption. Unless the benefits of the technology are clearly understood, the practice and exercises that faculty are engaged

Table 1. Overview of faculty workshops

THEME I—COMPUTER PRODUCTIVITY (Basic Computer Skills)	
The track is designed to provide an introduction to computers to faculty with little or no experience in technology. Faculty learn a variety of productivity software as well as using the World Wide Web.	Introduction to Windows
	Introduction to Microsoft Word
	Windows File Management
	Introduction to MS PowerPoint
	Using Netscape Navigator and the WWW
THEME II—COURSE MANAGEMENT SOFTWARE	
The track promotes the understanding and use of course management software used at the university. In particular, strategies for students' assessment and evaluation in an online learning environment are discussed. Effective use of asynchronous interaction tools (such as discussion boards) is reviewed.	Planning a Course Web Site and Instructional Communication Strategies
	Setting Up a Course in Prometheus/Blackboard
	Posting and Managing Files in Prometheus/Blackboard 5
	Issues in Using Course Management Systems
	Assessment Strategies and Online Learning—Prometheus / Blackboard Testing Feature
	Online Course Interactions, Collaborations, & File Sharing
THEME III—WEB-BASED & LIBRARY RESEARCH	
The track focuses on enhancing faculty use of library resources in their area of research. An overview of subject-specific library databases is provided. In addition, library and Web resources are integrated and made available for classroom use.	Researching Using the Library's Social Sciences Database
	Researching Using the Library's Science/Engineering Database
	Researching Using the Library's Arts and Humanities Database
	Researching Using the Library's Business and Management Database
	Web Sites in Course Instruction & Detecting Cyber-Cheating
	Finding Web Information Using Advanced Search Engines
	Integrating Subject-Specific Web Sites into Course Instruction

Table 1. Overview of faculty workshops (cont.)

THEME IV—WEB DESIGN AND DEVELOPMENT (Web-Based Learning)	
The track covers the key milestones for Web site development: from planning and design to actual development and online content publication, hands-on practice with different Web development packages, and step-by-step instructions to successfully build and manage a course Web site.	Web Site Planning and Design
	Creating Web-Ready Images Using Adobe Photoshop, Adobe GoLive
	Using Adobe Acrobat to Create Web-Ready PDF Files
	Building Web Pages (Dreamweaver, Macromedia Flash)
	Web Publishing
THEME V—TEACHING WITH VIDEO (Multimedia Production)	
The track covers professional video creation, leveraging the use of the university studios. Topics include the technology and the management of video projects, as well as the steps for video conversion and distribution on-line.	Teaching with Video Series (Four-Part Series Combined)
	Image Control
	Video Compression, Single Camera Techniques & Storyboarding
	Capturing, Editing, and Publishing Video
THEME VI—STATISTICAL ANALYSIS USING SAS SYSTEM SOFTWARE	
The track offers faculty an opportunity to practice with the statistical analysis software package (SAS); both introductory-level and advanced-level statistics are covered.	SAS Introductory Workshop
	Intermediate Data Analysis
	Categorical Data Analysis
	Time Series Data Analysis

with at the Institutes will not have the lasting impact required to better prepare students in understanding the demands of the digital economy (Netzley, 1999). Giving tools to share experiences and providing—even limited—monetary resources to experiment with classroom implementation are key factors to foster innovation. The successful results of this approach, captured by the survey data collected over the multiple editions of the Institutes and discussed in the next section, represent an opportunity for better understanding the drivers and the obstacles for technology deployment in the classroom.

Faculty Satisfaction with Development Programs

Evaluations of individual workshops, as well as program-wide evaluations, were conducted in several editions of the Institute (see Appendices 1 and 2 for sample survey instruments and satisfaction outcomes). Aggregate results showed high satisfaction with the Initiatives. Overall, participant satisfaction was constantly very high in the different editions of the programs. Faculty enthusiasm was extended to all the workshops, in spite of the intensive schedule and the amount of new material presented. The feedback (Figure 2) shows that both content and formats were on target:

- responses average positive results constantly above the mean;
- participants were satisfied with the events and with the organization;
- several new projects were started as a result of ideas and skills attained in the Institutes;
- participants continued to repeatedly use support facilities and applications presented at the workshops; and
- a few participants started using Web-based applications in their courses, or moved to an advanced level of online course implementation (i.e., streaming technology) using pedagogical strategies discussed at the Institutes.

Figure 2. Faculty overall satisfaction with the Institute

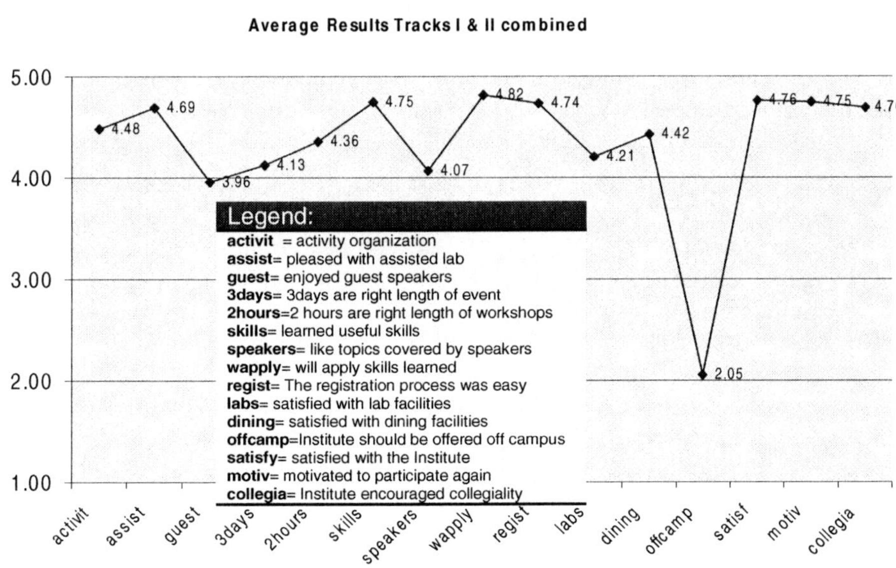

Open-ended responses to the survey confirmed the positive outcomes. However, they also highlighted key needs, specifically related to faculty placement in workshops/themes (see, for example, in Appendix C, the comments in caps). In particular, participant placement would be more effective if based on the individual level of technology experience. If attendees have limited experience with a technology and lack the necessary prior support, they risk impacting the pace of the program. Over the years, it was long debated whether faculty should take a brief competency test for placement in different learning tracks. This hypothesis was discarded as inappropriate for an academic audience, and as a negative element towards obtaining and motivating attendees' participation in the program.

To address the above-mentioned issue, key program changes were implemented. The themes remained the umbrella for the workshop content and objectives, but faculty were given the opportunity to move across tracks and self-select the workshops they were most interested in at any particular point. While in the 1999 and 2000 Institutes editions, faculty who enrolled in Theme I (Computer Productivity) remained in the same track throughout the Institute; from the year 2001 and onwards, faculty were allowed to swap themes, and workshops within a theme. This approach significantly increased satisfaction with the pace of the program, as faculty could transfer based on their evaluation of the difficulty level of the track/workshop. Results from the Summer 2001 edition of the Institute show that faculty took advantage of the relocation opportunity. They also show a clear trend in the type of content that was perceived as most relevant (as presented in Figure 3).

Faculty Emerging Needs

Faculty self-selected the workshops that they were interested in attending, although they were strongly encouraged to participate fully in the development themes (Table 1) they initially registered to attend. It is interesting to note that in spite of the prior level of experience with the technology, faculty chose to participate in the 'advanced themes' or those themes that covered more than the basic productivity skills covered in Theme I.

Participants also self-selected those workshops that they felt were meeting their learning objectives at their pace. The largest number of participants chose Theme II. Theme II was advertised as an intermediate track focusing on Web-based courses and course design. Themes IV and V had the next highest number of participants. These 'advanced themes' focused on two specific areas—distance education and video production. There was a decline in the interest for Theme I, and this will probably continue as faculty become less interested in the basics of productivity software and move into more advanced uses. Figure 3 shows the distribution of participants based on their self-selection to specific themes/workshops. Future programs will need to factor in the general advancements in participants' skills and interest.

With the increase in proficiency or mastery of the basics, it is necessary to tailor programs more specifically to faculty needs. Faculty will quickly diverge on what skills they need,

Figure 3. Faculty emerging interest areas

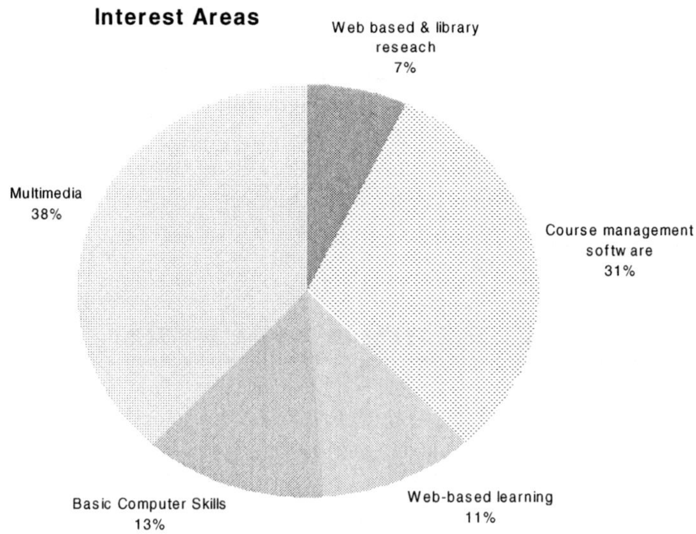

Figure 4. Faculty satisfaction by workshop type (Summer 2003)

2003 Edition	Workshop Type	No. of Registrants	No. of Participants	Overall Mean	Content & Format Mean	Instructor Mean	Technology Aids	Course Objectives	Overall Satisfaction
June	**Blackboard**	36	29	4.16	3.90	4.48	4.72	3.81	4.45
July	**Blackboard**	43	33	4.39	4.54	4.87	4.76	3.82	4.68
August	**Blackboard**	38	31	4.36	4.20	4.73	4.68	4.05	4.47
		117	**93**	**4.30**	**4.21**	**4.69**	**4.72**	**3.89**	**4.53**
June, July, August	**Acrobat**	81	48	4.34	4.03	4.45	4.49	4.34	4.33
June, July, August	**Dreamweaver**	52	31	4.50	4.25	4.65	4.78	4.42	4.18
June, July, August	**Photoshop**	40	19	4.51	4.36	4.65	4.70	4.26	4.38
		173	**98**	**4.45**	**4.21**	**4.58**	**4.66**	**4.34**	**4.30**
June, July, August	**Open Lab**	56	16	4.65	4.67	4.95	4.83	4.38	5.00

Legend **1=Strongly Disagree** **2=Disagree** **3=Neither Agree Nor Disagree** **4=Agree** **5=Strongly Agree**

Open lab

and desire to move further along their personal and skill development curve. The more instructors begin to experiment and use various technologies, the more their individualized needs will grow. This suggests that future programs should probably focus on offering tailored sessions (and less standard workshops), and more support staff should be available for 'open labs'—that is, sessions for individualized project tutoring. To evaluate the perceived effectiveness of the customized approach, the 'open lab' format was implemented in the Summer 2003 Institute edition. The results from the post-program evaluation survey show that the 'open lab' obtained the highest satisfaction scores compared to the other content areas (Figure 4). Future editions will continue to apply the 'open lab' model and will collect additional data on effectiveness. Although the 'open lab' approach is a more resource-intensive workshop type (as a higher number of staff instructors need to be available for tutoring sessions), it is also the approach that may increase faculty continued interest and participation.

Lasting Concerns

While these programs have been redesigned over the years to better address faculty needs (in terms of content expansion, pacing of instruction, and continued access to resources), there are a number of lasting concerns that hinder faculty use of classroom technologies. The main issue still faced by faculty often remains the lack of time and funds to undertake technology-based projects. While the Institutes provide grants for an initial project implementation, the grant amount is limited and can only suffice for small projects. Innovation is hindered by the lack of resources. The number of projects launched after each of the summer initiatives increased over the years, but the ratio between the number of Institute participants and the number of new projects launched per year is extremely low. While faculty will participate in the training events—a 'build it and they will come' model (Irani & Telg, 2002)—and would eventually implement technology-based projects for classroom projects if awarded a grant, the number of full implementations have not met expectations.

A major factor that discourages faculty from investing time and resources in the implementation of new technologies for instructional use is also the limited role that such efforts play in the portfolio. Particularly in research institutions, such as the university implementing this program, major attention is placed on faculty scholarly work. The teaching portfolio and academic success represent only a limited portion of the faculty evaluation scheme. Unless innovation efforts and curriculum development initiatives are fully recognized as a relevant part of the faculty portfolio, there is little opportunity for growth and innovation. Currently, most of the innovation efforts rely on the motivation and strenuous commitment of a few instructors (Hall & Elliott, 2003) who decide to devote personal time and resources to technology implementation. If these efforts were better recognized both informally and formally, the situation could improve. This would call for a review of the tenure evaluation criteria, an endeavor extremely hard to accomplish and rarely driven by stakeholders outside the faculty council community, as the centers and partners organizing the Institutes.

Conclusion and Future Issues

The proliferation of wireless campuses, the experimentation of concepts such as the 'agora campus' (Watters, Conley et al., 1998), and the increased demand for classroom technology use by students (Deden, 1998; Kraemer, Bergin et al., 1986) call for an expansion of technology implementation across disciplines. Regardless of the content being taught, it is increasingly important that faculty leverage the use of technologies in their own field, either through lab experiments, targeted assignments, or hands-on laboratories.

Achieving technology literacy university-wide remains a very difficult proposition, but one that is increasingly being met. Universities have been addressing issues related to the need for faculty training through offering state-of-the-art development programs that increase theoretical and hands-on skills. These programs show high levels of reach and display progress in the right direction. This chapter described one such initiative based on a four-year implementation of summer development programs at the George Washington University in the United States. Key success factors have been identified in the ability to offer a variety of workshop formats paired with other content-rich events (such as guest speakers, discussion sessions, and the like), and with the ability to offer flexible and tailored programs. These programs allow high reach and impact throughout the university schools and disciplines.

While faculty 'technology literacy' is being achieved, its implementation in the classroom remains episodically reliant on the goodwill of the individual faculty participants. Faculty demonstrates a high motivation in learning new technologies but is continually faced with competing requirements that hinder the full implementation of technology-driven projects in the classroom. Lack of sufficient funding is the substantial problem. Programs can be designed to motivate faculty participation and acquisition of advanced technology skills. However, implementation will fail until faculty will be rewarded for their efforts through the relevant evaluation instruments, such as tenure evaluation criteria that reward technology-based innovation in the classroom. Only then will universities be able to achieve technology literacy campus-wide and also sustain it over the years.

References

Deden, A. (1998). Computers and systemic change in higher education. *Communications of the ACM, 41*, 58-63.

Hall, M. & Elliott, K.M. (2003). Diffusion of technology into the teaching process: Strategies to encourage faculty members to embrace the laptop environment. *Journal of Education for Business, 78*, 301-307.

Irani, T. & Telg, R. (2002). Building it so they will come: Assessing universities' distance education faculty training and development programs. *Journal of Distance Education, 17*, 36-46.

Kraemer, K.L., Bergin, T. et al. (1986). Curriculum recommendations for public management education in computing. *Public Administration Review, 46*, 595.

Morales, L. & Roig, G. (2002). Connecting a technology faculty development program with student learning. *Campus-Wide Information Systems, 19*, 67-72.

Netzley, M.A. (1999). Introduction: Are we requiring what our students most need? *Business Communication Quarterly, 62*, 7-9.

Summers, T.A. & Vlosky, R.P. (2001). Technology in the classroom: The LSU College of Agriculture Faculty perspective. *Campus-Wide Information Systems, 18*, 79-84.

Watters, C., Conley, M. et al. (1998). The digital agora: Using technology for learning in the social sciences. *Communications of the ACM, 41*, 50-57.

White, J.T. & Myers, S.D. (2001). You can teach an old dog new tricks: The faculty's role in technology implementation. *Business Communication Quarterly, 64*, 95-101.

Appendix A

Example of Individual Workshops Evaluation Form and Aggregate Results

Content and Format	Strongly disagree/ Disagree[1]	Neither agree nor disagree	Agree/ Strongly agree[2]	N/A
The topics covered are useful to me.	1.8%	3.2%	93.3%	1.3%
There was an appropriate amount of hands-on practice.	5.7%	4.0%	45.9%	43.7%
There was sufficient time to cover the course objectives.	9.2%	8.4%	77.9%	3.2%
The material was well organized and easy to follow.	5.0%	7.2%	85.1%	1.7%

[1] Cumulative data (strongly disagree+disagree).
[2] Cumulative data (strongly agree+agree).

Instructor	Strongly disagree/ Disagree	Neither agree nor disagree	Agree/ Strongly agree	N/A
The instructor demonstrated knowledge of the subject.	.4%	1.0%	98.0%	.7%
The instructor presentation was easy to understand.	.7%	5.7%	89.1%	1.0%
The instructor was skilled in listening.	1.5%	5.7%	88.7%	3.9%
The instructor encouraged questions.	1.2%	6.9%	88.6%	2.7%
The instructor answered questions clearly.	1.5%	4.5%	91.1%	2.2%
The instructor stayed focused on objectives.	1.1%	4.4%	89.4%	4.9%
The pace was:	Too fast 17.3%	Too slow 5.0%	Just right 58.0%	18.3%

Appendix A (cont.)

Technology Aids	Strongly disagree/ Disagree	Neither agree nor disagree	Agree/ Strongly agree	N/A
I was able to clearly hear the instructor.	2.9%	2.0%	93.3%	1.7%
I was able to clearly see the instructor.	13.8%	4.0%	81.2%	1.0%
I was able to clearly see the *visual aids* used by the instructor.	17.0%	7.2%	72.3%	3.0%

Your overall satisfaction	Strongly disagree/ Disagree	Neither agree nor disagree	Agree/ Strongly agree	N/A
I would take another course from this instructor.	3.1%	4.7%	89.5%	2.4%
I would recommend this course to others.	3.5%	4.7%	87.7%	3.7%

After class, you will:	Strongly disagree/ Disagree	Neither agree nor disagree	Agree/ Strongly agree	N/A
Apply the skills you learned here.	2.5%	4.9%	88.4%	4.2%
Use the class material for reference.	2.0%	4.0%	88.7%	5.2%

Appendix B

Program Evaluation Instrument

Format	Strongly Disagree	Disagree	Neither Agree nor Disagree	Agree	Strongly Agree	Not Applicable
I liked the way the activities were organized.						
I was particularly pleased with the inclusion of:						
Assisted lab time						
Guest speakers						
Kick-off dinner						
I found three days to be the right amount of time for the Institute.						
I found two hours to be the right amount of time for the workshops.						
Do you recommend revising the format of the Institute? How?						
Content	Strongly disagree	Disagree	Neither agree nor disagree	Agree	Strongly agree	Not applicable
I learned useful skills.						
Guest speakers covered interesting topics.						
I will apply the skills I learned here.						
Please indicate other presentation topics that you would find useful for future editions of Institute.						

Appendix B (cont.)

Registration	Strongly disagree	Disagree	Neither agree nor disagree	Agree	Strongly agree	Not applicable
Was it easy to register?						
How did you hear about the Institute? ___Press release __Departmental memorandum __Faculty/colleagues _Information session __Other (please specify)						
What would make registration easier for you?						
Facilities	Strongly disagree	Disagree	Neither agree nor disagree	Agree	Strongly agree	Not applicable
I am satisfied with the computer lab facilities.						
I am satisfied with the dining facilities.						
I would prefer that the Institute was offered off-campus.						
Please list any comments on facilities.						
Overall Satisfaction	Strongly disagree	Disagree	Neither agree nor disagree	Agree	Strongly agree	Not applicable
I am satisfied with the Institute event.						
This Institute motivated me to participate in other learning tracks.						
The Institute environment encouraged collegiality.						
What do you think was the *most* successful Institute event? 1. 2. 3.						
What do you think was the *least* successful Institute event? 1. 2. 3.						

Appendix C

Open-Ended Comments

GENERAL

1. All in all, a successful class. The instructors were all fine, bright, cheerful and helpful. Thanks for a memorable experience.
2. *INSTRUCTORS WERE VERY PATIENT! (+ ENTHUSIASTIC). I THINK YOU SHOULD TRY TO SCREEN A LITTLE MORE IN TERMS OF PARTICIPANTS, I.E. I SAT BESIDE A PERSON WHO DIDN'T KNOW HOW TO USE WINDOWS AT ALL (OR EVEN THE MOUSE!) YET THIS PERSON WAS IN TRACK II. THIS WAS VERY DISTRACTING AND FRUSTRATING FOR EVERYONE!*
3. Ask what will be most immediately useful? Probably Web Courseware. Ask about the software included in the sessions and how we appropriately acquire it to use? I need repeat sessions for most of the topics to really use the knowledge!
4. In fact all INSTITUTE staff was good.
5. Very good—a bit too much to digest, but the possibilities & procedures are clearer.
6. Overall, it was an excellent workshop—well organized and well presented.

CONTENT

7. I think it was great. Looking forward to Track III.
8. I found the TV speaker's talk to be of limited practical usefulness. I enjoyed the office of Gen. Counsel Deputy, but would like to have heard more from him.

FORMAT

9. The 3-day intensive experience is excellent. Have guest speakers at either lunch or breakfast but not both on a single day. The breakfast was good because of collegiality, meeting fellow students.
10. Format was good.
11. I thought the 90-minute break for lunch was great—enough time to quickly check e-mail/phone & make it back for lunch & speaker.
12. Mixing hands-on and presentations are the best.

FACILITIES

13. Lab 205 was very good (306 in Track I was not as good because of the high tables).
14. Can't believe we got fed at all! Thanks!!!
15. 2 computers I tried had something wrong w/ MS Office (i.e. No PowerPoint/Word). Some variation in the snack for the breaks (other than cookies) would be appreciated. Breakfasts were great (lots of variation). Lunches were good & always nice to have a speaker.

Chapter XI

Technology for Management, Communication, and Instruction: Supporting Teacher Development

Silvia L. Sapone
California University of Pennsylvania, USA

Kim Johnson Hyatt
Duquesne University, USA

Abstract

This chapter introduces a pedagogically sound experience for teachers and teacher candidates as they prepare or continue to learn about the use of technology for the K-12 classroom. The authors hope that learning about fundamental technology skills will not only inform teachers about how to effectively meet the needs of a diverse student population, but also expand their knowledge base in terms of professional growth.

Technology changes the way teachers interact with curriculum and engage in discourse with students and their families, peers, and administrators; therefore, it is essential to address how it can be utilized for management, communication, and instructional purposes in order to enhance the learning environment. This chapter argues that districts need to develop a plan that incorporates technology training for all teachers to create a positive impact on teaching and learning.

Introduction

How does one provide a pedagogically sound experience for teachers in K-12 school systems and teacher candidates at the university level as they learn about the use of technology? New technologies present us with an opportunity for reconceptualizing the pedagogy of learning. Shifts in learning paradigms due to the growth of the Internet are described as: a shift from linear to hypermedia learning, from instruction to construction and discovery, from absorbing material to learning to navigate and how to learn, from school to lifelong learning, and from one-size-fits-all to customized, self-directed learning (Tapscott, 1998; Gray, 1999). Technology has the potential to transform the way we teach, manage, and communicate. It changes the way teachers engage in discourse with students and peers, and interact with curriculum.

Today's school children are the first generation of the "digital age." They are being raised in a society that is changing rapidly as a result of the influx of new technologies. The Presidential Committee of Advisors on Science and Technology (PCAST, 1997) and the U.S. Congress Office of Technology Assessment (1995) in Washington have stated that it is incumbent on the U.S. educational system to make provisions for all children to obtain the skills that are needed to become technologically literate citizens. Therefore, what does this mean for educators?

Technology is available in our classrooms, and it is changing the way educators think about teaching and the way students think about learning. Therefore, it is important for teachers to have a good understanding of ways these technologies can best be integrated into the curriculum to meet the needs of diverse student populations. In his book, *The Road Ahead,* Bill Gates made the statement, "One thing is clear, we don't have the option of turning away from the future. No one gets to vote on whether technology is going to change our lives" (1995, p. 74). The pace of innovation in digital information and communications technologies is accelerating, promising to revolutionize how we work, live, and learn (Brown, 2000; PITAC, 1997, 2000). Since many of the students are already surrounded by technology on a daily basis, teachers alike must acquire and develop skills to understand and integrate technology into the classroom environment. Accomplishing this vision will ultimately depend on the dedication, skill, and ongoing professional development of tomorrow's teachers (PITAC, 1997, 2000). Hence, this chapter will explore various perspectives about how technology can be utilized for management, communication, and instruction in the classroom.

Perspectives on Technology for Management

As the bell rings each morning, teachers commence their daily routine of recording attendance, passing out work for students returning from an absence, collecting homework from the previous night, and reviewing due dates for work already assigned. As the day progresses, teachers work on grading papers, recording grades in their gradebooks, writing letters or calling parents, and informing administrators and guidance counselors about progress alerts and/or behavioral issues. These expectations, along with numerous others, are often referred to as management tasks. Since these daily tasks remain constant, a question arises about how technology can be utilized to impact the efficiency and effectiveness of this work. Teachers need to be spending less time on management tasks and more time on planning and instructional tasks. Therefore, by introducing user-friendly tools with proper training, teachers will feel confident implementing technology into their classroom. There are many options for using technology to assist with management tasks. The most popular tools are electronic gradebook programs, personal digital assistants (PDAs), and laptop computers.

Gradebook Programs

Gradebook programs should be a requisite element in the classroom of the twenty-first century. According to Vockell and Fiore (1993):

> *"An electronic gradebook can provide, at a moment's notice, a complete report on a student's progress in a professional and easy-to-read format. In addition, a gradebook program will weight and average scores quickly and accurately and perform many extra tasks with little or no additional effort."*

With the use of an electronic gradebook, teachers have the ability to communicate with students about their progress on a daily, weekly, or monthly basis. It takes the element of surprise out of the once-a-semester report card, and keeps students and parents alike updated on a regular basis. "If you teach and you're not using an electronic gradebook, you're losing a chance to reclaim some of what is a teacher's greatest impoverishment—time" (Stanton, 1994).

An extension to the electronic gradebook is the use of online grading. The benefits enable parents to be directly involved with their child's progress when it is convenient for them. Without this connection to the classroom, the majority of teacher and parent contact stems from concerns about academic work, discipline, and/or social issues (Hyatt & Sapone, 2002). There is usually not enough time to write or call parents whose children exhibit academic excellence on a particular assignment and/or on a regular basis.

The Pinnacle System, which was outlined in *T.H.E. Journal* (2001), describes five different reports that can be sent to parents:

1. an absence notice when their child is marked absent and a parent has not called,
2. a warning if their child's grades slip below a certain point,
3. a weekly attendance record,
4. a standard grade report, and
5. a snapshot of their child's grade in every teacher's gradebook.

Although, these reports open the lines of communication between children and parents, some students feel it is a violation of their privacy. They cannot hide their grades, lack of attendance, and/or missing assignments from parental eyes (Dunn, 2001).

Critics of electronic gradebooks believe they are too impersonal. They cannot accurately reflect students' level of performance due to the special needs of each individual. Guskey (2002) concludes that "grading requires careful planning, thoughtful judgment, a clear focus on purpose, excellent communication skills, and an overriding concern for the well-being of students—qualities that no computer possesses." He also thinks that they "lead educators who use them to believe that mathematical precision necessarily brings greater objectivity and enhanced fairness to grading." In addition to the impersonal side of electronic grading is the potential problem of hacking if the gradebook is not properly secured. A hacker could change grades and/or retrieve personal information, not only with an electronic gradebook, but even easier with an online gradebook. Therefore, measures must be taken to ensure privacy for the individuals who access them. Finally, the issue of cost becomes an important factor when considering school-wide adoption. It is not always in the budget, especially since many school districts need the money for new books, athletic equipment, and other necessary materials.

The benefits of using an electronic gradebook outweigh the lack of objectivity a teacher may feel when inputting scores. It is recommended that school districts utilize a standard gradebook program. If teachers are provided with uniform training, it will be easier to submit required classroom reports, assist those individuals having difficulty, and increase communication between teachers, parents, students, and administrators. Because there are a lot of companies that produce electronic gradebooks, it is best for districts considering adoption to invite representatives to in-service workshops to demonstrate the products. The faculty required to use the gradebook would be able to ask questions, interact with the product, and make informed recommendations about adoption. For additional information on gradebook software, refer to *Your Guide to Gradebook Software on the Web:* www.educational-software-directory.net/teacher%27s/gradebook.html.

- *1st Class Software* [Win]—Has a variety of reporting and graphing options.
- *A2Z Gradebook* [Win]—Stores grades, calculates averages, and generates reports. Merge files from multiple teachers to create comprehensive reports.

- Altissima [Win]—Gradebook with capabilities for keeping comments on students.
- Class Action Gradebook [Win, Mac]—Tracks grades, attendance, and seating. Generates reports, letters, and graphs.
- Class Mate Grading Software [Win]—Teachers grading package.
- ClassMaster [Win, Mac]—An electronic gradebook that calculates, records, reports, and forecasts student and class performance.
- ClassBuilder [Win, Mac]—Gradebook software with Palm support.
- ClassRoom Windows [Win]—Free gradebook and class management program for teachers.
- Easy Grade Pro [Win, Mac]—An electronic gradebook that can store student, assignment, score, and attendance data on all classes and subjects for a year. Data can be manipulated and analyzed in a variety of ways.
- Easy Gradebook [Win]—Shareware gradebook program.
- Excel-lent Gradebook [Win]—A gradebook program that runs inside of Microsoft Excel. Shareware.
- EZ Grader [Win, Mac]—Manage lesson plans, class information, and grading software.
- Grade Machine [Win, Mac]—For grading and classroom management, and for getting a quick, detailed, school-wide picture of any student's performance.
- Grade Point [Win]—Helps you create progress reports, average grades, prepare report cards, create student rosters and checklists, publish seating charts, plan for small flexible remedial groups, and track missing assignments.
- Grade Speed [Win]—Prides itself in its simplicity.
- Gradebook1 [Win, Mac]—Features password protection, auto-save, easy backup, birthday reminders, score calculator. Shareware.
- Gradebook 2.0 [Win]—Many features and report options.
- Gradebook Power [Win]—More than 40 academic reports including attendance and seating charts. Import and export to school administrative software. Supports block schedule, traditional, and trimester school years.
- GradeBusters [Win, Mac, Palm, Casio]—Electronic grade book system with free upgrades for life.
- GradeGenie—Gradebook and attendance program. Many configuration options for customization. Security features.
- GradeGuide [DOS]—Used for analyzing and reporting students' grades.
- Gradekeeper [Win, Mac]—Gradebook software that can also create a Web site so parents and students can check their grades online.
- Gradepoint [Win]—A database software gradebook for managing student grading activities.
- GradeQuick [Win, Mac, Palm]—Calculates grades, tracks attendance, creates reports, and more.

- *Grades* [Mac]—Tailored for university, college, and high school professors to administer students' grades, exams, assignments, and grade reporting.
- *Gradesheet.com* [Win]—Gradebook server software.
- *GradeSource*—Web-based instructor course management tool with student-viewable Web page reports.
- *GradeStar Gradebook* [Win]—Gradebook for teachers at all levels. Many features for tracking grades, attendance, reports, and customization.
- *Integrade Pro* [Win, Mac]—Allows teachers to show at any time a complete list of a students' scores, missing assignments, and up-to-the-minute calculated grades. A variety of printed reports are possible.
- *J&S Gradebook* [Mac]—Unlimited number of students, activities, and classes. Customizeable progress reports and statistics. Web publishing with iGradeô add-on program.
- *MasterGrade* [Win, Mac]—Culmination of extensive software development, field testing, and research into usability and satisfaction of existing teacher gradebook software.
- *MicroGrade* [Win, Mac]—Computerized gradebook program that offers secure grade posting with free WebGrade service.
- *MyGradebook.com*—Web-based gradebook.
- *The Pretty Good Grading Program (PGGP)* [Win, Mac]—Gradebook software specifically for the elementary teacher.
- *Teachers Aid* [Win]—Software for tracking students' grades and more.
- *Teaching Software* [Win]—Helps keep track of student grades, calculate various averages, produce summaries, and post the grades onto the World Wide Web.
- *ThinkWave* [Win]—Gradebook software and complete classroom organizer. Manages attendance and lesson plans. Allows publishing grades to the Web and facilitates e-mail to parents.
- *Tiny Red Book* [Palm]—Gradebook software for the PalmOS.
- *VARed Software* [Win]—Handles any grading system or size class. Plots, statistics, attendance, and seating charts.

PDAs and Laptop Computers

What is a PDA, you might ask? According to Dunne (2001):

> *"A PDA is a digital organizer, or personal digital assistant (also called a handheld). Calendar, notepad, and address books are common features on a PDA, but many also download e-mail and other materials from a computer. PDA offerings are steadily expanding—modems come with some models and can be purchased as an add-on*

to others. Much like a traditional computer, PDAs consist of a display screen (the screen is usually a touch screen, and it is called a LCD display), a processor, memory, and an operating system."

PDAs can be used in the classroom for a variety of management tasks by both teachers and students. A survey completed by Eib and Welton (2004) for the Department of Defense Education Activity (DoDEA) is best summarized through an organizational chart of what PDAs can provide for teachers and students.

Besides the obvious benefits, there are also a few issues to consider when purchasing PDAs. They can be difficult to learn how to use because it takes practice to input information accurately and efficiently. And, in terms of student use, if treated like a textbook (e.g., loaning it to a student for the year), it becomes the responsibility of the parent to replace batteries and pay for lost or damaged units. Parents may not possess the money for these additional yearly school costs. It also becomes the responsibility of the student to remember to bring it from home to school. (Some students can't remember to bring a pencil!) In terms of teacher use, it can be used for seating charts and other management tasks; however, any substitute teacher brought into the building would also need to be trained in order to keep records up-to-date. Overall, a PDA is more

Teacher Use

Initial survey results show that teachers feel that using PDAs as educational tools is beneficial. Teachers report using PDAs in the following ways:

- Beaming study guides for tests to students
- Observing student behavior and keeping notes
- Recording individual student work
- Tracking student activities each week
- Editing students' writing
- Developing PDA simulations for teaching specific skills
- Collecting data
- Developing students' organizing skills
- Integrating pictures into presentations

Effect on Student Learning

When asked how students were using the technology, teachers gave the following responses:

- Recording assignments
- Taking notes on lectures and readings
- Sending work form home to their folder
- Beaming information to a tutor for evaluation
- Beaming responses to partners and editing information
- Completing electronic quizzes and beaming the results to a teacher
- Self-assessing work and progress
- Taking notes on animal behavior on a zoo field trip
- Increasing the number of assignments students complete

cost efficient and portable than a laptop; however, a laptop can perform additional management tasks.

For teachers, laptop computers (also called notebooks) can be utilized for recording attendance, passing out assignments, collecting homework, reviewing due dates, and informing administrators and guidance counselors about progress alerts, and/or behavioral issues could be completed with a click of the mouse. There are also computer programs to assist with designing and grading tests, review sheets, group projects, and the like. For students, a laptop makes burdensome backpacks obsolete. Instead of carrying heavy books, texts can be downloaded. Therefore, students cannot forget their books and/or homework assignments because they can access their work at school. Students can also record daily and/or weekly assignments and note upcoming events or project due dates. Conferencing with teachers about graded assignments would also change the way teachers and students interacted on a daily basis. Students could reflect on their progress after receiving feedback from the teacher.

Besides the obvious roadblock of cost, there are potential problems with using laptops in schools: getting into inappropriate Web sites, downloading music, playing games, e-mailing during class, and so forth (Angelo, 2002). Also, as discussed previously, computers must be secure so that hackers cannot retrieve or change information. If cost is a factor, school districts should look into funding options for technology integration. And, since technology changes so often, leasing could also be considered, even if it means piloting a program using a specific grade.

Perspectives on Technology for Communication

Until the use of e-mail and the World Wide Web, communication between the school and the home had a negative stigmatism attached to it for years. As previously mentioned, a parent phone call usually meant reporting bad news about behavior and/or grades. Also, these phone calls did not occur frequently enough to inform parents in a timely manner about potential problems with their children. Since "communicating with parents is a time-consuming task for teachers" (Huseth, 2001), it doesn't happen as often as it should using traditional methods of phone calls, mid-semester progress reports, and end-of-semester reports. Therefore, with the use of technology, communication links between the school and the home can be enhanced in terms of timeliness and frequency. It can also reverse the stigmatism, so that communication becomes a positive experience for all. One way for teachers to interact directly with the home is via the World Wide Web using Web pages. This type of technology is a productive way to make announcements to parents and the community about upcoming events at the school, requests for classroom resources such as guest speakers, and classroom information updates for parents and students.

In terms of classroom updates, the following information could be included on an individual teacher's Web page:

- daily or weekly agenda of items covered in class,
- homework assignments and project due dates,
- Web links for support or enrichment,
- extra credit opportunities, and
- an e-mail address.

Web tools provide parents the details about the classroom environment, expectations, and assignments (Meyer, 2000; Huseth, 2001; Flake 2001; Viebranz, 2003). With additional software programs, many schools are becoming proactive and using the home-to-school communication system in combination with a management system that allows access to grades, schedules, report cards, daily and period attendance, and so forth (White, 2003).

Although making it more convenient to communicate between the school and the home, technology is less personal than picking up the phone. However, e-mail seems to be an appropriate means for most communication subject matter. It alleviates numerous attempts to make contact and allows the receiver the option to reply. Teachers and parents will need to use discretion as to when e-mail is more appropriate than the phone, especially for sensitive issues. And even though the details of the classroom environment can be accessed online, parents may still feel the need to speak to teachers. That is why parents will also need to be given information about the appropriateness of contacting teachers via e-mail or phone. The goal of using technology is to provide the opportunity for parents to engage in conversation with their children about their learning before contacting the teacher.

Perspectives on Technology for Instruction

Designing and implementing effective education and training materials—especially when they incorporate and/or integrate new technologies—is a difficult task, because course design and its implementation are often likely to extend the competencies of any one individual (Hoskisson, Stammen, & Nelson, 1996). We often use the phrase "no longer the sage on the stage, but the guide on the side" to describe how teachers could no longer be the fountain of all knowledge because new data and knowledge were being created at such rapid rates that no one person could keep track of it all (Held, Newsom, & Peiffer, 1991). Changing roles requires changing pedagogy.

Research reminds us that technology generally improves performance when the application directly supports the curriculum standards being assessed (Cradler, McNabb, Freeman, & Burchett, 2002). A review of studies conducted by the CEO Forum (2001) emphasizes that "technology can have the greatest impact when integrated into the curriculum to achieve clear, measurable educational objectives." As we look at the integration of technology implementation, we need to rethink the way we teach, how we build curriculum and the way we support and evaluate faculty." Educational technology includes books, chalk and blackboard, pen and paper, television, radio, computers, PDAs, but only potentially. These only become educational when and where they are embedded into activities designed with explicit pedagogical intent. Teachers define and shape the pedagogical setting in which they apply technology. In order for the technology to foster active learning will depend on the strategies teachers employ. Insights from cognitive research and classroom practice suggest that for media to engage students, help them structure their learning experiences, and apply their understanding, the teacher needs to become less of a sole purveyor of knowledge and more of a facilitator (Jones et al., 1995; Means, 1994; Saettler, 1990). Imagine students having access to a plethora of information with the skills of knowing how to retrieve it. Such capabilities may affect the way that teachers design instruction. Knowledge is dynamic rather than some fixed amount of information; hence, a transformation of the teacher's role needs to shift from "teaching," as disseminating information, to "learning," by facilitating students to develop lifelong learning skills. In order for this shift to happen, teachers must develop technology skills for instruction in the following areas: Web literacy, PDA usage, and streaming video.

Web Literacy

Teachers must have the ability to validate the information they find on the Internet. They must be prepared to apply "critical thinking strategies, from decoding Web addresses to understanding the pattern of links to searching for the owner of a site" (Salpeter, 2003). David Warlick refers to the American Library Association's Nine Information Literacy Standards for Student Learning (www.ala.org/aasl/ip_nine.html) as "learning literacy's"— essential skills that "help people learn in an information-rich, highly networked, and rapidly changing world" (Salpeter, 2003). Teachers must be prepared to locate, analyze, synthesize, and critique information. The ability to search for information online is one of the most basic digital literacy skills. An understanding of directory structure and the use of keywords to conduct searches becomes important. Although locating information is the first challenge when utilizing the Internet, an equally important set of literacy skills involves using and interpreting information. Teachers must be prepared to provide and design the "right kind" of assignments that utilize technology. Therefore, how can we move from learning from technology to learning with technology?

Webquests, originated by Bernie Dodge and Tom March, offer what Dodge refers to as "inquiry-based (activities) designed to use learners' time well, to focus on using information rather than looking for it." Webquests are built around tasks, which provide a context for student work. They can afford students the opportunity to not only engage in the content via technology, but also provide a context in which students participate cooperatively with their peers. Webquests can offer a great way to not only enrich the curriculum, but also provide the avenue to analyze and synthesize information students find online. In terms of instruction, teachers are using technology to link pedagogy and content.

PDAs

PDAs are changing the way teachers access and work with information. Not only can PDAs serve as a management tool, but they can also serve as an instructional tool. The PDA can facilitate the process of authentic assessment by gathering information in a variety of multimedia formats in real-world situations. Teachers can plan for students to utilize the handheld devices for collecting and analyzing data, as well as write parts of their assignments directly on their PDAs. Software applications such as text editor, spreadsheet with charts, and databases can be synchronized with desktop computers to allow the user to take notes "in the field." PDAs also allow for wireless access to the Internet. In this respect, students will now have mobile access to course-related material inside and outside the classroom.

Today, one of the most popular assessment tools is the electronic portfolio. This is a record of a student's work over time, which is used to document achievement and improvement (Stiggins, 1994). The Learner-Profile for Palm OS is a comprehensive tool that helps educators design standards-based criteria and track student progress. Data is collected in the PDA, transferred to a desktop, and then used to produce a wide variety of reports on the students' progress.

Health and Physical Education teachers may utilize the PDAs with the Vivonic Fitness Plan for the Palm OS. This is software that allows the user to collect information about their nutritional intake and their physical activity to see whether they have met their fitness goals. Palm Fitness is another type of software that focuses on health-related fitness. With this software, teachers can collect fitness data on curl-ups, push-ups, pull-ups, and so forth. On a general basis, the PDA may be used in all the disciplines to do word processing and create line, bar, scatter, pie, and stock charts.

The use of PDAs for instruction is endless. Teachers can make their own Palm Digital Media books or course materials. Handouts and readings could be converted into electronic books and organized using embedded hyperlinks and images (Juniu, 2002). While there are many benefits to using a PDA, the most important benefit for educators and students is the PDA's ability to extend the learning environment beyond the classroom. With PDAs, students and teachers are now able to access the Internet, send and receive their assignments wirelessly through modems or wireless cards, take notes, perform calculations, read books, organize coursework, collect data, manage activities and courses, and instantly beam information to others (Juniu, 2002). Because of their portability, teachers can carry these devices from class to class or wherever they go and capture information while interacting with their students. Although exciting, teachers thinking about the use of PDAs need to consider cost, capacity, portability, expandability, color display, and software availability.

Streaming Video

Streaming video is television content that can be delivered to a computer via the Internet (Nelson, 2003). Streaming video offers immediacy and individual control, while videotapes offer a wider range of content and centralized control. Videotapes only require common classroom technology—a TV/VCR. Used in conjunction with one another, these two technologies can deepen student engagement with lessons, strengthen understanding of the connections between history and current events, and offer a practical way for students to make up missing assignments or review material covered in class (Nelson, 2003). Cable networks such as CNN, C-SPAN, The History Channel, Discovery Channel, and A&E offer free streaming video on their Web sites. By using both streaming video and videotapes, teachers are able to provide their students with many different viewpoints on the same topic. In addition, they are able to bring experts into the classroom and have flexibility in how they deliver a lesson.

Summary of Technology for Management, Communication, and Instruction

Today, everything is changing so rapidly that not only has technology made life easier for the teacher, but it has also complicated it (Nisan-Nelson, Paula, 2001). While the mention of technology immediately brings to mind the use of some type of computer or equipment, it does not necessarily include instructional design. Although the technological tools shared in this chapter provide opportunities for the enhancement of student learning, three issues that concern educators emerge when using technology in the classroom:

1) information overload and lack of useful instructional format,
2) problems with identifying the necessary skills and attitudes to maximize effectiveness, and
3) effectively designing and evaluating different learning formats (Hargis & Houston, 2000).

In the past, the failure of new technologies being integrated in the classroom has been blamed on the teachers' inability to adapt it to their teaching style (Cuban, 1986).

Research has suggested that there is a tendency for teachers to stay with instructional strategies with which they are familiar and comfortable, and which are the accepted status quo at their schools (Tobin & Dawson, 1992). That is why selecting appropriate technologies should be based on desired learning outcomes and students' needs, rather than on teaching styles.

Technology adds tools that facilitate access to people, content, strategies, activities, guidance, and opportunities to apply new information, making learning a personal process (Hargis & Houston, 2000). A Report to the Nation on Technology and Education: Meeting the Technology Literacy Challenge (Department of Education, 1996) states that computer skills and the ability to use technology to improve learning, productivity, and performance has become as fundamental to a person's ability to navigate through society as traditional skills like reading, writing, and arithmetic. The Technology Literacy Challenge that envisions a 21st century where all students are technologically literate requires fulfilling four main goals:

1) All teachers in the nation will have training to help students learn to use computers and the Internet.
2) All users will have modern multimedia computers in their classrooms.
3) Every classroom will be connected to the information superhighway.
4) Effective software and online learning resources will be an integral part of every school's curriculum.

Research continues to provide reasons that support the use of technology within school communities to enhance the academic performance of today's youth. Is also suggests that the amount of support teachers receive can affect the way they relate to problems when using technology (Bandura, 1986; Delongis, Coyne, Dakof, Folkman, & Lazarus, 1982). Preparing students for the workforce is an area where technology plays a pivotal role in reaching educational goals. When students learn to use applications, such as word processors, spreadsheets, and the Internet, they acquire some of the prerequisite skills for workforce preparedness (Cradler, 1994). However, learning how to use software is likely taught separately from lesson content. Often, the result is that students' exposure to technology is often split off from the rest of the curriculum and from the world beyond the classroom, where they will be expected to participate as productive citizens after they graduate (Brown, 2000; Maddux, Johnson, & Willis, 1997; PITAC, 1997; Valdez et al., 2000). Therefore, it is requisite that technology be integrated with curriculum goals, not taught as a separate entity. Using technology correctly will increase the teachers' ability to guide and inspire their students to learn throughout their school years and in their careers.

In order to significantly impact the professional development and education of teachers so that they are able to utilize the full potential of technology in the classroom, we must provide training on the integration and use of technology minimally in the areas of management, communication, and instruction. As schools continue to purchase more and better technology, the benefit to students and their learning will increasingly depend on how well teachers are prepared to use these new tools. A constructivist pedagogy combined with purposeful technology integration creates a rich learning environment for students (Grabinger, 1996). It is not the computer alone that will impact student learning, but a transformation in our way of thinking towards student-centered classrooms in which technology becomes something that students learn with and not from. Teachers cannot be intimidated to use technology in the classroom; they must embrace this paradigm shift in order to promote lifelong learning for themselves, as well as their students (Flake, 2001).

References

Angelo, J.M. (2002). Virginia district re-boots its iBook program. *District Administration, 38*, 20-21.

Anonymous. (2001). Electronic gradebook products change the way teachers do business in the classroom. *T.H.E. Journal, 29*, 72-74.

Brown, M. (2000). Cool science tools. *Technology & Learning, 20*, 18.

Cradler, J., McNabb, M., Freeman, M., & Burchett, R. (2002). How does technology influence student learning? *Learning and Leading with Technology, 29*, 46-52.

Dunn, L. (2001). Medill news service. *PC World.Com,* (July 11), 1.

Dunne, D. (2001). What is a PDA? *Darwin Magazine.* Retrieved from *www.darwinmag.com/learn/curve/column.html?ArticleID=56*

Eib, B.J. & Welton, F. (2004). Which educational technology is best for your school? *Principal Leadership, 4*, 56-58.

Flake, J.L. (2001). Teacher education and the World Wide Web. *Journal of Technology and Teacher Education, 9*, 43.

Gates, B. (1995). *The road ahead* (p. 74).

Grabinger, R.S. (1996). Rich environments for active learning. In D. Jonassen (Ed.), *Handbook of research for educational communications and technology* (pp. 665-692). New York: Simon & Schuster Macmillan.

Gray, D. (1999). The Internet in lifelong learning: Liberation or alienation? *International Journal of Lifelong Education (18)*2, 119-26.

Guskey, T. (2002). Computerized gradebooks and the myth of objectivity. *Phi Delta Kappa, 83*, 775-780.

Hargis, J. (2000). Electronic leaf project. *Science and Children, 37*, 20-23.

Hicks, S.J. & Young, B. (2001). The Internet academy and beyond. *Journal of Technology and Teacher Education, 9*, 63.

Huseth, M. (2001). The school-home connection. *Learning and Leading with Technology, 29*, 6.

Hyatt, K. & Sapone, S. (2002). *(T.E.A.M.S.) Teaming in elementary and middle schools.* Longmont, CO. Rocky Mountain Press.

Juniu, S. (2002). Implementing handheld computing technology in physical education. *JOPERD, 73*, 43-48.

Lindroth, L. (2004). Technology in your classroom. *Teaching K-8, 1,* 22-24.

McAnear, A. (2003). Help beyond the classroom. *Learning and Leading with Technology, 28*, 58.

Means, B. (1994). *Technology and education reform.* San Francisco: Jossey Bass.

Meyer, R. (2000). It takes a cybervillage. *School Library Journal*, 20-25.

Nelson, M.R. (2003). On tape or online. *Access Learning, 9*, 8-10.

National Center for Education Statistics. (2000). *Teachers' tools for the 21st centruy: A report on teachers' use of technology* (NCES 2000-102). Washington, DC: Department of Education. Retrieved January 2000 from *nces.ed.gov/pubsearch/pubsinfo.asp?pubid=2000102*

Nisan-Nelson, P.D. (2001). Technology integration: A case of professional development. *Journal of Technology and Teacher Education, 9*, 83.

Norby, S. (2003-2004). Hardwired into history. *Educational Leadership, 4*, 48-53.

Patterson, J.C. (2001). Kids on the run: Mobile technology. *Technology & Learning, 21*, 44.

Reese, J. (2003). A teacher's guide to using technolgy in the classroom. *Multimedia Schools, 10*, 44.

Salpeter, J. (2003). Web literacy and critical thinking: A teacher's tool kit. *Technology & Learning, 23*, 22-34.

Sologuk, S., Stammen, R., & Vetter, R. (2001). A collaborative approach for creating curriculum and instructional materials. *Journal of Technology and Teacher Education, 9*, 199.

Stanton, D. (1994). Gradebooks, the next generation. *Electronic Learning in your Classroom, 14*, 54-57.

Tapscott, D. (1998). *Growing up digital.* New York: McGraw-Hill.

U.S. Congress Office of Technology Assessment. (1995). *Teachers & technology: Making the connection.* OTA-EHR-616. Washington, DC: U.S. Government Printing Office (ED 386 155).

Viebranz, G. (2003). School-to-home collaboration tool makes education a team effort for Wisconsin district. *T.H.E. Journal, 31*, 16.

Chapter XII

Mentoring and Technology Integration for Teachers

Junko Yamamoto
Mt. Lebanon School District, USA

Mara Linaberger
Pittsburgh Public Schools, USA

Leighann S. Forbes
Slippery Rock University, USA

Abstract

This chapter addresses the acquisition of technology literacy skills through the use of a variety of mentoring programs for educators. A case is made for mentoring all individuals in an institution in order to improve the overall integration of technology in a variety of settings. The chapter also provides concrete examples of three models of technology mentoring: Technology Champions, Technology Collaborators, and Technology Cohorts. Characteristics of effective mentoring are discussed as well as future trends in mentoring through the use of online technologies. The authors believe that through coming to an understanding of the factors influencing implementation of mentoring plans and the benefits and drawbacks of several mentoring models, the reader will be able to select an appropriate mentoring model to meet organizational and individual training needs.

Introduction

Many of us remember a mentor who has touched our professional lives and the qualities that made the mentor great. This chapter examines mentoring, its value in technology instruction, and the elements key to choosing an appropriate mentoring model. It also describes models of mentoring and elements of successful mentoring programs. Additionally, the role of a mentor is defined and the need for mentoring as a supplement to other types of professional development programs is examined. Through building an understanding of the role of a mentor, the need for mentoring, and the importance of technology mentoring, the reader will be able to select a technology mentoring model that meets diverse needs. Three models for mentoring, *Technology Champions, Technology Collaborators*, and *Technology Cohorts*, are presented as well. Finally, future trends in mentoring are shared.

Current thinking on technology integration points out the need for personnel to have "...easy access to professionals with expertise in technology and pedagogy" (SouthEast Initiatives Regional Technology in Education Consortium, n.d.a, para. 21). On the surface it may seem as though the availability of a technical guru or curriculum expert would be sufficient to meet the need of individuals trying to integrate technology. Closer examination of the problem, however, reveals a greater benefit to implementing technology training through mentoring. Unlike the gurus and experts, a mentor is someone who is personally invested in the success of his or her protégé. By implementing a technology mentoring program, institutions can support the development of ongoing collaboration while also providing technical and instructional support.

A Definition of Mentorship

What is mentoring? For the purposes of this chapter, mentoring will be defined as a type of situated professional development in which an experienced individual (the mentor) guides an individual with less experience (the trainee or protégé). While often seen as a tool for initiating new employees, a more thorough definition of mentoring includes opportunities to improve the practice of experienced individuals as well.

Why Technology Mentorship?

One obvious reason for implementing mentoring is to address the differing levels of technology proficiency within an organization. The Apple Classroom of Tomorrow (ACOT) study (cited in SouthEast Initiatives Regional Technology in Education Consortium, n.d.b), identifies five stages of technology incorporation: entry, adoption, adaptation, appropriation, and invention. As individuals move through these stages at differing rates, organizations may need to address all five stages at the same time. In order to meet these diverse needs, professional development will have to be tailored to the learner's stage of instructional evolution (Maney, 2000).

Not only does technology mentoring help to address multiple stages, it can also increase the use of technology in an organization. According to a study conducted by the Mid-Atlantic Regional Technology Education Consortium (MARTEC), "...mentoring and coaching is an ongoing process that goes much further to increase teachers' use of technology by showing a higher retention of knowledge among teachers" (2001, para. 1). Mentoring can increase training time and appropriate use of technology, thereby increasing student success and further motivating teachers to continue learning to integrate technology into instruction.

Adult learners learn best when training acknowledges their experience and is project based (Knowles, 1984). Educators frequently learn to use technology at their own pace in conjunction with classroom-based needs. To address these instructional needs of teachers, mentoring must focus not on technical how-to, but rather on strengthening instruction through the use of technology. Mentoring allows this training to be tailor-made for the content area and the teaching style of each individual. For these reasons, mentoring is an ideal match for training in educational technology.

Unfortunately, not all schools have flexible technology training for employees. Tarleton (2001), for example, indicates that most technology training for teachers tends to be "one-shot group workshops...in the areas of basic computer operation or use of a specific software program" (p.26). Such training may be a starting point for trainees who are new to a piece of hardware or software, but ongoing and flexible learner-centered training must not be neglected. Technology mentoring can help to meet this need.

Mentoring Models

Providing flexible training can be a daunting task for any organization. Choosing a mentoring model that meets the needs of the organization is crucial to the success of any technology training initiative. The following examples illustrate three potential models for mentoring: *Technology Champions*, *Technology Collaborators*, and *Technology Cohorts*. Using their general frameworks, finding an appropriate way to introduce technology mentoring into a new or existing professional development program should seem less daunting.

Technology Champions

The University of Michigan Business School defines information *Technology Champions* as "faculty members who strive to have a significant impact by creatively using technology to support teaching, learning or research" (2003, para. 1). For our purposes, a *Technology Champion* integrates technologies into teaching and is willing to assist colleagues on an as-needed basis.

A more formal example of the *Technology Champion* model is a university setting in which Computer-Assisted Language Learning (CALL) workshops for the instructors were initiated. Language instructors across the university chose specific sessions they were interested in attending. Instructors who needed further assistance called, asked questions via e-mail, or visited the language media center director, who was serving as their mentor. This director also offered similar educational opportunities to local K-12 language teachers via in-service training and a Multimedia in Language Teaching Workshop.

As these protégé-instructors in K-12 and higher education started to use technology in their classrooms, opportunities for professional interaction through a multimedia showcase were created. The protégé-instructors brought their completed projects to such events, and explained how they were used to support lesson objectives.

In a more informal example of the *Technology Champions* model, a high school teacher with years of teaching experience but little technology know-how wanted to incorporate technology into her teaching. She approached a teacher in the same department who felt comfortable with technology and requested weekly training sessions.

They covered a variety of topics associated with Microsoft Word, including a mini-lesson on copyright laws when the protégé learned to insert images harvested from the Internet into her documents. The pair also completed Web-based projects. The mentoring relationship continued to evolve as the protégé expressed the types of activities she wanted to do in class.

The main benefit of the *Technology Champions* model is the individualized attention afforded in the relationship. Protégés choose topics and create materials that are immediately useful in their classroom. In addition, the mentor-protégé pair agrees on the focus of the tailor-made training. This, in return, increases interest as well as the retention of knowledge and skills. Finally, mentors model appropriate use of technology, emphasize the role of pedagogy, and provide ongoing support and feedback.

Among the drawbacks of the *Technology Champion* approach is the lack of a requirement to use technology. Implementing this model often addresses only those individuals with a desire to integrate technology, not an entire staff. In addition, training is mainly based on the protégé's needs, so the training may take a back seat to other work when a protégé or mentor becomes busy. Because mentors often do not receive formal training, the quality of mentors may vary in this model. Finally, according to Rowley (1999), there is a relationship between compensation and commitment. In this model, release time or financial reward may not be available to the mentor or protégé, thus impacting its success.

Technology Collaborators

The *Technology Collaborators* model recruits teachers or workers who have demonstrated facility or expertise with technology to work with and mentor colleagues. Rather than using these "experts" as technology teachers or technology support, they work with a number of staff members in a facilitative manner. *Technology Collaborators* are expected to mentor protégés in a more formalized manner. One *Technology Collaborator* may have multiple protégés with whom teaching or work-based duties are shared.

Collaborative planning and sharing of instructional duties requires the roles of mentors and protégés to be clearly defined and communicated before implementing the model.

In one case, two elementary school *Technology Champions* became *Technology Collaborators* when they were given teaching schedules that included collaborative teaching periods. In addition to teaching side-by-side in a computer lab with their protégés, these *Technology Collaborators* had common planning time with these co-teachers. These collaborative teams determined the content and activities to be addressed with technology. Initially, the *Technology Collaborator* mentors created the activities; however, as the novice teacher-trainees grew in their ability, they created technology lessons independently.

When the novice teachers taught their classes, the *Technology Collaborators* were present. At first the mentors served as leaders in these instructional situations. They modeled effective techniques and strategies for utilizing technology. As time passed, the mentors stepped back and allowed their protégés to take on a more dynamic role.

Benefits of the *Technology Collaborators* model are that it acknowledges and capitalizes upon the technology expertise of available personnel. In this model, one staff member may mentor several individuals. Those familiar with technology share their knowledge with others, building a strong sense of community. This model saves on funding for training and provides for staff learning during normal work hours.

The major drawbacks to the *Technology Collaborators* model lie in planning and implementation. Without adequate articulation of roles prior to the launch of such a model, the protégés may not fully comprehend the need to actively participate in the learning situations that the *Technology Collaborator* (mentor) provides. Trainees may believe the mentor will always be there to help them to plan and remedy things, and thus choose to take a passive role in their own learning. To implement this model, instructional duties and schedules must be revised to allow the mentor to become an effective guide-by-the-side. In the end, *Technology Collaborators* can only be effective if stakeholders believe in its ability to transform all members' technology skills.

Technology Cohorts

The *Technology Cohort* model is another formal model that addresses the needs of many individuals. *Technology Cohorts* use recognized instructional technology leaders as mentors to a cohort of experienced teachers. In this model, the cohort is composed of teachers already recognized as strong instructors. *Technology Cohorts* are framed around attending a series of training sessions. The training sessions are spaced out over several months and provide information and practice with hardware, software, and best practice to enable teachers to integrate technology into instruction.

In one example of a *Technology Cohort*, "...teachers were trained in the use of the Internet, electronic mail, presentation packages, desktop publishing, database, spreadsheet, and digital photography, as well as in use of the scanner and its associated software" (*Case Studies...*, 1999) Each teacher (protégé) took the information and skills from the trainings and applied them to a personal project. The goal of the project was to integrate technology into instruction through the use of both formal and informal methods. Formal mentoring existed in this model, as the mentors were available to answer both instructional and technical questions on an on-call basis. Informal mentoring existed in this model as the participants developed their own support network. The collaboration, excitement, and desire to learn often led the protégés in this model to become *Technology Champions* in their own workplaces.

The benefits of using *Technology Cohorts* are easy to see. Many individuals are able to receive training and support at the same time. Allowing participants to develop their own project ensures the authentic use of the training, while ongoing support and networking allows protégé-teachers to relax and try something new. Protégés who lack confidence in integrating technology progress into advanced stages of technology use resulting in a more learner-centered environment (SouthEast Initiatives Regional Technology in Education Consortium, n.d.b).

While the *Technology Cohorts* model is a powerful mentoring tool, drawbacks exist that may prohibit its use. First, a cadre of knowledgeable and skilled trainers must be assembled and be made available to provide technical and instructional support to the participants. Second, entities must be able to release both the mentors and protégés for not only multiple trainings, but for follow-up meetings and consultations as well. The time and money spent on the cohort approach can be quite substantial.

Characteristics of Effective Mentoring

While each of the preceding models addresses different needs, they are all built upon common characteristics necessary for successful mentoring. In an effective mentoring program, all of the following characteristics should be present:

- *Roles are clearly articulated:* An expectation that the protégé will become an independent practitioner must be communicated. Ideally, all stakeholders will participate in the planning process and develop a common understanding about roles and responsibilities.
- *Ownership is promoted in protégés:* Mentors must first listen to ideas about the types of activities the protégé wants to create. Putting those wants and needs in the center of the training promotes motivation.
- *Clear instructional goals are set:* Attention to pedagogy is important. Instructional objectives, assessment criteria, and instructional procedures should be clearly defined so they will not be overlooked as a protégé becomes occupied with the actual use of technology.
- *Training is project-based and hands-on:* Creating products, lessons, or units that protégés can use right away will make learning meaningful.

- *Sharing of ideas is encouraged:* Mentors should provide opportunities for protégés to exchange ideas through workshops or showcases. This will give the protégés a chance to share their achievements with colleagues.
- *Ethical use of technology is promoted:* Mentors must model the ethical use of technology and teach protégés how to keep themselves abreast of relevant changes in copyright laws and guidelines.
- *Feedback is offered:* Mentors must create a cycle that encourages feedback on technology-based lessons in a timely manner.
- *Professional goals are modeled:* Finally, as noted in Rowley (1999), good mentors must consistently model a commitment to continuous learning.

Even with all of these characteristics present in both the mentor and the protégé, mentoring may still fail if not supported by the administrative leadership. To provide an environment in which mentoring can be effective, leaders must provide mentors and protégés with both technical support and instructional support (Cooley & Johnston, 2001). Support must be continuous and may include such things as equipment for the mentoring project, reimbursement or release time for mentoring meetings, and a limit on the number of protégés per mentor (MARTEC, 2001). The International Society for Technology in Education's Educational Computing and Technology Standards for Technology Facilitation (2001) provides excellent guidelines that can easily be tailored for mentoring in a variety of institutional structures.

Future Trends

According to Cetron and Cetron (2004), federal and state funding for school districts is on the decline. This undoubtedly puts pressure on schools to cut expenses. Mentoring, while valuable, is not a highly visible activity and may be at risk during cost-cutting. The use of online mentors is one potential area for cost savings. Web-based mentoring can include listservs, peer-mentoring via formal online courses, and professional development Web sites. Even though online mentoring can be seen as a cost-saving solution, it should not be used as a replacement for face-to-face mentoring opportunities. Face-to-face and online models should co-exist to serve the diverse needs of learners.

Mentoring and Listservs

An informal online mentoring situation, a *listserv* is an "online support group" in which participants post questions and responses. Participants subscribe to a listserv at no cost and receive postings from members as e-mail messages. Listservs frequently have postings about professional conferences and calls for papers for publications.

Mentoring in Formal Online Learning

A wide variety of Internet-based distance education programs are currently available worldwide, and many of these online learning programs include a mentoring component. Today's distance education student may be formally or informally mentored by faculty, staff, classmates, or leaders from industry.

Duquesne University's Educational Doctorate program in Instructional Technology (EdDIT) provides its candidates with numerous opportunities to mentor and be mentored. The EdDIT program employs a dual *Technology Cohort* and *Technology Collaborator* model. Faculty mentors, acting as *Technology Collaborators*, provide guidance through regular e-mail correspondence. Students, members of a *Technology Cohort,* often mentor one another through weekly synchronous chats, e-mails, phone calls, and one-on-one meetings.

Mentoring in "Online Communities"

A third online mentoring resource is a professional development site such as Tapped In (ti2.sri.com/tappedin/). According to the Tapped In vision statement:

> *"The increasing demand for continuous professional development means that providers must expand face-to-face programs to include online activities and content that engage teachers anytime, anywhere. The growing recognition that no single organization can satisfy teachers' ongoing professional development needs requires that educators and providers form communities to share strategies, resources, and support." (SRI International, n.d.)*

Tapped In provides teachers with the means to develop their own mentoring strategy on an as-needed basis.

Developed in 1997, Tapped In is an online meeting place that aims to meet this challenge. Much more than just a listserv discussion, Tapped In also incorporates live chats, professional development workshops, and collaborative projects. At Tapped In, individuals can find a mentor and/or be a mentor on their own time, free of cost. Students and colleagues alike can join and use the resources available on the virtual campus. With so many options, online professional development sites like Tapped In are basically mentoring a la carte!

Conclusion

Mentoring improves organizations by addressing the diverse training needs of individuals. Organizations should evaluate the needs and dynamics of their own institution to identify, modify, and implement a suitable mentoring model. The models presented in this chapter, *Technology Champions*, *Technology Collaborators*, and *Technology Cohorts,* are a sampling of the many technology-based models that exist.

Different learning styles and curriculum objectives within any given institution beg the use of mentors. Although no secret formula exists for selecting a mentoring model for an institution or individual, characteristics common to successful mentoring have been identified. Good mentors plan for mentoring, offer instructional feedback, and model continuing professional growth (Rowley, 1999). Mentoring is most effective when it is custom designed to meet the needs of the participants, occurs on an as-needed basis, and is individualized. Mentoring, whether it occurs in the traditional face-to-face format or in an online setting, allows personnel to improve skills and continuously develop.

According to the How People Learn Framework, teachers learn through many experiences, including their own practice, interactions with others, specific training, degree programs, and experience outside the classroom (Bransford, Brown, & Cocking, 2000). Thus, mentoring must be offered in concert with other professional development opportunities. "When offered in tandem with traditional methods of professional development, mentoring reinforces the material covered in workshops, incorporates knowledge, and creates more motivation to follow up on the part of both the teacher and the mentor" (MARTEC, 2001, para. 3).

Keeping in mind the expectation that participants will continue to grow, the mentoring model best suited for an organization will "...differ, depending upon the existing resources (human and technological) at a site, the visions the sites have developed for how technologies are to be used and what problems they can address, and the leadership and support that are available to meet those goals" (Cooley & Johnson, 2001, p. 74). Prior to choosing a mentoring model, organizations must consider the benefits and drawbacks of the models presented in this chapter, as well as the resources, vision, leadership, and support available for implementation. A model that supports the goal of ongoing growth can then be chosen with confidence.

References

Bransford, J.D., Brown, A.L., & Cocking, R.R. (Eds.). (2000). *How people learn: Brain, mind, experience, and school* (Expanded ed.). Washington, DC: National Academy Press.

Case Studies: Northwest Tri-County Intermediate Unit. (1999). Retrieved November 23, 2003, from *www2.sis.pitt.edu/~etia2/case_studies/nw/nw_5.htm*

Cetron, M. & Cetron, K. (2004). A forecast for schools. *Educational Leadership, 61*(4), 22-29.

Cooley, N. & Johnston, M. (2001). *Supporting new models of teaching and learning through technology.* Arlington, VA: Educational Research Service.

International Society for Technology in Education. (2001). *Educational computing and technology programs: Technology facilitation initial endorsement.* Retrieved February 14, 2004, from *cnets.iste.org/ncate/n_fac-stands.html*

Knowles, M.S. (1984). *Andragogy in action: Applying modern principles of adult learning* (1st ed.). College Park, MD: Jossey-Bass.

Maney, K. (2000). *Professional development and evaluation criteria for ACOT model of instructional evolution.* Retrieved January 26, 2004, from *www.osn.state.oh.us/stateconf2001/archive/handouts/maney3.pdf*

Mid-Atlantic Regional Technology Education Consortium. (2001). *Mentoring for effective technology integration in K-12 schools: What works?* Retrieved February 8, 2004, from *www.temple.edu/martec/techmentors/mentoring_vs_workshops/index.html*

Rowley, J.B. (1999). The good mentor. *Educational Leadership, 56*(8), 20-22. Retrieved January 20, 2004, from *www.ascd.org/cms/objectlib/ascdframeset/index.cfm?publication=http://www.ascd.org/ed_topics/el199905_rowley.html*

SouthEast Initiatives Regional Technology in Education Consortium. (n.d.a). *Factors that affect the effective use of technology for teaching and learning.* Retrieved January 20, 2004, from *www.seirtec.org/publications/lessondoc.html*

SouthEast Initiatives Regional Technology in Education Consortium. (n.d.b). *Promising practices in technology: Recognizing and supporting teaching with technology.* Retrieved November 19, 2003, from *www.seirtec.org/ACOTstages.html*

SRI International. (n.d.). *About Tapped In.* Retrieved January 20, 2004, from *ti2.sri.com/tappedin/Web/about.jsp*

Tarleton, B. (2001). Teachers and computers: Are teachers up to speed? *Tech Directions, 61*(1), 24-26.

University of Michigan Business School. (2003). *Introducing: Information technology champions.* Retrieved February 6, 2004, from *www.bus.umich.edu/NewsRoom/ArticleDisplay.asp?news_id=1352*

Endnote

The authors would like to thank Jeanette Clement, Marie Martin, and Nicole Roth for their review of the initial manuscript and suggestions for revision.

Chapter XIII

Information Systems Education for the 21st Century: Aligning Curriculum Content and Delivery with the Professional Workplace

Glenn Lowry
United Arab Emirates University, UAE

Rodney Turner
Victoria University, Australia

Abstract

In this chapter, we consider how information systems educators might revise curriculum content and adopt student-centered/active learning pedagogical approaches to achieve a better fit between the workplace and the university 'studyplace'. In considering ***What to Study****, numerous research findings suggest a repertoire of 'soft' skills that are seen as essential to success for new IS professionals. The research findings discussed in this chapter present evidence that traditional business subjects such as Marketing, Economics, or Finance do not equate to the 'other' or soft business skills that employers of IS graduates are seeking in new hires. Soft skills are cultivated elements of professionalism that derive from example, reflection, imitation, and refinement of attitudes, personal capabilities, work habits, and interpersonal skills. Soft skills are* *seldom taught in dedicated subjects in tertiary information systems curricula. Somehow, the soft areas such as teamwork, communication skills, ability to accept direction, and others are expected to be* picked up *along the way through an unspecified, osmotic process. Turning to* ***How to Study****, a critical and contentious issue is determining the appropriate learning environment to best help new graduates develop soft skills and higher order thinking. Course delivery paradigms may be characterized as traditional, passive 'teacher-centered learning' and active 'student-centered learning'. We argue that student-centered/active learning approaches may be more effective in helping students to cultivate and refine soft skills than those currently in use. The chapter concludes with a discussion of IS curriculum reform issues and strategies for reducing confusion, overcoming tradition and inertia, finding resources, and neutralizing vested interests, to meet the educational needs of students.*

Note: The term information systems will be used to mean management information systems, business information systems, and informatics throughout this chapter.

Introduction

Information systems professionals contribute to the achievement of business and organizational goals through the use of information technology. The information systems profession is team-oriented and project-based.

Students are first and foremost concerned with future employability. Employers, on the other hand, often indicate that they want new graduates who can be immediately productive in their environment.

Are the aspirations of students and employers fundamentally incompatible? How can IS educators help to find a workable and satisfying balance?

In the sections that follow, we will consider how information systems educators might modify curriculum content and pedagogical approach to achieve a better fit between the workplace and the university 'studyplace'.

Education for Yesterday's Workplace: Why We Must Rethink Curriculum Content and Delivery Methods

The authors began their careers in the 1960s, before the development of the IS profession. As young academics, our students typically studied computing in science faculties, often in mathematics and computer systems engineering departments. Curriculum content consisted of a mixture of mathematics, such as discreet mathematics and numerical analysis, of computer science focused on the properties and (mostly) limitations of the hardware of the day, and first-, second-, and third-generation *high-level* procedural programming languages. We recall students whose professional preparation consisted of the ability to build machines and to program in eight or ten languages, such as machine language, Assembly language, Algol, FORTRAN, and COBOL. After several years service as a journeyman programmer, the more 'people-oriented' programmers became *systems analysts*. Systems analysts were very experienced programmers who had an interest in clients and their needs, who understood the need for information systems to contribute to organizational goals. A great deal has changed, yet tertiary curricula and delivery methods have changed more slowly in content and delivery than the needs of the professional workplace.

Universities have rapidly begun to lose their short-lived and always shaky monopoly on professional entry into information systems careers. A growing number of aspiring young IT professionals are selecting certification by software vendors over university study as a means of preparation and career entry. After one year of focused technical study, followed by an inexpensive, independent examination, many newly certified vendor-trained *solution developers*, *systems administrators*, and *Web site developers* command salaries and working conditions equal to or often superior to new information systems graduates.

The critical question facing information systems educators in the new century is, surely:

> *"How can university information systems courses add enough value to students that they will choose to study in higher education for a full university degree rather than opt for a one-year certification course leading to a similar economic and status outcomes in the short term?"*

What to Study? Balancing 'Hard' and 'Soft' in the IS Curriculum

It is true that the preparation of IS professionals must encompass a body of knowledge and a repertoire of technical skills identified by various professional bodies (Cheney, Hale, & Kasper, 1990; Davis, Gorgone, Feinstein, & Longenecker, 1997; Gorgone & Gray, 1999; Underwood, 1997; Lidtke, Stokes, Haines, & Mulder, 1999; Cohen, 2000; Mulder & van Weert, 2000; ACM-AIS, 2002).

Until recently, assessment of the degree of alignment of IS curricula with the models of the various professional bodies has been mainly accomplished through qualitative means during accreditation-linked self-study and site visitations. Snoke and Underwood (2002) have developed a practical and replicable empirical methodology for determining the coverage of core capabilities by various information systems curricula.

The persistent research finding that employers want graduates who possess better business skills is often interpreted by academics to mean that more traditional, formal business subjects such as Accounting, Economics, Business Finance, and Marketing should be taught alongside traditional technical or 'hard' skill subjects such as systems analysis/design and programming in particular languages (Trauth, Farwell, & Lee, 1993; Van Slyke, Kittner, & Cheney, 1997). Somehow the other 'soft' areas such as teamwork, communication skills, ability to accept direction, and others are 'picked up' through an unspecified, osmotic process.

Studies conducted in other practice-oriented business disciplines such as Accounting (Stewart, 1997) have indicated that students may not fully appreciate the importance of non-technical skills sought by prospective employers.

Several writers, including Ang (1992), Ang and Jiwahhasuchin (1998), and Young and Keen (1997), have noted the long-term shift from programming and other technical subjects to business analysis and people-oriented skills in IS curricula and in employer requirements expressed in recruiting advertisements over the past two decades. Ashley and Padgett (1997) reported results of a 1996 study of the evaluation of the IS curriculum by IS graduates. The study covered business and non-business courses along with traditional IS courses and compared results with a similar study in 1990 (Beise, Padgett, & Ganoe, 1991).

Some of the results appear to go against conventional wisdom. In the non-business area, foreign languages rated quite poorly in both periods. In their business courses, Introduction to Information Systems and Business Communication rated highly, but core business subjects such as Economics, Business Law, Statistics, Quantitative Methods, and even Accounting rated below the average. Predictably, the IS courses such as "Systems Analysis & Design" rated highly, whereas COBOL was becoming less important, and procedural languages such as Pascal, ADA, and BASIC were rated low, but with little change between 1990 and 1996. Lu and Wang (1998-1999) investigated the skills and knowledge needs of IS graduates in Hong Kong. Respondents were mainly mid-level managers, with a smaller proportion of IS professionals. They found communication skills, management issues, and project management skills were among the more desirable; technical skills sought included programming, systems analysis and design, data communications, and database. They also noted a relative lack of possessed skills in all IS core areas. A number of recommendations were proffered to address the problem including the adoption of the IS curriculum model with modification to suit local Hong Kong needs.

Athey and Plotnicki (1998) investigated the changing skill requirements in the IS fields. They found that while there was a reduction of demand in some areas such as COBOL, none had completely disappeared and the levels of demand varied across different parts of the USA. They noticed a strong growth in Internet technologies and client-server technologies, suggesting that any IS program lacking these components would be failing the student.

Khalil, Strong, Kahn, and Pipino (1999) presented a framework of competencies for IS curriculum inclusion. They identify a mismatch between the needs of organizations for delivering high-quality information-to-information consumers and what graduating IS professionals are equipped with. They suggest substantial curriculum changes in respect to skills in information quality (IQ) necessitating the re-education of educators.

Wong (1996) noted the need for IS people who are experts in areas of IT and IS; those who realize the importance of business functions and understand how to fit IT and IS into a business, helping it to gain strategic advantages over its competitors. Westfall (1999-2000) noted that there is a need to address the IT technology-related or hard skills, and interpersonal/management or soft skills in the IT curriculum. He proposes a 'learning needs model' to address some of the problems associated with keeping up to date with developments in the rapidly changing field.

The past few decades have been characterized by a rapidly and constantly changing business environment. Lee, Trauth, and Farwell (1995) argued that technological and sociological developments facilitated by evolving information technology and changing business needs has made it necessary for IS professionals to develop a wider range of non-technical skills than was previously the case. Similar views have been expressed by many others, including Burn, Ng Tye, and Ma (1995), Cafasso (1996), Lowry, Morgan, and FitzGerald (1996), Main (1995), and Morgan, Lowry, and FitzGerald, (1998). Competition for the best entry positions has been heightened by IS outsourcing (Slaughter & Ang, 1996). Students have become more aware of the need to insure that they develop "career resilience" (Waterman, Waterman, & Collard, 1994) to prepare themselves to manage their own careers through regular self-evaluation and ongoing, self-initiated training and skills development.

Gupta and Wachter (1998) saw a need for IS students to develop skills and abilities in various areas, including teamwork, creativity, and communication, and proposed a capstone course to achieve these aims. Kakabadse and Korac-Kakabadse (2000) highlight the changing role of the IS/IT professional and identified skills and competencies required for development in the early twenty-first century.

Identifying the skills sought by employers of new IS graduates is critical for educators in designing curricula and advising students. Van Slyke et al. (1997) found that specific technical skills were less important than basic technical skills and non-academic skills. In a study across various IS job classifications, Doke and Williams (1999) found that systems development skills and interpersonal skills were common across classifications, but programming skills were more important for entry-level IS positions. Similar results were obtained by Turner and Lowry (1999a) in a pilot study of 102 students and 54 employers of IS graduates. An earlier study by McLean, Tanner, and Smits (1991) found that employers believed that staff are motivated primarily by "hygiene factors" such as income, security, and other material components that in and of themselves cannot produce job satisfaction, but without which job satisfaction cannot occur (Herzberg, 1968). Wrycza, Usowicz, Gabor, and Verber (1999) found that knowledge and skills needed for work in small businesses is different from that required for larger enterprises. They also found that contemporary firms had a stronger need for IS specialists than they did for computer programmers.

The findings reported in this chapter present a snapshot of some of the evidence that 'business subjects' such as those comprising many undergraduate business or commerce courses do not equate to the business skills that employers of IS graduates are seeking in new hires. The work presented here is part of an ongoing research program that investigates the views of other major stakeholders including employers, currently enrolled students, and academics (Turner & Lowry, 1999b, 2000, 2001, 2002a, 2002b, 2003, 2004).

We argue that IS practitioners, employers, and students see little value in some of the more formal business subject areas that often form the core of an IS degree offered in a business or commerce faculty. These stakeholder groups see more value in the development of soft skills useful in client interaction. The findings have serious implications for IS educators and IS curriculum design.

Importance of Non-Technical Business Subjects in the IS Curriculum

In a previous study of the content of information system curricula, the authors (Turner & Lowry, 1999b) began to suspect that the "other business skills" desired of new IS graduates were not synonymous with traditional business curriculum subjects. The results indicated that of nine business subjects that are typically included in IS curricula, only three—Accounting, Business Ethics, and Management—were judged to be important by students and employers.

Students and employers were asked to indicate what they considered to be the most and least important non-information systems subjects. Their responses are shown in percentages in Table 1. Nine subjects were evaluated by students and employers as "Most Important" in the three columns to the left, and as "Least Important" in the three right-hand columns. For convenience, the superscripted numbers in parenthesis indicate the first, second, and third most and least important subjects, from student and employer perspectives.

There is a surprising level of agreement between students and employers. Assessments of "Most Important" subjects differ only in the rank order, with students viewing Management as most important, Accounting as second most important, and Business

Table 1. Perceived importance of non-technical business subjects

Most Important	student	employer	Least Important	student	employer
Accounting	(2) 13.5	(1) 21.3	Accounting	9.9	1.9
Business finance	6.6	11.6	Business finance	(2) 13.5	6.4
Business ethics	(3) 12.5	(3) 14.8	Business ethics	11.6	7.1
Business law	8.3	4.5	Business law	9.2	(3) 14.1
Business statistics	6.9	9.0	Business statistics	11.2	12.2
Economics	5.6	2.6	Economics	(3) 12.5	(2) 16.0
Foreign language(s)	7.6	3.2	Foreign language(s)	(1) 14.2	(1) 23.1
Management	(1) 24.1	(2) 17.4	Management	3.3	3.2
Marketing	10.9	10.3	Marketing	10.2	9.6

Ethics as third. Employers ranked them as Accounting, Management, and Business Ethics. There was less agreement regarding least important non-information systems subjects, with students rating Foreign Languages first, Economics second, and Business Law third.

These results suggest that employers and students share some degree of agreement regarding the relative importance of non-IS business subjects. The results have interesting implications for tertiary educators. Clearly, students should be advised to include study of Management, Accounting, and Business Ethics in their courses. Unless there is some compelling reason to include further non-IS business subjects, such as fulfilling the requirements for a second major or a dual qualification, study toward acquisition of soft skills may be a better choice for students than additional non-IS subjects.

Methodology of the 2001-2002 Follow-Up Study

A follow-up study to further explore the "other business skills" aspect of the IS curriculum was conducted in 2001. A multipart questionnaire was devised that solicited views on the importance of formal business subjects and soft skills that may be found in the curriculum of many IS degrees. Demographic data were also gathered.

Web-based survey distribution was used. Mehta and Sivadas (1995) demonstrated that e-mail-based surveys generated response rates comparable to those of postal surveys, but significantly faster, at lower cost, and of a higher quality. On the other hand, Tse et al. (1995), in an internal survey of Hong Kong University staff, experienced a much lower return rate for e-mail surveys (6%) compared with conventional mail (27%) that they attribute to the possibility of participant identification with e-mail. Comley (1996) found comparable response rates from the two methods. Comley also indicated that electronic data collection methods are often self-selecting due to recipients irregularly checking e-mail messages and that they consequently have the potential to introduce bias. Although this is a problem for representative samples, it is less of a problem for targeted groups as in the present study.

The questionnaire was set up using Microsoft FrontPage 2000. Data were captured using Microsoft Access 2000. Electronic surveys have the advantage of being pre-coded and free of ambiguity of response in that only one response per item can be selected. They have the disadvantage that they risk missing those who do not have access to computers and the Web. This was not seen to be a problem for the group being surveyed.

During the first half of 2001, invitations to participate were sent by e-mail to 1,008 IS professionals throughout Australia who had attended job fairs in the previous 12 months. Twenty-eight unusable responses were eliminated from the analysis. A total of 136 usable replies were received, representing an overall response rate of 13.5%—acceptable for unsolicited surveys of this type, but lower than hoped. Analysis of the data was carried out using SPSS R10. A similar questionnaire was also sent to 2,000 IS decision makers. A total of 137 usable returns were received along with 241 failed deliveries giving a 7.8% effective return.

Respondent Level of People Contact

Respondents were classified into one of two groups depending on the perceived level of 'people contact' they normally encounter in their job, shown in Table 2.

A review of Table 2 indicates that roles involving higher contact with people account for 56% of the responses, with roles involving lower personal contact with users at 44%. As the Web Development role is arguably a role involving higher client contact, the percentage of roles involving lower people contact would decline to only 35%, with those requiring higher contact growing to 64%. Either view is consistent with the view expressed by Ang (1992) that the importance of technology-oriented roles would decline, while roles involving client interaction would grow in importance, a view supported by the data in Table 1.

Respondent Organizational Level

Table 3 shows the position occupied by the IT/IS respondent from the employer group. The job titles represented in Table 3 indicate that the majority of respondents were in a position to either appoint or direct the activities of IS staff.

Table 2. Principal work function and level of respondent people contact

	Frequency	Lower People Contact %	Higher People Contact %
Lower People Contact Roles			
Applications Programming	34	25.0%	
Web development	12	8.8%	
Systems programming	4	2.9%	
Network administration	10	7.4%	
Higher People Contact Roles			
System support	32		23.5%
Project administration	13		9.6%
IT sales	2		1.5%
IT staff supervision	6		4.4%
Education / training	5		3.7%
Recruiting / staff placement	2		1.5%
Consulting	16		11.8
Total	**136**	**44 %**	**56%**

Table 3. Organizational level of respondents

Function	Number of responses	Percent
IT / IS / Computing manager	108	78.3
CIO / Chief Information Officer	9	6.5
IT Consultant	5	3.6
IT / IS Team Leader	4	2.9
Not identified	3	2.2
Manager, recruiting & personnel	2	1.4
Project Manager	2	1.4
Personnel Consultant	2	1.4
Recruitment Officer	2	1.4
Company Secretary/ Finance Manager	1	0.7
Total	**138**	**100**

Ranking Academic Subjects

The instrument contained two sections pertaining to academic preparation of graduates. These two sections separately covered the technical areas of an IS business degree and the other academic areas that are not specific to IS. A seven-point Likert scale (1 = irrelevant through to 7 = essential) was used to measure the response for each question. For each group mentioned above, the mean and standard deviation for each question was computed, as shown in Table 4.

Table 4 shows the respondents' views of the importance of academic subjects. The data clearly indicate that core business subjects such as Accounting [3.98 (lower), 4.25 (higher)], Economics [3.38 (l), 3.83(h)], Law [3.62 (l), 4.42 (h)], and Statistics [4.00 (l), 4.32 (h)] rate rather low in importance among practicing IS professionals. With a score of "4" being the mid-range and representing a neutral response, these *core* business subjects are seen as less important by practitioners in the discipline of IS.

Management [5.43 (l), 5.63 (h)], Ethics [4.85 (l), 5.24 (h)], and Organizational Behavior [4.68 (l), 5.08 (h)] rate closer to "5" or higher, indicating these are somewhat more important—especially Management, which rates in the Fairly Important to Very Important range. In all cases, respondents in higher people contact roles rated these areas as more important than did those in positions that involve lower people contact. Overall, these results are unexpected given the popular claims that IS graduates need more understanding about business. Communications and Report Writing, often regarded more as a soft skill rather than an academic discipline in its own right, was rated the most important [5.82 (l), 6.18 (h)] of the academic areas, supporting many anecdotal reports that

Table 4. Comparative importance of academic subjects (n=136)

	Low (l)	High (h)	
Subject	**mean (σ)**	**mean (σ)**	
Communications & Report Writing	5.82 (1.27)	6.18 (0.81)	
Analysis & Design	5.82 (1.16)	5.91 (1.05)	
Database design	5.65 (1.27)	5.47 (1.24)	
Business Applications	5.62 (1.04)	5.68 (1.17)	
Client server applications	5.60 (0.99)	5.72 (0.86)	
Use operating systems	5.52 (1.03)	5.66 (1.15)	
Apply OOPs	5.45 (1.03)	5.12 (1.39)	
Management	5.43 (1.11)	5.63 (0.96)	
Knowledge of PC apps	5.40 (1.21)	5.46 (1.24)	
E-Commerce/E-business development	5.23 (1.44)	5.41 (1.04)	
Project Management	5.10 (1.07)	5.70 (1.17)	*
Web design/development	5.05 (1.71)	4.88 (1.39)	
LAN & Data Communications	5.02 (1.27)	5.38 (1.25)	
Large System experience	4.92 (1.23)	5.28 (1.15)	
Apply 3GLs	4.87 (1.31)	4.57 (1.47)	
Business Ethics	4.85 (1.68)	5.24 (1.48)	
Data mining/Data warehousing	4.78 (1.38)	4.74 (1.35)	
Organizational Behavior	4.68 (1.42)	5.08 (1.38)	
Mathematical Modeling	4.38 (1.40)	4.14 (1.48)	
CASE applications	4.38 (1.11)	4.61 (1.47)	
ERP implementations & operations	4.32 (1.31)	4.61 (1.45)	
Knowledge base/Expert systems	4.25 (1.48)	4.67 (1.35)	
Operations Research	4.22 (1.15)	4.34 (1.35)	
Marketing	4.18 (1.64)	4.47 (1.41)	
Business Finance	4.10 (1.50)	4.46 (1.48)	
Business Statistics	4.00 (1.43)	4.32 (1.38)	
International Business	3.98 (1.66)	4.43 (1.51)	
Accounting	3.98 (1.51)	4.25 (1.58)	
Psychology	3.63 (1.73)	3.75 (1.79)	
Business or Commercial Law	3.62 (1.54)	4.42 (1.48)	*
Economics	3.38 (1.50)	3.83 (1.48)	
Foreign Languages	2.78 (1.83)	3.45 (1.68)	*
n =	**60**	**76**	
* significantly different at 0.05% level			

employers value and seek these skills. It should also be noted that a subject entitled "Communications & Report Writing" has been included in some business degree programs in the past.

Of the academic disciplines covered in the survey, only three were significantly different at the 0.05% level. These were Project Management, Business or Commercial Law, and Foreign Languages. Not surprisingly the "higher people contact" group rated these areas as significantly more important than other groups.

Even for respondents in low client contact roles, only 13 roles achieved a rating of 5.0 or more, with 19 roles rated at between 4.92 and 2.78 on the seven-point Likert scale. Respondents in high client contact roles rated 15 roles above 5.0, with 17 roles failing to achieve a rating above 4.88.

Some of the subjects that failed to achieve a rating of 5.0 included technical areas such as Large System Experience, Data Mining/Data Warehousing, Applying 3GLs, CASE Applications, ERP Implementations & Operations, and Knowledge Base/Expert Systems. Clearly, the respondents were not seeking additional technical knowledge, but value the soft skills of Communications and Report Writing (5.82) highest of those considered.

The results of subjecting the data to the Kruskall-Wallis procedure are shown in Table 5. In this non-parametric test, variables achieving a score of less than 0.05 are significant.

The data were subjected to the Kruskall-Wallis procedure. The ability to apply OOPs, CASE Applications, Database Design, E-Commerce & E-Business Development, Large System Experience, the Ability to Apply 3-GLs, LAN & Data Communications, and Web Design and Development all achieved significance. To some extent, the authors believe that the data reflect the particular concerns of the pool of respondents and that caution should be used in generalizing the findings in curriculum decisions. For example,

Table 5. IS/IT/CS subjects comparison: Kruskall-Wallis procedure results

Subject	df	Asymp. Sig.
Apply OOPs	1	0.00
CASE applications	1	0.00
Database design	1	0.00
E-Commerce/E-business development	1	0.00
Large System experience	1	0.00
Apply 3GLs	1	0.00
LAN & Data Comms	1	0.02
Web design/development	1	0.03
Client server applications	1	0.06
Project Management	1	0.08
Analysis & Design	1	0.13
Knowledge base/Expert systems	1	0.14
Use operating systems	1	0.21
Business Applications	1	0.22
Data mining/Data warehousing	1	0.42
ERP implementations & operations	1	0.57
Knowledge of PC apps	1	0.73

although Large Systems Experience and the Ability to Apply 3GLs achieved significance, other research confirms the declining importance of these subjects (Ang, 1992; Ang & Jiwahhasuchin, 1998; Young & Keen, 1997).

Ranking Soft Skills

A third section in the survey solicited rankings of the importance of a range of so-called 'soft' skills. The results are presented in Table 6. Comparisons between the 'higher' and 'lower' people contact groups were made. In all cases, Mann-Whitney U tests were used to establish any statistical differences between the two classifications. Table 6 shows that soft skills in the main are rated substantially higher than hard academic skills. Although the higher people contact grouping tended to rate these soft skills above the rating by the lower people contact grouping, only one variable (Problem Definition Skills) was rated significantly higher by the more client-oriented respondents. Only one soft skill—Able to Prepare Multimedia Presentations—was rated lower than 5.0 by both groups. *ALL* other soft skills were rated at 5.0 or higher by *both* groups.

Table 6. Comparative importance of soft skills (n=136)

	Lower	Higher
Skills	**mean (σ)**	**mean (σ)**
Problem solving skills	6.38 (0.56)	6.49 (0.58)*
Work as a team	6.47 (0.70)	6.57 (0.62)
Meet deadlines	6.37 (0.66)	6.34 (0.70)
Quickly acquire new skills	6.32 (0.62)	6.41 (0.66)
Work under pressure	6.42 (0.74)	6.42 (0.80)
Independently acquire new skills	6.32 (0.72)	6.38 (0.71)
Time management	6.23 (0.79)	6.20 (1.06)
Handle concurrent tasks	6.15 (0.73)	6.17 (0.87)
Able to interact with people of different backgrounds	6.05 (0.72)	6.20 (0.73)
Problem definition skills	6.03 (0.71)	6.30 (0.75)
Able to work with people from different disciplines	6.03 (0.71)	6.05 (0.76)
Work independently	6.30 (1.03)	6.25 (0.87)
Written communication skills	6.10 (0.86)	6.25 (0.83)
Client focused service ethic	6.07 (0.92)	6.24 (1.06)
Willing to undergo ongoing professional dev.	6.03 (0.94)	6.29 (0.85)
Think creatively	5.93 (0.99)	6.20 (0.80)
Place organizational objectives first	5.72 (0.87)	5.74 (1.01)
Accept direction	5.87 (1.03)	6.16 (0.73)
Business analysis skills	5.63 (0.86)	5.62 (1.15)
Oral presentation skills	5.70 (0.93)	5.86 (1.17)
Information seeking skills	5.68 (1.02)	5.95 (0.91)
Leadership potential	5.08 (1.09)	5.25 (1.07)
Good sense of humor	5.00 (1.30)	5.26 (1.39)
Able to prepare multimedia presentations	4.52 (1.44)	4.89 (1.05)
n =	**60**	**76**
* significantly different at 0.05% level		

All but one soft skill achieved a mean rating exceeding 5.0 for both groupings. Seventeen (out of 24) of the soft skills were rated in excess of 6.0 by the higher people contact group of practitioners. Fifteen of the lower people contact group rated these higher than 6.0. Closer inspection of Tables 4 and 7 reveals that the highest rated IS area, Analysis & Design, rated below all but seven of the soft skills in Table 7.

Teamwork, Problem-Solving Skills, Ability to Work Under Pressure, and Ability to Quickly Acquire New Skills Independently are each rated quite highly, close to essential, by IS practitioners, irrespective of the level of people contact their work activity involves. Only one soft skill, Ability to Prepare Multimedia Presentations, rated relatively low, and it could be argued that this is not a true soft IS skill.

Comparison Between IS/IT Professionals and IS/IT Employers

Table 7 shows the mean and standard deviations of ratings by IS/IT professionals and IS/IT employees for hard skills and business subjects.

Of the 14 subjects/skills that achieved a mean rating of 5.0 or more, the highest rating by both practitioners and employers was achieved by Communications & Report Writing, a soft skill. Eleven technical subjects and two 'other business subjects'—management and business ethics—achieved mean ratings of 5.0 or more. The value placed on these two subjects is consistent with earlier findings by the authors shown in Table 1.

A remaining pool of traditional business subjects—including Marketing, Business Finance, Operations Research, Mathematical Modeling, International Business, Business Statistics, Accounting, and Business or Commercial Law—failed to achieve a mean rating exceeding 4.35. Three other subjects—Psychology, Economics, and Foreign Languages—ranked quite low; none achieving even a neutral rating of 4.0 by either group. The low ratings achieved by these subjects by both practitioner and employer groups suggests that the IS curriculum would be improved by their replacement by other, more relevant, subjects that help students develop their 'business skills'.

The data regarding non-IS business subjects were subjected to the Kurskall-Wallis procedure. Only three subjects—Accounting, Management, and International Business—achieved significance. Both Accounting and Management emerged as two of the three most highly ranked non-technical subjects in the earlier study by the authors (Turner & Lowry, 1999b). International business was not included in the 1999 study and was added as a result of insights gained from that work. While business ethics was identified in the 1999 study as one of three most highly ranked non-technical business subjects, it was ranked a bit lower in the later study.

Table 9 shows the mean and standard deviations of ratings by IS/IT professionals and IS/IT employees for soft business skills.

Table 9 shows a marked similarity between practitioners and employers in their ratings of the importance of soft business skills. Once again, consistent with Table 6, only the ability to prepare multimedia presentations failed to achieve a mean rating of 5.0. All other soft business skills were highly rated by both IS practitioners and employers.

Table 7. Comparative ratings of hard skills by IS practitioners and employers

	IS/IT Professionals		IS/IT Employers	
Skills	**Mean**	σ	**Mean**	σ
Communications & Report Writing	6.02	1.05	6.09	0.81
Analysis & Design	5.87	1.09	5.63	1.26
Client server applications	5.67	0.92	5.37	1.15
Business Applications	5.65	1.11	5.76	1.20
Use operating systems	5.60	1.10	5.39	1.27
Database design	5.55	1.25	5.12	1.16
Management	5.54	1.03	5.20	1.10
Knowledge of PC apps	5.43	1.22	5.41	1.37
Project Management	5.43	1.16	5.60	1.24
E-Commerce/E-business development	5.33	1.23	4.78	1.38
Apply OOPs	5.26	1.25	4.61	1.51
LAN & Data Comms	5.22	1.27	5.55	1.22
Large System experience	5.12	1.19	4.54	1.53
Business Ethics	5.07	1.57	5.23	1.52
Web design/development	4.96	1.54	4.67	1.15
Organizational Behavior	4.90	1.41	4.92	1.34
Data mining/Data warehousing	4.76	1.36	4.66	1.36
Apply 3GLs	4.70	1.41	4.15	1.58
CASE applications	4.51	1.32	3.80	1.42
Knowledge base/Expert systems	4.49	1.42	4.20	1.37
ERP implementations & operations	4.48	1.39	4.33	1.61
Marketing	4.35	1.52	4.39	1.34
Business Finance	4.30	1.50	4.54	1.47
Operations Research	4.29	1.26	4.32	1.26
Mathematical Modeling	4.25	1.44	3.97	1.49
International Business	4.24	1.59	3.69	1.56
Business Statistics	4.18	1.40	4.33	1.38
Accounting	4.13	1.55	4.68	1.38
Business or Commercial Law	4.07	1.55	4.12	1.45
Psychology	3.70	1.76	3.85	1.46
Economics	3.63	1.50	3.68	1.47

Nine soft skills achieved significance when subjected to the Kruskall-Wallis procedure. These include Time Management, Oral Presentation Skills, Good Sense of Humor, Willingness to Undergo Professional Development, Ability to Prepare Multimedia Presentations, Ability to Quickly Acquire New Skills, Ability to Meet Deadlines, the Ability to Work under Pressure, and Well-Developed Written Communication Skills. It is interesting to note the position of the Ability to Prepare Multimedia Presentations in Table 10, as it was the only soft skill to fail to receive a rating of 5.0 or more from IS practitioners and employers.

Table 8. Non-IS subjects comparison: Kruskall-Wallis procedure results

Subject	df	Asymp. Sig.
Accounting	1	0.00
International Business	1	0.01
Management	1	0.01
Business Finance	1	0.09
Mathematical Modeling	1	0.12
Business Statistics	1	0.24
Business Ethics	1	0.41
Foreign Languages	1	0.68
Psychology	1	0.74
Economics	1	0.78
Marketing	1	0.78
Operations Research	1	0.79
Organizational Behavior	1	0.84
Business or Commercial Law	1	0.92
Communications & Report Writing	1	0.92

Table 9. Comparison of importance placed on soft skills by IS/IT professionals and employers

	IS/IT Professionals		IS/IT Employers	
Skills	**Mean**	**σ**	**Mean**	**σ**
Work as a team	6.52	0.66	6.39	0.81
Problem solving skills	6.44	0.57	6.37	0.68
Work under pressure	6.42	0.78	6.27	0.75
Quickly acquire new skills	6.37	0.64	6.15	0.73
Independently acquire new skills	6.35	0.72	6.23	0.71
Meet deadlines	6.35	0.68	6.13	0.81
Work independently	6.27	0.94	6.22	0.65
Time management	6.21	0.95	5.98	0.84
Problem definition skills	6.18	0.74	6.14	0.74
Willing to undergo ongoing professional dev.	6.18	0.89	5.93	0.89
Written communication skills	6.18	0.85	6.04	0.76
Client focused service ethic	6.16	1.00	6.09	0.94
Handle concurrent tasks	6.16	0.81	6.08	0.81
Interact with people of different backgrounds	6.13	0.73	6.03	0.85
Think creatively	6.08	0.89	6.09	0.71
Work with people from different disciplines	6.04	0.74	6.10	0.82
Accept direction	6.03	0.89	5.98	0.84
Information seeking skills	5.83	0.96	5.82	0.93
Oral presentation skills	5.79	1.07	5.56	0.88
Place organizational objectives first	5.73	0.95	5.74	0.97
Business analysis skills	5.63	1.03	5.51	1.04
Leadership potential	5.18	1.08	4.99	0.94
Good sense of humor	5.15	1.35	5.58	1.14
Able to prepare multimedia presentations	4.73	1.25	4.32	1.38
n =	**136**		**138**	

Table 10. Soft skills comparison: Kruskall-Wallis procedure results

Skills	df	Asymp. Sig.
Time management	1	0.00
Oral presentation skills	1	0.01
Good sense of humor	1	0.01
Willing to undergo ongoing professional dev.	1	0.01
Able to prepare multimedia presentations	1	0.01
Quickly acquire new skills	1	0.01
Meet deadlines	1	0.03
Work under pressure	1	0.05
Written communication skills	1	0.05
Leadership potential	1	0.07
Work independently	1	0.10
Independently acquire new skills	1	0.11
Work as a team	1	0.20
Business analysis skills	1	0.33
Able to work with people from different disciplines	1	0.35
Client focused service ethic	1	0.36
Handle concurrent tasks	1	0.36
Accept direction	1	0.43
Able to interact with people of different background	1	0.43
Problem solving skills	1	0.54
Problem definition skills	1	0.56
Think creatively	1	0.65
Information seeking skills	1	0.71
Place organizational objectives first	1	0.80

Curriculum Content Discussion

Information technology is central to the work of computer scientists and information systems professionals. Computer scientists are more oriented toward the technology, while information systems professionals are more oriented toward the users of technology. The model curricula of relevant professional bodies such as the Association of Information Technology Professionals (Davis et al., 1997) and the Australian Computer Society (Underwood, 1997), IRMA-DAMA (Cohen, 2000), and ACM-AIS (2002) have noted and acknowledged the different roles performed by information professionals.

There has long been agreement that the IS curriculum should comprise some combination of technical subjects and non-technical business subjects, and that graduates also need soft business skills. There is far less agreement about what the mix between these should be and how best to prepare students in some areas, notably in the development of soft business skills.

Overall, the data indicate that IS/IT practitioners perceive soft skills as very important while hard skills, especially some of the more traditional core business subjects such as Accounting or Economics, are rated lower, perhaps expecting a satisfactory level of technical skill as a given. The data were obtained from a wide representation of professionals across the spectrum of functional areas that require different types and levels of hard and soft skills.

While we agree with the general view that soft skills have become increasingly important, we argue that the traditional business subjects are *not* the business skills primarily sought in studies of the IS marketplace. Does the study of traditional business subjects such as Marketing, Business Law, or Economics directly help the students to develop a repertoire of soft business skills? The findings suggest that in reality it is not more core business subjects that are needed, but an appreciation of business processes and activities that are not always covered in IS degree programs.

How to Study? Active Learning Approaches for the IS Profession

Of equal importance to curriculum content is adoption of effective learning strategies. Until fairly recently, the traditional lecture/tutorial/readings approach was the accepted and arguably the most effective pedagogical strategy. It was the only means available to reach a larger audience at one time and provided a means for bringing order to the tertiary education process. In the absence of better methods, this hoary paradigm has served since the golden age of Pericles. The advent of the personal computer, the Internet, and other enabling technologies have freed the education process from traditional bounds of time and space, enabling asynchronous learning without the necessity of face-to-face attendance for the purposes of imparting and receiving information. The role of the academic has shifted inexorably from that of expert knowledge giver and oracle to coach, mentor, and guide to active learners. The emphasis has shifted from teaching to learning.

We believe that the knowledge and intellectual skills required of an information systems graduate are neither contentious nor difficult to identify. The same may be generally said for desired personal attributes and interpersonal skills. A critical issue and the one *likely to be contentious* is the appropriate learning environment to best prepare graduates to engage in higher-order thinking. Delivery paradigms can be characterized as 'teacher-centered learning' and 'student- centered learning'. We suggest that student-centered/active learning approaches may be a better way than those currently in use.

Teacher-centered learning is characterized by didactic teaching, passive learning, the teacher as the 'expert', and the control of learning rests with the academic. The learning of the students is directed by the academic and is often based on what the academic believes the student needs to learn. Savery and Duffy (1995) observe that this approach can lead to students focusing on determining what knowledge they require to pass the subject rather than the instructional objectives of the program, a phenomenon well known to educators—or to most of us who have been students.

Student-centered learning places the student into active, self-directed learning, learning by enquiry, and ownership of the learning goals. Active learning strategies may be suitable for better preparing information systems students for professional practice. For example, in the Problem-Based Learning (PBL) approach, complex, real-world problems or cases are used to motivate students to identify and research concepts and principles they need to know in order to progress through the problems. Students work in small learning teams, bringing together collective skill at acquiring, communicating, and integrating information in a process that resembles that of inquiry (Bentley, Sandy, & Lowry, 2002).

Didactic learning, that is 'teaching what is known', cannot be achieved in the information systems discipline, as knowledge is increasing rapidly and adding more into an already crowded curriculum is difficult (Lowry & Doroshenko, 1996; Lowry et al., 1996). Information systems professionals work in environments that are project oriented, problem and task based. Hence, students need to be able to determine 'what they know', identify 'what needs to be known' and how to 'gain the knowledge or skill' to solve a problem or task. Learning how to acquire and apply these skills is part of the active learning approach. The active learning approach provides students with lifelong learning skills suitable to the IS profession.

Active Learning

Active learning offers an approach that can lead to a better alignment between educational delivery and the information systems professional work environment. As active learning focuses more on the educational process rather than content, learning is different; it has a broader focus, where understanding concepts is more important than a lot of detail. The active learning approach is shown in Figure 1, an active learning cycle diagram.

A cycle can be seen to follow four stages:

1. Work begins with *learning stimulus* in the form of a problem, project, inquiry, or practical work assignment. Students work together on a problem or in a situation that requires a studied and coordinated response.
2. Following a process of problem definition and exploration, students *diagnose* what they know, what they need to know, and what they do not know, in order to produce the desired result. Team members work independently, as a group, until they gain

Figure 1. Active learning cycle

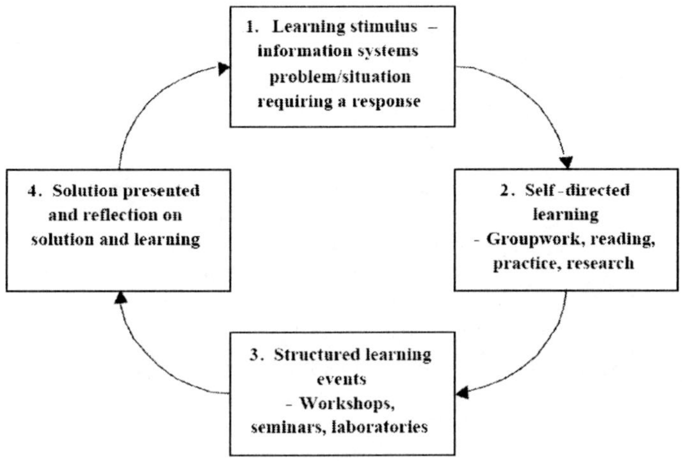

a better understanding of what needs to be done and develop a plan for its achievement.

3. Members then may participate in appropriate structured learning events such as workshops, seminars, and laboratory work, gaining insight and experience.
4. Meeting and communicating as often as they feel is necessary, students collectively develop solutions to problems, deliverables for projects, reports resulting from the group's research effort, or a report from a work experience integrated with formal study.

There are several approaches to student-centered active learning: Problem-Based Learning, Project-Based Learning, Inquiry-Based Learning, and Work Integrated Learning. Table 11 summarizes each of these pedagogical approaches.

Why Adopt Active Learning Strategies for IS Education?

Benefits perceived by both staff and students (Bentley, Lowry, & Sandy, 1999a, 1999b, 1999c; Bentley, Sandy, & Lowry, 2002) include:

- increased motivation,
- improved problem solving,

Table 11. Active learning approaches

APPROACH	DESCRIPTION
Problem-Based Learning	Problem-Based Learning is an Active Learning strategy that may be suitable for better preparing information systems students for professional practice. In the problem-based approach, complex, real world problems or cases are used to motivate students to identify and research concepts and principles they need to know in order to progress through the problems. Students work in small learning teams, bringing together collective skill at acquiring, communicating, and integrating information in a process that resembles that of inquiry.
Project-Based Learning	An Active Learning approach that focuses on developing a product or creation. The project may or may not be student-centered, problem-based, or inquiry-based. Project-based learning uses open-ended assignments that provides students with a degree of choice, and extends over a considerable period of time. **Teachers** act as facilitator, designing activities and providing resources and advice to students. Instruction and facilitation are guided by a broad range of teaching goals. **Students** collect and analyze information, make discoveries, and report their results. **Projects** are often interdisciplinary.
Inquiry-Based Learning	A student-centered, Active Learning approach focusing on questioning, critical thinking, and problem-solving. IBL is expressed by the idea "involve me and I understand." The IBL approach is more focused on using and learning content as a means to develop information-processing and problem-solving skills. The system is more student-centered, with the teacher as a facilitator of learning. There is more emphasis on "how we come to know" and less on "what we know." Students are involved in the construction of knowledge through active involvement. The more interested and engaged students are by a subject or project, the easier it will be for them to construct in-depth knowledge of it. Learning becomes easier when it reflects their interests and goals and piques their natural curiosity.
Work-Integrated Learning	WIL is a hybrid approach that achieves learning outcomes through a combination of alternating periods of traditional academic pedagogy with extended periods of practical experience in the professional workplace. Work-Integrated Learning is a mature pedagogical strategy that is often referred to as "sandwich" and "end-on" courses.

- improved time management,
- improved self-directed learning skills,
- improved research skills, and
- improved group work skills.

Students have suggested that the problems we use are realistic and relevant to the work of information systems professionals. We have not found any appreciable differences between students' assignment and exam performances when the course is taught in a traditional mode versus when active learning is used. Other benefits arise; for example, a tutor—who in the previous semester taught programming to the students, and who subsequently had the same students in an active learning class—noted the increased enthusiasm and motivation shown by students in their group work and approach to learning.

In improving self-evaluation skills, students probably for the first time in a course have to write down their reflections on their learning in their diaries. Early in the semester, diary entries indicate the need to spend more time on reading and practice and to consider the number of hours spent on the subject. Many seem to realize the necessary commitment required for effective tertiary study.

A working group report by Ellis et al. (1998) observed that active learning suits the information systems and computing fields as:

- IS and computing are, for the most part, problem driven.
- Lifelong learning is necessary due to the rapidly and continually changing nature of the industry.
- Practitioners must constantly update their skills and competencies in order to keep abreast of new technology.
- The project group is the predominant mode of operation within the industry.
- IS and computing cross discipline boundaries.

According to Woods (1996, p. 12), "PBL is about learning subject knowledge in the context of using and developing process skills." Boud and Feletti (1991, p. 14) describe Problem-Based Learning as:

> *"... a way of constructing and teaching courses using problems as the stimulus and focus for student activity. It is not simply the addition of problem-solving activities to otherwise discipline-centered curricula, but a way of conceiving of the curriculum that is centered around key problems in professional practice. Problem-based courses start with problems rather than an exposition of disciplinary knowledge."*

A large body of knowledge relating to active learning, especially in the disciplines of Health and Law, is available.

Preparing for the Workplace in the StudyPlace

The major learning characteristic in Problem-Based Learning is the presentation of the problem before any knowledge is given. The knowledge is acquired and applied back to the problem. Students must identify what knowledge needs to be gained to solve the problem, acquire the knowledge, and relate it to the problem.

Savery and Duffy (1995) present a case to show that active learning is consistent with the principles of instruction arising from constructivism and that active learning is an ideal approach to learning. They argue that learners must be constructors of their own knowledge, and must be presented with active learning situations and tasks from the environment in which they will work. Savery and Duffy are adamant that the learning objectives and resources are not presented with the problem as in case-based approaches, as this latter approach does not help to develop "metacognitive" skills associated with problem solving or with professional life. Active learning uses authentic problems from practice to motivate student learning and develop attitudes and skills required for lifelong learning. Real-world problems are messy and complex.

Authentic real-world problems in the professional context help students gain ownership of the learning experience. Ellis et al (1998) identify a spectrum of problem definitions from the teacher constructing and fully specifying the problem, to the teacher constructing an open-ended problem, through to students constructing the problem themselves. Learning and problem solving usually take place in small groups (5-7). Students acquire the process of problem solving through collaboration, along with the team skills of negotiation, decision making, and allocation and management of work.

The use of increasingly complex problems draws upon the higher-order thinking skills of analysis, synthesis, and evaluation. After the completion of each problem, students develop a framework for use in the next problem. This concept is referred to as 'scaffolding'. For example, beginners in active learning need to build upon the processes of active learning rather than learning knowledge content. Learning support to assist in building these frameworks should be considered and resources provided to assist the scaffolding process (Ellis et al, 1998; Greening, 1998). The problems can be sourced or adapted from real examples. Initially the problems should be well structured to provide clues and scaffolding to guide the students in their learning.

Active learning is both a curriculum design and a teaching and learning strategy. It is said to develop higher-order thinking. Students are placed in the active role of problem solvers (practitioners) as they are confronted with a situation (ill-structured problem) that reflects the real world. These are often complex problems that do not have black-and-white answers. The learning process must be monitored, not just the learning at the end. Essentially, in active learning the problem drives the students' learning. Active learning is different from the case method approach; the presentation and problem-solving approach are different.

Characteristics of active learning include:

- is context-based using real-life situations;
- focuses on thinking skills (problem solving, analysis, decision making, critical thinking);
- requires integration of interdisciplinary knowledge/skills/behaviors;
- is self-directed and develops lifelong learning skills;
- is shared in small groups.

All these characteristics are currently used in a range of teaching and learning approaches, but active learning puts all these together. Elements of each characteristic must be present for the learning approach to be characterized as active learning.

Subject-based learning tends to be linear and takes the approach where students are told the theory (what to know), and then learn it and are expected apply it to practice (given examples to illustrate how to use it). This can be termed a 'theory into practice' model. Active learning, however, starts from practice (with real-world situations); students then identify what they need to know, construct/discover the appropriate theory, and finally apply it to practice in solving the problem (Woods, 1994). This is a 'practice into theory into practice' cyclic model.

Savery and Duffy (1995) present a case to show that active learning is consistent with the principles of instruction arising from constructivism and that active learning is an ideal approach to learning. They argue that learners must be constructors of their own knowledge, and must be presented with active learning situations and tasks from the environment in which they will work. Savery and Duffy are adamant that the learning objectives and resources are not presented with the problem as in case-based approaches, as this latter approach does not help to develop "metacognitive skills associated with problem solving or with professional life."

The assessment of active learning therefore is different from traditional assessment. In active learning the process of learning is assessed as well as the content learning and outcomes. There is much discussion in the active learning literature regarding the forms of assessment and evaluation of active learning students. Its discussion here is beyond the scope of this chapter.

Active Learning Discussion

The fact is that many, if not most, information systems graduates will be employed in a project environment. Yet, we deliver the information systems curriculum in small, byte-sized, semester-long 'chunks' that resemble buckets containing defined areas of knowledge suitable for related study. In each subject, the academic is a hurdle to be gotten around by the students as they move 'forward' toward a passing result. If they repeat this exercise successfully enough times, once per required course, we say to them, "Now, you can go and integrate all of this," graduate them with their degrees, and send them out to meet their fate. How well, though, does skill at study, passing examinations, and producing student projects prepare information systems students for work in the professional project environment? Would they not be better served by working in a project environment, learning and practicing how to identify problems, frame questions, locate information and resources, work with and serve clients and colleagues, to ascertain and locate the knowledge and resources needed, to successfully plan and complete projects, from the beginning and throughout their period of study?

This chapter has presented a simple model for development of a 'compleat information systems graduate' to assist educators in developing curriculum content and choosing the learning approach. It is suggested this may be achieved through changing from a teacher-enabled to a student-enabled learning approach using active learning. This approach is in its infancy in the information systems discipline and is far from the fully integrated active learning curriculum used in many medical and law schools. The active learning approach appears to be a good match with the realities of professional information systems practice by providing a closer link between the learning and work environment.

Towards Substantive IS Curriculum Reform

Some Issues...

Some formidable barriers exist to substantive revision of IS curricula to emphasize acquisition and development of soft business skills. These include:

- **Confusion:** Research results that call for more 'business skills' have handily and traditionally been interpreted as meaning exposure of students to additional, formal business subjects. While an IS student may well gain knowledge and skill in marketing, economic analysis, or international business in that way, our findings suggest that it is the soft skills, rather than formal academic skill, that is wanted by IS/IT practitioners and employers.
- **Tradition and Inertia—Content:** It is easy to offer traditional business subjects, as they are already being taught anyway. In many institutions, the existing IS academic staff would have to acquire the additional academic background and skills needed to introduce a substantive soft skills emphasis into the IS curriculum. In most instances, there is unlikely to be sufficient time or interest in doing so.

- **Tradition and Inertia—Delivery Method:** Many, if not most, subjects are taught in a familiar lecture–practical mode. As a project- and team-oriented profession, information systems programs may well achieve a better match between the workplace *through* the studyplace through the adoption of active learning, student-centered delivery methods such as Problem-Based Learning and Work-Integrated Learning. Active learning requires a shift in the role of the academic from expert in control to coach and mentor. Active learning pedagogy requires more preparation for and involvement in the teaching/learning process by academics. It is more work; less time is available for research and other career-advancing activities.
- **Resources:** If a substantial portion of an undergraduate degree program were shifted from traditional business subjects to the acquisition and development of soft skills, who would develop, teach, and assess the new soft skills curriculum component?
- **Vested Interest:** Some academic institutions supplement the enrollment in less relevant or popular subjects through inclusion of those subjects in a popular curriculum such as Information Systems. In many institutions, economic incentives exist for students to be enrolled in subjects within a single administrative unit, such as a business or IT faculty.

And Some Recommendations...

There are, of course, no easy solutions to resolve the issues raised. In increasing order of difficulty, some of the barriers to meaningful reform and evolution of the IS curriculum might be surmounted over time and with sufficient dedication.

- **To Reduce Confusion:** Local course advisory and professional bodies can provide invaluable insight into the mix of technical and non-technical formal courses and soft skills appropriate for a given institution's service area. Focus groups and local replication of available studies should provide targeted, timely, and authoritative guidance for ongoing curriculum evolution.
- **Overcoming Tradition and Inertia—Content:** To some extent, prospective students have taken matters into their own hands by opting in larger numbers to bypass traditional university courses in favor of industry-sponsored/sanctioned entry gateways such as those offered by Microsoft, Oracle, SAP, and others. It is possible that students electing the non-academic alternative see more value in industry-focused training than in academic education, which they see as irrelevant to their career aspirations. A large number of traditional business subjects were rated low in importance by IS practitioners and employers in the tables in this chapter. Tertiary educators will need to reconsider the value of these traditional business subjects, and will have to extend ourselves to develop and deliver revitalized curricula that squarely address the expressed desire for soft skills that have been identified in a number of studies. Have another look at Table 4

(Comparative Importance of Academic Subjects) and Table 7 (Comparative Ratings of Hard Skills by IS Practitioners and Employers). Note the position of the majority of traditional business subjects in ratings of importance by IS practitioners and employers. What would your course advisory body or a local study of your service area suggest?

- **Overcoming Tradition and Inertia—Delivery Method:** Adoption of student-centered/active learning teaching strategies will require a willingness to devote a far greater proportion of academic time and effort to preparation and involvement in the teaching/learning process. As a practical matter, this will be difficult to achieve without some substantive revision of the academic career structure, especially the criteria for retention and promotion. The expectation of academics has grown so rapidly in the past two decades that it is unrealistic to expect a substantial additional commitment to development and delivery of student-centered/active learning courses *as well as* scholarly research productivity at the current level. If the research productivity 'ask' remains at the same level as at present (or even increased, a likely scenario given the increased competition for jobs in the academic sector), then it appears that we must reduce the *number* of subjects comprising an academic workload. Given the financial realities of higher education post-2000, it is unlikely that teaching loads will be reduced or that class sizes will be reduced to accommodate active learning without a substantial and sustained alternative source of funding for staff to take on the additional teaching effort that active learning entails. The only likely sources are from industry partners or from increased student fees. No easy answers here. In the long run, it may develop that lower-priced IS courses will be delivered through the Internet and massed, teacher-centered, face-to-face courses, with face-to-face active learning pedagogy available only at elite, high-cost institutions. No easy solutions here.
- **Finding Resources:** Always a problem, resources are easier to obtain from a body of satisfied clients, such as the firms who employ our graduates. If we are seen to consult with, listen to, and serve the interests of those firms, they will follow their self-interest in becoming industry partners, rich sources of guidance in curriculum planning and development, work experience for students, consultancies for academics, equipment, money, political weight in our own institution. We must learn to master what we teach about building client ownership to insure system acceptance and success.
- **Neutralizing Vested Interests:** Senior university managers may oppose substantive IS curriculum reform such as that discussed in this chapter for a number of reasons, including loss of revenue if students enroll in soft skill courses provided by another administrative unit. It is up to IS educators to develop strategies to address the turf issues that preoccupy some administrators. Building effective partnerships with the appropriate industries in our service area can provide a powerful voice to speak on our behalf to senior management. Accrediting bodies can also help in this way.

Table 12 summarizes these issues and recommendations in increasing order of difficulty.

Table 12. Summary of issues and recommendations for IS curriculum refinement

Issue	Recommendation
Confusion: Research results that call for more 'business skills' have handily and traditionally been interpreted as meaning exposure of students to additional, formal business subjects. While an IS student may well gain knowledge and skill in marketing, economic analysis, or international business in that way, our findings suggest that it is the soft skills, rather than formal academic skill, that is wanted by IS/IT practitioners and employers.	**To Reduce Confusion:** Local course advisory and professional bodies can provide invaluable insight into the mix of technical and non-technical formal courses and soft skills appropriate for a given institution's service area. Focus groups and local replication of available studies should provide targeted, timely, and authoritative guidance for ongoing curriculum evolution.
Tradition and Inertia—Content: It is easy to offer traditional business subjects, as they are already being taught anyway. In many institutions, the existing IS academic staff would have to acquire the additional academic background and skills needed to introduce a substantive soft skills emphasis into the IS curriculum. In most instances, there may be insufficient time or interest to do so. . A large number of traditional business subjects were rated low in importance by IS practitioners and employers in the tables above.	**Overcoming Tradition and Inertia—Content:** Many prospective students have taken matters into their own hands by opting in larger numbers to bypass traditional university courses in favor of industry-sponsored/sanctioned entry gateways such as those offered by Microsoft, Oracle, SAP, and others. It is possible that students electing the non-academic alternative see more value in industry-focused training than in academic education, which they see as irrelevant to their career aspirations. Educators will need to reconsider the value of traditional business subjects, and need to develop and deliver curricula to include soft skills.
Tradition and Inertia—Delivery Method: Many, if not most, subjects are taught in a familiar lecture–practical mode. As a project- and team-oriented profession, information systems programs may well achieve a better match between the workplace *through* the 'studyplace' through the adoption of active learning, student-centered delivery methods such as Problem-Based Learning and Work-Integrated Learning.	**Overcoming Tradition and Inertia—Delivery Method:** Delivery through student-centered/active learning requires more effort devoted to teaching preparation and delivery. Substantive revision of the academic career structure, especially the criteria for retention and promotion, would be required. If research productivity expectations remain as they are, additional funds will have to found from industry partners or from student fees to pay additional teachers. No easy solutions here.
Resources: If a substantial portion of an undergraduate degree program were shifted from traditional business subjects to the acquisition and development of soft skills, who would develop, teach, and assess the new soft skills curriculum component? We must learn to master what we teach about building client ownership to enlist influential industry partners.	**Finding Resources:** Resources are easier to obtain from a body of satisfied clients, such as the firms who employ our graduates. If we are seen to consult with, listen to, and serve the interests of those firms, they will follow their self-interest and become rich sources of guidance in curriculum planning and development, work experience for students, consultancies for academics, equipment, money, political weight in our own institution.
Vested Interest: Some academic institutions supplement the enrollment in less relevant or popular subjects through inclusion of those subjects in a popular curriculum such as Information Systems. In many institutions, economic incentives exist for students to be enrolled in subjects within a single administrative unit, such as a business or IT faculty.	**Neutralizing Vested Interests:** Senior university managers may oppose substantive IS curriculum reform such as that discussed in this chapter for a number of reasons, including loss of revenue if students enroll in soft skill courses provided by another administrative unit. It is up to IS educators to develop strategies to address the turf issues that preoccupy some administrators. Building effective partnerships with the appropriate industries in our service area can provide a powerful voice to speak on our behalf to senior management. Accrediting bodies can also help in this way.

Towards a Technology-Based Profession...

There has long been agreement that the IS curriculum should comprise some combination of technical subjects and non-technical business subjects, and that graduates also need soft business skills. There is far less agreement about *what* the balance between these should be and how best to prepare students in some areas, notably in the development of soft business skills.

While we agree with the general view that soft skills have become increasingly important, we argue that the traditional business subjects are *not* the business skills primarily sought in studies of the IS marketplace. Does the study of traditional business subjects such as Marketing, Business Law, or Economics directly help the students to develop a repertoire of soft business skills? The findings suggest that in reality it is not more core business subjects that are needed, but an appreciation of business processes and activities that are not always covered in IS degree programs.

While study after study has called for soft skills acquisition and development by IS students, some IS programs have a clearer and better-developed vision than others of what those skills are and how they may be introduced and cultivated. The growing emphasis on soft skills in IS education is an indication that what began as a fundamentally technology-oriented discipline is, indeed, evolving into a technology-based profession. We can watch someone else claim that knowledge and the opportunities that it offers, or we can embrace it ourselves, hoping that there is still time.

References

ACM-AIS (Association for Computing Machinery Association for Information Systems). (2002). *IS 2002—Model curricula and guidelines for undergraduate degree programs in information systems*. Retrieved November 28, 2003, from *www.acm.org/education/curricula.html#IS2002*

Ang, A.Y. (1992). Australian information systems curricula: A comparison between the views of academics and professionals. *Interface, 14*(3), 7-12.

Ang, A.Y. & Jiwahhasuchin, S. (1998). Information systems education in Thailand: A comparison between the views of professionals and academics. *Journal of Global Information Management, 6*(4), 34-42.

Ashley, N.W. & Padgett, T.C. (1997). *Information systems graduates: Evaluation of their IS curricula.* Retrieved November 28, 2003, from *www.westga.edu/~bquest/1998/infosys.html*

Athey, S. & Plotnicki, J. (1998). The evaluation of job opportunities for IT professionals. *Journal of Computer Information Systems, 39*(Spring), 71-88.

Beise, C.M., Padgett, T.C., & Ganoe, F.J. (1991). What information systems graduates are really doing: An update. *Computer Personnel, 13*(2), 4-11.

Bentley, J., Lowry, G., & Sandy, G. (1999a). Towards the compleat information systems graduate: A problem-based learning approach. In B. Hope & P. Yoong (Eds.), *Proceedings of the 10th Australasian Conference on Information Systems* (pp. 65-75). Wellington, NZ: Australian Computer Society/ACIS.

Bentley, J., Lowry, G., & Sandy, G. (1999b, December 9-11). Initiatives in information systems: Matching learning to professional practice. *Proceedings of the 1st Asia Pacific Conference on Problem-Based Learning* (pp. 56-68). Hong Kong: The University of Hong Kong.

Bentley, J., Lowry, G., & Sandy, G. (1999c). *Problem-based learning in information systems education: Preparing students for professional practise in a project environment*. South African Computer Society. Retrieved December 2, 2003, from *www.cs.wits.ac.za/~philip/SAICSIT/SAICSIT-99/electronic/ideas/Bentley.pdf*

Bentley, J., Sandy, G., & Lowry, G. (2002). Problem-based learning in information systems analysis and design. In E. Cohen (Ed.), *Challenges of information technology education in the 21st century* (pp. 100-123). Hershey, PA: Idea Group Publishing.

Boud, D. & Feletti, G. (Eds.). (1991). *The challenge of problem-based learning*. New York: St. Martin's Press.

Burn, J.M., Ng Tye, E.M.W., & Ma, L.C.K. (1995). Paradigm shift—cultural implications for development of IS professionals. *Journal of Global Information Management, 3*(2), 18-28.

Cafasso, R. (1996). Selling your soft side helps IT. *Computerworld, 18*(35), 60-61.

Cheney, P., Hale, D., & Kasper, G. (1990). Knowledge, skills and abilities of information systems professionals: Past, present and future. *Information Management, 9*(4), 237-247.

Cohen, E. (2000). *Curriculum model 2000 of the Information Management Association and the Data Administration Mangers Association*. Retrieved November 28, 2003, from *www.irma-international.org/downloads/pdf/irma_dama.pdf*

Comley, P. (1996). *The use of the Internet as a data collection method.* Retrieved December 1, 2003, from *www.sga.co.uk/esomar.html*

Davis, G., Gorgone, J.T., Feinstein, D.L., & Longenecker, H.E. (1997). *IS'97 model curricula and guidelines for undergraduate degree programs in information systems.* Association of Information Technology Professionals.

Doke, E.R. & Williams, S.R. (1999). Knowledge and skill requirements for information systems professionals: An exploratory study. *Journal of IS Education, 10*(1), 10-18.

Ellis, A., Carswell, L., Bernat, A., Deveaux, D., Frison, P., Meisalo, V., Meyer, J., Nulden, U., Rigelj, J., & Tarhio, J. (1998). *Resources, tools, and techniques for problem-based learning in computing. Proceedings of the 3rd Annual SIGCSE/SIGCUE ITiCSE Conference on Integrating Technology into Computer Science Education,* Dublin, Ireland.

Gorgone, J.T. & Gray, P. (1999). *Graduate IS curriculum for the 21st century*. Retrieved December 1, 2003, from *www.computer.org/proceedings/hicss/0001/00011/00011003abs.htm*

Greening, T. (1998). *Scaffolding for success in PBL*. Retrieved December 1, 2003, from *www.utmb.edu/meo/*

Gupta, J.N.D. & Wachter, R.M. (1998). A capstone course in the information systems curriculum. *International Journal of Information Management, 18*(6), 427-441.

Herzberg, F. (1968). One more time: How do you motivate employees. *Harvard Business Review, 46*(1), 53-62. Retrieved November 28, 2003, from *www.cs.adelaide.edu.au/%7Echarles/ACS/ACS0.pdf*

Kakabadse, A. & Korac-Kakabadse, N. (2000). Future role of IS/IT professionals. *Journal of Management Development, 19*(2), 97-154.

Khalil, O., Strong, D., Kahn, B., & Pipino, L. (1999). Teaching information quality in information systems education. *Informing Science, 2*(3), 53-59.

Lee, D.M., Trauth, E.M., & Farwell, D. (1995). Critical skills and knowledge requirements of IS professionals: A joint academic/industry investigation. *MIS Quarterly, 19*(3), 313-340.

Lidtke, D., Stokes, G., Haines, J., & Mulder, M. (1999). *ISCC'99: An information systems-centric curriculum'99: Guidelines for educating the next generation of information systems specialists*. Retrieved November 2003 from *www.iscc.unomaha.edu*

Lowry, G.R. (1997). Postgraduate research training for information systems: Improving standards & reducing uncertainty. In D.J. Sutton (Ed.), *Proceedings of the 8th Australasian Conference on Information Systems* (pp. 191-202). Adelaide, South Australia: Australian Computer Society & ACIS Executive.

Lowry, G.R. & Doroshenko, E.E. (1996). Object orientation in software engineering education: Integrating concepts, methodology development models, and CASE in the curriculum. In M. Purvis (Ed.), *Proceedings of the 1996 International Conference on Software Engineering: Education and Practice* (pp. 336-343), Dunedin, New Zealand. Los Alamitos, CA: IEEE Computer Society Press.

Lowry, G. & Turner, R. (2005). Softening the MIS curriculum for a technology-based profession. In M. Khosrow-Pour (Ed.), *Encyclopedia of information science and technology* (pp. 2539-2545). Hershey, PA: Idea Group Reference.

Lu, M.T. & Wang, P. (1998-1999). Knowledge and skills of IS graduates: A Hong Kong perspective. *Journal of Computer Information Systems, 39*(Winter), 40-46.

Main, R. (1995). Telstra winnows the best and brightest graduates. *Computerworld, 18*(12), 36.

McLean, E.R., Tanner, J.R., & Smits, S.J. (1991). Self-perceptions and job preferences of entry-level information systems professionals: implications for career development. *Proceedings of the Special Interest Group on Computer Personnel Research Annual Conference* (pp. 3-13). Athens, GA: ACM.

Mehta, R. & Sivadas, E. (1995). Comparing response rates and response content in mail vs. email surveys. *Journal of the Market Research Society, 37*(4), 429-439.

Morgan, G.W., Lowry, G.R., & FitzGerald, D.G. (1998). Development staff characteristics and service stability in leading Australian-owned information technology firms. *Proceedings of the 1998 International Conference on Software Engineering:*

Education and Practice (pp. 96-103), Dunedin, New Zealand. Los Alamitos, CA: IEEE Computer Society Press.

Mulder, M. & van Weert, T. (2000). *Proceedings of the Informatics Curriculum Framework 2000 for Higher Education* (ICF-2000). Paris: UNESCO.

Savery, J.R. & Duffy, T.M. (1995). Problem-Based Learning: An instructional model and its constructivist framework. *Educational Technology, 35*(5), 31-38.

Slaughter, S. & Ang, S. (1996). Employment outsourcing in information systems. *Communications of the ACM, 39*(7), 47-54.

Snoke, R. & Underwood, A. (2002, August 9-11). IS curriculum evaluation for core capabilities: A methodology for determining the coverage. *Proceedings of the Americas Conference on Information Systems,* Dallas, TX.

Stewart, G. (1997). The perceptions of professional practice by IT students. In D.J. Sutton (Ed.), *Proceedings of the 8th Australasian Conference on Information Systems* (pp. 739-744). Adelaide, South Australia: Australian Computer Society & ACIS Executive.

Trauth, E., Farwell, D., & Lee, D. (1993). The IS expectation gap: Industry expectations versus academic preparation. *MIS Quarterly, 17*(3), 293-307.

Tse, A.C.B., Tse, K.C., Yin, C.H., Yi, K.W., Yee, K.P., & Hong, W.C. (1995). Comparing two methods of sending out questionnaires: E-mail vs. mail. *Journal of the Market Research Society, 37*(4), 441-446.

Turner, R. & Lowry, G. (1999a). The compleat graduate: What students think employers want and what employers say they want in new graduates. In S. Lee (Ed.), *Preparing for the Global Economy of the New Millennium. Proceedings of Pan-Pacific Conference XVI* (pp. 272-274). Fiji: Pan-Pacific Business Association.

Turner, R. & Lowry, G. (1999b). Reconciling the needs of new information systems graduates and their employers in small, developed countries. *South African Computer Journal, 24*(November), 136-145.

Turner, R. & Lowry, G. (2000). Motivating and recruiting intending IS professionals: A study of what attracts IS students to prospective employment. *South African Computer Journal, 26*(4), 132-137.

Turner, R. & Lowry, G. (2001). What attracts IS students to prospective employment: A study of students from three universities. *Managing Information Technology in a Global Economy* (pp. 448-452). Hershey, PA: Information Resources Management Association.

Turner, R. & Lowry, G. (2002). The relative importance of 'hard' & 'soft' skills for IT practitioners. In M. Khosrow-Pour (Ed.), *Issues and trends of information technology management in contemporary organizations* (pp. 1-10). Seattle, WA: Information Resources Management Association.

Turner, R. & Lowry, G. (2003). Education for a technology-based profession: Softening the information systems curriculum. In T. McGill (Ed.), *Issues in information systems education* (pp. 156-175). Hershey, PA: Idea Group Publishing.

Turner, R., Fisher, J., & Lowry, G. (2002). Retaining information systems staff—what may work, and what probably doesn't. *Proceedings of the Pan Pacific Business Conference* (pp. 279-281), Bangkok, Thailand.

Underwood, A. (1997). *The ACS core body of knowledge for information technology professionals*. Retrieved from *www.acs.org.au/national/pospaper/bokpt1.htm*

Van Slyke, C., Kittner, M., & Cheney, P. (1998). Skill requirements for entry-level IS graduates: A preliminary report from industry. *Journal of Information Systems Education, 9*(3), 7-11.

Waterman, R.H., Waterman, J.A., & Collard, B.A. (1994). Toward a career resilient workforce. *Harvard Business Review, 69*(July-August), 87-95.

Westfall, R.D. (1999-2000). Meta-skills in information systems education. *Journal of Computer Information Systems, 40*(Winter), 69-74.

Wong, E.Y.W. (1996). The education and training of future information systems professionals. *Education + Training, 38*(1), 37-43.

Woods, D.R. (1996). *Problem-Based Learning: Helping your students gain the most from PBL* (3rd edition). Retrieved December 1, 2003, from *chemeng.mcmaster.ca/pbl/pbl.htm*

Wrycza, S., Usowicz, T.W., Gabor, A., & Verber, B. (1999). The challenges and directions of MIS curriculum development in respect of transformation of business requirements. *Proceedings of ITiCSE'99* (pp. 177-178), Krakow, Poland.

Young, J. & Keen, C. (1997). The emerging importance of broader skills and personal attributes in the recruitment of Australian IS professionals. *Proceedings of the 8th Australasian Conference on Information Systems,* Adelaide, South Australia.

Chapter XIV

Business Graduates as End-User Developers: Understanding Information Literacy Skills Required

Sandra Barker
University of South Australia, Australia

Abstract

This investigates the introduction of 'real-life' scenarios with undergraduate business students to enhance their understanding of end-user development of database applications. It identifies the problems experienced with end-user development due to incomplete information, incorrect design procedures, and inadequate software knowledge. End-user development of small-scale applications by non-IS/IT professionals is becoming increasingly popular in the workplace, and it has been identified by many researchers as having some managerial risks associated with it. Conversely it has also been identified in the research that the benefits of application development by these 'end-users' mostly outweigh the managerial risks. By allowing access to 'real-life' situations, improving their information literacy skills, and identifying the design issues relevant to good database development, students will be given an insight into how businesses use and store data, and be more aware of the requirements for their future employment.

Introduction

Since the introduction of personal computers (PCs) in the early 1980s, there has been a shift in the use of computer systems from being predominantly the domain of information systems (IS) professionals to almost anyone within an organization (Barker & Monday, 2000). The proliferation of relatively inexpensive hardware and software has meant that employers can now afford to have computers within their organization. Subsequently businesses are increasingly requiring business graduates to not only have good information literacy skills, but also some knowledge of the concepts of application development (Barker & Monday, 2000). Govindarajulu (2003) identified that the introduction of end-user computing (EUC) is becoming "crucial for increasing productivity in many firms" (p. 152). In 1993, Brancheau and Brown presented a paper that reviewed the previous 10 years of research into end-user computing. They commenced their paper by defining end-user computing as the "adoption and use of information technology by personnel outside the information systems department to develop software applications in support of organizational tasks" (1993, p. 439). Using this definition for EUC brought the understanding that the phenomenon of EUC included the development of applications by end-users. This paper (Brancheau & Brown, 1993) has become one of the most cited pieces of literature in the field of end-user computing and end-user application development, and subsequently Brancheau and Brown's definition of EUC is widely supported by current researchers in the field. Edberg and Bowman (1996) defined user-developed applications (UDAs) as "any computer-based application for which non-IS professionals (end-users) assume primary responsibility" (p. 168).

This chapter will reflect on the experiences of the author and the business students in the development of small-scale database applications and the issues that should be addressed in regard to the information literacy skills required to undertake this type of development. However, it is important to first determine who end-user developers are and why they are becoming such an important part of today's business.

Who are End-User Developers?

The first research relating to EUC was published in the late 1970s (McLean, 1979; Codasyl Report, 1979, cited in Cotterman & Kumar, 1989). In the 1970s computing was identified with mainframe computers, and end-user computing appeared to relate to one of three types of computer use: indirect use (where computing tasks were undertaken for the requester), intermediate use (where instructions were given by the person requesting the information as to the format the information would take), and direct use (where information was retrieved by the user using a terminal).

The introduction of the personal computer (PC) in the early 1980s led to EUC being reported as "...a rapidly growing and irreversible phenomenon" (Alavi & Weiss, 1985, p. 6) which has attributed major advantages to organizations including "enhanced productivity of professional and white-collar workers, overcoming the shortage of DP professionals, provision of user-friendly and responsive systems, and overcoming the implementation problems of transferring this process to the user" (p. 6). The research into EUC has led to a number of differing definitions being developed dependent upon the researcher's experience and how they classified end-users.

Rockart and Flannery (1983) identified six classifications of end-users dependent upon their function within the organization. These classifications were:

- non-programming end-user,
- command-level end-user,
- end-user programmers,
- functional support personnel,
- end-user computing support personnel, and
- data processing programmers.

These classifications expanded upon those defined by the Codasyl Report by being more prescriptive with their definition of how the end-users interacted with the technology. Early researchers (e.g., Rockart & Flannery, 1983) reported on a producer/consumer dichotomy when it came to describing end-users, while other researchers (Wetherbe & Leithseier, 1985, as cited in Cotterman & Kumar, 1989) reported on the comparison between the end-user operator and the end-user developer.

Leithseier and Wetherbe (1986) amended their research to include a third component, that of the amount of control that the manager or user has over the computer resources. Cotterman and Kumar (1989) developed taxonomy of end-users based upon this research. It was already apparent at this early stage in the research into EUC that some end-users (i.e., non-IS trained users) were undertaking some application development.

Anecdotally, the increased availability of PCs within organizations, together with the increased level of computer literacy being taught during the primary and secondary education programs, leads the candidate to believe that there are more 'end-users' in employment. A recent study in the United States (Govindarajulu, 2003) highlighted the types of end-users by classification within the User Cube (developed by Cotterman & Kumar, 1989). This paper clearly identified that:

1. the development of applications by end-users contributed to an increased momentum of end-user computing in that area;
2. an understanding of the variance in end-users in an organization will assist in the formulation of management policies directed at the issues related to end-users, and;
3. the classification tool developed in the paper allows a researcher to study end-users based on interaction between user types, support required by end-users, the types of applications developed, and the support systems available (Govindarajulu, 2003, p. 158).

Personal productivity tools (e.g., Microsoft Office, Lotus Office, etc.) are being marketed as being more user friendly, leading end-users to become creative within their everyday working requirements. The so-called wizards are giving end-users more confidence with the software, without having to understand the programming language on which the spreadsheet, database, Web page, or presentation is based. Therefore, with end-users becoming more prevalent in business, and businesses identifying the needs and benefits of end-users developing their own applications, business students need to be exposed to the realities of the jobs they may be entering upon graduation.

User-Developed Applications

The implementation of UDAs has increased due to the perception that they offer greater user control and increased flexibility, encourage innovation, and reduce the workload of the IT department (Monday, 2001). Hobbs and Pigott (2001) found that the force behind end-user development is that users are able to identify their requirements more readily than others and are therefore able to tailor the application to accurately reflect these needs. Consequently it has been noted that UDAs now represent a significant proportion of information systems being utilized in business (McGill, 2002).

However, there is significant evidence that businesses are only just identifying the problems associated with UDAs. While undertaking risk analysis and evaluation, organizations often overlook the risks involved with the proliferation of UDAs (Janvrin & Morrison, 2000). These risks can include incorrect design, inadequate testing, poor maintenance (McGill, 2002), and lack of familiarity with development methodologies or application software (Panko & Halverson, 1996).

It is therefore apparent that more responsibility is being placed on the end-user developer to be conversant with design methodologies, data modeling techniques, theory related to effective and user-friendly input, output and interface design, the intricacies of application software, and documentation techniques to ensure that the application they develop is robust and useful to the organization.

Monday (2001) states that feedback over a number of years from local businesses and professional organizations "highlighted a growing need for business graduates with a greater understanding of the opportunities afforded by 4GLs, and a competency in understanding the business needs and developing small-scale applications for local users," which can be applied to the day-to-day business problems.

Teaching Strategy

In the late 1990s, non-IS business graduates found that they required assistance from previous tutors in the design and implementation of small-scale databases required in their employment. It was this feedback that led to the redesign of a course that would provide students with an active introduction to the problems of end-user development of databases.

Graduates highlighted that many of them (and others in their organizations) were required to develop database applications. Mostly these end-users demonstrated little understanding of the concepts of problem solving, information gathering, analysis, and design and implementation issues for database applications. They did not recognize the implications of the process of application development, or the quality of the applications developed, for the organization (Barker & Monday, 2000).

The graduates raised concerns as they were being required to design and build applications using Microsoft software; however, they had only been introduced to the software's applications generators or "wizards" in the computer literacy course. It was as these graduates explored the need for more advanced features of the software that they began to understand the potential and the limitations of using only the wizard or basic features of the software.

The need of graduates to design and build small-scale applications was raised as an issue. Although a number of the graduates became proficient in the tools of the software, they had only a limited understanding of design principles in relation to data structure, inputs including data validation, outputs, and the interface. Thus the applications tended to fail in terms of 'user friendliness' and failed to achieve the level of accuracy and efficiency expected in data input and output. Winter, Chudoba, and Gutek (1997) suggest it is likely that the UDAs will fail in terms of user friendliness and accuracy of data input and output because of the lack of attention paid to the role of IS literacy in helping the end-user to be efficient and effective.

This first semester course, developed as a result of this graduate feedback, concentrates on data management, systems development theory, and small-scale database construction using Microsoft Access. The course is taught using case studies written in consultation with business, or based on the industrial experience of the staff working on the program.

Kreber (2001) describes case studies as "the detailed description of a particular real-life situation or problem as it happened in the past or as it could happen in the professional life of the student." The use of case studies is encouraged in higher education, as it tends to involve students in a more active learning process. This can be seen to be in line with the four phases of Kolb's experiential learning theory, as students experience concrete experience, abstract conceptualization, reflective observation, and active experimentation. Here students are more likely to "foster the skills of self-directed learning" (Kreber, 2001). Knoop (1984, cited in Kreber, 2001) introduced a problem-solving model based on Kolb's theory.

This model is distinguished by five steps:

1. Identify the problem.
2. Distinguish the problem from the underlying symptoms.

3. Generate alternate problem-solving strategies.
4. Evaluate the alternatives and select best strategy.
5. Develop plan of implementation of best strategy.

Students' experiences apply to this model, as they must first determine any information not presented in the case study that they deem necessary to solving the problem they have been presented. This takes place with the use of a Web-based discussion board available to all students through the course Web site. The course coordinator assumes the role of the primary contact person within the business and responds accordingly to student questions, allowing some latitude for the students to think about the process they are undertaking. All students have access to the questions asked by other groups or individuals and consequently to the answers given by the 'business'.

Case studies used in these course alternate between service and manufacturing business sectors, as this is where the majority of graduates find employment. The content of the case study centers on the information needs of a small business or one department within a larger organization. Students are required to understand the corporate structure and information needs of the department, as well as the organization as a whole.

'Real-Life' Experiences

The case study is presented to the student groups as though it was a project brief from a real organization. Over the past two years, the cases have been presented by actual organizations, and the course coordinator has acted as intermediary to ensure that all groups of students are able to access the same information about the business and its requirements.

Students are challenged by the strict time constraints of the assessment; they have 13 weeks to complete the database task. Tutors encourage students to spend the initial weeks advancing their knowledge of the software to be used by undertaking set exercises from a related textbook. Practical workshop sessions are provided for on-campus students so that they are able to ask questions and discuss alternative features that are available in the software being used. External students are given access to an asynchronous Web-based discussion board for software-based queries. While undertaking this learning students commenced the information-gathering phase of the system development.

Even though students are given a large amount of information in the case study presented, they are required to determine any important information missing from the documentation and consult directly with the business to uncover the relevant data. It is this area in which the students experience major difficulties. The problems that they encounter include: minimal understanding of the process, requests for unnecessary information, inability to reword questions if inadequate reply is received, not asking any questions, and not referring to the Web discussion board which therefore leads to the making of incorrect assumptions. One of the main problems experienced by students in this situation is the ability to decipher what information is necessary and what is just background data about the organization. This inability to decide on the necessary information generally leads students to encounter problems later on in the project when trying to achieve a more complex application than is actually required.

As has been highlighted in the EUC literature, most end-user developers do not generally undertake design tasks in relation to the development of their applications. As the students are learning the features of the software at the same time as they are attempting to design the spreadsheet or database application, they have a tendency to launch directly into the physical design and implementation. This tends to cause the most problems in the case of database construction. Students who do not use data modeling techniques to identify the entities and attributes required, together with the primary keys and table relationships, experience the greatest difficulty with producing a sound, effective, and usable application.

Misuse of or lack of validation and GUI controls were the major weaknesses across the assignments. None of the databases proved to be totally robust and user friendly, however several achieved a good level of development.

Finally, students experienced problems due to the lack of testing of the application. In the production of the database, students tended to enter the data after the construction of the tables and therefore did not test the input screens for functionality and user-friendly design. Applications were therefore not tested for validation techniques, meaningful error messages, and usability and effective macros. A number of the students commented that the wizards were not capable of achieving the full requirements of the users; however, the case studies were all tested prior to the delivery to ensure that the wizards were sufficient for the development of these applications.

Student Issues

The case studies used in this course exposed the students to the problems faced with not knowing or understanding the business type they are assessing. The lack of knowledge of the business processes particularly in the manufacturing industries initially causes the students major concerns, as they not only have to understand the nature of the business, but also the problem necessary to be solved. At the completion of the course, many students have commented about what they have learned, not only about problem solving issues and the use of the software application, but also about the business they were assessing.

The students do not tend to experience the problems inherent in the information-gathering phase of the process, as most of the information is disseminated through the case study documentation and the discussion board. One way that students might experience this problem would be to remove the discussion board from the available facilities, thus making each group responsible for their own information gathering. Although this would simulate the process more accurately, this is generally not considered a viable option in the teaching area of large groups of students where the same questions would be presented numerous times.

Students are not given inaccurate information or time delays due to intra-organization conflicts however; they are only given the information they ask for, and this can sometimes lead to the introduction of poor or incomplete information. Occasionally, due to onshore and offshore teaching commitments, students are unable to contact the business which, in part, simulates the situations experienced by the author in the inability to contact key project personnel due to roster issues. Although the students only experience delays of three to four days maximum, it impacts on their time management quite considerably as they tend to delay starting the assignment until quite close to the due date rather than managing their time as they would in industry.

Case studies are carefully produced to ensure that all the tasks required to be completed or implemented are achievable with the software being utilized. As this is not always the case in business, students are not exposed to these issues. The course aims to give the students some awareness of the limitations of the software (as experienced by non-IS professionals) and therefore they tend to appreciate these limitations without actually experiencing them fully.

Conclusion

Although there is still room for refinement of the case study delivery of this course, students are rising to the challenge of dealing with 'real-life' business problems. Some students are relying heavily on other groups or group members to lead the way without understanding the importance of the system development phases. It is these students who present only partially completed or poorly designed applications, and as such further research is required into better ways to deliver the case study approach.

The aim of this course is to help students recognize the importance of the steps required to achieve a good quality software application even though they are non-IS professionals. It also seeks to encourage students to recognize the implications of their actions and choices for the organization, and not just their immediate needs. Emphasis, thus, is not purely on building a good quality, robust software application, but in presenting a more holistic view of user and organizational needs.

The fact that businesses are requiring graduates that they employ to have the ability to design and build their own small-scale software applications shows that it is imperative that business courses contain a significant level of information literacy. The course discussed in this chapter is a step towards addressing this requirement.

References

Alavi, M. & Weiss, I.R. (1985). Managing the risks associated with end-user computing. *Journal of Management Information Systems, 2*(3), 5-20.

Barker, S. & Monday, A. (2000, December). Business students in information systems: Wizards or apprentices? *Proceedings of the Australasian Computing Education Conference,* Melbourne, Australia.

Brancheau, J.C. & Brown, C.V. (1993). The management of end user computing: Status and directions. *ACM Computing Surveys, 26*(4), 437-482.

Cotterman, W.W. & Kumar, K. (1989). User cube: A taxonomy of end users. *Communications of the ACM, 32*(11), 1313-1320.

Edberg, D.T. & Bowman, B.J. (1996). User-developed applications: An empirical study of application quality and developer productivity. *Journal of Management Information Systems, 13*(1), 167-185.

Govindarajulu, C. (2003). End users: Who are they?. *Communications of the ACM, 46*(9), 152-159.

Hobbs, V.J. & Pigott, D.J. (2001, May). Facilitating end user database development by working with users' natural representations of data. *Proceedings of the IRMA Conference*, Toronto, Canada.

Janvrin, D. & Morrison, J. (2000). Using a structured design approach to reduce risks in end user spreadsheet development. *Information and Management, 37,* 1-12.

Kreber, C. (2001). Learning experientially through case studies? A conceptual analysis. *Teaching in Higher Education, 6*(2), 217-228.

Leithseier, R.L. & Wetherbe, J.C. (1986). Service support levels: An organized approach to end user computing. *MIS Quarterly, 10*(4), 337-349.

McGill, T. (2002). User developed applications: Can end users assess quality? *Journal of End User Computing, 14*(3), 1-15.

Monday, A. (2001, May). The reality of teaching large groups of local and international business students to develop end-user applications. *Proceedings of the IRMA Conference*, Toronto, Canada.

Panko, R.R. & Halverson, R.P. Jr. (1996). Spreadsheets on trial: A survey of research on spreadsheet risks. *Proceedings of the 29th Hawaii International Conference on System Sciences* (pp. 326-335), Maui, Hawaii.

Rockart, J.F. & Flannery, L.S. (1983). The management of end user computing. *Communications of the ACM, 26*(10), 776-784.

Winter, S.J., Chudoba, K.M., & Gutek, B.A. (1997). Misplaced resources? Factors associated with computer literacy among end-users. *Information and Management, 32,* 29-42.

Section III

Problems Accessing Technology that Hinders Literacy

Chapter XV

Narrowing the Digital Divide: Technology Integration in a High-Poverty School

June K. Hilton
Jurupa Valley High School, USA

Abstract

Empirical data from a secondary school that took steps to increase technology integration in its classrooms with the long-term goal of raising student achievement are presented. Results from the analysis of this data indicate positive effects from the implementation of two grants designed to bridge the digital divide. Research confirms that the results from this case study are consistent with the methods for success in implementing technology as a tool to improve student achievement. Future study should involve further data collection via teacher evaluations of the professional development process and the analysis of the results from standardized test scores to confirm the positive impact of technology on student achievement.

Introduction

In December 2000, former U.S. Secretary of Education Richard Riley released the new educational technology plan, *eLearning: Putting a World-Class Education at the*

Finger Tips of All Children. This report was a result of an 18-month study by educators, administrators, policy-makers, and the private sector to rethink and revise the national strategy for the effective use of technology in elementary and secondary education. The report outlined five national goals for technology education which include:

> *Goal 1: All students and teachers will have access to information technology in their classrooms, schools, communities, and homes.*
>
> *Goal 2: All teachers will use technology effectively to help students achieve high academic standards.*
>
> *Goal 3: All students will have technology and information literacy skills.*
>
> *Goal 4: Research and evaluation will improve the next generation of technology applications for teaching and learning.*
>
> *Goal 5: Digital content and networked applications will transform teaching and learning. (U.S. Department of Education, 2000, p. 4)*

While these goals are certainly worthwhile, the question arises, "Are they attainable for all students and all teachers?" According to Brogan (2000, p. 57), "Many teachers did not grow up with computers and are not receiving the training they need to operate them. Some children do not have a computer at home whereas others may have several." This fact is corroborated by Lori Meyer (2001), who reports that 82% of teachers surveyed by the National Center for Education Statistics (NCES) indicated they were not given enough time outside their regular teaching duties to learn, practice, or plan how to use computers and other technologies. This same study also revealed that the more hours teachers had spent in training, the more prepared they felt to use computers and the Internet for instruction.

In addition to insufficient teacher training, another concern is availability of technology to students and teachers at different schools. The lack of technology based on socioeconomic level known as the "digital divide" has changed its focus in recent years. What used to be considered as simply the difference between those who had computers (the wealthy) and those who did not (the poor) is now changing to focus on how the technology is used in the classrooms. Bushweller and Fatemi (2001) report that in high-poverty communities, schools have one computer for every 5.3 students. This is slightly above the national average of one computer for every 4.9 students. However, this same study found that in schools with fewer than 11% of the students qualifying for free/reduced lunch, 74% of the classrooms had Internet access, while in schools with 71% of the students qualifying for free/reduced lunch, only 39% of the classrooms had Internet access. Also of concern was the fact that teachers tended to infuse technology into lessons much less with low-achieving students than with high achievers. The teachers cited tight time constraints, which made it difficult to cover the prescribed curriculum—an even more difficult task with students who have weaker skills or less motivation (Bushweller & Fatemi, 2001).

Clearly it is necessary for all educators to understand not only the importance of technology integration in raising student achievement, but also the methods for breaking down the barriers to this integration in schools on the "wrong side" of the digital divide. Previous research has focused on state or district measures to address these issues. What is needed is an in-depth look on how a high-poverty secondary school moved toward narrowing the digital divide during a two-year period, and the empirical evidence gathered on the issues of staff development and accessibility to technology.

Background

The issue of technology implementation and its effect on student achievement has received much publicity in recent years. As schools are being held more accountable for meeting state and national standards through their performance on standardized tests, the focus on improving student achievement through technology becomes an even greater issue. The question arises, "What factors impact the effectiveness of technology as a tool to raise student achievement?" Archer (1998) believes that computers can raise student achievement and even improve a school's climate. Levinson (2000) agrees, but adds that many factors, such as staff development, infrastructure, and effective instructional materials, influence the effectiveness of technology. Thus, if schools are to be effective in utilizing technology to raise student achievement, these factors must be addressed. Simply put, if schools are to realize benefits from education technology, teachers and students must have adequate and equitable access to hardware and network connections; states and districts must give schools the capacity to use technology well by devising a thoughtful technology plan, and offering adequate teacher training and technical support; and teachers and students must use technology in effective ways (Jerald, 1998). The following paragraphs will address each factor in more detail.

Accessibility

Accessibility to technology is the first step in implementing a technology plan. The hardware and software needs to be in place before its effectiveness can be evaluated. According to Skinner (2002), "Nationally, in 2001, there were just over four students to every instructional school computer, and the number of students per Internet-connected computer in schools dropped from 7.9 in 2000 to 6.8 in 2001" (p. 53). While these numbers are not uniform between students in high-poverty and low-poverty schools, the gap between the two is narrowing. In schools defined as high poverty (75% or more of the students eligible for the federal free and reduced lunch program), 60% of the classrooms were wired in 2000, compared to 77% of the classrooms in all public schools (Skinner, 2002, p. 55).

Connectivity

Another area of concern with respect to accessibility is connectivity. While schools may have the hardware necessary to connect to the Internet, it does not imply that they are connected. Again, while improvements have been made in connectivity, it is not equal among all schools. Two findings regarding connectivity by school characteristics are:

1) In schools with the highest concentration of students in poverty (75% or more students eligible for free or reduced-price school lunch), a smaller percentage of instructional rooms were connected to the Internet (60%) than in schools with lower concentrations of poverty (77-82% of instructional rooms).
2) In schools with the highest minority enrollment (50% or more), a smaller percentage of instructional rooms had Internet access (64%) than in schools with lower minority enrollment (79-85% of instructional rooms) (Cattagni, Farris, & Weststat, 2001).

Clearly, there is not equal access to technology for all students and teachers. This fact makes it extremely difficult for schools with high-poverty and/or high-minority populations to address the first factor of technology effectiveness—infrastructure via accessibility and connectivity.

Staff Development

A second factor of importance in implementing a technology plan is staff development. The research on this topic is prolific. Trotter (1999) reports that nearly four out of every ten teachers who do not use software for instruction say they do not have enough time to try out software, and almost as many say they do not have enough training on instructional software (p. 39). While teachers may have computers at home, using computers for instruction often requires different skills, and many educators are not trained in these skills. Additionally, a lack of time available to receive training is another major obstacle in staff development. K-12 experts agree that the biggest impediment to teachers' ability to learn and use technology integration strategies is time—often there are simply not enough hours in the day or days in the year for teachers to become techno-wizards (Sandham, 2001). It becomes necessary then for schools and school districts to provide time and support to their staff to overcome these barriers.

The type of training that is provided to teachers is also important. Fatemi (1999, p. 7) found that training on "integrating technology into the curriculum" was more helpful to teachers than training in "basic technology skills." A 1997 report from the National Center for Education Statistics (NCES) found that teachers not only need to learn how to use a computer system and the applications, but also need to receive training on the use of available instructional software and how to access other technology resources (p. 67). Since many educators already have a computer at home, they know how to operate it. What is needed is how to use it for instruction.

Interestingly, the type of staff development offered as well as the way computers are used for instruction differs according to school characteristics.

> *"Ninety-one percent of teachers in schools with 6 to 20 percent minority enrollments and 90 percent of teachers in schools with 21 to 49 percent minority enrollments reported that basic training was available to them, compared with 81 percent of teachers in schools with 50 percent or more minority enrollments. Furthermore, 94 percent of teachers in schools with less than 11 percent of the students eligible for free or reduced-price school lunch, 90 percent of teachers in schools with 11 to 30 percent of students eligible, and 91 percent of teachers in schools with 31 to 49 percent of students eligible for free or reduced-price school lunch reported that training in the use of the Internet was available to them, compared with 80 percent of teachers in schools with 50 to 70 percent of students eligible and 79 percent of teachers in schools with more than 70 percent of students eligible for free or reduced-price school lunch." (Smerdon et al., 2000, p. 80)*

Thus, the type of training a teacher receives will influence how they use that technology in the classroom.

Unfortunately, disparities about how the computer is used for instruction are also aligning along ethnic, achievement, and language lines.

> *"A National Center for Education Statistics study last year found that 45 percent of teachers in schools that served predominantly minority students used computers or the Internet for instruction during class as compared with 56 percent of their colleagues in schools with few minority students. Schools targeted for poor performance are dealing with other issues. Technology is last on the totem pole." (Reid 2001, p. 17)*

Smerdon et al. (2000) concur, presenting the following findings:

1) *"Teachers in lower minority enrollment schools were generally more likely than teachers in the highest minority enrollment schools to assign students to use these technologies for multi-media presentations (49 percent of teachers in schools with less than 6 percent minority enrollments and 48 percent in schools with 6 to 20 percent minority enrollments compared with 36 percent of teachers in schools with 50 percent or more minority enrollments) and CD-ROM research (55 percent of teachers in schools with less than 6 percent minority enrollments and 50 percent in schools with 6 to 20 percent minority enrollments compared with 38 percent of teachers in schools with 50 percent or more minority enrollments)."*

2) *"Teachers in schools with smaller proportions of minority enrollments were more likely to use computers or the Internet for Internet research (57 percent of teachers in schools with less than 6 percent minority enrollments and 52 percent in schools with 6 to 20 percent minority enrollments compared with 41 percent of teachers in schools with 50 percent or more minority enrollments)"* (p. 28).

Equally disturbing is the evidence that teachers of students with different ability levels are also using the computer differently. Manzo (2001) reports that in most places the general application of technology with low-achieving students is for "drill and practice" in academic skills. Becker (2000) states, "Teachers of low-achieving classes use substantially more skills-based software, while teachers of advanced students use a mix of more sophisticated programs." Likewise, students with limited English proficiency (LEP) are being treated differently than their fully English proficient counterparts when it comes to computer-based instruction. Zehr (2001) has found that even when LEP students are fortunate enough to get as much time on school computers as their English-proficient classmates, they tend to use it in less meaningful ways (p. 28). One reason for this is that in order for LEP students to get the most out of technology, they need teachers who are trained both to help them learn English and to use computers effectively in instruction. Unfortunately, this combination is rare. Based on these reports it is obvious that teacher technology training must include both quality and quantity. In order for all teachers to meet the second criteria—appropriate training—it must include the methods necessary to reach all students regardless of race, ability, or language skills.

Effective Use

The third factor for a successful implementation of technology is effective use. As has already been shown, teachers of students with different backgrounds use technology differently. With proper support and training, effective use for all students is possible. Smerdon et al. (2000) reported that teachers in high-minority schools were generally more likely than teachers in low-minority schools to cite the lack of support regarding ways to integrate telecommunications as a barrier to technology use. Additionally, teachers in high-poverty and high-minority schools generally were less likely to report that training in Internet use was available to them. Administrators and other district personnel must find the means and the money to support their teachers in addressing this issue. The major concern in this area deals with the ability of school districts to provide a technology coordinator or specialist conversant in technology use. All workers trained in technology need some type of expert support to help them with problems or when questions arise. The proportion of schools with a full-time technology coordinator increased only one percentage point from 1996 to 1998, to 30%, while an additional 10% have part-time coordinators. The rest (60%) rely on teachers or other volunteers, district staff, or outside consultants (Jerald & Orlofsky, 1999). Once again, high-poverty schools also faired worse than low-poverty schools in this area. Only 19% of schools where more than 70% of students are eligible for the federal free and reduced-price lunch program reported having a full-time coordinator, down seven percentage points from two years ago (Jerald & Orlofsky, 1999).

It becomes obvious upon review of this data to begin to question why efforts are not being made to address this lack of support. One need only look at where districts are spending their money. Jerald and Orlofsky (1999) point out that almost 60% of district spending goes toward hardware and networks, while only 13% is allocated for training and support. This percentage is well below the generally accepted value, 30%, mentioned by industry analysts. Obviously, districts must prioritize when preparing budgets, and rethink how and where the money is spent. While having state-of–the-art hardware is admirable, it does no one any good if it sits unused in the classrooms.

One way to be sure that more of a budget goes toward training and support is to utilize the wealth of funds and grants offered by private companies and government agencies. Use of these funds allows resources to be allocated differently because there are more funds available for the same amount of categories. This is especially true for schools serving high-poverty and/or minority communities. Effective use of grant funds can do much to address the issues raised in the preceding paragraphs and begin to close the digital divide at all levels.

The next section takes an in-depth look at one school's attempt to implement a technology plan that addressed the issues of infrastructure, training and support, and the effective use of technology for a high-poverty community. In doing so, the ability of technology to raise student achievement can then be realistically evaluated.

A Case Study in Technology Implementation

Background

Jurupa Valley High School (JVHS) is located in the western end of Riverside County, California. School personnel include 110 classroom teachers, seven guidance coordinators, one nurse, one psychologist, one language/speech/hearing specialist, one full-time deputy sheriff who also serves as the school resource officer, and seven campus supervisors. The school comprises a total of 60 classified staff, which includes office staff, classroom aides, custodians, and other paraprofessionals. The school administration consists of a principal and three assistant principals whose areas of responsibility include curriculum and instruction, pupil personnel services, athletics, and extracurricular activities. Student enrollment during the 2002-2003 school year was 2,765. The student ethnicity breakdown was 54.1% Hispanic, 41.7% White, 1.5% African-American, and 2.6% Other (Asian, American Indian/Alaska Native, Pacific Islander, Filipino), classifying the school as a majority minority school. More than 950 students (36.3%) participate in the Free/Reduced Lunch Program, qualifying the school as a moderate- to high-poverty school. Additionally, approximately 15% (392) of the students were designated as English Development Students (ELD). Figures 1 and 2 illustrate the increase in student population for the past six years, as well as the current student ethnicity breakdown.

Figure 1. Student population trends 1995-2001

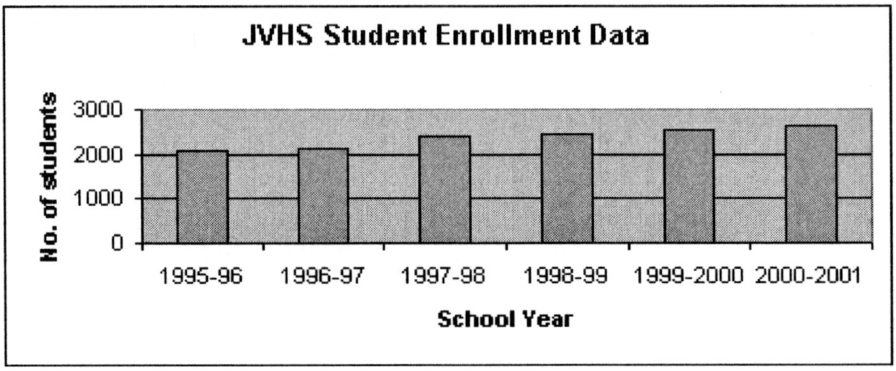

Figure 2. Student ethnicity breakdown

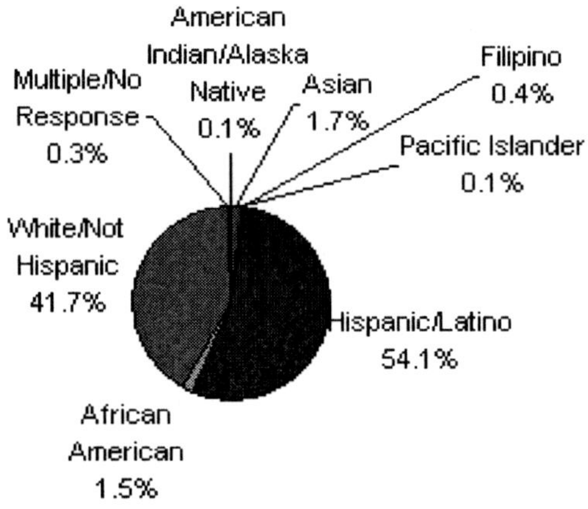

Table 1. SAT mean scores, 1998-2003

	1998	1999	2000	2001	2002	2003
School Verbal Mean	454	446	454	454	448	447
State Verbal Mean	491	492	479	481	490	494
National Verbal Mean	505	505	505	506	504	507
	1998	**1999**	**2000**	**2001**	**2002**	**2003**
School Math Mean	473	463	480	480	467	467
State Math Mean	516	513	491	493	516	518
National Math Mean	512	511	514	514	516	519

Academic data over the past three years indicate that Jurupa Valley High School remains below the state and national averages on the SAT Math and Verbal sections. The means both sections between the 1998 and 2003 graduating classes remain flat. Table 1 and Figure 3 outline these trends.

Data from the SAT9, which served as the state recognized test for indicating academic performance from 1998-2002, shows mixed results. Longitudinal trends indicate that the time between freshman and sophomore year reflects a decrease on the SAT9, while between sophomore and junior year reflects an increase. All scores, however, are below the state level for all grades during the five-year period. Table 2 and Figure 4 reflect the SAT9 data during the five-year period from 1997-2002.

Figure 3. SAT verbal and math scores, 1998-2003

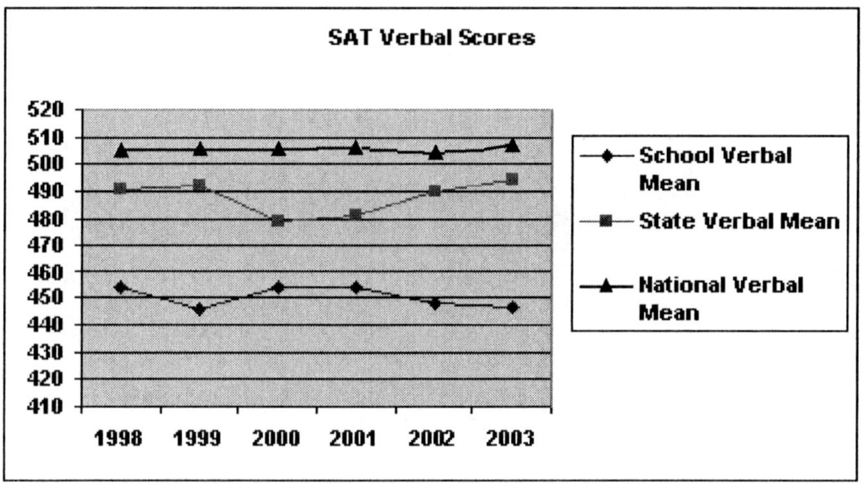

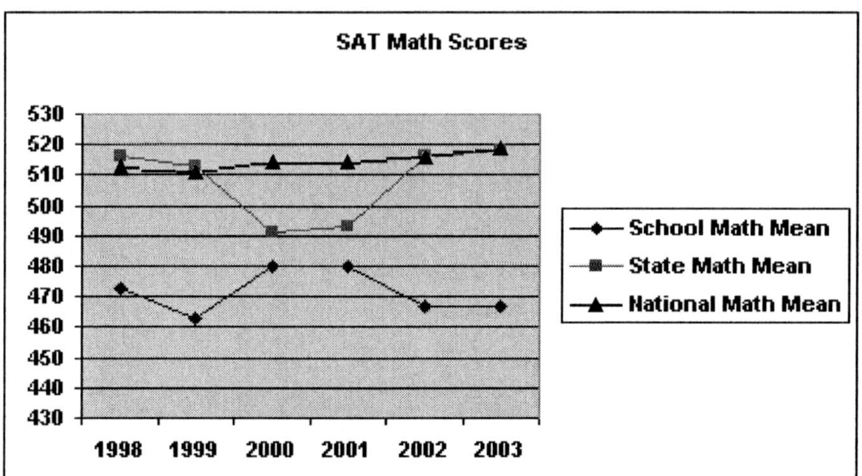

Table 2. SAT9 results, 1997-2002

Reading	1997-1998	1998-1999	1999-2000	2000-2001	2001-2002
Grade 9	28	27	27	26	30
Grade 10	25	24	22	24	25
Grade 11	33	28	29	27	25
Math	**1997-1998**	**1998-1999**	**1999-2000**	**2000-2001**	**2001-2002**
Grade 9	42	39	40	42	51
Grade 10	33	37	32	33	38
Grade 11	36	38	39	34	37

Figure 4. SAT9 reading and math results, 1997-2002

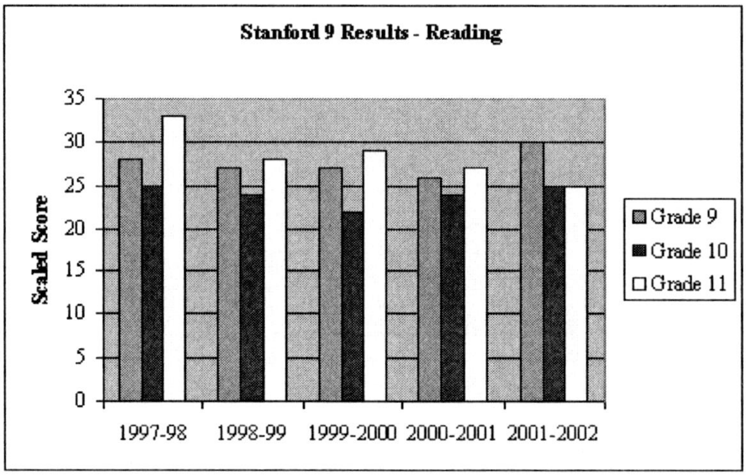

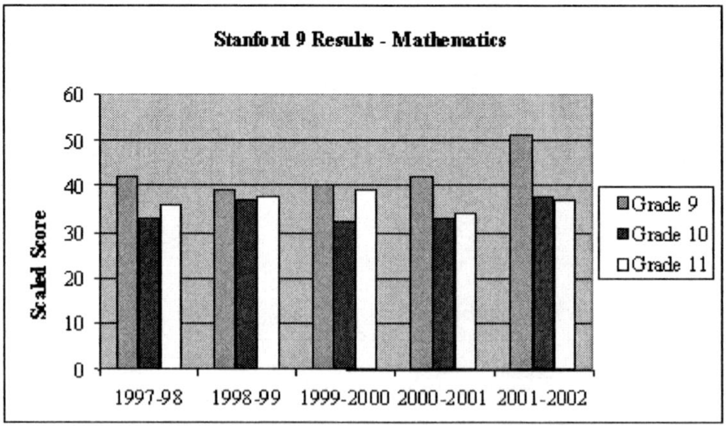

Since the school did not reach its targeted API growth index for either the 2000-2001 or 2001-2002 school years, it was accepted into the Immediate Intervention/Underperforming Schools Program (IIUSP). The school received $500,000 during both the 2001-2002 and 2002-2003 school years to implement its Action Plan, approved by the state to improve student achievement. Although the school exceeded its API growth target for the 2002-2003 school year, it still received IIUSP funding for the 2003-2004 school year as well.

The Technology Implementation Process

There were two technology grants that significantly impacted Jurupa Valley High School's technology plan. The National Association of Secondary School Principals (NASSP), which teamed with the GTE Foundation, underwrote the first grant. This grant, called PACT, Promoting Achievement Through Creative use of Technology, consisted of grants ($50,000 over two years) to six middle schools and high schools in selected urban areas of California, Texas, and Florida to improve teaching and learning through technology literacy. The goal of the grant was to raise student achievement through the implementation of technology as outlined in the NASSP document (1996), "Breaking Ranks: Changing an American Institution," a widely regarded secondary school reform initiative. The grant was written by the principal and submitted in April 1999. The school was notified in late May 1999 of their selection as one of the six grant recipients. Second-year funding was contingent upon successful completion of Year One goals.

A second grant that also assisted in the implementation of Jurupa Valley's technology plan was the Digital High School (DHS) Program. The Digital High School Program serviced all secondary schools in the state of California, providing provided assistance so that these schools were able to install and support technology, as well as to provide staff training. All California secondary schools were placed on a four-year installation cycle beginning in 1998-1999. Jurupa Valley was designated a "Year Three" school, indicating that the grant would be written and approved by the State Department of Education during the 1999-2000 school year, with installation of equipment during the 2000-2001 school year. The installation support was provided through the Technology Installation Grant, a one-time $300 per student amount. Based on student enrollment during 1999-2000, this amounted to $752,000. Following the Technology Installation Grant, all schools submitted a final report and a Certification of Completion of the Installation Grant. Schools submitting this certification were eligible to receive a Technology Support and Staff Training Grant in the second fiscal year following the year in which they were selected for the Technology Installation Grant. The Technology Support and Staff Training Grant is an ongoing $45 per student per year. Based on student enrollment during the installation year, Jurupa Valley received almost $118,000 for the 2001-2002 school year. The above funding was contingent upon the Jurupa Unified School District providing an equivalent local match, as well as the funds being appropriated each year by the State Department of Education. Due to reductions in the state budget, funding for continued staff development and training was discontinued for the foreseeable future.

These two grants provided the monetary support needed to implement the school's technology plan and address the issues most often raised concerning effective technology implementation. The next section presents the results from the implementation of these two grants.

Results

The first empirical data to review is the increased use of the computer lab. In 1998-1999, prior to the implementation of either grant, five teachers and their classes utilized the newly designed computer lab. During Year One of the PACT Grant (1999-2000), this number increased 400% to 25 teachers. Figure 5 outlines the breakdown of use by department.

While this was a tremendous increase in use, only 25% of the staff was using the lab to augment classroom instruction. Three of the four departments most utilizing the computer lab—Special Education, Foreign Language, and Science—also had content-specific software purchased and installed on the computers in the lab as a result of Year One PACT Grant funds. A paraprofessional was also employed using PACT Grant funds during 1999-2000 to assist teachers and students in the lab.

Year Two of the PACT Grant (2000-2001) saw the computer lab used more frequently. While the number of teachers using the lab decreased slightly to 19, this was more a result of the lab being used for staff development than fewer teachers wishing to use the lab. The lab was closed intermittently to train the Math Department on a newly purchased software program, as well as to train all staff on a newly acquired Career Education software program. The lab was also closed every Monday and Thursday to permit technology training for teachers, thus restricting the number of times a teacher could use the lab to five sessions per teacher per semester. This amounted to once per month per teacher. Figure 6 depicts computer lab use during the 2000-2001 school year.

Figure 5. Computer lab use, 1999-2000

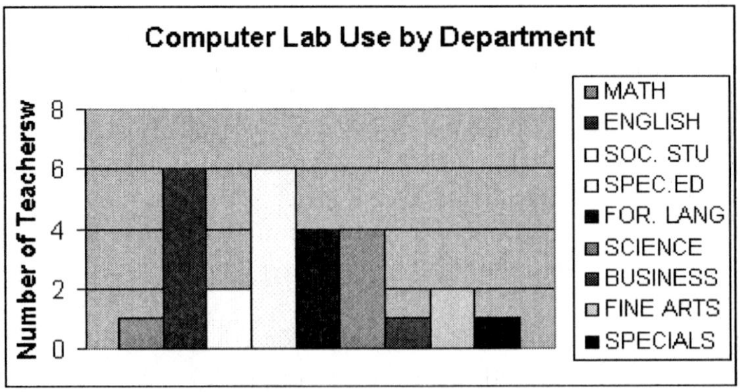

The Foreign Language Department, which includes the English Language Development students, increased their use of the lab during 2000-2001. This was an attempt to provide limited English Proficient students the opportunity to learn language skills via software programs and Internet research assignments. The PACT Grant funds also funded the employment of a technology-savvy long-term substitute to assist, when needed in the lab, as well as to install the multimedia equipment purchased through the DHS Grant in the individual classrooms. Eight additional computers were purchased, bringing the total computers in the lab to 36. This reduced the student/computer ratio to 1:1 in the lab. All computers had a high-speed Internet connection and were networked to a printer.

A second area of empirical data to review is staff development. Most of the PACT Grant funds in Year Two were dedicated to technology training. Training was open to all staff, with first semester preference given to the Mathematics and English Departments. These departments were identified first as they directly related to the core areas targeted by the SAT9, the district criterion referenced tests, and the benchmarks listed in the DHS Grant proposal. Each teacher was given the choice of attending a weekly, three-hour session lasting for 15 weeks. Sessions were offered during both the morning and afternoon. Teachers were provided with substitute coverage during school hours or hourly compensation at the contracted rate for after school hours. The company that provided the technology training also offered the session for professional advancement credit on the salary scale through Long Island University. By the end of the 2000-2001 school year, approximately 60% of the staff received this training. Figure 7 highlights the percentage of each department that participated in this professional development opportunity.

It should be noted that staff members already competent in technology use were encouraged *not* to sign up for training. While individual competency was certainly a personal evaluation, some departments such as Science and Business Technology already had members that were not in need of training, thus making their percentages

Figure 6. Computer lab use, 2000-2001

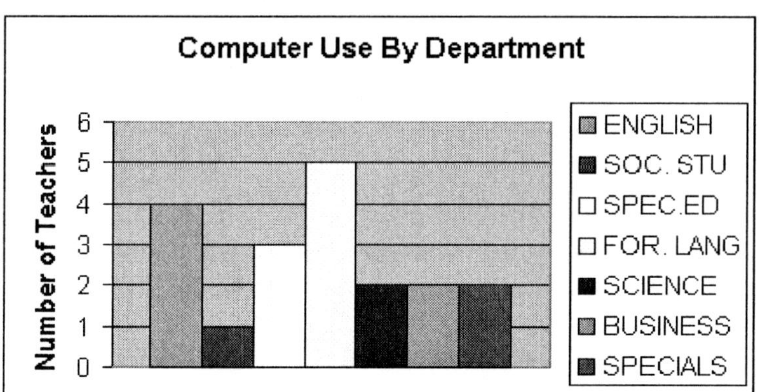

Figure 7. Staff development by department via PACT Grant funds

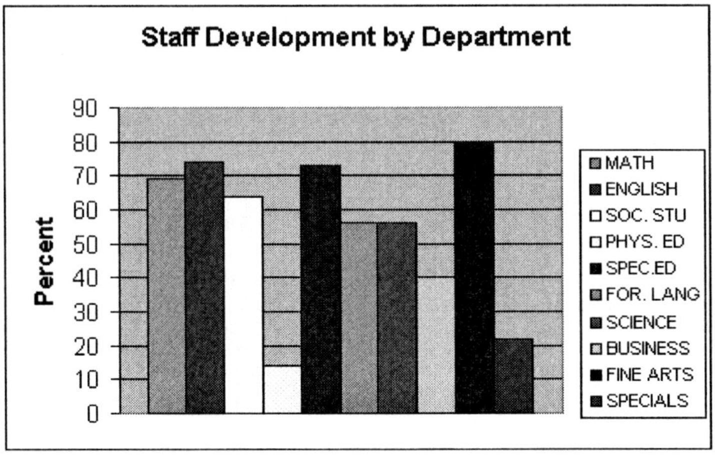

seem low in comparison to other departments. As seen from the chart, departments such as Physical Education and Specials (Agriculture, ROTC) had low participation primarily due to their personal perception of lack of relevance to their curriculum.

The funding from the Digital High School grant provided for the installation of a multimedia computer, television, and VCR in every classroom, along with a high-speed Internet connection via a T1 line. These funds also supplied money for a part-time computer specialist to maintain the school's local area network (LAN) and troubleshoot problems that arose in both the computer lab and individual classrooms.

There is no question that monies received from these two grants provided the school with a tremendous opportunity to reduce the "digital divide." The empirical data presented in the preceding paragraphs sheds light on why it is important not simply to have available monies, but to spend those monies in appropriate areas. In the following section, some possible explanations of these findings are discussed.

Discussion

Jurupa Valley High School has approached the technology implementation process in a manner that maximizes the probability of success in raising student achievement. Both grants provided monies not only to equip classrooms, but also to provide staff development. Many districts in general and schools in particular fail in the area of staff development. Teachers must be provided with time to learn how the technology works, as well as how to integrate it into the classroom.

The Chicago Public schools experienced a similar influx of money for technology. According to a report on the Chicago School System's approach to staff development, Wisnewski (1999) reports, "The district recognized the need for training during school hours as well as on Saturdays and during the summer. Teachers were released from duty for five days so they could receive training while keeping tabs on the substitute teachers in their classrooms" (p. 23). JVHS provided similar training to its staff with the same opportunity to "keep tabs" on their classes. The school also provided flexibility by alternating morning and afternoon sessions, and providing hourly compensation. Trotter (1999, p. 40) reports that training seems to make a positive difference to those who received it, particularly when it came to confidence levels, use of digital content, and willingness to experiment. His findings highlight the importance of training in both basic skills and integration. One interesting finding from his report on a study conducted by the Institute for Research on Learning was that teachers who received 11 or more hours of curriculum-integration training were five times as likely to say they feel "much better prepared today" to integrate technology into their classroom lessons than teachers who received no such training (Trotter 1999, p. 40).

Jurupa Valley offered its staff 45 hours of training in basic skills and curriculum integration with PACT Grant funds. The importance of training is echoed by Levinson and Grohe (2001, p. 55), who state, "The pressure point for effective technology implementation is training and staff development. It should account for 30-50 percent of your hardware investment if the new technologies are to bring about the benefits which we think they can." Zehr (1997) concurs, stating that if a school's equipment is to be used well, at least 30% of a technology budget should be spent on professional development. The school indeed invested a large part of the funds from the PACT Grant in technology training.

What makes technology training so critical is its likelihood to lead to implementation. As Fatemi (1999, p. 7) points out:

> *"A lack of training is the most important obstacle inhibiting the use of digital content. Teachers who received technology training in the past year are more likely than teachers who had not to integrate technology into their classroom lessons and are also more likely to use and rely on digital content for instruction, spend more time trying out software and searching for Web sites to use in class."*

Trotter (1999) found that teachers who received training were more likely to use software to enhance instruction in their classrooms, to rely on software and the Internet in classroom instruction to a "very great" or "moderate" extent, and to spend time trying out or teaching themselves about software, as well as searching the Internet for information and resources to use in the classroom (p. 40). Personal observation indicated that many teachers who participated in the training did indeed attempt to integrate technology into their classroom during and after training. For example, English teachers continued to utilize the computer lab after first-semester training as evidenced by the computer lab sign-up sheets.

In addition to staff development, accessibility to equipment was another area where the funds from these grants were put to good use. The National Center for Education Statistics (2001) reported that by the fall of 2000, the ratio of students to instructional computers in public schools had decreased from 5 to 1, and that the ratio of students to instructional computers with Internet access in public schools improved from 9 to 1 in 1999 to 7 to 1 in 2000. The same report, however, also found that the ratio of students to instructional computers with Internet access was still greater in schools with the highest concentration of students in poverty (9 to 1) than in schools with the lowest concentration of poverty (6 to 1). The computers purchased by Jurupa Valley with both grants over the two-year period reduced the student-computer ratio to 8 to 1, a slight decrease from the reported average of 9 to 1.

While it is important to have computers available to students, a greater concern is computer use. Anderson and Ronnkvist (1999) have concluded that although computing capacity for instruction has improved substantially over the past several years, there are a number of "major deficiencies." For example, they found that most of the computers in schools do not have the capability to run a large variety of multimedia software and are also limited in how they can access graphical information on the Internet. Fortunately, the computers purchased with the DHS funds were multimedia capable, state of the art, and able to process graphics as well as text. Although the computers located in each classroom at Jurupa Valley are capable of handling a large amount and variety of data, their use is restricted because of their limited numbers. Since each academic classroom currently houses only one computer, student use on this one computer is not possible. The computer lab, which affords a 1:1 student/computer ratio, is where student access is possible and most frequent. Smerdon et al. (2000) listed three findings concerning preparatory tasks and computer availability, and classroom instruction and computer availability.

1) Among teachers who reported having computers located in their classrooms, those who had more than five classroom computers were more likely than those with fewer classroom computers to report doing various preparatory activities (lesson plans, etc.) "a lot".
2) Teachers' reports of assigning students to use computers or the Internet for various instructional purposes differed by the number of computers in their classrooms; for example, 59% of teachers with one computer in the classroom reported *not* assigning students to use computers or the Internet to solve problems or analyze data, compared with 40% of teachers with two to five computers and 23% of teachers with more than five computers.
3) Conversely, teachers with more than five computers in their classrooms were most likely to report assigning problem-solving or data analysis computer work to a "large extent," followed by teachers with two to five computers and teachers with one computer (21% compared with 9% and 5%, respectively).

At Jurupa Valley, the availability of the computer lab assists teachers in assigning their students problem-solving or data analysis tasks. The difficulty lies in the inability to use the computer lab due to staff development and other teacher training activities. Teachers have assigned student projects and/or reports requiring in-class PowerPoint presentations, which allow student use of the sole classroom computer during scheduled class periods; however, individual use is limited.

Finally, the monies from these grants have permitted the computer lab to be available after school for students to use. The computer lab was open this past school year, two days a week for four-and-one-half hours, staffed by faculty receiving contracted hourly compensation. This has helped make computers available to those who do not have one at home. A recent report on after-school equity with computers found that 80% of high school students from families with annual household incomes of at least $75,000 reported using a computer at home, while only 18% of students from families with household incomes between $10,000-$15,000 reported using a computer at home (Sandham, 2001). By allowing students the opportunity to use a computer with Internet access, the school has afforded them the same opportunity to improve their research, problem-solving, and data analysis skills.

Conclusion

Technology, when implemented correctly via a sound technology implementation plan, can provide the means for raising student achievement. The issues that need to be addressed are both technical and organizational. Obviously, the hardware and infrastructure must be in place, but it will not begin to raise student achievement if both the faculty and students do not utilize it. A sound technology plan must include components for training, support, and maintenance. As Wisniewski (1999) explains, "The challenge is to ensure that teachers use the technology in ways that help children learn better than if there were no technology" (p. 23). This cannot occur if provisions are not made to address these issues. This is where the organizational element becomes crucial. As the NCES report (1997) found, "You need to ensure that the technology is used properly and that it is systematically maintained and supported" (p. 75). The only way to ensure proper use is to train the users on the equipment. It is clear that the barriers to the use of computers and the Internet for instruction most frequently reported by public school teachers were insufficient numbers of computers, lack of release time for teachers to learn how to use computers or the Internet, and lack of time in the schedule for students to use computers in class. In fact, while it is true that most schools now have computers and the Internet available somewhere in their schools, this availability is still somewhat limited in the classroom (Smerdon, 2000). A sound technology plan must incorporate methods to reduce or eliminate these barriers.

The results from this case study reflect the efforts of Jurupa Valley High School to address these barriers. While computers were limited to one per classroom, a computer lab with a student/computer ratio of 1:1 was made available to teachers. Training was provided to all staff of sufficient duration (45 hours per teacher), and time both inside and outside the school day allowed teachers flexibility in selecting a training session. Additional incentives in the way of professional development credit or hourly compensation were also provided.

Support for technology was made available through the use of a part-time technology coordinator, paraprofessional, and tech-savvy, long-term substitute to assist teachers in the computer lab as well as in their classrooms. The school also made the computer lab available to students during after-school hours for those who did not have access at home. This effort did much to help students who otherwise would not be able to develop literacy in technology skills. These are also key areas that need to be considered when developing a plan.

The funds provided by the two grants studied here allowed the school to allocate money in areas that most schools and districts neglect—training and support. As seen in the research, differences in the implementation of a technology plan vary markedly by school characteristics. Jurupa Valley used these funds to provide not only hardware and software, but also training and support in order that teachers and students could effectively use the available technology. What is needed now is the collection of longitudinal data to study the effects of this implementation on student achievement. Data from standardized tests can now be collected and analyzed to determine the effects the implementation of technology has on raising student achievement. This has been the debate for the past several years. As Levinson 2000 states, "Before we can address whether technology use is impacting student outcomes, we should address how well the technology—and its contextual variables, such as staff development, tech support, and materials—is implemented" (p. 58). This case study has addressed the degree to which technology in a high-poverty school has been implemented. The school addressed the major issues well with the assistance of grants. While the implementation of a technology plan is a dynamic process, it has been set in motion using sound principles. Thus, future research may now focus on the effect this technology has on an important educational issue—increasing student achievement.

References

Anderson, R.E. & Ronnkvist, A. (1999). *The presence of computers in American schools.* Irvine, CA: Center for Research on Information Technology and Organizations, University of California, Irvine.

Archer, J. (1998). The link to higher scores. *Education Week–Technology Counts 1998, 18*(5).

Becker, H.J. (2000, January). Findings from the teaching, learning, and computing survey: Is Larry Cuban right? *Proceedings of the Council of Chief State School Officers Annual Technology Leadership Conference,* Washington, DC.

Brogan, P. (2000). Educating the digital generation. *Educational Leadership, 58*(2), 57-59.

Bushweller, K. & Fatemi, E. (2001). Dividing lines. *Education Week–Technology Counts 2001, 20*(35), 10-11.

Cattagni, A., Farris, E., & Weststat. (2001). Internet access in U.S. public schools and classrooms: 1994-2000. (NCES 2001-071). Washington, DC: National Center for Education Statistics, U.S. Department of Education..

Fatemi, E. (1999). Building the digital curriculum. *Education Week–Technology Counts 1999, 19*(4), 5-8.

Jerald, C.D. (1998). By the numbers. *Education Week–Technology Counts 1998, 18*(5).

Jerald, C.D. & Orlofsky, G.F. (1999). Raising the bar on school technology. *Education Week–Technology Counts 1999, 19*(4), 58-62.

Levinson, E. (2000). Technology and accountability: A chicken-and-egg question. *Converge,* (November), 58-59.

Levinson, E. & Grohe, B. (2001). The times they are a-changin'. *Converge,* (May), 54-56.

Manzo, K.K. (2001). Academic record. *Education Week–Technology Counts 2001, 20*(35), 22-23.

Meyer, L. (2001). New challenges. *Education Week–Technology Counts 2001, 20*(35), 49-54.

National Association of Secondary School Principals. (1996). *Breaking ranks: Changing an American institution.* Reston, VA: Author.

Reid, K.S. (2001). Racial disparities. *Education Week–Technology Counts 2001, 20*(35), 16-17.

Sandham, J.L. (2001). Across the nation. *Education Week–Technology Counts 2001, 20*(35), 67-68.

Sandham, J.L. (2001). Time, leadership, and incentives. *Converge,* (July), 39-42.

Skinner, R.A. (2002). Tracking tech trends. *Education Week–Technology Counts 2002, 22*(35), 53-56.

Smerdon, B., Cronen, S., Lanahan, L., Anderson, J., Iannotti, N., & Angeles, J. (2000). *Teachers' tools for the 21st century: A report on teachers' use of technology.* (NCES 2000-102). Washington, DC: National Center for Education Statistics, U.S. Department of Education.

Trotter, A. (1999). Preparing teachers for the digital age. *Education Week–Technology Counts 1999, 19*(4), 37-43.

U.S. Department of Education. (2000). *eLearning: Putting a world-class education at the finger tips of all children.* Retrieved from *www.ed.gov/Technology/Elearning/index.html*

U.S. Department of Education, National Center for Education Statistics. (1997, October). *Technology @ your fingertips—a guide to implementing technology solutions for education agencies and institutions.* Washington, DC.

U.S. Department of Education. (2000). *The power of the Internet for learning: Moving from promise to practice.* Retrieved from *interact.hpcnet.org/Webcommission/index.htm*

Wisniewski, M. (1999). Counting on computers. *Electronic School,* (September), 22-24.

Zehr, M.A. (2001). Language barriers. *Education Week–Technology Counts 2001, 20*(35), 28-29.

Zehr, M.A. (1997). Teaching the teachers. *Education Week–Technology Counts 1997, 17*(11), 24-26.

Chapter XVI

Digital Access, ICT Fluency, and the Economically Disadvantaged: Approaches to Minimize the Digital Divide

Ellen Whybrow
University of Alberta, Canada

Abstract

The digital divide is a complex phenomenon inextricably linked to income security and not easily addressed through programs that provide simple solutions of training and access. This chapter details the importance of digital access and fluency as they relate to economic disadvantage and explores a variety of models that are used to address the problem. The chapter argues that programs addressing digital divide issues require a multi-faceted approach to address a variety of needs that exist as a result of the condition. While there may be a clash between community, educational, and employer groups, the chapter proposes an alliance model of stakeholders working towards common goals as well as their own organizational interests.

Introduction

The rapid increase of information and communication technologies (ICTs) has irrevocably changed the nature of educational and work environments in Western countries in the past decade. As recently as the mid-1990s, the use of technology in most post-secondary programs was limited to the use of PowerPoint for instructional delivery and word processors for assignments. In a few short years, ICT tools such as course management systems, synchronous capability, the Internet, and wireless devices, have provided students new conditions with which to obtain, manage, communicate, and construct knowledge. Graduates of educational programs bring these skills to the workplace, making access to emerging technologies and the cultural capital needed to be fluent in their use a prerequisite for academic, social, and future vocational success (Wilhelm, Carmen, & Reynolds, 2002; Pew Research Center, 2002).

A continuing dilemma in the field of adult education is the issue of access and equity for students from economically disadvantaged backgrounds. Levine and Nidiffer (1996) found that post-secondary enrollment rates have improved in the previous half-century for all students with barriers to education, with the exception of those students with economic barriers. ICT is constantly evolving and continues to be costly for students who are economically disadvantaged and, in many cases, have had limited or superficial access to these tools (Statistics Canada, 2003; Wilhelm et al., 2002; US Department of Commerce, 2000). As proficiency with ICT is increasingly linked with job and income security (Krahn & Lowe, 2002), becoming proficient beyond the basic use of these technologies has become a key requirement for economically disadvantaged adults to realize vocational and therefore economic aspirations. How educators and the society that they serve accommodate the economically disadvantaged is a key question to those who consider the accessibility of education to be a core value.

Education has long been viewed as a means to equalize social and economic disparity within society. Access to and equity in education are the characteristics that facilitate such equal opportunity. However, educational organizations are limited in tackling such a complex problem. Instead, the answer lies in alliances of various organizations—both public and private—working towards common goals while fulfilling their own organizational interests. The focus of this chapter is to explore the relationship between economic restructuring, the economically disadvantaged, and the need for ICT fluency in this new and ever-changing environment. The chapter will review quantitative and qualitative data describing the phenomenon and will synthesize various approaches developed in response. Finally, the chapter will suggest directions for program response and areas for further research.

Background: Defining the Population and Access Barriers

One of the challenges in undertaking a review of this nature is defending its relevance. Colleagues see technology ubiquitously in use throughout educational institutions and know that student loan programs and scholarships open doors for the disadvantaged to obtain an education, which increases job opportunities once completed. The solution is simple: if you are poor, get an education and the technical skills you will need to get a job. What is less obvious is that there are links between technology and economic restructuring happening at national and global levels which impact personal job and income security for the poor and increasingly the middle class.

What is evident from the literature is that there is no clear or universally accepted definition of who is economically disadvantaged or poor. Some countries like the U.S. use an absolute measurement, which defines poverty as a state in which a person is unable to provide even the most basic needs of food, clothing, and shelter. Other countries such as Canada and Britain use relative measurement, which defines poverty at a specific level compared to median income (Dickens & Ellwood, 2003). These definitions come under criticism from various factions; absolute measures may indicate that poverty has fallen (Institute for Research on Poverty, 2002) or been eliminated (Sarlo, 1992), while relative measures indicate an increase (Dickens & Ellwood, 2003). What is easier to identify is that certain groups are at a disadvantage economically regardless of the criteria used; visible minorities, single-parent families, particularly those headed by women, the educationally deficient, and those living in large metropolitan or rural areas have higher rates of poverty (Institute for Research on Poverty, 2002). Absolute measurements would obviously exclude people who can afford technology access, while relative measurements mean that people can own technology or have home access and still fall within a definition of being poor. For the purposes of this review, relative definitions and the term "economically disadvantaged" will be used from this point forward.

Some futurists have reviewed the progress of other technologies and predicted that the issues of the digital divide will fade away of their own accord as ICTs proliferate everyday life (Sargent & Tucker, 1997). The Pew Research Center (2003) has found that although Internet access has increased for Americans (58% had home access in 2002 compared to 49% in 2000), its growth has been slowing since late 2001; the report draws comparisons to the adoption rate of the telephone which slowed during the Depression. The report's survey indicates that a sizeable number of people remain offline and Internet cost is a substantial disincentive for some of the offline population. While it is logical to make historical comparisons to other technologies, this chapter argues that ICT differs substantially from previous technologies such as the telephone. ICT, referring to electronic media consisting of hardware and software, and telecommunications technology such as the Internet go beyond simplistic two-way audio connections to allow for place- and time-independent communication, as well as research, knowledge construction, and management functions. ICT tools also differ from other technologies because they are constantly evolving, making the requirements to continually upgrade hardware and bandwidth important. In a previous report, Pew (2000) reports that, while US Internet access had increased dramatically, half of all Americans remain offline and 57% of non-users have no plans of acquiring access. Many of these non-users (39%) cite cost as a disincentive to going online.

It is also important to emphasize that access can mean more than access to hardware. Mitchell (1999) notes that access involves general connectivity that is available in your surrounding community, as well as what you can pay to service your home. It also involves the cultural aspect embedded in software design. The language and relevance of most information is targeted at the well-educated middle class. These features also pose additional access barriers, which are far less quantifiable than variables such as ownership or home Internet access, but important to note nevertheless.

ICT and Economic Disadvantage: The Polarization of the Workforce

Not being online or technically proficient has economic consequences. The obvious is that information, such as job postings, is increasingly available exclusively online. However, there are other reasons related to the restructuring of Western economies that make being a technology "have-not" significant. Technology has produced patterns of work that "deskill" or eliminate human labour (Shalla, 1997). Krahn and Lowe (2002) have analyzed computer use, income, and working patterns that exist within the Canadian economy and have arrived at the succinct label of "Good Jobs/Bad Jobs." This is a condition in which companies, in efforts to compete globally, have increasingly moved to a structure revolving around a small core group of highly paid workers who are supported in their creation, communication, and management functions by a periphery of part-time or contracted unskilled, semi-skilled, and even skilled workers. Highly paid staff are more likely to use computers and use them in advanced ways. Their use of computers means that they are more likely to be developing transferable skills. Peripheral workers, although many may use computers, tend to use technology to process data, rather than to create or manage information. This raises the issue of enskilling and deskilling (pp. 289-292). Those who use computers in advanced ways along with other advanced skills improve their employment prospects, while those whose use of technology is marginal or automated find their career prospects limited. This polarized workforce is increasingly a worldwide phenomenon. In the US, Goode and Maskovsky's (2001) collection of ethnographic studies note the effects of this polarized workforce and the corresponding decline in wages and job security for low or semi-skilled people.

The polarization described above can affect a broad spectrum of people including many in the middle class (Ehrenreich, 1990). Lack of technology access, a problem more prevalent among the economically disadvantaged, makes the problem more acute because there are fewer chances for self-directed study. It can be argued that providing access through schools, libraries, and community centres provides a remedy for deskilled or unskilled workers. To a certain extent this is true. If we examine studies of disadvantaged and at-risk children, special programs to provide technology home access are associated with increased school performance; the question remains whether it is logical to assume that similar programs for adults increase skills important for work. A.T. Kearney's (2002) study of children's technology access and its relationship to career preparation for technology-related careers shows that access is only part of the issue. In a workforce survey of youth in the Silicon Valley, it was found that while school (99%) and home (86%) computer and Internet access were very high, youth from lower socioeconomic backgrounds were much less interested in obtaining the education needed to take advantage of the region's major economic activity. As with other characteristics, social networks were extremely important in determining the educational and career path of youth. It is reasonable to assume that adults seeking retraining to improve economic prospects also have the same influences and limitations.

Experiences of Digital "Have-Nots"

The connection between technology literacy and economic security was well-entrenched in the minds of many participants in a qualitative study of economically disadvantaged adults pursuing post-secondary education (Whybrow-Howes, 2000). For those most concerned with changing their economic circumstances, it was important not only to be computer literate, but also to study in a computer-related field to take up a more secure role in the knowledge economy. Interviews with the participants—most of whom were disadvantaged by relative and not absolute measurements—indicated that adult students planning to go back to school were able to save for technology purchases and did not find the cost unreasonable. Those students who were not able to purchase computer systems relied primarily on institutional labs or other community services. Access was most difficult for non-computer owners in highly technologically intensive programs. Since many in the study were, at best, recent computer owners, they often perceived their literacy as substantially behind the literacy of fellow students. As with children, social networks were important in filling in access and literacy gaps, although these networks were not always reliable in achieving these goals.

Stanley (2003) notes the psychosocial issues of relevance, fear, and self-concept that hinder the acquisition of computer literacy. Cost was, in many cases, a minor issue that was used to justify rather than explain one's lack of computer literacy. Some participants in her study put off ICT purchases because they did not see it as relevant to their lives and lacked an understanding of the potential of ICT to expand social, educational, and economic opportunities. Many did not "see" themselves as computer users, who were perceived as not part of their culture or sub-culture. Many participants did purchase ICTs only to avoid their use because they did not want to appear incompetent or not being able to learn in front of their families or partners. Her research indicates "ownership does not always accurately reflect computer literacy" (p. 409).

Solving the Problem

For many educators interested in social justice issues, the problems associated with the economically disadvantaged, the phenomena of a polarized workforce, and the need for ICT proficiency remains difficult and, at times, seemly unsolvable. While action at the individual level is always important, in general, complex problems require multi-faceted solutions and a coordination of efforts on the part of individuals, educational institutions, communities, and governments. A review of the literature indicates three general models with which to address ICT and the economically disadvantaged. All models have strengths and weaknesses, and these will be reviewed. Finally, a fourth model will be proposed which builds upon the strengths of all models to provide multiple partnerships, formal and non-formal educational opportunities, and the ability to produce more meaningful changes.

Formal Education: The Computer Course Model

The most basic and easily categorized response is the "computer course." It is a unit that is easily described, scheduled, and delivered to clients. The service provider may be a community college, non-profit organization, or adult education centre. The "course" is usually marketed to individuals, and its successful completion leads to either more courses, certification, or both.

The blueprint of the course is curriculum. A variety of curriculum responses to the phenomenon of ICT and the economically disadvantaged have been proposed and implemented through the years. Early pre-"Internet" literature focused on the notion of computers as keys to equity, access, and quality (Congress of the US, 1993; Guthrie, Garms, & Pierce, 1988). This point of view states that information technologies provide low-cost learning opportunities, which, in turn, lead to greater educational access for all, and increased equity for those most marginalized in education through expanded

Figure 1.

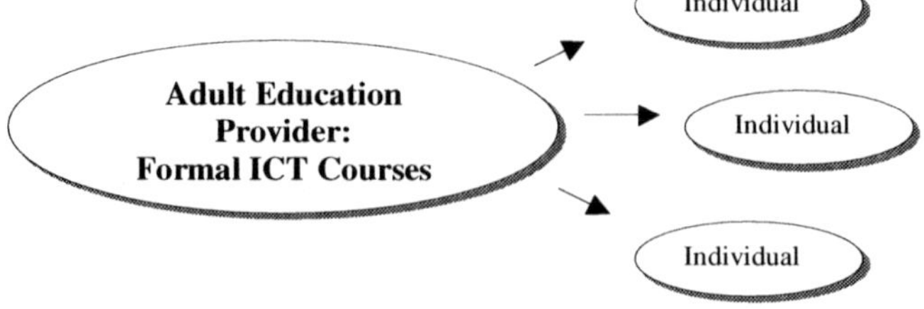

individualization and interaction. Computer programs that address a wide range of instructional and remedial needs allow students to work at their own pace until mastery of concepts is achieved. However, literature of the day also suggests substantial evidence that students in low socioeconomic schools receive inferior computer instruction, which emphasizes drill and practice, transmission methods, and lower-order thinking skills, while students from high-income schools spend more time making judgments, inferences, and evaluation of the content. "Affluent students are thus learning to tell the computer what to do, while less affluent students are learning to do what the computer tells them" (Watt, as quoted by Resta, 1992, p.122).

The traditional view of technology as a transmitter of knowledge is still very prevalent. Features of this approach are skill-based modules to acquire technology skills, carefully packaged Web-based, or CD-based materials to learn other content and traditional tests. An example of this approach is the European Computer Driving license, which has been widely adopted in the European community and is being used through programming in some countries to certify "the skill level achieved by socially disadvantaged people" (European Centre for Development, 2001, p. 17). Payne (2002), in his review of work-based skills, notes national and international political support for these easily understood approaches, but also notes the approach leads to a decontextualization of learning without specific relevance to the learner. While a computer driving license provides an easily recognizable qualification, it is this writer's viewpoint that it will not fundamentally change the economic conditions in which people find themselves.

Kozma and Wagner (2003) have noted the features of instructive and constructive curriculum approaches to ICT and the economically disadvantaged. Instructive approaches, which emphasize direct instruction, allow explicit progression, frequent feedback, and coverage of basic skills. Instructive approaches are often packaged as computer-assisted instruction and can frequently be purchased off the shelf or from publishers, which provides an easily incorporated resource for adult education programs. This approach meets the formal academic and linguistic needs of the disadvantaged by providing early success, obvious mastery of skills, and frequent assessment. These features of the instructive approach are useful, but limited to basic skill development. If we define ICT fluency as the development of advanced skills to create, communicate, and manage complex problems, then the instructive approach has boundaries in terms of creating these opportunities for learning.

Constructive approaches provide skills acquisition by rooting learning in real-world problems. Students work individually or in teams on projects that require the acquisition and use of ICT skills to solve problems that are meaningful to them. Constructive approaches build on ill-structured learning projects to encourage the application of ICT to problem solving. This in turn encourages "higher-level skills, such as the ability to search for information, reason with models, analyze data, and communicate ideas" (p. 12). Constructive approaches address not only specific academic and linguistic needs, but are more suited to addressing the social dimension important to working with the disadvantaged. Kozma and Wagner identify the need to create supportive learning communities through collaborative projects, as well as the need to connect learners with "outside community resources" (p. 9). A comparison of the instructive and constructive approaches is detailed in Figure 2. Both approaches cover the same skills.

Figure 2.

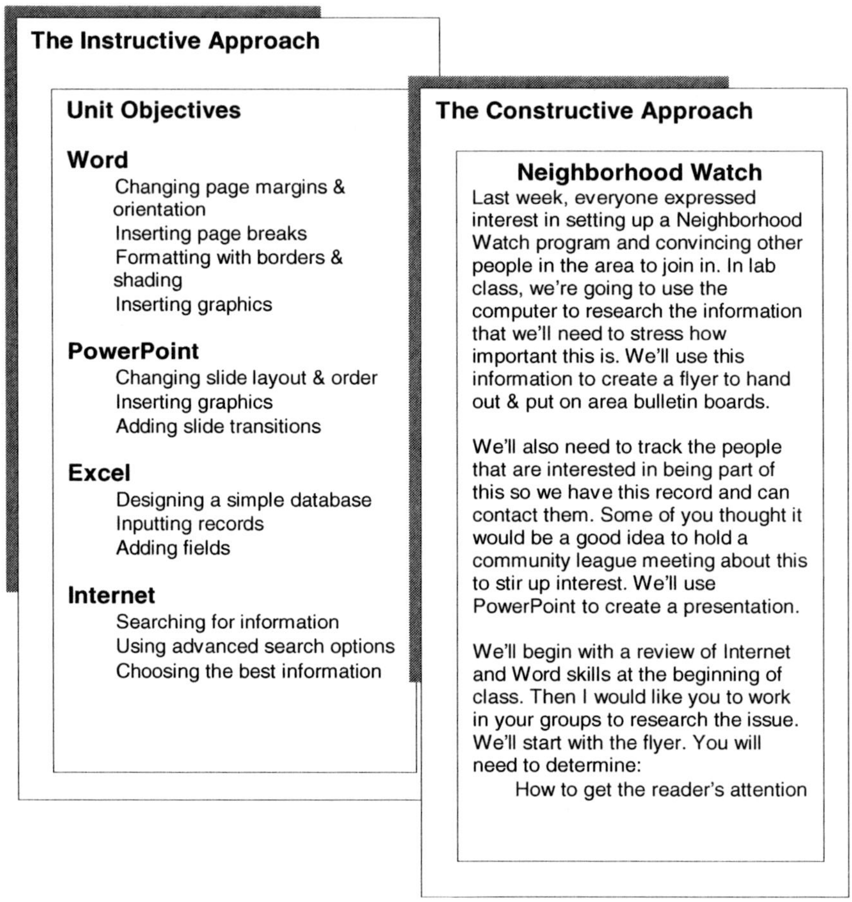

There are definite advantages to the instructive approach. Students and instructors know what is being covered, instruction is provided in a manageable and step-by-step approach. More importantly, the curriculum is also easily understood by funders, employers, and the students themselves. However, it is the constructive approach that provides a more memorable learning experience by focusing on task-oriented learning experiences. Skills are covered through working towards solutions of real-world problems. This poses obvious planning and instructional challenges, and a learning environment in which the instruction and goals are continuously negotiated. The lack of linearity is somewhat disconcerting to instructors and students alike. Students may finish a course without a clear understanding of what they know. If their goal in enrolling is to improve employment prospects, this is an additional disadvantage. Despite its disadvantages, the constructive approach holds numerous advantages. Studies at the post-secondary level that use a problem-based, interactive approach show positive outcomes in increased student learning (Springer, Stanne, & Donovan, 1999). It is reasonable to assume that the same holds true with non-traditional learners. The approach also provides a community learning experience, which may reduce anxiety about acquiring new skills and provide learners with a social network of computer users within their culture. In this sense, it is the approach that most likely can be used to fulfill the social needs identified by Kozma and Wagner (2003, pp. 18-20). The authors note that both approaches can be blended to maximum effect; a constructive approach can be the primary methodology, with a regular checklist review and conventional mastery-based testing to keep students focused on what they are learning. Linking to external standards or testing is an important feature to build into an ICT program, as it provides benchmarks for students to aim for as well as a recognizable certification.

Non-Formal Education: Post-Secondary/Community Centre Partnership Model

While the delivery of formal courses is appealing to many economically disadvantaged individuals, the onus still remains on the individual to seek out and enroll in formal offerings. This may leave out those with scheduling, transportation, and childcare barriers. Others may be intimidated by or simply uninterested in enrolling in courses if they perceive themselves as not fitting in with the culture of the other students. Stanley (2003, p. 414) notes that local community centres can play an important role in educational delivery by minimizing barriers. They can also create learning experiences that extend beyond the formal confines of the course structure to a learning environment that provides a range of non-formal opportunities that embed technology literacy in the heart of the community. Partnerships between adult education providers and community centres allow each entity to build on its expertise and expand the opportunities available to people beyond what one service provider can deliver.

As with the Computer Course model, the partnership model may also market formal education to low-income communities. A limited example of this is the approach certain educational organizations have taken in marketing their programs in low-income areas. Roach (2000) reports the efforts community colleges in the Washington area have taken to become more visible to economically disadvantaged communities. Some have established satellite campuses or restructured curriculum to provide less theory and more practical training to suit the needs of employers in the area. Minority student groups provide support and networking opportunities for low-income students once admitted to these programs.

These efforts, however, do not constitute a true example of a partnership. The efforts are still conventional educational organizations marketing formal course-based learning opportunities to individuals in these communities. Such efforts will provide opportunities to those who are already motivated to change their circumstances, and have academic and personal skills, as well as the support to reach long-term goals. In some communities, this may only be a few individuals. The problem still remains of the larger community. How

Figure 3.

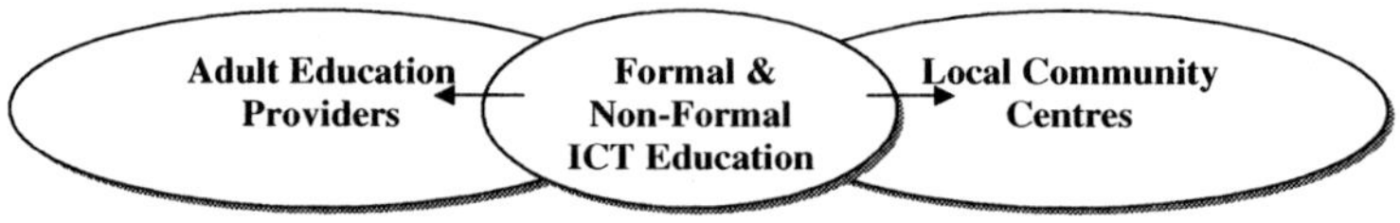

do we ensure ICT access and meaningful educational opportunities that will minimize economic disparity and maximize social mobility?

The partnership model, in its truest form, implies reciprocity between partners. The educational institution that provides ICT expertise receives opportunities to research or to provide its on-campus students real-life experiences in civic participation rather than theoretical academic review. Partner low-income communities receive ICT hardware, software, ICT expertise, and a variety of educational opportunities, which range from formal course offerings to less-structured opportunities. Educational opportunities flow both ways (Figure 3).

The Chronicle of Higher Education (2002) reports "service-learning programs" that are run from Florida's Miami-Dade Community College, whose faculty and students have contributed 280,000 hours to various agencies in South Florida. This commitment has led to the development of a Technology and Learning Center in the low-income community of Overtown, and provided computers and Internet access, computer literacy courses, and a variety of after-school or summer camp opportunities. A key component to this project is an understanding that the educational institution does not solve problems for the community, but sees itself as creating "problem-solving capacity" with its partner organization.

Not all educational/community partnerships are of a front-line nature. MIT (Schön, Sanyal, & Mitchell, 1999) has been supporting the work of community activists since the 1970s through a Community Fellows Program (CFP). Each year, 12 to 15 activists and organizers from urban low-income communities come on campus for a year to reflect and reorganize work in their respective communities. Since the 1990s, the CFP has become increasingly focused on technology as an educational, organizational, and income-generating tool within their communities. MIT realizes many benefits from this program such as research opportunities, meaningful engagement experiences for its Department of Urban Studies and Planning, and dialogue with its CFP fellows.

One result of MIT's commitment to community engagement is the Computer Clubhouse concept (Resnick, Rusk, & Cooke, 1999). The clubhouse seeks not only to teach basic computer skills among low-income youth, but also to provide conditions in which participants become producers rather than consumers of ICT. Radical constructivist principles of learning are central to this mission. Developing learning communities where youth and adult mentors collaborate with others on projects of interest is a key feature of the clubhouse. Roles are not set. A youth participant may become a mentor on certain projects where he or she is the clubhouse expert. On other projects, the youth or adult mentor may become the learner in this dynamic environment. Curriculum is negotiated though "design experiences" (pp. 268-271) that encourage creative expression and problem solving. Sample projects include online art galleries, robotics, or programming computer games. Such projects engage youth in ways formal education fails to do and provide a deeper learning experience that is interdisciplinary by nature.

While the computer clubhouse focuses on youth, another MIT initiative encompasses the entire community to engage empowerment and activism. Shaw and Shaw (1999) report the results of a computer network system placed in a low-income community by the MIT media laboratory. The effect of simultaneous chat and discussion board forum, which was leading edge at the initiation of the project, demonstrates the capacity of low-income communities to use ICT for community improvement. Parental involvement in schools increased, community projects were organized, and dialogue around a variety of topics exploded among residents who largely did not know their neighbors in a decayed and dangerous urban environment.

Employer Recruitment: The Job Training Model

Non-formal education is a possible solution to pull back disadvantaged youth from the hinterland of unemployment, poverty, or worse. Other partnerships keep ICT available and meaningful for the larger community. However, certain adults require more direct and quick intervention. These may be individuals who are already motivated. Others may be those from the middle class who have fallen on hard times and need a helping hand to get back in the workforce. In these cases, the partnership model may not adequately meet immediate learner needs. Stanley (2003, p. 9) also notes that although economically disadvantaged people would benefit from an ICT curriculum that creates "pathways" to careers, many service providers dealing with this group are not equipped resource-wise or through their own social networks to provide these opportunities.

An obvious context within which to structure ICT approaches for the economically disadvantaged is to link technology skills to current and emerging workforce needs. There are compelling reasons to do this. Khirallah, McGee, and Goodridge (2001) report

Figure 4.

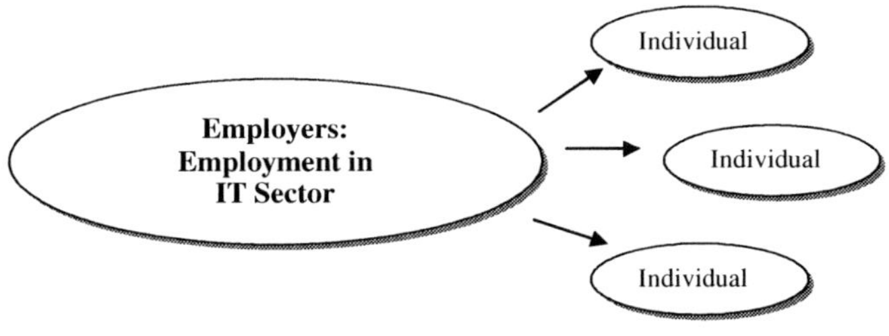

the need for IT workers; 77% of 500 US companies surveyed see the digital divide as a key issue. Some companies such as Hewlett Packard and Cisco Systems have digital divide programs in place to encourage science and technology interest among children and see this as a long-term strategy to influence education to fill future needs. Adults are more immediately focused on career aspirations, so initiatives that promote economic relevance are important. Other types of linkages are employment initiatives that connect the disadvantaged to minority workforce associations or minority-owned companies. Roach (2000) reports employer interest in recruiting minorities into the IT industry. Associations of IT-based companies have actively recruited minority applicants and created summer internship programs through advertising in low-income communities or specialized recruitment programs. Other companies work with African-American colleges to offer "internships, workshops, scholarships, and seminars." Some employers have banded together to form their own partnerships to sponsor training for the disadvantaged. Finally, minority-owned companies can play an important role by providing role models of success in the IT industry, mentorship, and an avenue for networking.

Holistic Initiatives: Multiple Alliance Model

Employer initiatives to recruit and train economically disadvantaged individuals provide immediate solutions, particularly to those who become employed as a result. As noted above, these initiatives meet the needs of some but not others. These types of projects are geared to industry needs and are dependent on the health of specific industries. It would appear that these initiatives are primarily in effect where the IT industry is predominant and experiencing a labour shortage. This has the effect of making large initiatives specific to a geographical region or cycles of economic activity. This also leads to questions about long-term benefits of such programs. A crucial question is whether the training and subsequent employment enskill or deskill the individual. Selwynn (2003, p. 8) notes the "narrowing of adult education...around business and industry-friendly skills and competencies..." and calls for emancipatory goals for ICT adult education that provide learners with opportunities to use ICT to their own advantage. However, programs of an emancipatory focus or those that stress critical pedagogy can lose momentum among participants and funders if they fail to create recognizable certification, employment, or change.

In the previous models, the various service providers and potential employers of economically disadvantaged individuals are restricted to offering disparate pieces. Missing from these disconnected opportunities are the motivations and goals of the economically disadvantaged, both as individual participants and as members of their respective communities. Each of the players in previous models brings its expertise to the problem. Adult education and post-secondary institutions provide ICT expertise and formal courses, and seek enrollment in these. Employers provide immediate job opportunities and want a pool of qualified workers from which to draw. Both surround the larger hub of the community centre, which provides access to a community of learners and potential employees. Yet each of these entities is limited to a certain extent to these

Figure 5.

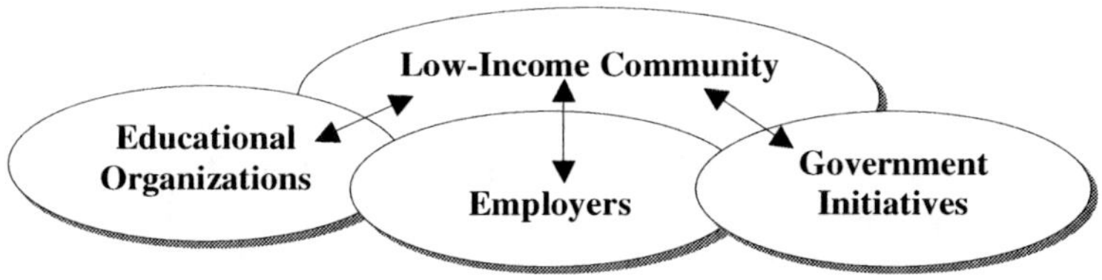

domains. Linking through formal alliances allows each to build on the strength of others. More importantly, an alliance allows momentum toward political solutions.

Conservative policies towards digital divide issues as exemplified by the Bush administration focus on market force correction rather than social programs (Powell, 2001). However, others debunk the power of market forces and call for government intervention to address disparities. To a certain extent, the mixture of educators, community groups, and industry are an unlikely alliance. Selwynn (2003, pp. 13-14) notes, "It is naïve to imagine the effective development of ICT-based adult education without the involvement of the IT industry and other private sector actors..." but acknowledges the clash between "private interest and public good." Kozma and Wagner (2003, p. 25) see the involvement of "national, state or provincial and local governments..." that provide focused job training as well as resources that address larger issues of "community environments." This may involve direct funding to special needs programs, but may also involve indirect incentives such as tax credits to encourage industry involvement. Industries that sell IT infrastructure have a vested interest in such initiatives and can be recruited as partners. Khirallah et al. (2001) report certain IT industries have either developed educational programs or installed infrastructure at partner schools and homes. Such industry involvement, if harnessed and encouraged to the larger community, has reciprocal benefits to business and the general public. An alliance model allows each player to contribute its specific expertise and in so doing, meet some of its own objectives.

Conclusion

It is unlikely that any of the models described will be successful without leadership from the economically disadvantaged themselves. As a group, they exist without any unifying characteristics other than their disenfranchisement from the mainstream. Some are from the middle class and have fallen on some hard times and simply need some support to re-establish themselves. The situations of others is more dire, and it is debatable whether educational assistance of any kind is really helpful beyond programs that focus on children or youth. The extent to which the cultural capital of technology is a barrier to the educational and vocational aspirations of those on the wrong side of the digital divide is not entirely clear, and descriptions of economically disadvantaged adults' experiences in this changing environment are not extensively detailed in the literature. Research of a qualitative nature could more extensively inform program development. Extensive long-term quantitative evaluation of the success of formal education ICT courses and job training initiatives to produce long-term economic improvement is needed, as well as the evaluation of the impact of non-formal community-based initiatives.

While post-secondary institutions can provide services and formal courses, they are unable to completely respond to such a complex problem. It remains the role of community leaders to organize their constituents and network with service providers in education, the government, and industry sectors to make a case for action. Ultimately, all players have an interest in working towards the goal of economically healthy communities.

References

A.T. Kearney & Silicon Valley Network. (2002). *Joint venture's 2002 workforce study: Connecting today's youth with tomorrow's technology careers.* San Francisco: A.T. Kearney. Retrieved June 18, 2004, from *www.atkearney.com/shared_res/pdf/Workforcestudy_S.pdf*

Congress of the U.S. (1993). *Adult literacy and new technologies: Tools for a lifetime.* Washington, DC: Office of Technology Assessment. (ERIC Document Reproduction Service No. ED361473).

Dickens, R. & Ellwood, D. (2003). *Whither poverty in Great Britain and the United States? The determinants of changing poverty and whether work will work.* Retrieved January 23, 2004, from *www.nber.org/books/bcf/dickens-ellwood3-10-03.pdf*

European Centre for the Development of Vocational Training. (2001). *National actions to implement lifelong learning in Europe: A contribution to the consultation process launched by the European Commission Memorandum.* Retrieved February 1, 2004, from *europa.eu.int/comm/education/policies/lll/life/life/country_en.pdf*

Ehrenreich, B. (1990). *Fear of falling: The inner life of the new middle class.* New York: Perennial Library.

Goode, J. & Maskovky, J. (Eds.). (2001). *The new poverty studies: The ethnography of power, politics, and impoverished people in the United States.* New York: New York University Press.

Guthrie, J.W., Garms, W.I., & Pierce, L.C. (1988). *School finance and education policy: Enhancing educational efficiency, equality and choice.* Englewood Cliffs, NJ: Prentice-Hall.

Institute for Research on Poverty. (2002). *Who was poor in 2002?* Retrieved January 15, 2004, from *www.ssc.wisc.edu/irp/faqs/faq3.htm*

Khirallah, D.R., McGee, M.K., & Goodridge, E. (2001). Divided we fall. *Information Week,* (830).

Kozma, R. & Wagner, D. (2003, November). *Reaching the most disadvantaged with ICT: What works?* Paper presented at the National Center for Adult Literacy. Retrieved January 22, 2004, from *www.literacyonline.org/ICTconf/OECD_Koz-Wag_final.pdf*

Krahn, H.J. & Lowe, G.S. (2002). *Work, industry, and Canadian society* (4th edition). Toronto: ITP Nelson.

Levine, A. & Nidiffer, J. (1996). *Beating the odds: How the poor get to college.* San Francisco: Jossey-Bass.

Mitchell, W.J. (1999). City of bits hypothesis. In D.A. Schön, B. Sanyal, & W.J. Mitchell (Eds.), *High technology and low-income communities: Prospects for the positive use of advanced information technology.* Cambridge, MA: MIT Press.

Payne J. (2002). *Basic skills in the workplace: A research review.* Retrieved January 26, 2004, from *www.lsda.org.uk/files/pdf/1426.pdf*

Pew Research Center. (2003). *The ever-shifting Internet population: A new look at Internet access and the digital divide.* Retrieved January 16, 2004, from *www.pewinternet.org/reports/pdfs/PIP_Shifting_Net_Pop_Report.pdf*

Pew Research Center. (2002). *The Internet goes to college: How students are living in the future with today's technology.* Retrieved January 9, 2004, from *www.pewinternet.org/reports/toc.asp?Report=71*

Pew Research Center. (2000). *Who's not online: 57% of those without Internet access say they do not plan to log on.* Retrieved January 3, 2004, from *www.pewinternet.org/reports/toc.asp?Report=21*

Powell, M. (2001, March 29). *Agenda and plans for reform of the FCC.* Hearing before the Subcommittee on Telecommunications and the Internet. Retrieved January 9, 2004, from *energycommerce.house.gov/107/hearings/03292001Hearing144/print.htm*

Resnick, M., Rusk, N., & Cooke, S. (1999). The computer clubhouse: Technological fluency in the inner city. In D. Schön, B. Sanyal, & W. Mitchell (Eds.), *High technology and low-income communities: Prospects for the positive use of advanced information technology.* Cambridge, MA: MIT Press.

Resta, P. (1992). Organizing education for minorities: Enhancing minority access and use of the new information technologies. *Education and Computing, 8*(2), 119-127.

Roach, R. (2000). Capitalizing on the digital divide. *Black Issues in Higher Education, 16*(27).

Sargent, N. & Tucker, A. (1997). *Pandora's box?* (Companion Papers on Motivation, Access and the Media). Leicester, England: National Institution of Adult Continuing Education. (ERIC Document Reproduction Service No. ED423441).

Sarlo, C.A. (1992). *Poverty in Canada.* Vancouver, BC: The Fraser Institute.

Schön, D., Sanyal, B., & Mitchell, W.J. (Eds.). (1999). *High technology and low-income communities: Prospects for the positive use of advanced information technology.* Cambridge, MA: MIT Press.

Selwynn, N. (2003, November). *ICT in non-formal youth and adult education: Defining the territory.* Paper presented at the National Center for Adult Literacy. Retrieved January 22, 2004. from *www.literacyonline.org/ICTconf/OECD_Selwyn_final.pdf*

Shalla, V. (1997). Technology and the deskilling of work. In A. Duffy, D. Glenday, & N. Pupo (Eds.), *Good jobs, bad jobs, no jobs: The transformation of work in the 21st century.* Toronto: Harcourt Brace Canada.

Shaw, A. & Shaw M. (1999). Social empowerment through community networks. In D. Schön, B. Sanyal, & W. Mitchell (Eds.), *High technology and low-income communities: Prospects for the positive use of advanced information technology.* Cambridge, MA: MIT Press.

Springer, L., Stanne, M.E., & Donovan, S. (1999). Effects of small-group learning on undergraduates in science, mathematics and engineering, and technology: A meta analysis. *Review of Educational Research, 69*(1), 21-51.

Stanley, L.D. (2003). Beyond access: Psychosocial barriers to computer literacy. *Information Society, 19*(5), 407-416.

Statistics Canada. (2003). *Digital divide in schools: Student access to and use of computers.* Retrieved November 29, 2003, from *www.statcan.ca/Daily/English/030623/d030623b.htm*

The Chronicle of Higher Education. (2002). Community service—learning initiatives bridge the gap between America's technology haves and have-nots. *The Chronicle of Higher Education, 48*(43), A28.

U.S. Department of Commerce. (2000, October). *Falling through the Net, toward digital inclusion: A report on Americans' access to technology tools.* Washington, DC: National Telecommunications and Information Administration. Retrieved January 5, 2001, from *www.ntia.doc.gov/ntiahome/digitaldivide/*

Whybrow-Howes. (2000). *Technology access and equity issues for financially disadvantaged adult learners.* Unpublished Master's Thesis, University of Alberta, Edmonton, Alberta, Canada.

Wilhelm, T., Carmen, D., & Reynolds, M. (2002). *Connecting kids to technology: Challenges and opportunities.* Retrieved November 29, 2003, from *www.digitaldividenetwork.org/content/stories/index.cfm?key=244*

Section IV

Examples and Guide that Promote Instructional Technology Literacy

Chapter XVII

Learning to Become a Knowledge-Centric Organization

George Stonehouse
Northumbria University, UK

Jonathon D. Pemberton
Northumbria University, UK

Abstract

The importance of knowledge to an organization's competitive performance is widely recognized. A knowledge-centric organization is one within which the creation and management of knowledge are at the heart of its strategic thinking, operations, and activities. Knowledge-centricity can only be achieved if knowledge, and the behaviors and systems associated with its creation and management, are deeply embedded within the organization. In fact, given the dynamism of organizations and their environments, knowledge-centricity is likely to be a holy grail that organizations seek but may never find. Similarly, knowledge-centricity will evolve as a concept, as knowledge of the processes of learning, knowledge creation, and management develops over time. This chapter, therefore, represents a snapshot of the current status of the concept and offers advice on how organizations can begin to make progress towards becoming knowledge-centric. On the basis of research, the chapter identifies the primary characteristics of a knowledge-centric organization, and the tools and techniques necessary for knowledge-centric organizational development.

Introduction

The creation and management of knowledge have become the focus of much management literature and research. Organizations have recognized the role of knowledge in achieving and sustaining competitive advantage, and have begun to devote considerable attention to its management. At the same time, organizations have realized that the escalating pace of technological change, the associated shortening of product lifecycles, globalization, and increasing competition require the creation of new knowledge at an ever-increasing rate (Stonehouse & Pemberton, 1999; Von Krogh, Nonaka, & Abel, 2001; Zack, 1999). Knowledge-based innovation has become the modern business imperative and continuous knowledge creation the only means by which competitive advantage can be sustained. The importance of communications and information technology (CIT) in the creation and management of knowledge has been widely documented, to the extent that there is a widely held view among managers that CIT is synonymous with knowledge management (KPMG, 2000). Indeed, developments like the Internet, extranets, intelligent databases, and groupware have made significant contributions to the creation and management of knowledge, enhancing the abilities of organizations to capture, share, store, and manipulate knowledge.

There is danger, however, in overstating the role and importance of technology. It is necessary to adopt a socio-technical perspective, where equal emphasis is placed upon the social architecture of organizations in terms of leadership, culture, structure, and systems as key forces in knowledge creation and management. Whereas technology acts largely as a knowledge enabler through which *explicit* knowledge can be captured, stored, and disseminated, it is the social architecture that largely governs an organization's ability to develop and exploit *tacit* knowledge as a key source of competitive advantage (Stonehouse, Pemberton, & Barber, 2001). The intangibility of tacit knowledge greatly limits the potential of technology in its development and management within the organization. The importance of tacit knowledge is increasingly recognized by both managers and academics alike, with the consequence that far greater attention is now paid to the social forces at work within organizations (Senge, 1990; Stonehouse & Pemberton, 1999).

This chapter develops the concept of knowledge-centricity as a socio-technical phenomenon through which organizations can enhance their abilities to create and manage both explicit and tacit knowledge, and hence to create and sustain competitive advantage. In practical terms, the chapter introduces the *knowledge-creation audit*, a tool for assessing the ability of the organization to create new knowledge, and the *knowledge-centricity matrix*, which provides a template for mapping the degree to which an organization is knowledge-centric.

The Concept of Knowledge-Centricity

A knowledge-centric organization is one within which knowledge is regarded as the fundamental source of superior performance and, as a direct consequence, its creation and management are embodied in its mission, strategy, social architecture, operations, and performance. In other words, knowledge is critical to the mission of the organization and forms the central focus of all its endeavors.

At this juncture, it is useful to distinguish between the concept of a 'learning organization' and that of a 'knowledge-centric organization'. While there are several areas of commonality, there are also important differences between the two concepts. Central to a learning organization are the twin concepts of organizational learning and learning about learning. Organizational learning can be equated with knowledge creation, while the notion of learning about learning is employed in developing aspects of leadership, culture, structure, and infrastructure within the organization which expedite learning processes (Stonehouse & Pemberton, 1999). The knowledge-centric organization incorporates both these facets of a learning organization, but goes beyond in several respects. Knowledge-centricity is perhaps best viewed as a mindset within an organization within which knowledge, and its creation and management, are all-pervasive and are at the core of the being of the organization.

Recognition of the value of knowledge as the major determinant of organizational effectiveness has been a relatively recent development, with the result that there is significant variation in the extent to which organizations have adopted practices and procedures which are designed to maximize their potential for knowledge creation and management. Even when the value of knowledge has been embraced, the development and implementation of a social architecture and the systems that most effectively facilitate the formation of new knowledge inevitably take considerable time and effort. Progress towards knowledge-centricity is, therefore, best regarded as a process of organizational development over time. KPMG refers to this process as the *knowledge journey,* which consists of five stages or states: knowledge-chaotic, knowledge-aware, knowledge-enabled, knowledge-managed, and finally, knowledge-centric organizations (KPMG, 1997). The progress of an organization towards knowledge-centricity can be monitored within this conceptual framework. For organizations seeking success, the journey today must be regarded as a race rather than a leisurely voyage, given the pace of technological change and increasing scale of competition (Tissen, Andriessen, & Deprez, 2000). The race to become knowledge-centric can only be won if organizations take a systematic approach to the journey.

A road map for knowledge-centricity will begin with an audit of facilitators and inhibitors of knowledge creation and management in the organization (Stonehouse et al., 2001), together with a mapping of knowledge requirements, sources, repositories and flows in relation to the mission, strategy, and operations of the business. The processes of continuous organizational development towards the desired goal of knowledge-centricity will then focus in a systematic way on factors such as leadership, culture, structure, infrastructure, systems, staff training, professional development, reward systems, empowerment, and so forth. In this sense, a complex array of organizational factors comes into play when examining the issue of knowledge-centricity.

It is useful to consider the factors and features of each stage of the knowledge journey in more detail as precursors to considering the tools of analysis, namely, the knowledge-creation audit and knowledge-centricity matrix, employed in assessing the extent to which an organization is moving towards knowledge-centricity.

A *knowledge-chaotic* organization has not yet recognized the importance of knowledge, and its use is consequently often ad hoc and inconsistent. Organizations at this stage of development typically duplicate information through incompatible systems and as a result of an unwillingness of individuals to share knowledge (Pemberton & Stonehouse, 2002). Most importantly, poor leadership and a lack of vision are typically apparent in the knowledge-chaotic organization.

At the next stage, the *knowledge-aware* organization is one within which there is recognition of the value of knowledge and the need to organize it. Following on from this, there will have been some moves to identify the sources of knowledge and the processes associated with its creation and management. Typically, some systems have been introduced, but there has been an emphasis of technology and a failure to recognize the importance of their social context within the organization. Similarly, their implementation is uneven across the organization. Finally, there are no coordinated plans for dealing with knowledge as an organizational resource for the improvement of performance.

When knowledge management has begun to benefit the business, the organization can be regarded as being *knowledge-enabled*. Standard knowledge management processes and tools are evident, knowledge resources are evaluated, and knowledge systems are in place. On the other hand, some technological barriers to knowledge sharing and dissemination remain, particularly a lack of structured knowledge repositories. Many of the socio-technical aspects of the organization required to facilitate knowledge development, in terms of its culture, remain unaddressed at this stage and represent a significant hurdle in moving to the next phase of the knowledge journey (Pemberton & Stonehouse, 2002).

A *knowledge-managed* organization has developed an integrated framework of procedures to create and manage information and knowledge. Most of the technological and cultural issues of knowledge transfer and sharing have largely been overcome. In addition, the organization will have developed a knowledge strategy that is reviewed and improved on a continual basis. Leadership of the knowledge strategy will normally be provided by a knowledge champion at the senior management level within the organization.

The ultimate stage of development is the *knowledge-centric* organization, within which knowledge and its role in innovation permeates its mission and strategy. At the same time, the development and exploitation of knowledge assets, supported through integrated knowledge management tools and technology, form the basis of the organization's competitive advantage. The social architecture of the organization in terms of its leadership, culture, structure, and infrastructure fully support the creation and management of knowledge, and knowledge measurement systems are broadly in place. A critical distinguishing feature of the knowledge-centric organization, in contrast to one that is merely knowledge-managed, is the recognition of the importance of individual tacit knowledge in creating organizational knowledge, and a commitment to a philosophy of 'learning about learning' throughout the enterprise. As one of the respondents to Huseman and Goodman's research put it, "knowledge-centricity can be regarded as a systems approach to transfer learning and leverage learning across the whole company" (Huseman & Goodman, 1998).

From a practical perspective, managers require tools that assist them in gauging the stage of development of their organization in terms of the knowledge journey. To this end, the use of two such tools, the knowledge-creation audit and knowledge-centricity matrix, can assist in this process. These tools are distinct but interrelated. The former serves the purpose of gathering data on the ability of the organization to create and manage knowledge in terms of its social architecture (leadership, culture, structure, and infrastructure), while the latter is a means of representing the status of the organization in relation to knowledge-centricity. It is important, however, to recognize that the development of these analytical frameworks is an ongoing and continuous process.

The Knowledge-Creation Audit

The knowledge-creation audit is a process that assists organizations in evaluating their ability to create and manage knowledge. The audit process consists of the following six stages:

1. An introduction to the concepts of knowledge-based competitive advantage, knowledge creation, and management.
2. Completion of the knowledge-creation audit questionnaires by selected individuals within the organization.
3. Completion of knowledge-creation audit questionnaires by groups within the organization.
4. Analysis of individual and group questionnaires by the audit team.
5. Discussion of audit findings with key members of the organization.
6. Identification of individual and organizational development requirements necessary to progress on the journey to knowledge-centricity.

The audit is conducted with employees at all levels across the organization. On its own, this provides a useful way of assessing the organization's approach to knowledge management issues. It must, however, be supplemented by interviews with senior personnel to examine areas of strategy and management, issues not generally familiar to all employees. Furthermore, observation of the working environment to validate the claims made by interviewees and questionnaire respondents allows a more thorough assessment of whether the knowledge-centric characteristics are indeed present. Ultimately, this final assessment is made by the researcher in light of the pluralistic research conducted.

The process employs a questionnaire devised by the authors. Several other authors have developed similar mechanisms, including the knowledge management diagnostic (Bukowitz & Williams, 1999) and the knowledge management toolkit (Skyrme, 1999). In its most recent format, this audit questionnaire allows the organization to self assess in terms of:

- Leadership and vision
- Culture and structure
- Processes
- Explicit knowledge
- Tacit knowledge
- Knowledge monitoring, gathering, storage, and dissemination
- Markets and customers
- Knowledge measurement
- Human infrastructure
- Technology infrastructure

Within each section, a number of sub-themes are examined, where respondents within an organization indicate the strength of agreement with a number of statements using a five-point Likert scale. More detailed discussion is provided in Pemberton, Stonehouse, and Francis (2002).

The major outcomes of the process are a profile of the organization's ability to create and manage knowledge, and a raising of awareness of knowledge and its importance to the performance of the organization. Without such an assessment it is very difficult for an organization to identify its current status in terms of the knowledge journey and the development areas required for future progress.

The Knowledge-Centricity Matrix

The knowledge-centricity matrix consists of a template upon which the organization can represent its current stage of development. The knowledge-creation audit is a valuable means of gathering the data necessary to complete the template for a specific organization.

The matrix is illustrated in Table 1. It is recognized that there is an element of subjectivity in devising the desirable and critical criteria, but justification is largely rooted in research in this area.

Furthermore, the authors' experience of research and consultancy in the areas of knowledge management, organizational learning, and performance have played a major part in identifying the key elements perceived to be important in identifying the features of the knowledge-centric organization (Pemberton & Stonehouse, 2002; Pemberton et al., 2002; Stonehouse et al., 2001).

Supplementary sources, including published case studies and annual company reports, have also been used alongside materials from the management literature (Birkinshaw,

Table 1. The knowledge-centricity matrix

ISSUES	FEATURE	DESIRABLE	CRITICAL
Strategic	Knowledge issues are addressed in the organization's business strategy		✓
Measurement	Mechanisms exist to quantify knowledge assets	✓	
Structural	Flatter structure with fewer layers to facilitate more effective knowledge transfer		✓
	The use of group-based teams, ideally cross-functional, designed to encourage knowledge sharing	✓	
	Decentralization of decision making to capitalize on individual and team expertise	✓	
Leadership	The existence of a knowledge champion at senior management level		✓
	Management awareness of knowledge issues accompanied by an open and inclusive attitude to decision making		✓
Infrastructure	Technical infrastructure to support knowledge transfer with tools (e.g., knowledge maps) to facilitate this		✓
	Support systems, both human and technical, that avoid 're-inventing the wheel'	✓	
	Effective communication channels encompassing verbal, electronic, and written formats		✓
Cultural	Incentives for sharing knowledge, ideally built within appraisal regimes, emphasizing personal and organizational benefits		✓
	High trust and supportive environment encouraging individual responsibility		✓
	Allocation of time within the organization to actively encourage communication and knowledge transfer	✓	
Individual	Recognition of the individual's knowledge by:		
	▪ Individual		✓
	▪ Co-workers	✓	
	▪ Managers		✓

2002; Chase, 1997; Horne, 1998; Kippenberger, 1998; McCampbell, Clare, & Gitters, 1999; Mouritsen, Larsen, & Bukh, 2001; Petrash, 1996).

It should be noted that the matrix is primarily designed as a tool for use in large to medium companies for assessing the extent to which a company has progressed along the road to knowledge-centricity. The potential for its application in small and medium-sized businesses is currently under exploration.

Certain features are deemed to be essential to knowledge-centricity because they are central to the ability of an organization to create and manage knowledge, and to the integration of knowledge into organizational strategy. Other features are regarded as desirable in that they support knowledge-centricity, but are not of such central importance. A knowledge-centric organization will possess all of the essential characteristics and a majority of those regarded as desirable.

The matrix is constantly being improved on the basis of ongoing research, and it is recognized that the incorporation of the weightings of the features will allow the knowledge-centricity matrix to become a more flexible tool in the future.

Case Study: European Design Center - Black & Decker

In order to show how the audit tool and matrix can be used, a case study of Black & Decker's European Design Center (EDC) is used to illustrate the practical application of the these techniques. The case study was constructed on the basis of research conducted in the European Design Center in 2001, and it effectively illustrates how the tools can be employed in an organizational setting (Pemberton et al., 2002).

Black & Decker is the world's largest producer of power tools and related accessories; the company is currently valued at $5 billion and is a Fortune 200 global corporation (Black & Decker, 2001). Its success is built on the development and introduction of new innovations before its competitors, and a means by which it retains competitive differentiation and superior performance. The European Design Center (EDC), based in northeast England and the focus of the research discussed in this chapter, employs more than 100 personnel with its engineers, designers, and programmed managers, in conjunction with the marketing team, responsible for the development of many of Black and Decker's global products.

Adopting the pluralistic approach to research outlined in the previous section, a series of informal face-to-face interviews with senior personnel were conducted to gain a feel for the organization's approach to knowledge management issues. Semi-structured interviews were subsequently carried out with five managers in January 2001 to gather opinions and facts to better understand the organizational factors that influence knowledge creation, sharing, and management processes.

The knowledge-creation audit questionnaire, having been employed previously in other organizations, was then revised and adapted for the EDC, and after a pilot survey, it was distributed to a random sample of 30 employees from different areas, of differing status, and across different groupings within the EDC in February 2001. All 30 questionnaires were returned, with the computer-coded responses analyzed using Excel and SPSS.

A detailed account of the analysis and findings of both the audit questionnaire and interviews are reported in Pemberton et al. (2002). A summary of the key findings is given here:

- Two areas are identifiable as strong features of the organization. The role of tacit knowledge is recognized as an integral part of the EDC's business, and there is consensus that the technology infrastructure to support knowledge management initiatives within Black & Decker is essentially in place.
- Neutral responses are recorded for culture and structure, the role of explicit knowledge, knowledge repositories, and market leverage.
- Four areas were perceived as particularly weak within the EDC, these being leadership, processes, knowledge measurement, and human infrastructure.

A more detailed analysis of the sub-themes presented in the knowledge audit identified a number of perceived strengths and weaknesses:

Areas of Strength

- Knowledge experts are recognized and their expertise is sought on a day-to-day basis by coworkers.
- Customers and competitors of the company recognize that the organization uses its know-how and knowledge to develop innovative products.
- Technology exists that permits and encourages coworkers to share their knowledge in the form of documents and multimedia objects.

Areas of Weakness

- Managing the company's knowledge is not considered a core management skill in which every manager and professional has some familiarity.
- Gathering, storing information, and knowledge-sharing behaviors are not recognized and rewarded by the company.
- Leadership is generally perceived as lacking a knowledge vision and failing to emphasize the role of knowledge within the organization.
- Processes and procedures to monitor external knowledge sources, particularly in relation to that of competitors, are weak.

Table 2. Black & Decker (EDC) knowledge-centricity matrix

ISSUES	FEATURE	DESIRABLE	CRITICAL
Strategic	Knowledge issues are addressed in the organization's business strategy		✓
Measurement	Mechanisms exist to quantify knowledge assets	×	
Structural	Flatter structure with fewer layers to facilitate more effective knowledge transfer.		✓
	The use of group-based teams, ideally cross-functional, designed to encourage knowledge sharing	✓	
	Decentralization of decision making to capitalize on individual and team expertise	✓	
Leadership	The existence of a knowledge champion at the senior management level		✓
	Management awareness of knowledge issues accompanied by an open and inclusive attitude to decision making		×
Infrastructure	Technical infrastructure to support knowledge transfer with tools (e.g., knowledge maps) to facilitate this		✓
	Support systems, both human and technical, that avoid 're-inventing the wheel'	✓	
	Effective communication channels encompassing verbal, electronic, and written formats		✓
Cultural	Incentives for sharing knowledge, ideally built within appraisal regimes, emphasizing personal and organizational benefits		×
	High trust and supportive environment encouraging individual responsibility		×
	Allocation of time within the organization to actively encourage communication and knowledge transfer	✓	
Individual	Recognition of the individual's knowledge by : ▪ Individual ▪ Co-workers ▪ Managers	 ✓ 	 ✓ ×

- While tacit knowledge is generally perceived as a strength of the organization, there is limited encouragement for knowledge experts to share their expertise via formal and informal mechanisms.
- Few systems are in place to formally measure and manage its knowledge resources.

From these results, together with observations of the research team, the information gathered was incorporated into the knowledge-centricity matrix so as to model the extent of knowledge-centricity within the European Design Center.

On the criteria detailed previously, and on the evidence collated and analyzed, Black & Decker could not be viewed as knowledge-centric at the time of the research. Encouragingly, knowledge is clearly seen a strategic imperative. The critical features relating to structure and infrastructure are also apparent, witnessed by significant investment in information and communications technologies, and a refining of the work environment to accommodate teams and communities within a generally flat structure. On the downside, the matrix identifies leadership and culture as being weak areas of the organization. In particular, managers appeared not to recognize that knowledge management underpins core business processes and is consequently not fully integrated into the natural flow of work. Culturally, a lack of trust and incentives for sharing knowledge is visible, presenting a significant barrier to knowledge sharing. This is strongly related to the individual, and while within the organization there is a respect and acknowledgement of the value of knowledge between individuals and coworkers, recognition of individual knowledge by managers appeared to be missing. This links closely with the idea that the management of knowledge is not firmly embedded within organizational culture.

A caveat to these comments is that this research refers explicitly to Black & Decker's European Design Center. Although designated a primary global design center, exactly how the EDC mirrors other areas of the organization is not clear, and further research is needed to corroborate these findings, if generalizations are to be made. However, given the observations based on the EDC, it is unlikely that it can be viewed as knowledge-centric.

Conclusion

Within a knowledge-centric organization, knowledge, through its creation and management, as well as its deployment throughout the organization's strategies, processes, and products, is viewed as a fundamental force behind superior organizational performance. The journey towards knowledge-centricity is therefore an imperative for organizations seeking competitive edge. This journey can be facilitated by the employment of frameworks and tools that allow organizations to diagnose their current position and progress towards becoming knowledge-centric. The knowledge-creation audit and the knowledge-centricity matrix are two such frameworks. Inevitably, the frameworks are imperfect to some degree, but nevertheless represent valuable ways of assisting organizational development towards the desired end of knowledge-centricity. At the same time, other instruments of organizational change and development must be employed.

Of course, the journey towards knowledge-centricity is a learning process, and a recognition that many facets of an organization's operations and strategy need to be addressed. Without doubt, technology has been the impetus for moving the issue of knowledge and its management center-stage - the huge investments made by companies are testament to this fact. Yet, research over the last few years has demonstrated that other features must be considered if knowledge is truly to be exploited as an organizational resource. More specifically, the leadership of the organization is of critical importance. As illustrated in the case study above, unless senior managers are fully committed to creating and managing knowledge, and unless they provide leadership that creates a culture of trust, empowerment, sharing, questioning, critical reflection, and innovation, then the organization will find it extremely difficult to become knowledge-centric. The mindset of leaders and managers, and its embodiment in the culture of the organization, together with the supporting technological infrastructure, is a critical determinant of an organization's likely success in being viewed as knowledge-centric. Sustaining knowledge-centricity, however, ultimately depends upon continuous learning and organizational development.

Acknowledgments

The authors would like to thank Mark Francis for his collaboration in this research and his former employer, Black & Decker, for allowing the work to be undertaken and reported.

References

Birkinshaw, J. (2002). Managing internal R&D networks in global firms. *Long Range Planning, 35*(3), 245-267.

Bukowitz, W. & Williams, R. (1999). *The knowledge management field book.* London: Financial Times Prentice-Hall.

Black & Decker. (2001). *A bright future based on a solid past.* Retrieved October 3, 2002, from *www.mmdp.co.uk*

Chase, R. (1997). Knowledge management benchmarks. *Journal of Knowledge Management, 1*(1), 83-92.

Hall, R. & Andriani, P. (2002). Managing knowledge for innovation. *Long Range Planning, 35*(1), 29-48.

Horne, N. (1998). Putting information assets on the board agenda. *Long Range Planning, 31*(1), 10-17.

Huseman, R.C. & Goodman, J.P. (1998). *Knowledge organizations: Their emergence and impact on corporate training*. Annenberg Center for Communications, University of Southern California, USA.

Kippenberger, T. (1998). Sharing knowledge at BP. *The Antidote, 3*(1), 38-40.

KPMG. (1997). *The knowledge journey: A business guide to knowledge systems.* Retrieved December 6, 2001, from www.kpmgconsulting.co.uk.

KPMG. (2000). *Knowledge management research report 2000*. Retrieved October 3, 2002, from *www.kmadvantage.com/docs/KM/KPMG_ KM_Research _Report_2000.pdf*

McCampbell, A., Clare, L., & Gitters, S. (1999). Knowledge management: The new challenge for the 21st century. *Journal of Knowledge Management, 3*(3), 172-179.

Mouritsen, J., Larsen, H., & Bukh, P. (2001). Valuing the future: Intellectual capital supplements at Skandia. *Accounting, Auditing and Accountability Journal, 14*(4), 399-422.

Pemberton, J., Stonehouse, G., & Francis, M. (2002). Black & Decker - Towards a knowledge-centric organization. *Knowledge and Process Management, 9*(3), 178-189.

Pemberton, J. & Stonehouse, G. (2000). Organizational learning and knowledge assets - An essential partnership. *The Learning Organization, 7*(4), 184-193.

Pemberton, J. & Stonehouse, G. (2002). The importance of individual knowledge in developing the knowledge-centric organization. In E. Coakes, D. Willis, & S. Clarke (Eds.), *Knowledge management in the socio-technical world: The graffiti continues.* London: Springer-Verlag.

Petrash, G. (1996). Dow's journey to a knowledge value management culture. *European Management Journal, 14*(4), 365-373.

Senge, P. (1990). *The fifth discipline: The art & practice of the learning organization.* New York: Doubleday.

Skyrme, D. (1999). *Knowledge networking: Creating the collaborative enterprise.* Oxford: Butterworth Heinemann.

Stonehouse, G. & Pemberton, J. (1999). Learning and knowledge management in the intelligent organization. *Participation and Empowerment, An International Journal, 7*(5), 131-144.

Stonehouse, G., Pemberton, J., & Barber, C. (2001). The role of knowledge facilitators and inhibitors: Lessons from airline reservations systems. *Long Range Planning, 34*(2), 115-138.

Tissen, R., Andriessen, D., & Deprez, F.L. (2000). *The knowledge dividend.* London: Financial Times Prentice-Hall.

Von Krogh, G., Nonaka, I., & Abel, M. (2001). Making the most of your company's knowledge: A strategic framework. Long Range Planning, 34*(4), 421-439.*

Zack M. (1999). *Knowledge and strategy*. Oxford: Butterworth-Heinemann.

Chapter XVIII

Fundamentals of Multimedia

Palmer W. Agnew
State University of New York at Binghamton, USA

Anne S. Kellerman
State University of New York at Binghamton, USA

Abstract

This chapter introduces multimedia, defined as interacting with information that employs most or all of the media: text, graphics, images, audio, and video. Students and faculty need to learn to create and use high-quality multimedia documents, including references, lecture materials, reports, and term papers. The authors provide a framework for understanding multimedia in its rapidly changing context. They discuss a wide spectrum of multimedia end-user devices that range from smart cell phones and powerful PCs to intelligent cars and homes. They also propose a vision of pervasive multimedia any time and anyplace, and discuss related issues, controversies, and problems. Typical problems are excessive complexity and a plethora of choices that paralyze many potential users. The chapter concludes with a discussion of possible solutions to major problems and probable future trends.

Introduction

Multimedia is interacting with text, graphics, images, audio, and video. Creators and users of multimedia employ end-user devices that range from PCs and interactive televisions to smart phones and PDAs. People exchange multimedia using delivery methods such as dial-up and cable-modem access to the Internet, mailed DVDs, and Internet2. Multimedia communications can be more effective and interesting than communications that are limited to text.

Most of us will create, as well as use, multimedia throughout the remainder of our lives. Almost all future work and everyday life will involve dealing with multimedia wherever we are by using the end-user devices at hand. Examples of use include sending images to Aunt Lizzie by way of a cell phone, and writing and wirelessly posting a report on the Internet concerning worldwide petroleum sources, while standing near an oil well in the Middle East.

The objectives of this chapter are to:

- provide a framework for efficiently acquiring new knowledge and skills in the rapidly changing multimedia arena;
- discuss a vision for effective multimedia creation and use, by nearly everybody, nearly anywhere, and at any time;
- delineate the major issues, controversies, and problems that litter the path toward achieving that vision; and
- discuss some corresponding solutions and recommendations, many of which involve skills that instructional technologists, teachers, and students need.

Background

Figure 1 shows a high-level view of people and components involved in creating and using multimedia. Some providers create multimedia content, information, titles, or applications that employ multiple media and are interactive. These authors create this content by employing end-user device hardware and software. They then typically store the resulting content on servers. The content is delivered to other, often different end-user devices employed by users, customers, or readers by means of delivery networks that range from mailing diskettes or DVDs to using local area networks or the Internet. By no means are all authors professional creators; the most interesting aspect of multimedia is that it is now sufficiently inexpensive and almost sufficiently easy that almost anybody can create as well as use multimedia. Other providers include a wide range of individuals, companies, and governments that play a wide variety of roles. For example, some providers provide products and services that are important to the delivery of multimedia to end-users.

Figure 1. Framework

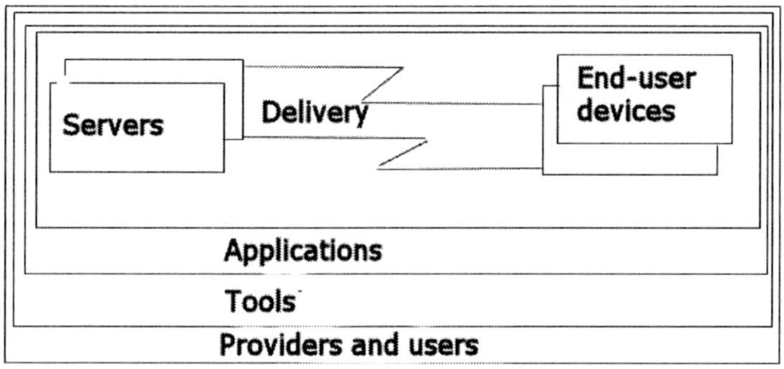

Figure 1 is a framework in which you can add newly acquired knowledge about multimedia. For example, if you think you might want to provide an on-demand multimedia tutorial for your students to use from their cell phones, you need to have an authoring end-user device, a way to deliver this content to your users, and tools to allow you to create content for the desired end-user platform. You should know that, at least in the US, wireless delivery will be problematic. The good news is that network providers are improving their products and services, with the goal of handling wireless high-quality images and video within the next couple of years.

Creators and end-users employ a variety of tools. Some tools operate on the individual media. Other tools, called multimedia authoring systems, assemble multimedia media and add interactivity. Individual media tools include editors for text, images, graphics, audio, and video. Tools that generate HTML with associated Web browsers are examples of multimedia authoring systems. Table 1 provides some specific examples. A great many can be found at Maricopa Community College's Web site, Multimedia Authoring (Maricopa Community College, 2004).

One correct conclusion that you can draw from the table's examples is that creators of multimedia often need to obtain and master separate tools for each medium, as well as one or more authoring tools that combine several media. To the extent that multimedia creators and users are different people, users are also faced with multiple choices of tools with which to play back the media, such as browser plug-ins for a variety of streaming audio and video formats. Users may also need one or more authoring systems' so-called "run-time environments," if not the full authoring systems.

Multimedia tends to be large in terms of storage space and network bandwidth. Whereas a text page occupies only about 3,000 bytes, five minutes of high-quality video can occupy up to 1 Gigabyte (1 GB). Solutions involve squeezing multimedia by compressing it using a range of sophisticated technologies. As you can see from Table 2, desktop computers routinely come with 80 GB of hard-drive storage space, whereas mobile

Table 1. Typical multimedia software

Medium	Tools
Text	Microsoft Word, Corel WordPerfect, Tex, Latex
Graphics (i.e., vectors)	Corel Draw, Adobe Illustrator, Macromedia Fireworks, Adobe ImageReady, Macromedia Flash
Image (i.e., bitmap)	Adobe Photoshop, Jasc Paint Shop Pro, Macromedia Fireworks
Audio	Sony Sound Edit Pro, Sony Sound Forge for Windows, Sony Acid, Cakewalk products
Synthetic Video (animation)	AutoDesk AutoCAD, Discreet 3D Studio (MAX), Virtus 3D Website Builder, Macromedia Flash, Electric Image Amorphium Pro, Alias Maya
Captured Video	Adobe Premiere, Avid, Media 100 products, Ulead Media Studio Pro, Microsoft MovieMaker, Apple iMovie
Authoring Systems for All Media	Macromedia Director, Macromedia Dreamweaver, Click2learn Toolbook, Microsoft Front Page, Adobe Page Mill, Microsoft PowerPoint with Producer

devices have far less space. Multimedia requires networks that are fast enough to ensure that multimedia plays correctly. Cable modems, Digital Subscriber Lines, and special techniques of streaming are required and often perform adequately, but note the typical network data rate of PDAs in Table 2.

Assume that you have set up an environment such as the one in Figure 1. Now comes the really challenging part: creating the content or coaching others to create content. If you are coaching students, you should know that creating multimedia projects can help your students to achieve goals that include developing higher-order thinking skills and interpersonal skills, learning content by engaging multidisciplinary subjects, and developing technical competence and media literacy that will empower the students throughout their lives (TeleEducation NB, 2002). Furthermore, employing multimedia will allow you to improve students' efforts outside formal classroom settings and allow you to

Table 2. Typical end-user devices

Property	Desktop Computer	PDA and Cell Phones
Storage	80 GB hard drive	128 MB Flash RAM card
Processor clock rate	2.4 GHz	400 MHz
Operating system	Windows XP	PocketPC
Display diagonal, inches	17.0	3.8
Network for delivery	Cable modem, wireline, typical speed of 400 K bits/sec	Wireless, typical speed of 16 Kbits/sec

Table 3. Sample content-preparation guidelines

Guideline
Provide user-selectable options for multiple learning styles.
If you present text and audio on the same page, make sure that both use the same words. Nobody can read one set of words while listening to different words.
Remember that any movement on a page, such as video or animation, strongly distracts a user from non-moving information such as text.
Use colors to facilitate readability, appeal to different audiences, and reflect different cultures.
Use background music sparingly, to set a mood.
Prepare text for skimming rather than for reading long passages in detail. Computer monitors tire the eyes because they have resolutions that are much less than resolutions of printed pages.
Organize multimedia information carefully and consistently.
Have important information no more than three clicks (or levels) deep.
Do not use copyrighted media in any content that you sell, unless you obtain the owner's permission. Be careful what copyrighted media you use, even in an educational context.

For extensive details, consult *Distributed Multimedia* (Agnew & Kellerman, 2002).

piggyback on these efforts inside the classroom. Victory, however, is not merely receiving any old PowerPoint presentation, even with audio, animation, and video. Having an arsenal of past examples and setting up Olympic scoring of students' results (Agnew, Kellerman, & Meyer, 1996) helps elevate the standards of content quality. Guidelines such as those in Table 3 can help you as either a coach or creator.

Issues, Controversies, and Problems

Early adopters and pioneers routinely create multimedia. Today, with affordable hardware and software, people who are not media professionals can prepare interactive documents that contain multiple media. They can communicate using these media either in real time, using streaming, or asynchronously, using e-mail. Using multimedia tools, they can structure their information to greatly facilitate understanding. They can send this multimedia information to remote locations, with some certainty that it will be received rapidly and understood successfully. Tomorrow, lacking such skills will seriously impact almost all professionals' and students' lives, job satisfaction, and job performance. Content created by early adopters and pioneers has made multimedia literacy part of the expected price of admission to many roles.

Complexity and too many choices stymie the rest of us. Unfortunately, arcane skills are still required to set up digital environments and then use them for serious information preparation or even for living-room enjoyment.

Our professional colleagues and teaching friends confirm that multimedia is changing fast and furiously, making it difficult for them to keep up in a field that they view as diverging from their respective professional areas. They are elementary school teachers, biology teachers, instructional technologists, literature professors, and so forth. Nevertheless, new multimedia capabilities are superb ones that such professionals need. What best characterizes humans, all over the world, is our ability to communicate orally and in writing. Multimedia can make this communication even better, if done well.

Dramatic price declines in software and hardware allow many more of us to set up the environments we need to both create and use multimedia. For example, we have watched PC cams (small video cameras that connect to PCs for both storage and control) drop in price below $100, then below $30, and now below $10. The difficulty all of us find is that to learn what we specifically need to know, we must either spend hours on the Internet or buy books, often blindly. If only the cost and time spent learning to use the affordable hardware and software were decreasing as well.

Vendors have conflicting motivations. It would be easier for users if Microsoft could indeed integrate all required support into its operating system. Governments and competing vendors have widely divergent motivations. As a result, authors are required to either guess at which formats and data rates their audience requires or supply several different views of the same content.

Book stores display many shelves of books on different media and on enhancing Web pages. You are led to believe, with some truth, that to learn to create multimedia, you need a yard of books. Very few books tell how to create meaningful content where content is targeted to academic or serious professional uses.

Mismatch of equipment between home and school. People are using digital cameras, both standalone and inside cell phones, in record numbers. They are learning how to use them on their own, just blundering through. Electronic gadgets including computers at home are proliferating. Home computers tend to be good ones that far outperform what is available in most K-12 schools and many universities. In school, children are exposed to old equipment without getting sufficient quality instruction in its use and without educators taking advantage of the motivational aspects of using the equipment to enhance education. The Salvation Army prefers to reject any computer that is more than three years old; can schools do the same?

Creating high-quality content is difficult today, and few are experienced in it. The available tool often drives the content, rather than conversely. A tragically famous example of this is NASA's chart justifying its tests of foam striking a Space Shuttle's wing. The authors produced bullet after bullet of PowerPoint text at random levels of hierarchy and importance. Unfortunately, they buried the only important fact (that their test set-up had been totally unrelated to the real world) in a sentence fragment at the bottom of the page, rather than making it the title, or at least phrasing it as an unambiguous complete sentence.

Dr. Edward Ayers (2004) understands that few scholars have done what he has done over the last decade, namely scholarly research on multimedia narration (Ayers, 2004; valley.vedh.virginia.edu).

Solutions and Recommendations

Early adopters and pioneers routinely create multimedia. To help students and teachers achieve multimedia literacy as part of life's expected price of admission, educational technologists must continue learning, coaching, and mentoring the rest of the academic community. Academics in universities must work together. As an example of the kinds of successes cooperation can have, Dr. Meyer (a computer science professor) and Dr. Driver (a literature professor) worked together to inspire literature students to compose multimedia documents. Each provided relevant expertise (Driver & Meyer, 1999).

Young people are intrinsically early adopters and pioneers. While it is charming when students teach teachers, it is teachers who can best apply the required pedagogy to achieve the desired results.

Complexity and too many choices stymie the rest of us. A viable approach is to identify a small set of tools and stick with it for several years, ignoring incremental advances in hardware and software. This includes taking advantage of tools that ship with major software. For example, both Microsoft and Apple ship moderately functional video-editing software as parts of their current flagship operating systems.

Mismatch of equipment between home and school. Parents need to get involved, working with teachers to encourage home equipment use for creation of rich media content in support of pedagogical goals.

Creating high-quality content is difficult today, and few are experienced in it. As it becomes easier to assign multimedia, this will become more common. Future teachers need coaching in how to use multimedia in the classroom, as in the text, *Multimedia in the Classroom* (Agnew et al., 1996). Teaching teachers in colleges and universities does not consist of imparting isolated media skills, but rather of showing how to put it all together in a learning environment. One key is exhibiting exemplary multimedia content achieved by relevant people. It is not useful to present George Lucas's work for students to emulate; work produced by students in prior years is far more helpful. Like many subjects, the hardest part of teaching multimedia is getting started.

Teachers need to develop pedagogical goals for both teaching basic multimedia literacy and using multimedia to teach other subjects. This requires that they understand what is required to create and use multimedia to achieve pedagogical goals and that they then implement paths to reaching these goals that are consistent with their existing environments. They must be able to assess results along multiple dimensions. Merely using multimedia is not enough when the goal is quality content supported by rigorous arguments. Teachers and educational technologists will routinely need to advise, recommend, approve, and obtain parts of the framework required for multimedia.

Educators will need to improve their multimedia creation and playback environments, as prices and quality of tools continue to decline, and in step with the mainstream and with overall mission objectives. For example, the military now uses high-speed computers, high-bandwidth delivery connections, and sophisticated multimedia simulations to instruct soldiers on how to carry out missions. Whereas K-12 teachers might have more modest requirements, everyone involved in multimedia must learn to communicate intelligently and efficiently with vendors of multimedia products and services. A major part of this is learning when to search the Web and when to telephone a help line. Experience will assist educators in knowing what multimedia they and students can produce and use with what they have on hand, and what multimedia is suitable for what their intended users will have on hand.

Everyone should be able to recognize and produce quality multimedia content. Those who can do this will need to be generous with their time and talents, and help others to do likewise. Available tools must not drive content in undesirable directions, such as PowerPoint's leading from sentences to sentence fragments to sloppy thinking. Using tools must not be allowed to become the end in itself.

Suitable goals include preparing teachers and students who are routinely able to create and deliver a multimedia proposal, resume, presentation, set of instructions, or report using appropriate selections from alternative media. In many cases the media will need to be suitable for nationwide or even worldwide distribution over the Internet. This requires some understanding of the available bandwidths of connections that range from reasonably fast broadband to abysmally slow cellular wireless. It also requires selection between real-time and asynchronous communication and suitability for a wide variety of end-user devices.

Creating multimedia requires people to be able to:

- acquire and prepare images and graphics for inclusion in documents;
- repurpose slides and analog photos into digital forms for playback on TVs, PCs, cell phones, and PDAs;
- create and incorporate video using either economical PC cams or high-quality Mini-DV camcorders;
- prepare animation for illustration and instruction; and
- employ voice recognition software for communicating with devices that are too small to have workable keyboards.

Examples of specific skills include:

- converting media from one form to another for use in various situations and on various devices;
- using tools that allow processing of several media files in one batch, such as in converting an entire folder of several images from one format to another at once; and
- organizing raw and completed information for effective later re-use and collaborative use.

All of these skills require particular attention to what is actually feasible to achieve meaningful results.

Moreover, everyone must know about the rights that educators and others have with respect to using media created by others. Rights may differ between content used as is and altered content.

Future Trends

For better or for worse, future uses of multimedia in educational and other contexts will be driven by improvements in technologies. Moore's Law famously predicts that processor power and internal memory capacity will continue to double every year or two, without significant increases in cost. Less famously, other important technologies are improving at even faster rates. A decade ago, the available hard drive space on a typical home computer sufficed for storing barely 30 minutes of moderate-quality video; now a typical computer can store about 30 hours of high-quality video. Increasingly, economical hard drives have allowed many users to afford personal video recorders, such as TiVo, as well as sophisticated in-home video editing. A decade ago, transcontinental telephone connections were so scarce and expensive that long-distance telephony was a cash cow; now a glut of worldwide fiber-optic cable bandwidth allows Dell to route help-line calls to Indonesia as cheaply as to Indiana.

Companies including Intel, IBM, and AT&T are severely threatened by rapid technological progress that gives customers the opportunity to pay vastly fewer dollars for the same products and services. Many companies see multimedia as their only hope for convincing customers to purchase far more products and services, for at least the same number of dollars. It works. Most owners of digital still cameras now use more hard-drive space for storing images than they used for all purposes just a few years ago. New, tiny video cameras that temporarily store video on expensive flash RAM cards will permanently fill up even more storage space on hard drives.

This trend toward rapid improvement in technologies means four things to us all, as creators and users of multimedia. First, we must beware of pressures to use more of the products and services that do not benefit us, merely because they are increasingly economical. Second, we must try to make excellent use of newly affordable methods for achieving our goals. Third, we must encourage providers of multimedia products and services to make major improvements in ease of learning and ease of use, rather than merely dumping in more and more capabilities with attendant increases in confusion. Fourth, we must continually keep abreast of research on assessments of multimedia technologies, especially ones which include best practices. One way to keep abreast is to subscribe to Kotlas's newsletter, *CIT Infobits* (2004) and review the list she compiled on Assessments of Multimedia Technology in Education.

Conclusion

We will all communicate using technologies that range from today's e-mail and Word documents to tomorrow's video instant chats. Each communication will be significantly enhanced by our ability to easily and effortlessly use appropriate media and to allow the recipient to selectively access content in a variety of forms. We will build on skills acquired at home, in K-12 schools, and in higher education. We can expect to learn continually as technologies improve. As vendors expect to sell more of their hardware and software, we hope their motivations will include making equipment easier and quicker to learn and use, as well as more economical to buy. We must help one another, even if it requires cross-disciplinary activities. The best authors need to take advantage of multimedia to create multimedia and to help the rest of us learn to create it and use it.

References

Agnew, P., Kellerman, A., & Meyer, J. (1996). *Multimedia in the classroom*. Needham Heights, MA: Allyn & Bacon.

Agnew, P. & Kellerman A. (2002). *Distributed multimedia—technologies, applications, and opportunities in the digital information industry, a guide for users and providers* (2nd edition). Cincinnati: Atomic Dog Publishing.

Assessments of Multimedia Technology in Education: Bibliography. (Information Resource Guides Series #IRG-11), Institute for Academic Technology (IAT). Compiled by Carolyn Kotlas, MSLS, University of North Carolina. This document includes government, private industry, and K-12. Retrieved February 10, 2004, from *www.unc.edu/cit/guides/irg-11.html*

Ayers, E. (2004). Doing scholarship on the Web: 10 years of triumphs—and a disappointment. *The Chronicle of Higher Education,* (January 30), B24-B25.

Driver, M. & Meyer, J. (1999). *Engaging students in literature and composition using Web research & student constructed Web projects.* Retrieved February 10, 2004, from *csis.pace.edu/~meyer/hawaii/*

Educase. (2003). *Information resources library on articles with multimedia applications and campus learning.* Retrieved February 10, 2004, from *www.educause.edu/asp/doclib/subject_docs.asp?Term_ID=364*

Koltas, C. (2004). *CIT infobits.* Retrieved February 10, 2004, from *www.unc.edu/cit/infobits/index.html*

Maricopa Community College. (2004). *Multimedia authoring*. Retrieved February 10, 2004, from *www.mcli.dist.maricopa.edu/authoring/*

TeleEducation NB. (2002). *The significant difference phenomenon.* Retrieved February 10, 2004, from *teleeducation.nb.ca/significantdifference/*

Chapter XIX

What Literacy for Software Developers?

Jaroslav Král
Charles University, Czech Republic

Michal Žemlička
Charles University, Czech Republic

Abstract

There is a paradigm shift towards service orientation. Service orientation requires an education less oriented to a strictly computer-oriented knowledge, and education containing basics of thinking of empirical sciences and, to some degree, also humanities. The reason is, among others, the fact that the service interfaces in the service-oriented system should be user oriented—they should be based on knowledge, habits, and languages of a user problem domain. It is, however, difficult for many computer people to use user domain knowledge, as they often are overly proud of their computer knowledge (and underestimate knowledge of other disciplines—knowledge domains of the system users inclusive). We call this attitude 'hacker syndrome'. The hacker syndrome is the main obstacle to do analysis and to apply modern software practices like agile programming and service-oriented software architectures. Hacker syndrome prevention can be based on curricula ensuring training of the knowledge important for the development of service-oriented systems. Such a training can enhance job and career opportunities of software experts in near as well as in far future.

Introduction

It is well known that the main reasons for software project failures and the increase of software development expenses are the errors in the early stages of the project lifecycle. According to the studies of the Standish Group (1994), the errors are due to the management failures and inability of users to formulate their requirements properly. Comparing the studies of the Standish Group from 1994 and 2003, we find that the effects of management failures are becoming more important, whereas the reasons caused by improper user involvement are less important and the influence of the faults of developers is becoming marginal.

The statistics on the reasons of the failures of software systems show that the defects in requirement engineering are frequent and very costly to repair. It can be hardly caused by project management, as one can hardly suppose that the management errors (e.g., a lack of resources) influence requirements specification more than other phase of software development. The requirements specification is selectively influenced by snags in the communication and collaboration of developers and users. It is also confirmed by the fact that the agile programming (Beck et al., 2001) and especially the extreme programming (Beck, 1999) require permanent communication/collaboration of users and developers. It—as well as the experience of the authors—implies that the communication between users and developers cannot be reduced to communication between users and the project leader. It contradicts the recommendations of the Standish Group (1999) as the project manager then becomes the bottleneck of the project. It would also lead to a situation when developers do not understand properly what they should do.

We can conclude that all the members of the development team ought to understand their tasks, that is, what users really need and want. If the developers are not allowed, are unable, or do not want to communicate with users, they must use spoiled/imprecise information, if any, about their tasks. They are then unable to develop a satisfactory requirements specification.

On the other hand the users do not have a deeper insight what requirements are feasible, difficult, or easy to meet. The users then have no good vision what they can and should require. They will not understand the philosophy and the offers of software and how to best use them. The result will then probably be a system not fulfilling the user needs enough. The users will be unable to use the system properly. The developed software would not then bring the expected effects, if any.

The successes of agile programming, and also long-term experiences of the authors from practical projects and teaching university students, indicate that a permanent and intensive communication and close collaboration between users and development team is the most important precondition of the successes of software projects. This has strong implications on the desired knowledge profile of software developers and their education.

Communication Problems Between Developers and Users

The earlier noted conclusions are supported by the fact that, according to Denning (2003), communication skills and abilities are supposed to be critical for almost all information (computer) technology professions. The condition of any good communication/collaboration is, however, not only the ability to communicate and corresponding knowledge, but also the willingness to communicate. The developer must moreover accept the second side of the communication as partner and not consider him to be a 'dumb guy' who does not know what is the purpose of interrupt #10. The arrogance of developers (e.g., Král & Töpfer, 2000; see also the discussion below) is unavoidable if the computer world is like a paradise for them, whereas the world of the user is not interesting, gloomy, boring, vague, if not something like a hell for clever computer people. Developers are often unable to understand the user world. Under such conditions, the communication skills and knowledge are useless.

The communication problems between users and developers are amplified by the tendency to switch prematurely from the documents in natural (informal) language (i.e., the language of experts understandable to both sides) to designing and writing of programs. This tendency is typical for many developers and is sometimes supported by management being nervous that no instruction or line of code has been written yet.

The role of natural language in requirements specification is often underestimated, in spite of the fact that it supports intuition and can be during the current stage of the project as accurate as possible and so inaccurate as necessary. The disadvantage of natural language is that there is no possibility to make formal proofs for natural language documents. Formal proofs can be replaced by formalized inspections.

Developers are often introverts communicating with computers much of their time, thus having less time and willingness to interact with human beings. They then have less human-to-human communication skills. The problem is that the basic natural language skills must be developed in childhood. University students should learn and practice expert language style. For example, the Faculty of Mathematics and Physics of Charles University, Prague, and the Faculty of Informatics of Masaryk University, Brno, have lessons on expert style.

The above facts confirm the known fact that the bottleneck of software development (especially information systems development) is the quality of communication between users (possibly all) and developers (also possibly all, if appropriate). Such a communication is possible only under the condition that the communication parties understand each other and are willing to communicate.

Software development is the matter of developers. To be more specific, the developers must find out requirements and edit them into a concise document—a requirement specification (RS). The information in the RS is mainly the information from the user knowledge area. So the developers must be able to understand it and learn basic knowledge of the user knowledge domain. This is a difficult task. The main issue is, however, different.

The main issue is the willingness to collaborate with users in a peer-to-peer way (Král & Töpfer, 2000). Our experience indicates that the willingness and ability to collaborate with users is correlated with the ability to think empirically and to use mathematics, especially mathematical statistics. It seems to be confirmed by the fact that the software project managers in the Czech Republic are often graduates in empirical sciences. The main barriers at the developers' side are prejudices, overestimation of the importance of computer-oriented skills, and too high conceit of computer knowledge. This is typical for hackers. We shall therefore call this attitude 'hacker syndrome'.

Hacker Syndrome

By hacker syndrome we understand psychological profile, attitudes, and abilities typical for hackers and in a weaker form for many computer professionals. Hacker syndrome is occurring in many highly specialized professions; in this chapter we shall discuss the case of software developers only.

Manifestation of Hacker Syndrome

The main manifestations of the hacker syndrome are:

- Pride of the ability to program well, and overestimation of the importance of programming/software knowledge and underestimating other knowledge domains.
- Poor social skills; unwillingness to interact with real-life world with its vagueness, unpredictability, and emotions.
- The love for computers, dislike of social activities.
- Tendency to consider the people without hacker syndrome to be dumb/stupid.
- Tendency not to use documents, especially the ones in natural (expert) language; inability to understand real-life processes.

Some Czech companies developing information systems—especially the information systems having service-oriented architecture (Král & Žemlička, 2004d, 2005)—do not like to hire the people apt to have hacker syndrome, such as computer science graduates (Král & Töpfer, 2000). The companies complain that the software specialists are arrogant in teams and during the collaboration with users. We have heard an opinion that it is easier in a company to train people in programming than to induce programmers or information technology experts to give up bad habits.

On the other hand, companies active in computer graphics evaluate high some students who had lessons in artistic computer graphics, computer music, humanities, and those having core knowledge of experimental sciences (sociology, econometrics, etc.). Such knowledge is usually not available in the companies. People with this knowledge are usually able to collaborate with the experts who are not computer professionals.

People with hacker syndrome hate documentation, and also often hate the methods and attitudes of experimental sciences and situations when there is incompleteness and uncertainty of real-life data and processes. It is especially apparent when it is necessary to use tools of mathematical statistics. People with hacker syndrome have the tendency to shortcut solutions and, it seems, to voice extreme political opinions.

The properties of service-oriented software systems (SOSS; Král & Demner, 1979; Král & Žemlička, 2004a, 2004c, 2005; Barry & Associates, 2003), except the systems in e-commerce, depend substantially on the properties of the interfaces of the services. Examples of such systems are enterprise systems, manufacturing control systems, CRMs, and so forth; we call such systems 'software confederations' (Král & Žemlička, 2003b). The interfaces of the services should be user oriented, that is, understandable by users (Král & Žemlička, 2004b). User orientation of interfaces is a cornerstone of good software engineering properties of service-oriented systems. It is yet another reason why developers should understand user knowledge domain.

Hacker Syndrome and Empirical Attitude

On the basis of our long-time pedagogical experience and on the experience from practical projects, we believe that the tendencies to be hackers—being usually talented, introvert, and often too self-evident individuals—sometimes lead to asocial tendencies like creating viruses. It shows that hacker syndrome is usually a deep property of the psychology of individuals. As such it is very complicated to cure, and it may be too late to cure it at universities.

One approach to prevent hacker syndrome is to emphasize stronger on the education of experimental sciences in computer professional curricula. The education should be targeted so that it should present not only the final results of the sciences but, what is more important, the ways the results were empirically achieved. It usually means the use of methods of mathematical statistics with good examples of applications in the software development and requirements specification as well.

The inability and unwillingness to use mathematical statistics is strongly correlated with hacker syndrome. This fact is underestimated, although without knowledge of mathematical statistics as a tool of experimental inference, it is not reasonably possible to analyze software metrics, to apply CMM (SEI Institute), to formulate requirements, and to manage projects (compare Critical Chain Method by Goldratt, 1997). Hackers are usually unable to work in a team—this is known as the design anti-pattern Corncob (Brown, Malveau, McCormick, & Mowbray, 1998).

The manifestations of hacker syndrome (overestimation of own knowledge, no understanding for real-world problems, no understanding for mathematical statistics, rash decisions) can appear in attitudes of some young scientists from abstract sciences (Motl, 2004).

We assume that the individuals tending to have hacker syndrome have psychological dispositions that can be influenced by upbringing and education. The problem is that current curricula (IEEE & ACM, 2001; Gorgone et al., 2002; Davis, Feinstein, Gorgone, Longenecker, & Valacich, 2001; Dickey 2003) overemphasize the technical problems of information technology and therefore amplify the hacker attitude. It is to a high degree true for the proposal CC-2004 by ACM. Even weak symptoms of hacker syndrome may negatively influence software (especially information systems) development. It is therefore desirable to change the curricula structure to prevent the cultivation of hacker syndrome symptoms. It must be done as soon as possible, as the fully developed hacker syndrome is very difficult (and often impossible) to cure.

Prevention of Hacker Syndrome

Hacker syndrome is quite incurable when it is fully developed. We believe that hacker syndrome develops from too strong an emphasis on education of classical programming and programming languages, and to some degree of classic mathematical disciplines—that is, teaching only the subjects where everything is precise and expectable/precomputable. Such a discipline can also be mathematical statistics, if taught as part of classical mathematics and not as a data analysis tool.

As noted previously, the prevention of the hacker syndrome should be based on the combination of programming, with education of methods of experimental sciences and of mathematical statistics as a tool of experimental sciences. It appeared to be a very complicated task. Two large Czech universities (Charles University in Prague and Masaryk University in Brno) tried to solve this problem. They introduce in their undergraduate curricula lectures of some experimental sciences (physics, computational linguistics, biometrics, econometrics) to show "how the experimental sciences think/work". These lectures are now followed by one-semester lectures on probability and mathematical statistics. These lectures were designed similarly as lectures of other mathematical disciplines, and were not completed by applications of probability and mathematical statistics in problems of software development.

Since the lectures require quite complex mathematical background, they are scheduled during the last year of undergraduate study. The knowledge obtained there therefore cannot be sufficiently applied in computer science lectures. Other reasons also exist: computer science teachers often are not immune to hacker syndrome, and the knowledge also restricted the opportunities to show how the experimental sciences analyze reality.

The positive effect of the lectures is apparent but more significant effects were expected. The main problem is not only the very rare use of mathematical statistics in computer science lectures but also the fact that mathematical statistics is taught too late—when the hacker syndrome is often already developed. Probability and mathematical statistics cannot be taught sooner as there is no sufficient mathematical background. It is necessary to invent a compromise solution based on the fact that the knowledge from high schools is almost sufficient for the simple application of some statistical methods.

Hacker Syndrome and Service-Oriented Systems

Service-oriented systems become a dominant paradigm of software development. Quality-of-service-oriented systems—especially those like decentralized systems of products or CRM (Dyché, 2002)—strongly depend on user orientation of service interfaces (Král & Žemlička, 2003b). Using suitably chosen services is possible to reach the situation when, for documentation of the services, the description of their interfaces is sufficient (Král & Žemlička, 2005).

The interfaces are well designed only if the users as well as the developers understand them equally. This is an area where people with hacker syndrome are not excellent as interface designers. Dominant is the knowledge and experience of the users. Computer knowledge is less important here.

A well-designed interface enhances the system modifiability and reduces the need of never-ending re-implementation. The re-implementation will usually be more a matter of particular services than of the whole system. The services—thanks to good interface design (if user oriented)—will tend to be stable in time (Král & Žemlička, 2005), and the frequency of its changes will be reduced. It is therefore expected that the need for knowledge that the hackers are proud of will be significantly reduced in the near future.

It should be taken into account that hacker knowledge becomes obsolete very quickly. It therefore cannot be in it its extreme form a good investment. The rise of service-oriented systems means a qualitative shift of software engineering—it is a new paradigm. As such, service orientation requires new ways of thinking, new best practices and tools, and new working styles. Governing of any new paradigm requires years, and many people will never accept it and be able to master it. Service orientation is extremely hard to accept for people with hacker syndrome.

Education of IT Experts

Enhancement of Empirical Thinking and the Knowledge of Humanities

We have seen that it is an issue that the theory of statistics seemingly must be taught too late. A good compromise can be to organize the lectures on statistics as a two-stage process. The first stage can be a collection of lectures focused to empirical sciences and the basics of mathematical statistics. The lectures should be presented in more or less informal style, so that almost no knowledge on mathematics and statistics beyond the high school level would be necessary. The lessons should contain examples from information technologies. Occasional knowledge repetition and supply should need, at most, a few lessons.

It is possible to find enough examples from computer science, where it is possible to be sufficient with quite elementary knowledge of mathematical statistics such as mean value, contingent intervals, and so forth. Other results can be used without proofs. It is the case of central limit theorem and the distribution of the sum of independent random variables. The second stage should have the character of traditional lectures, where it is possible to use sufficient background from mathematics, some empirical sciences, and more advanced examples from information technology.

The second stage of mathematical statistics undergraduate education should therefore be taught during the second year or at the beginning of the third year of undergraduate study. Involved lectures should again use some examples from the first stage to show that more advanced techniques give substantially better results. The lectures should discuss the problems of software metrics and bad habits such as the inaccessibility of data, the statistical analysis of which is published.

Advanced lecture on mathematical statistics should be included in post-graduate study. The lecture should repeat basic knowledge on mathematical statistics and add methods of the theory of estimation, testing and analysis of time series, and so forth.

If some university provides a so-called secondary profession (as it is usual in Germany), it is important that computer scientists who are going to work in systems analysis should select such a secondary profession that contains enough empirical (not purely speculative) science.

It is also desirable that there be humanities (sociology, econometrics, mathematical models of psychology, etc.). Knowledge from psychology, theory of teams, and teamwork are also important. The lectures on philosophy, politics, and some arts proved themselves to be useful at Masaryk University in Brno, Czech Republic.

Lecture share is 50-60% computer science and mathematics, 20% experimental sciences basics, and 10-15% others (humanities, artistic computer graphics, computer music, politics).

Computer scientists should have insight into disciplines that influence them fundamentally: laws and economy. Even simple courses oriented to law and economic aspects of computer science can fundamentally influence success of the students in the Czech Republic: It can help them in negotiating agreements but also in the design of the functions of developed systems. They will learn to get to know and accept disciplines, the principles and habits of which may be quite different from their 'computer-pure world'.

We assume that lectures demonstrating exercises of experimental philosophy in computer science are missing. Lectures on basics of expert language style are part of curricula at both Charles and Masaryk universities. These lectures belong in both cases to feared ones.

Examples of Application of Experimental Attitude in Entry Courses of IT Study

The problem when students learn statistics too late can therefore be solved so that entry-level programming (or special) courses repeat basics of probability and mathematical statistics, and use them in solving tasks from the IT world. Possible examples of empirical inference are:

1. Determining when to stop testing of a software unit, preferably using data from a software project.
2. Estimating how many defects are contained in the given software unit.
3. Finding out whether a programmer writes his/her code with significantly more or less defects than the other programmers do; deciding how to cope with the varying complexity of software units.
4. Choosing an optimal server capacity according to statistical parameters of the client's loads and the number of clients.
5. Analysis whether a system is worn out and should be rewritten.
6. Examining statistical indicators of software metrics quality.
7. Determining how to select hardware resources for the software systems growing with time.
8. Using regression analysis and relation $\text{Effort} = c \times \text{Length}^{1+a}$.
9. Researching data availability and bad habits in publications on software metrics; applying Large Numbers Law.
10. Studying probability of company bankruptcy in relation to number and size of orders.
11. Comparing statistical analysis of the systems of cooperating services.
12. Determining basic statistical method of network administration.
13. Comparing Critical Path Method to Critical Chain Method (Goldratt, 1977).
14. Using statistical tools in marketing (time series, correlation).
15. Experimenting with simulation programs showing treacherousness of statistical methods.
16. Using basic knowledge on hashing methods (mean value, standard deviation).
17. Statistical aspects of data or software quality.

The use of tools for statistical analysis (specialized programs, a spreadsheet can be enough) from the examples from information systems practice is very important. The use of spreadsheets showing the outputs of other programs can be a good step to training for the development of service-oriented systems containing, as services, suitably encapsulated applications (Král & Žemlička, 2004b, 2005).

Primary and Secondary School Education

Primary schools should teach knowledge and abilities that are more difficult for children to learn as they get older. An example can be the abilities to communicate, especially to communicate in the native language. Lower school levels should unveil basic working habits and skills, knowledge of mathematics, and elementary pieces of the knowledge of sciences and humanities. Such knowledge is important generally, in IT as well.

The ability to precisely and clearly formulate knowledge (eventually in a written form) in one's natural language is very important for both requirements specifications (e.g., techniques of interviewing) and design of services' interfaces in service-oriented systems. It is therefore important to invest sufficient effort into unfolding communication abilities at primary and secondary schools. We should require from students discussions and explanations of knowledge, especially when the students are good (or excellent) in mathematics, sciences, and/or computers, and do not like to talk or explain. All people will need natural language and therefore their education (especially in primary school) should reflect that fact.

We assume that the pupils' language skills should be developed by learning foreign languages and also by improving communication abilities in one's native language. Discussions, essays, and papers seem to be suitable methods for this purpose. The situation in the Czech Republic is in respect worse than in, for example, the United States. It seems that they are better in science.

In the cases of professional articles, the emphasis should be on working with more sources and mainly on finding the most important facts from available source(s). It is quite common now in the Czech Republic for pupils to select words that look impressive and connect them, even if they do not know what the articles are about. It is therefore important that the pupil presenting an article understand what he or she is talking about. The pupil should use his or her own words instead of words that make no sense to him or her and the others in the class. The presentation of the pupil should be understandable by his or her classmates as well. The presenter should be somehow interested in his or her own understanding of the paper (to force the presenter to explain the topic sufficiently). It is also important to present the facts formally using basic terms of expert languages (including mathematical expressions if appropriate).

Students should learn not only how to work with sources that match or enhance each other, but they also must learn how to work with sources that differ or are antagonistic. The students should be able to detect which information is trustworthy and which is debatable. Further, the students should be able to prove the information—computationally, experimentally, or through discussion.

Students should also practice longer independent performances with logical structure of the text, understandability for listeners, and presentation of the core of the information. We assume that it is useful if at least some students can use information collected via direct communication with people active in a given domain.

The problem in Czech primary and secondary schools is that they provide many reasons for a reduced number of lessons on exact sciences and empirical activities (mathematics, laboratories, biological practices). The situation is getting even worse now. It restricts opportunities to provide analysis of different data. Such analyses are very easy and instructive using suitable software applications (for example, spreadsheets, which are usually taught anyway).

The students should face situations in which not everything is exactly known, computable, or predictable. They should learn that something can be vague, uncertain, and can be recognized only partially and incrementally. Laboratories can fit this purpose well. They cannot only enhance the students' interest in a given subject, but they can also inspire further development of new kinds of thinking. For the needs of the development of exact sciences' thinking, it is not as important that the laboratories provide experiments from physics, biology, or chemistry, as it is that the pupils have the chance to try something (both alone and with classmates) and that they measure and evaluate the experiments' results. Examples of possible topics include:

- the number of cells in view or a given area;
- the concentration of a solution (by titration or by densimeter/acidmeter);
- the measurement of resistance of the resistors;
- the decision whether the differences of two random samples are statistically important (we can use the simple technique using confidence intervals); and
- the critique of the statements from newspapers based on an improper evaluation of open data sets.

In all these examples the experiments/measurements should be followed by common evaluation of results of all groups and by related discussion.

The students should gain here team experience, that is, for the situation when they should divide the labor, each must do his/her part, and afterwards the partial solutions will be put together into one common result. For example, each team member can collect and record partial observations based on common arrangement or style.

Software Experts and the Future of Information Technologies

The experiences with service-oriented systems show that service orientation (especially in the case of software confederations) is a very effective paradigm, solving many software engineering requirements like stability, modifiability, reusability, user orientation, integration/cooperation with third-party products, and so forth. It is expected that influence of this paradigm will be very substantial in almost all areas of information technology. It will take some time, as the majority of computer professionals will have to change their habits, development processes, and programming attitudes and skills.

These changes will be very painful for people having hacker syndrome, especially when they are too object oriented. It is questionable whether they ever will be able to master service orientation.

Service orientation is a big challenge for the management of software vendors. They will have to change not only the development processes, but also their business strategies.

All these issues are crucial, as the advantages of service orientation are so important, and as such it will become a mainstream technology. Reusability, stability, and the key role of user orientation of service interfaces weakens to a high degree the need of strictly computer-oriented knowledge and empowers the importance of the ability to communicate with users. As stated above, this ability is likely to be strongly correlated with the ability to understand empirical sciences and with the ability to apply mathematical statistics. Mathematical statistics have important applications in software development processes (see for example methodology CMM) and in functions offered to management.

IT experts will have to concentrate more on service-oriented systems and therefore on empirical sciences and mathematical statistics. But this is probably not enough. Some issues must be solved in primary and secondary schools. Primary and secondary schools should give their pupils and students an opportunity to learn skills needed to evaluate and measure. The education should include the knowledge areas and especially skill domains that cannot be taught at universities (as they can be taught properly in earlier childhood). This includes communication skills in natural language and basic mathematical skills, which are useful not only for computer people, as they offers them ways to succeed outside IT, but also as a part of common education.

Conclusion

Service orientation is becoming the crucial paradigm of information technologies. Service orientation is a very important step to making software an engineering product of the quality similar to the quality of other high-tech products. It is achievable only under the condition that the profile of education of IT experts (especially of those who develop information systems) will be changed. Targets of the change are of two types: (1) restricting the occurrences and the reduction of the level of the manifestation of the hacker syndrome; and (2) providing future IT experts with the knowledge and skills needed for the era of service-oriented systems. Tools applicable to meet both targets are to a high degree the same, and they extend application domain of IT experts outside information technologies.

Necessary changes in the education of information technology experts are not a simple task; to a high degree they represent the end of the era when the main problem was to implement the requirements in a quite low-level programming (procedural) language. In the future we will specify declarative requirements in the terms of users. They will support the dynamic changes of business processes by users.

Changes in the education of SW/IT experts should be oriented to improvement of their ability to cooperate—both among themselves and with other people, especially with future users of their work. These changes in education should better the chance of IT experts to find jobs even outside information technologies and to be able to respond properly on (to cope with) quick changes of information technologies in future. This is very important, as the engagement of elderly computer-oriented experts in the development and/or application of new information technologies is not easy. It can be expected that the experts will change professions during their careers. The reason can be either the competition of younger colleagues or generally the decreasing job opportunities for information technology experts.

Acknowledgment

This research is supported in part by grants of the Czech Grant Agency, numbers 201/02/1456 and 201/03/0911.

References

Barry & Associates. (2003). *Web services and service-oriented architectures*. Retrieved from *www.service-architecture.com*

Beck, K. (1999). *Extreme programming explained: Embrace change*. Boston: Addison-Wesley.

Beck, K., Beedle, M., van Bennekum, A., Cockburn, A., Cunningham, W., Fowler, M., Grenning, J., Highsmith, J., Hunt, A., Jeffries, R., Kern, J., Marick, B., Martin, R.C., Mellor, S., Schwaber, K., Sutherland, J., & Thomas, D. (2001). *Agile programming manifesto*. Retrieved from *www.agilemanifesto.org*

Brown, W.J., Malveau, R.C., McCormick, I.H.W., & Mowbray, T.J. (1998). *AntiPatterns: Refactoring software, architectures, and projects in crisis*. New York: John Wiley & Sons.

Davis, G.B., Feinstein, D.L., Gorgone, J.T., Longenecker, J.H.E., & Valacich, J.S. (2001). *IS 2002: An update of the information systems model curriculum.*

Denning, P.J. (2003). The profession of IT: Great principles of computing. *Communications of the ACM*, 46, 15-20.

Dickey, M. (2003). *Model curricula for undergraduate programs in computer science and related fields*. Retrieved from *www.cs.washington.edu/homes/dickey/curricula/*

Dyché, J. (2002). *The CRM handbook: A business guide to customer relationship management*. Boston: Addison-Wesley Professional.

Goldratt, E.M. (1997). *Critical chain*. Great Barrington, MA: North River Press.

Gorgone, J.T., Davis, G.B., Valacich, J.S., Topi, H., Feinstein, D.L., & Longenecker, J.H.E. (2002). *IS 2002: Model curriculum and guidelines for undergraduate degree programs in information systems.*

IEEE & ACM (2001). *Computing curricula.* Retrieved from *www.computer.org/education/cc2001/final/*

Král, J. & Demner, J. (1979). Towards reliable real time software. *Proceedings of IFIP Conference Construction of Quality Software* (pp. 1-12). Amsterdam: North Holland.

Král, J. & Töpfer, P. (2000). *Education of software experts for a changing world.* In Z. Pudlowski (Ed.), *Proceedings of the 2nd Global Congress on Engineering Education* (pp. 267-271). UICEE.

Král, J. & Žemlička, M. (2003a). Software confederations—an architecture for global systems and global management. In S. Kamel (Ed.), *Managing globally with information technology* (pp. 57-81). Hershey, PA: Idea Group Publishing.

Král, J. & Žemlička, M. (2003b). Software confederations and alliances. *CAiSE'03 Forum: Information Systems for a Connected Society* (pp. 229-232). Maribor, Slovenia: University of Maribor Press.

Král, J. & Žemlička, M. (2004a). Requirements specification and software engineering properties of service-oriented systems. In M. Khosrow-Pour (Ed.), *Innovations through information technology* (pp. 265-268). Hershey, PA: Idea Group Publishing.

Král, J. & Žemlička, M. (2004b). Service orientation and the quality indicators for software services. In R. Trappl (Ed.), *Cybernetics and systems* (Volume 2, pp. 434-439). Vienna: Austrian Society for Cybernetic Studies.

Král, J. & Žemlička, M. (2004c). *Systemic of human involvement in information systems.* Technical report KSI MFF UK No. 2004/2. Charles University, Prague, Czech Republic.

Král, J. & Žemlička, M. (2004d). Towards design rationales of software confederations. In I. Seruca, J. Filipe, A. Hammoudi, & J. Cordeiro (Eds.), *ICEIS 2004: Proceedings of the 5th International Conference on Enterprise Information Systems* (Volume 1, pp. 105-112), EST Setúbal, Setúbal, Portugal.

Král, J. & Žemlička, M. (2005). Architecture, specification, and design of service-oriented systems. In Z. Stojanovic & A. Dahanayake (Eds.), *Service-oriented software system engineering: Challenges and practices* (pp. 182-200). Hershey, PA: Idea Group Publishing.

Motl, L. (2004). Global warming does not exist. *Neviditelný Pes,* (January 5).

SEI Institute. *Capability maturity model.* Retrieved from *www.sei.cmu.edu/cmm/cmm.html*

Standish Group. (1994). *The chaos report.* Retrieved from *www.pm2go.com/smapleresearch/chaos_1994_1.php*

Standish Group. (1999). *Chaos: A recipe for success.* Retrieved from *www.standishgroup.com/*, button 'public access'.

Chapter XX

Computer and Information Systems in Latin Paleography Between Research and Didactic Application

Antonio Cartelli
University of Cassino, Italy

Marco Palma
University of Cassino, Italy

Abstract

In this chapter the authors describe how ICT changed the way of approaching research and teaching for today's paleographers. First of all they report how new technologies changed the cataloging, the studying, and the spreading of information concerning ancient manuscripts all over the world. Next, the results of the experiences they carried out at the Faculty of Humanities are described: the first one concerns the creation of Web resources for teaching paleography; the second one is a database collecting data on women copyists in the Middle Ages; the third one is the practical application of a more general project called by the authors "Open Catalog"; the fourth and last one is an information system concerning the bibliography of ancient manuscripts. Finally, the authors describe how ICT introduced new research methods in paleography and especially how they made possible the creation of learning communities (i.e., learning, studying, and research communities).

Introduction

The experiences the authors describe in this chapter were borne from the lucky meeting of the different fields of study and research they are involved in. One author is a researcher in didactic and technologies of education; the other is a professor of paleography. This last discipline, while studying and analyzing ancient charters and manuscripts (i.e., those written in the Middle Ages) demands that scholars and scientists have good knowledge and skills, at least in ancient languages (i.e., Greek, Latin, or Romance) and history (i.e., Roman and Medieval). In today's high schools and universities, where students' backgrounds in the above disciplines are unfortunately not very deep and solid, the teaching of paleography offers many questions and problems, and sometimes, intensive work correcting students' misconceptions and wrong ideas must be planned.

In recent years ICT intervened more and more in changing the approach a paleographer must have with his/her disciplinary field, and ICT literacy became one of the essential elements of students' background. Furthermore, in the authors' opinion, teaching and research cannot be separated, and a special care in the analysis of problems, the suggestion of solutions, and the development of instruments to be adopted is needed. The above remarks induced the authors to plan special instruments for paleographic research and to introduce their use also in everyday teaching.

The authors agree on the following main conclusion: the use of the new technologies and especially of ICT produces relevant and positive effects on the management of paleographic research and on the teaching of the same discipline. These positive results agree with what we were taught some years ago by American researchers on learning communities and can be improved by the adoption of a systematic use of ICT in all fields of medieval studies.

Background

Borne as a scientific discipline about three centuries ago, paleography is based on comparison. Dating and localizing a medieval script, as well identifying a scribe, are the paleographer's essential tasks on which all historical speculations are founded. In other words a paleographer has to answer the following typical questions: who, when, where wrote a charter or a manuscript between late antiquity and the invention of printing?

Comparison is a relatively simple task when writing examples are kept in the same library, but in the overwhelming majority of cases, they are located in different places, so one needs images to be compared. Before the photographic era the only resources beyond memory were drawings and prints, by which paleographers tried to reproduce the distinctive features of a script. From the end of the nineteenth century onwards, photographs and microfilm made graphic analysis enormously easier. Recently, the increasing number of digital reproductions in CD-ROMs or the Internet represented a virtual repository of images easily available to scholars.

A more complicated problem had to be faced in the elementary teaching of paleography, where beginners need plates to practice reading and recognizing different scripts. It was not by chance that paleography was acknowledged as an independent subject after the publication of the first photographic albums. Still after that, reading sessions of medieval writing examples needed a plate for every pupil, not exactly an easy condition before the spreading of photocopies. Until some decades ago one could frequently witness quarrels among students about the use of the same plate.

In the Internet age libraries and universities are placing a growing number of images at the disposal of scholars, teachers, and students. Even so, medieval manuscripts are so numerous and scattered all over the world that it absolutely unimaginable is a complete virtual album. Conversely, teachers provided their students reproductions often taken from existing publications, which may cause some copyright problems. A serious problem can arise from the lack of information about images. Scholars need to know all of the research produced regarding the manuscripts they see on the screen; students may wish to be informed about date and script, and possibly check their readings against a transcription. So libraries and universities should plan a comprehensive offer, matching images with bibliographies, descriptions, and every aspect of scientific information. The main themes of such projects will depend on the purposes of the involved institutions, but they cannot ignore the nature of the public they are addressing, nor neglect the regular revision and development of their materials.

On these principles are founded two of the most interesting enterprises in the field, *Digital Scriptorium* in America and *Manuscripta mediaevalia* in Europe. In the first case (sunsite.berkeley.edu/scriptorium) several libraries in the United States joined their efforts to create a real database containing bibliographic information, descriptions, and high-quality images of their manuscripts. *Manuscripta mediaevalia* (www.manuscripta-mediaevalia.de), operated by the Deutsche Forschungsgemeinschaft, contains hundreds of digitized catalogs, a number of modern descriptions, and the complete reproductions of 89 manuscripts (as verified on February 23, 2004). Other renowned European libraries, like the British Library, the Bodleian Library, or the Bibliothèque Nationale de France, offer data taken from their catalogs and images of some of their manuscript treasures, but the way to a sufficient level of information still seems very long.

Some innovation may be found in the new *Open Catalog* of the manuscripts owned by the Biblioteca Malatestiana of Cesena (www.malatestiana.it/manoscritti), one of the best preserved libraries from the Italian Renaissance. Here one finds an increasing number of reproductions, a continuous flow of bibliographic information, and a growing number of descriptions. The project is helped by the reasonable size of the collection (429 medieval manuscripts), and the library's remarkable human and financial investment.

A census of paleographical didactic sites appears much more difficult, because of the manifold and uneven initiatives sponsored by different institutions or single teachers. According to a recent survey (De Angelis, 2003), the situation seems very far from the average e-learning structures of other disciplines, where a regular two-direction exchange between teachers and learners is a well-established tradition.

The Experiences Carried Out by the Authors

Two main thoughts induced the authors to introduce ICT in paleography: the former one concerns the easy access to multimedia materials that the Internet and especially the Web guarantee; the latter one depends on the hypothesis the authors share that ICT and especially the Internet cancelled the temporal gap existing between researching and teaching time (at least in paleography). Now scientists can immediately publish the results of research, so that the separation of the proposal of new scientific paradigms from their translation into educational and didactic materials becomes more and more difficult.

The problems the authors describe below, the solutions they hypothesized, and the instruments they carried out concern the following common aspects of the everyday work of scholars involved in the study of the Middle Ages:

a) the scripts commonly used in that period;
b) the persons involved in the writing activity and especially women copyists;
c) the need for the transformation of well-settled and well-defined catalogs in a new and more powerful instrument, the *Open Catalog;* and
d) the bibliography of manuscripts.

The Web Site "Didactic Materials" for Latin Paleography

It is well known that in the Middle Ages different scripts were used, and the study of their features is based on the analysis of charters and manuscripts. It has also to be noted that security and preservation reasons make it more and more difficult for scholars—and what is more important, for students—to access these materials.

Furthermore some remarks on the features of the organization of paleographic studies have to be considered: The proceedings of conferences and meetings, used by scholars to report the results of their studies, are normally printed some years later. Also, it is quite obvious that the lack of reference materials can make it very difficult, if not impossible, to explain the meaning and relevance of a hypothesis or a discovery.

These reasons induced the authors to create a Web site (www.let.unicas.it/links/didattica/palma/paldimat.html) to offer the didactic materials of the course of Latin paleography and to make available within it two kinds of documents: (1) plates reproducing some pages of ancient manuscripts in the different scripts adopted in the Middle Ages, with the transcription of their texts (for the sake of completeness, it is important to report here the name of those each Internet user can access on the site to date:

Beneventan, Caroline, Gothic, and Humanistic, i.e., four of the most important and widely used scripts between the eighth and fifteenth centuries); and (2) texts freely extracted and translated from printed or electronic documents, or made available by the authors, and collected in the following sections: Codicology, Beneventan script, Caroline script, Cataloging, Preservation, Written Culture, Gothic script, Mercantesca script, Palimpsests, History of Paleography, Humanistic script.

The experience carried out by the authors with the site of the didactic materials is mostly unique, not only for the systematic nature of the plates and for the presence of their transcriptions, but also for the documents reported among the texts; many of them are in fact papers concerning recent research topics, produced for special events (mostly conferences) and made available by the authors for didactic purposes. Therefore, the students attending the Paleography course are instantaneously led to the leading themes of the most recent research and to the debates of the paleographic community.

The Web Site "Women and Written Culture in the Middle Ages"

This experience derives from the research of Miglio and Palma (2002) carried out on women copyists and led to the planning of an information system; in the database of the system were stored the data concerning both the women and the manuscripts they wrote, up to the fifteenth century.

The main aim of the dynamic Web site (edu.let.unicas.it/womediev) interfaced with an RDBMS (Relational Data Base Management System), named by the authors *Women and Written Culture in the Middle Ages* (Cartelli, Miglio, & Palma, 2001), was to systematize the data emerging from the research while leading to an instrument that could help scholars find new elements for further study.

The data appearing relevant to the scientific community were:

For the scribes:

- the name of the woman as it appears in manuscripts;
- the qualification of the copyist, that is, if it is reported, if it is known, whether the woman was a nun or a lay; and
- the date or the period the copyist belongs to.

For the manuscripts:

- the shelfmark (i.e., town, library, and number of the manuscript);
- the place where the manuscript was written;
- the country to which the place of origin belongs;
- the date or the period the manuscript belongs to;

- the authors and titles of the texts; and
- the bibliography or the source of information about the manuscript.

Furthermore it appeared important to show for each woman the manuscript/s she wrote and vice versa, and if possible and available, at least an image of the copyist's hand.

The site, which does not give rise to a printed bulletin or other periodical printed matter, has the following main features:

1. It proposes itself as a continuous work-in-progress where everyone can suggest new data to include, by pointing out bibliographical information to the authors (their e-mail addresses are reported in the site).
2. It presents two separate sections: the first can be operated only by the editors who can insert, modify, and delete the stored data, thus ensuring the scientific validity of the information reported; the second is at everyone's disposal to obtain the list of all women and manuscripts in the database, or to make queries concerning women and manuscripts with specific qualifications.
3. The editors can enter the database without being obliged to physically sit at the computer the database lays in; they can also use the database management services wherever they are all over the world on the condition they can access Internet in some a way (by phone, by LAN, etc.).

Students attending the course of paleography not only used the materials reported in the site, but were also involved in the description of manuscripts and in the collection of the plates reproducing texts written by women. This work and the analysis of the different data led students to distinguish the different hands of women copyists and their way of writing manuscripts.

The Open Catalog of Manuscripts and the Martyrology of Arpino

The hypothesis of the *Open Catalog of Manuscripts* originated from the experience of the Web site of the didactic materials and from the results of other studies concerning the use of the Web for the publication of catalogs of manuscripts (Cartelli & Palma, 2003b).

In its final structure the *Open Catalog of Manuscripts* is an information system devoted to the management of documentary information, and is based on the use of the Internet and especially of the Web. It is composed of five sections that have to be intended in a flexible manner; that is, these sections will depend on the available resources and the different solutions that will be adopted: (1) the first section is devoted to the documents illustrating the history of the library involved and that of its manuscripts; (2) the bibliography ordered by shelfmark and, eventually, alphabetically and chronologically, is housed in the second section; (3) the third section houses the descriptions of the manuscripts, that is, the previous printed catalogs or the ancient handwritten catalogs (suitably digitized), and the new descriptions (according to nationally defined standards); (4) the fourth section is devoted to the images of the highest number of manuscripts in the library (potentially all); and (5) the fifth and last section consists of a communication subsystem including electronic blackboards, chats, forums, and special Web solutions granting the easier acquisition, writing, and editing of texts (Cartelli & Palma, 2002).

In the authors' opinion the *Open Catalog of Manuscripts,* while spreading, promoting, and producing information, can place the libraries at the center of the scientific information. It will give manuscript curators the instruments to recover the function they had in erudition times and they progressively lost for the increasing of bureaucratic tasks—to give impulse to research by involving scholars and students.

The Martyrology of Arpino (www.let.unicas.it/links/didattica/palma/martirin.html), as a single manuscript kept in the church devoted to Our Lady in Arpino (a small town in Central Italy), had the suitable features for the creation of an *Open Catalog* (Cartelli & Palma, 2003a) and was used for teaching as follows:

- Some make-up courses centered on the Martyrology were designed for students showing History and Latin gaps in their basic knowledge, since the manuscript was used as a chronicle from the fourteenth to sixteenth centuries and the historical events reported there had a counterpart in relevant events of that period.
- Students were directly involved in producing the Web pages of the Martyrology (with the acquisition and editing of texts and images).
- They were also involved in the description of the manuscript.
- Finally, students had to transcribe the text (i.e., to make readable the text containing many abbreviations and special symbols).

It must be noted that the use of computers and of their peripherals for the digitization of manuscripts and editing of texts was soon and easily accepted by all students, and there were no cases of rejection of those instruments, as often happened in institutional computing courses in the Faculty.

The Bibliography of Beneventan Manuscripts

The BMB experience (*Bibliografia dei Manoscritti Beneventani/Bibliography of Beneventan Manuscripts*) started in 1992 collecting the quotations of Beneventan manuscripts (i.e., medieval books written in the South Italian national script) by means of an MS-DOS program called BIBMAN. The BMB Web site (edu.let.unicas.it/bmb) was first developed in 1997 and was hosted in the Web site of the Faculty of Humanities at the University of Cassino with the main aim of: (1) making faster and easier for scholars the downloading of new bibliographic data about Beneventan manuscripts (nearly monthly), and (2) encouraging the creation of a virtual community that could find in the site services new opportunities to improve their studies.

The use of BIBMAN ended up producing three main problems:

a) *The incompatibility with the operating systems of today's PCs:* With the new Windows XP, as well as Windows NT, it was no longer possible to start applications in the native MS-DOS, and BIBMAN didn't work at all.

b) *The achievement of the physical limits of the data management:* In 2001 BIBMAN no longer succeeded in building a database from the materials collected until that date. New archives for the data collected in 2001 and 2002 were created, but the editors could not correctly manage them (an efficient control of the data needs a direct access to all materials collected until that date).

c) *The inability to cope with the management of Web bibliographies*: BIBMAN was planned to manage bibliographical references concerning printed matter, but during recent years many Web sites concerning research on the Middle Ages were born, and many institutions and research centers adopted the Web as the only medium for the publication of manuscript studies (Palma, 2003).

The solution to the above problems was represented, in the authors' opinion, by the *BMB Online* Web site. In this information system different people can store the quotations of Beneventan manuscripts, so they can be freely queried by general users. Persons entrusted with the task of collecting the quotations of Beneventan manuscripts are grouped into three categories:

1) *Contributors* can access a special Web area (by means of their ID and password) where they can see the bibliographical materials the administrators assigned them, and can write, modify, and delete bibliographic data.

2) *Scientific administrators* can manage all data, and write, modify, and certify bibliographic materials, this last operation being done only once, because when a record is verified, it can be no longer be accessed for revision.

3) The *system administrator* is allowed to do all operations, including the modification or deletion of certified data.

The access to certified bibliographic materials is possible according to five different query pages: (1) the first one asks for the author's name and gives back his/her quotations; (2) the second and third ones ask for a manuscript (by means of its ID code or shelfmark), and gives back all quotations in the database for that/those manuscripts; (3) the fourth one lets the user select one of the authors and gives back all quotations made by that author; and d) the fifth and final one lets the user input one or more words or part of them concerning the title, location, or bibliographical abstract of a given publication, and shows all bibliographic records matching the query constraints and the corresponding quotations of Beneventan manuscripts.

It should be noted that the system also includes a closed communication subsystem represented by an electronic blackboard granting an easy exchange of messages among contributors involved in the collection of bibliographic data.

During the last academic year, after attending the basic courses on cataloging, students were asked to produce bibliographic materials. The discussions that students had with administrators, professors, and among themselves; the use they made of the electronic blackboard and of the e-mail services for the exchange of messages; and last but not least, the chance to work in small groups on the same problems—these all very much helped them acquire the knowledge and develop the skills they could need in their daily work.

Conclusion and Further Hints

As can be easily deduced from what has been said until now, instruments and solutions reported in the above sections were planned at different times and suddenly introduced in teaching work. It must be noted that in paleography, more than in other disciplines, the assessment of the didactic process is made easier by the evidence of students' skills in reading, interpreting, and analyzing a charter or a manuscript; furthermore the small number of students involved in each of the above experiences made possible a quick and deep observation of the their behavior and learning. As a consequence, the scores students received on examinations were all positive and better than the ones their colleagues were awarded without the adoption of the above instruments.

The main results emerging from the analysis of the above data concern the confirmation of what has been found in the studies on communities of learners (Brown & Campione, 1994; Lave & Wenger, 1991), that is, the raising of individual features and the improvement of group experiences (mainly due to the use of ICT). First of all, professors observed that results were better with respect to the ones students obtained with traditional courses. Furthermore some results never observed before were detected in the development of the following skills: working in a group, an easier facing of complex tasks (thanks to the help that each student could have from companions), and the raising of the individuals' peculiarities within the community.

In conclusion, if the analysis and measure of the influence of ICT on the learning and teaching process are very difficult tasks, we can agree with the results of the studies on ICT supporting communities of learners (Collins & Bielaczyc, 1997; Scardamalia & Bereiter, 1996). Students involved in the above experiences, in fact, not only developed computing skills greater than the ones they could obtain in traditional computing literacy courses, but they were immersed in a metacognitive environment, submitted to cognitive apprenticeship strategies, and involved in the discussion and evaluation of the procedures they took part in—in other words, they experimented with all elements responsible for meaningful learning (Varisco, 2002).

In the authors' opinion the good results obtained from the experiences to date carried out in paleography will induce more and more professors to increase the use of ICT in their research and teaching work. The Faculty Center for ICT and online teaching, created in 2003 by the Faculty Council, will be very useful in this respect, because it will help professors find better solutions to introduce new technologies into their daily work.

References

Brown, A.L. & Campione, J.C. (1994). Guided discovery in a community of learners. K. McGilly (Ed.), *Classroom lessons: Integrating cognitive theory and classroom practice* (pp. 229-270). Cambridge, MA: MIT Press.

Cartelli, A., Miglio, L., & Palma, M. (2001). New technologies and new paradigms in historical research. *Informing Science (the International Journal of an Emerging Discipline), Special Issue—Widening the Focus, 4*(2), 61-66.

Cartelli, A. & Palma, M. (2002). Towards the project of an Open Catalogue. In E. Cohen & E. Boyds (Eds.), *Proceedings of IS 2002 Informing Science + IT Education Conference* (pp. 217-224), Cork, Ireland. Retrieved from *proceedings.informing science.org/IS2002Proceedings/papers/Carte188Towar.pdf*

Cartelli, A. & Palma, M. (2003a). Il Martirologio di Arpino come oggetto di ricerca e strumento didattico. *Tecnologie Didattiche (a cura dell'Istituto per le Tecnologie Didattiche del CNR), 28*(1), 65-72.

Cartelli, A. & Palma, M. (2003b). The Open Catalog of Manuscripts between paleographic research and didactic application. In M. Khosrow-Pour (Ed.), *Proceedings of the IRMA 2003 Conference—Information Technology & Organization: Trends, Issues, Challenges and Solutions* (pp. 51-54), Philadelphia, PA. Hershey, PA: Idea Group Publishing.

Cartelli, A. & Palma, M. (2004). BMB online: An information system for paleographic and didactic research. In M. Khosrow-Pour (Ed.), *Proceedings of IRMA 2004 International Conference–Innovations Through Information Technology* (pp. 45-47), Philadelphia, PA. Hershey, PA: Idea Group Publishing.

Collins, A. & Bielaczyc, K. (1997). Dreams of technology-supported learning communities. *Proceedings of the 6th International Conference on Computer-Assisted Instruction* (pp. 3-10), Taipei, Taiwan.

De Angelis, G. (2003). Repertorio critico di risorse digitali per gli studi di storia della scrittura latina e della produzione manoscritta nel medioevo [Siti didattici], *Scrineum, 1*. Retrieved from *scrineum.unipv.it/repertorio/index.html*

Lave, J. & Wenger, E. (1991). *Situated learning: Legitimate peripheral participation.* New York: Cambridge University Press.

Miglio, L. & Palma, M. (2002). Donne e cultura scritta nel medioevo: http://edu.let.unicas.it/womediev/. In L. Miglio & P. Supino (Eds.), *Segni per Armando Petrucci* (pp. 197-215). Rome: Bagatto Libri.

Palma, M. (2003). La catalogazione dei manoscritti in Italia. *Segno e Testo, 1*, 333-351. Retrieved from *www.let.unicas.it/links/didattica/palma/testi/palma8.htm*

Scardamalia, M. & Bereiter, C. (1996). Engaging students in a knowledge society. *Educational Leadership*, *54*(3), 6-10.

Varisco, B.M. (2002). *Costruttivismo socio-culturale. Genesi filosofiche, sviluppi psico-pedagogici, applicazioni didattiche*. Rome: Carocci.

Chapter XXI

The Role of Project Management in Technology Literacy

Daniel Brandon
Christian Brothers University, USA

Abstract

This chapter discusses the modern discipline of "project management" and the role of this discipline in technology literacy. Professional organizations that foster this literacy area are discussed as well as the coverage of this field in the academic community.

Introduction

A key component in technology literacy involves the management of technology resources. In industries that "build things," that management of technology is largely encompassed within the discipline of Project Management. Project Management is "the application of knowledge, skills, tools, and techniques to the project activities in order to meet or exceed stakeholder needs and expectations from a project" (Duncan, 1996). A project is defined as "a temporary endeavor undertaken to create a unique product or service" (PMI, 2000). In such industries, the first-level management job for a technical person is typically in a "project manager" role.

Background

Despite ongoing innovations in Project Management, many projects fail; in some industries, particularly information technology (IT), most projects still fail. A Standish Group study found that only 16% of all IT projects come in on time and within budget (Cafasso, 1994). Field (1997) discovered 40% of IS projects were canceled before completion. The problem is so widespread that many IT professionals accept project failure as inevitable (Cale, Curley, & Curley, 1987; Hildebrand, 1998).

Project Management in Professional Organizations

A number of professional organizations have developed around the world to address and foster this specific discipline. Most notable is the Project Management Institute (PMI, www.pmi.org), with about 140,000 members worldwide. Other major international organizations are the Association for Project Management (APM) and the International Project Management Association (IPMA) (Morris, 2001). These organizations have recognized that there is a distinct skill set necessary and level of technology literacy for successful project managers, and the organizations are devoted to assisting their members in developing, improving, and keeping current in these skills (Boyatzis, 1982; Caupin, Knopfel, & Morris, 1998).

The Project Management Institute has developed an index of project management skills and knowledge called the "Project Management Body of Knowledge" (PMBOK). The PMBOK has been developed through several iterations over many years; the first version was developed in 1976 (Cook, 1977). The latest version (PMBOK 2000) was released for certification testing beginning in January 2002 (PMI, 2000). It defines nine *knowledge areas* (KAs), which are organized into 37 *processes*. The processes are grouped into five *process groups* (PGs). This is illustrated in Figure 1 (PMBOK, 1996; Duncan, 1996). The KAs represent the technology literacy necessary for effective project management: scope management, time management, cost management, risk management, quality management, human resources, communication, and procurement.

PMI and the other international project management organizations each have a certification program, and for PMI the designation for the most important certification level is Project Management Professional (PMP). To obtain PMP certification an individual must have 4,500 hours of documented project management experience over a period of six years, have a BS-level college degree, and pass a rigorous four-hour examination. The first PMP exam was given in 1984 to about 30 people, and today there are over 30,000 PMPs worldwide (Foti, 2001).

These professional organizations recognize that while there is a large set of common technology literacy among industries, each industry (and each government sector) has its own specialized extensions in both the breadth and depth of this body of knowledge. PMI has a new book (PMI, 2002) that details the way project work is typically organized

Figure 1. PMI process groups and knowledge areas

	Initiation	Planning	Executing	Controling	Closing
Integration		Project Plan Development	Project Plan Execution	Overall Change Control	
Scope	Initiation	Scope Planning	Scope Verification	Scope Change Control	Scope Verification
		Scope Definition			
Time		Activity Definition		Schedule Control	
		Activity Sequencing			
		Activity Duration Estimation			
		Schedule Development			
Cost		Resource Planning		Cost Control	
		Cost Estimating			
		Cost Budgetting			
Quality		Quality Planning	Quality Assurance	Quality Control	
Human Resources		Organizational Planning	Staff Acquisition	Team Development	
Communications		Communications Planning	Information Distribution	Performance Reporting	Administrative Closure
Risk	Risk Identification	Risk Identification		Risk Response Control	
		Risk Quantification			
		Risk Response Development			
Procurement		Procurement Planning	Solicitation	Contract Administration	Contract Closeout
		Soliciation Planning	Source Selection		
			Contract Administration		

in a number of industries, as well as the US government. In addition PMI has books on PMBOK extensions for the largest industry sector of Project Management, the construction industry (PMI, 2003), and for US government (PMI, 2002). Many other books are also available on project management in particular industries such as information technology (Schwalbe, 2001).

Project Management in the Academic Community

Several universities have also recognized the fact that Project Management involves distinct skills and technology literacies, and that the traditional degree programs and courses in both business schools and other schools do not adequately cover and/or integrate these components (Brandon, 2003). *The Chronicle of Higher Education* (2001) recently reported that seven Philadelphia-area corporations established ties with four universities in that region to improve the business skills of computer science and IT students; most of these key skills involved the project management skill sets.

Perhaps self-evident from the previous paragraph is the fact that the knowledge and training needed by project managers covers both traditional business disciplines and disciplines involved with building or making things. Often the skills involved with building or making things would be found in an engineering curriculum, and also in information technology or computer science curriculums.

Since the skill sets needed by project managers are extensive, and since these skills involve both business and engineering disciplines, and also since most candidate students are degreed working adults, most schools have developed their project management curriculums as graduate school programs. A number of universities also have a single "Project Management" course, typically offered as a graduate course.

Graduate Degree Programs

An analysis of universities currently offering graduate project management programs indicates several types of programs being offered:

1. A master's-level general degree program (such as an MBA) with a specialization in Project Management
2. A full master's-level (generally MS) program in Project Management
3. A "certification program" of several Project Management courses

Some universities offer more than one of these program types. Also in some universities the program is offered in the School of Business (or Management), and in some schools the program is offered in the School of Engineering. In most universities, many of the courses appeared to be shared with other graduate degree programs; in other words not all the courses in the program are focused on project management.

Once a PMP status is obtained, an individual must earn 60 PDUs (Professional Development Units) every three years. Some universities offer a PMP Exam Preparation course or cover exam prep material in one of their Project Management courses. However, most graduate programs do not cover exam prep; in fact the graduate programs are more geared to providing the PDU credits for PMPs. Figure 2 summarizes the program types for most of the US universities offering Project Management programs "certified" by PMI. The list of such schools is on the PMI Web site (www.pmi.org). Out of the 19 schools listed, 11 offer a certificate program, six offer an MBA/MS specialization, and eight offer a full Master's in Project Management. In 14 of the 19 schools, the program is entirely in the Business (or Management) school.

Project Management Literacy Organization

Since so many resources have been put into the development and refinement of the PMBOK, and it has been so well received by the Project Management community, it seems prudent to organize university program courses around the processes defined within PMBOK. The issue then becomes how does one "slice and dice" the processes as shown in Figure 1 into distinct (but integrated) courses. The PMBOK document itself organizes its write-up by knowledge area. However, most classic overall project management books and textbooks are organized by process groups (Badiru, 1988; Cleland & King, 1988; Hajek, 1984; Kerzner, 1980; Meredith & Mantel, 1989; Royce, 1998; Verzuh, 1999). There are however a number of books concerning particular parts of Project Management and these cover particular knowledge areas, but they are not specifically written as "textbooks" (Fisher & Fisher, 2000; Fleming & Koppelman, 2000; Pinto & Trailer, 1999; Schuyer, 2001; Verma & Thamhain, 1996).

Looking at the universities currently offering degree programs to see how their curricula were organized, we defined three general types of organization:

1. *Step:* Courses are organized in the traditional manner from less depth to more depth over most of the knowledge areas. For example, the first course might be Introduction to Project Management, the next might be Intermediate Project Management, and the next would be Advanced Project Management.
2. *KA*: Follows the PMBOK knowledge areas (Scope, Time, Cost, ...).
3. *PG*: Follows the PMBOK process groups (Initiation, Planning, ...).

Most programs do not fit entirely into one of these molds, but they were categorized according to the best fit. Overall out of the 19 schools, 10 use primarily the Step method, six use primarily the KA method, and two use the PG area.

For schools offering certification, five use the Step method, six use the KA method, and none use the PG method. For schools offering the MBA/MS specialization, none use the KA method, one uses the PG method, and the rest use the Step method. For schools offering the full MS in Project Management, two use KAs, one uses PGs, and the rest use the Step method.

Project Management Content and Delivery in Programs

As can be seen from Figure 2, not all of the courses in a Project Management program are Project Management-specific courses. For most schools, the certification offering is made up of mostly Project Management-specific courses (the #PM in Figure 1 is the number of Project Management-specific courses). For the Project Management specialization, most schools use three to six Project Management-specific courses. For the full MS Project Management degree, the number of Project Management-specific courses is about one-third to one-half of the courses. These non-specific courses in the full MS degree program vary widely from school to school, especially if the degree is in the Engineering School instead of the Business School. Some of these non-Project-Management-specific courses are typically: General Management, Organizational Behavior, Leadership, Managerial Accounting, Information Technology, Finance, Human Resources, Quantitative Methods, Quality Assurance, Procurement and Contracting, and Risk Management.

Figure 2. Institutions offering graduate credit programs in project management

University	Organize	School	Certificate Program		MBA/MS Specialization		PM Masters Degree	
			# Courses	# PM	# Courses	# PM	# Courses	# PM
Amberton	KA	Business	4	4				
American Graduate Univ.	KA	Business					12	7
Boston University	KA	Business	8	8				
City University	KA	Business	6	6				
Colorado Technical University	Step	Both	6	6	13	6		
George Washington University	Step	Business					12	3
Int'l School of Info. Mgmt.	Step	Business	3	3	12	4		
Keller School of Management	KA	Business	6	4			14	6
Northwestern	Step	Engineering					12	4
Regis University	PG	Business			13	6		
Stevens Inst. Of Technology	Step	Business	4	4	12	4	12	6
U. of Management & Tech.	KA	Both	7	7				
U. of Wisconsin - Madison	KA	Business	6	6				
U. of Wisconsin - Platteville	Step	Business					12	5
University of Central Florida	Step	Engineering	5	1				
University of Maryland	Step + KA	Engineering					10	5
University of Texas - Dallas	Step	Business	6	1	10	1		
Western Carolina University	PG	Business					12	6
Wright State University	Step	Business			12	3		

Some universities are offering some, all, or portions of their courses in the form of distance learning. So the issue becomes where on the spectrum from "bricks to clicks" should a program position itself. There are many pros and cons on both sides of this issue, and most of those pros and cons depend on exactly how a course is made available online, as well as the university's overall vision, mission, and tradition. This issue encompasses most degree programs (not just Project Management), so we are not going to further debate it here, except to indicate that it is highly dependent on a particular school's mission, tradition, and demographics. As discussed below, the potential students for such a graduate program are working adults, so attention must be given to the best delivery for that market. Many schools are holding classes on weekends or evenings to accommodate the adult audiences for these types of programs (*San Diego Business Journal,* 2001).

Future Trends

The university programs surveyed above were all relatively new programs, so there is little or no data available for a statistical or comparative historical analysis at this time. In the future, one may be able to survey graduates from the different types of programs to determine the pros and cons of each type of technology organization based on surveys of graduates or performance metrics tied to graduates of the different programs.

The issue of course material organization is a difficult one for a learning environment. As discussed above, universities offering these programs are taking different approaches in this area. The Step approach is most appropriate for programs that have only two or three project-specific courses. The KA approach requires much more course preparation time, textbooks are limited, and instructors need depth in these skills. One possible curriculum design would be to use a combination of PG and KA. For PG, separation into two process 'super-groups—project planning and project control—may be appropriate, both covering scope, time, and cost. Separate KA courses would likely involve: Procurement, Risk, Quality, and Human Resources & Communications.

Conclusion

For a comprehensive Project Management literacy learning program, we have identified four dimensions to such literacy. The PMI PMBOK focuses on the dimension of breadth of the knowledge areas (and the 37 processes), but intentionally does not go into much depth. Going into depth gets into method and tool specifics. Thus the first two dimensions likely needed in a technology learning program beyond the PMP Certification are both the breadth and depth of these 37 processes.

The third dimension identified is industry particulars. While there is much commonality to project management in all industries, there is also much that is specific to each area. For example, task estimation for an IT project is much different than task estimation in a construction project. So this would be another added dimension to a program, certainly not for all industries, but for the major ones of concern in a school's region.

The fourth dimension we identified was that of time or "currency." This not only includes the use of current tools, but the practice of Project Management in the current business and technical environment. Textbooks addressing parts of this fourth dimension are just starting to become available (Klastorin, 2004). Issues such as virtual teams, international coverage, and Web-based systems are included in this dimension.

References

Badiru, A.B. (1989). *Project management in manufacturing and high technical operations.* New York: Wiley Interscience.

Boyatzis, R. (1982). *The competent manager: A model for effective performance.* New York: John Wiley & Sons.

Brandon, D. (2003). Developing a graduate program in project management. In *Technologies & methodologies for evaluating information technology in business.* Hershey, PA: Idea Group Publishing.

Cale, E.G., Curley, J.R., & Curley, K.F. (1987). Measuring implementation outcome. *Information and Management, 3*(1), 245-253.

Cafasso, R. (1994). Few IS projects come in on time, on budget. *Computerworld, 28*(50), 20.

Caupin, G., Knopfel, H., & Morris, P. (1998). *ICB IPMA competence baseline.* Zurich: International Project Management Association.

Cleland, D.I. & King, W.R. (1988). *Project management handbook.* Van Nostrand Reinhold.

Cook, D.L. (2002). Certification of project managers—Fantasy or reality. *Project Management Quarterly, 8*(2), 32–34.

Duncan, W. (1996). A guide to the project management body of knowledge. Project Management Institute.

Field, T. (1997).When bad things happen to good projects. *CIO, 11*(2), 54-62.

Fisher, K. & Fisher, M. (2000). The distance manager: A hands-on guide to managing off-site and virtual teams. McGraw-Hill.

Fleming, Q. & Koppelman, J. (2000). *Earned value project management.* Project Management Institute.

Foti, R. (2001). The case for certification. *PM Network,* (September).

Hajek, V.G. (1984). *Management of engineering projects.* McGraw-Hill.

Hildebrand, C. (1998). If at first you don't succeed. *CIO Enterprise Section 2,* (April 15).

Kerzner, H. (1980). *Project management. A systems approach to planning, scheduling, and controlling.* Van Nostrand

Klastorin, T. (2004). *Project management: Tools and trade-offs.* New York: John Wiley & Sons.

Meredith, S.R. & Mantel, S.J. (1989). *Project management, a management approach.* New York: John Wiley & Sons.

Morris, P. (2001). Updating the project management bodies of knowledge. *Project Management Journal,* (September).

Pinto, J. & Trailer, J. (1999). *Essentials of project control.* Project Management Institute.

PMI. (2000). *A guide to the project management body of knowledge.* Project Management Institute

PMI. (2002). *Government extension to the project management body of knowledge.* Project Management Institute.

PMI. (2003). *Construction extension to the project management body of knowledge.* Project Management Institute

PMI. (2002). *Project Management Institute practice standard for work breakdown structures.* Project Management Institute.

Royce, W. (1988). *Software project management.* Addison-Wesley.

San Diego Business Journal. (2001). (August 6), 23.

Schuyler, J. (2001). *Risk and decision analysis in projects.* Project Management Institute.

Schwalbe, K. (2001). Information technology project management. *Course Technology.*

The Chronicle of Higher Education. (2001). (August 10), A45.

Verma, V. & Thamhain, H. (1996). *Human resource skills for the project manager.* Project Management Institute.

Verzuh, E. (1999). *Fast forward MBA in project management.* New York: John Wiley & Sons.

Chapter XXII

Developing Technology Applications: Effective Project Management

Earl Chrysler
Black Hills State University, USA

Abstract

This chapter discusses the difficulties organizations have experienced when attempting to develop a new information technology application. The reasons for these difficulties are examined. A methodology for teaching a Software Project Management course that prepares students for conducting a successful project is presented in detail. The author hopes that educators will find the concepts and techniques presented useful and incorporate some of them in their courses.

Introduction

The literature related to the software development area is replete with case histories of software projects that have had major cost overruns, repeatedly missed deadlines, and even outright abandonment. Clearly, there is a need for providing those who will eventually be responsible for such projects with the concepts, techniques, and methodologies to bring their software projects to successful conclusions. The purpose of this chapter is to demonstrate a methodology for providing students with the experiences that will assure that they have the ability to develop the knowledge and skills necessary to become an effective member of a software development team. The basic approach is that of having students become members of a team responsible for developing a new software system in response to a request for proposal from a client.

Specifically, the student teams play the role of consulting firms and are required to perform all of the tasks required in a software development engagement for a client.

Background

One has only to review texts in the area of Project Management related to systems development to realize that new system development failures tend to be the rule rather than the exception. In his book *Project Management for Business and Technology*, Nicholas (2001) devotes an entire chapter to "Project Failure, Success, and Lessons Learned." Mantel, Meredith, Shafer, and Sutton (2001), in their book *Project Management in Practice*, state that a failure may occur when a project no longer meets the cost/benefit criteria. One of the major causes of a project no longer meeting the cost/benefit criteria is the lack of accurate project time and cost estimation techniques. For example, although one may find an estimation methodology presented in a favorable light in one book, for example the COCOMO (Constructive Cost Model), discussed by Jeffrey (1987) in *Critical Issues in Information Systems Research*, that model is not given strong support by Kemerer (1997) in *Software Project Management: Readings and Cases.*

The above implies that an improved educational experience would enhance the effectiveness of the Project Management performance of Management Information Systems program graduates. The objective of this chapter is to propose a course with the content and format that would provide MIS students with that educational experience.

Main Thrust of the Chapter

Course Approach

Those offering courses in Software Project Management and courses with similar titles, such as Software Engineering, typically use a case study approach to introduce students to the various phases through which a software development project progresses. The instructor must decide upon: (a) the source of a case that will have all of the features desired, (b) whether to have each student responsible for a case or to have the students form teams, (c) if a team approach is used whether each team should be assigned the same case or each team assigned its own case, and (d) the frame of reference that is provided in which to couch the case, that is, a team is an in-house information technology group or an external firm employed to design, develop, and install a new system.

It is suggested that placing students in the role of members of a consulting firm intent upon performing a system development engagement for a client has several values.

Firstly, the students will be required to learn to be effective members of a team. The reality of organizational relationships today is that the days of the corporate Lone Ranger are long since over. The typical situation today is the Task Force or Investigative Committee. These require one to contribute to the success of "the group" and not seek individual recognition. One must be a team player to be perceived as a loyal and therefore desirable employee.

Secondly, students are required to meet scheduled deadlines, with significant penalties for not meeting the due dates for components of the system (i.e., deliverables). Once again, this is important training for an organizational reality.

Thirdly, there are naming conventions and standards that must be adhered to in terms of the system deliverables. Once again, the concept of discipline is being implemented. This requirement prepares the students to expect that standards and naming conventions will be extant in their entry-level positions and, if they are not present, to suggest that they would be useful.

One then must determine the source of one or more cases. One could select a case from a text. One could also select one or more organizations on campus that need a new system and use these organizations as subjects of a case. One could also select one or more off-campus organizations that are in need of a new system and use such organizations as subjects of a case. Each of these situations has advantages and disadvantages.

If one selects a case from a text, it many times will be found that the case is: (a) too simple, (b) too difficult, and/or (c) unrealistic. Also, if one selects a case that is the core theme of a text, one would either have to repeat the same case each semester or change texts each semester to obtain a new case for the course. Neither of these is a desirable option.

If one selects an on-campus organization, first there is the responsibility of the instructor to locate these potential case studies on campus. The instructor must also consider that, should a team not perform in an exemplary manner, the reputation of the instructor, the course, and indeed the entire MIS program may be tainted.

Should one consider using an off-campus organization as the site for a case study, there is the chore of identifying organizations each semester to be amenable for having themselves be the subject of a case study. Once again, the team performing the project for such an organization must perform its tasks at a very high level of quality in order to assure that the reputation of the instructor, the course, and even the program will not be sullied. In addition, there is the concern that consulting firms in the area may take issue with student teams appearing to compete with them for software development contracts.

If one has professional experience in the information systems field, it is not overly difficult to design a small-scale case study that will provide students with exposure to the types of experiences encountered in a software development engagement. Also, by assigning the same project to all student teams, grading team performance is simplified. In addition, an instructor need not be concerned about one team copying deliverables of another team. If a team has exerted the effort required to develop any project deliverable, there is little willingness on the part of members of that team to share the results of their work.

One may believe that designing a new case study each time the course is offered would be an onerous task. In reality, the instructor can merely couch the case in a firm in different types of industries. While each case would appear unique, each would be designed to introduce the students to the same set of issues that require the same types of skills and problem-solving abilities. Also, since the instructor has designed the basic case, the desired deliverables are known in advance and a common grading scheme can be developed.

Course Design

The basic premise for the students is that they will be members of a small consulting firm that specializes in developing custom software for firms. The instructor presents the students with a terse Request For Proposal (RFP) that states a firm wishes to have custom software developed for a specific set of functions, such as sales analysis and inventory control. An example of such a subject firm is that of a retail dealer in collectibles such as paintings, sculptures, and so forth. The RFP also states in detail what types of processing the system must perform, for example, file maintenance of both a Customer Master File and an Inventory Master File, and transaction processing of sales of items in inventory owned by the firm and items held for sale on consignment from individuals. Also one or more reports will be specified, such as a Sales Analysis Report that indicates the sales within a specific starting and ending date of all items, with consignment sales shown separately.

The first stage of the course is that each student team must prepare a proposal in an attempt to obtain the contract to develop the software and train the client's employees in the use of the system. The teams should have access to proposals prepared by teams in previous semesters placed on reserve in the campus library for their guidance.

Proposal Construction

The students are told the potential client has employed a consultant to review all proposals and to recommend a firm to perform the project. The proposal must therefore be written to appeal to two audiences, the management group of the potential client and the consultant reviewing the proposals. This requires those writing the proposals to provide two sections of each part of the proposal, a management overview and a technical details portion directed to the consultant. The sections of the proposal and a summary of their contents are as follows.

Project Background

When preparing a proposal, the authors should bear in mind that the potential client personnel need some reassurance that the organization that is going to develop custom software for them truly understands the nature of their operations and, in general, what functions the software firm will need to perform to fulfill the current needs of the client. As a consequence, the initial section of the proposal should typically be titled "Background." In this section those preparing the proposal should describe the nature of the potential client's business. For example, "Zevco Manufacturing has as its main product line stereo equipment sold in the automotive after-market through installer-distributors." The organization chart of the prospective client should be presented. Then details of the business operations of the organization that relate to the project should be elaborated on. After assuring the client that the general nature of its business is understood, those writing the proposal should describe the events that precipitated the need for the software. All of the above information should have been gathered either from documentation provided by the client in the Request For Proposal or from interviews with representatives of the client organization.

Then the tasks required in the project should be listed, using specifics where they are known and generalities elsewhere. For example, "Zevco wishes to have new record layouts developed for its Customer Master, Accounts Receivable Master, Order Master, and Order Transaction files" is a specific requirement; whereas, "One or more reports based upon data found in the Order Master File are to be designed and programs developed to generate these reports on an as-required basis" is a general requirement. Obviously, the more specific requirements one knows and the fewer general requirements one must face, the easier it is to estimate project times and costs. The realities of life, however, are that there are typically many general requirements and few specific requirements in most projects. A major problem in some projects is when undefined requirements become known. As discussed later, this is the reason for the "Change Control" section of a proposal. The proposal organization section follows the background portion of the proposal.

Proposal Organization

This section of the proposal informs the reader of the manner in which the proposal is assembled. The section headings of the remainder of the proposal are listed and a brief description of the contents of each section is provided. It is also suggested that it be explained to the reader that within each section of the proposal, there will be information presented at the two levels previously discussed, a management summary level discussion followed by a technical details level discussion.

Project Organization

In the organization section, which appears next, the manner in which the project members will be organized is presented and discussed. The organization chart should then be developed in a general form.

Regarding the project organization, the proposal should indicate that the Project Manager is assigned responsibility for the entire project. Assigned to the Project Manager are appropriate support staff. The support staff are responsible for scheduling meetings with client representatives and among the Project Management team, and recording the minutes of all meetings. The support staff is also responsible for collecting team member progress reports and updating the project status database. Reporting to the Project Manager in line fashion will be a System Design Manager, a Programming Manager, a Quality Assurance Manager, a Support Services Manager, and a Training Manager. The responsibilities and duties of each managerial position and the responsibilities and duties of the professionals in each of these areas should be presented.

If the project under study is relatively large, it is quite likely that within the systems and programming groups, there will be sub-groups, each with a group leader. In such an instance the proposal preparing team should expand the organization chart to indicate that an additional level or levels of personnel will be required. Regardless of the size of the project, the proposal should present such a description of the project organization since this is, after all, a class exercise.

Project Phases

The next several sections of the proposal provide the reader with descriptions of the phases through which the project will pass. The first phase is the Requirements Definition phase.

- *Requirements Definition:* In this section of the proposal, the team should describe to the client the tasks that will be required to determine the information processing requirements of the system. In the management summary level presentation on this topic, only general descriptions of the processes need to be set forth. In the technical details level coverage, the client should find the names and position titles of all of the organization personnel who will be interviewed, the types of information that will be gathered during these discussions, and so forth. The next phase to be addressed is the system logic phase.
- *System Logic:* This portion of the proposal should inform the client that a specific deliverable—that is, a tangible product—will be provided at this point. The nature of the deliverable is a system logic flowchart that presents graphically the general nature of the manner in which the system will function. An example of such a flowchart should be provided at this point.

Master files are given general names, such as Accounts Receivable Master file. Transaction files are identified, logically, by the type of transactions they contain: for example, Sales Order Transactions or Accounts Receivable Transactions. Outputs are labeled based on their contents, such as Outstanding Receivables Report or Inventory Error and Exception Report.

The basic purpose of the general system logic flowchart is to determine if all parties agree that the underlying system concept is sound. As an example, if a specific program is to update multiple files for a given transaction, the flowchart will allow those reviewing the system logic to verify that all files that are to be updated are shown as being processed by the program. Also, the flowchart can be used to verify that the sequence in which the processing will occur is correct and that the proper version of each file is being used in each program. If there are any questions regarding the manner in which the final system will function, the earlier such questions can be addressed and resolved, the more smoothly and efficiently the entire project will progress. At the management summary level, a general description of the flowchart would be adequate. A more in-depth description of how one uses such a flowchart to trace how the data flows through the programs, into files, and out of files onto reports can be presented in the technical details area.

- *Program Logic:* After being given an overall or conceptual view of how the system will function by the general system flowchart, the client should then be introduced to the program logic section. In the management-level discussion, the reader should be informed that analysts document in narrative form the step-by-step processing logic of each program. The technical details portion of this section is where a list of the contents of a set of program specifications is presented. An outline of such specifications, as shown in Figure 1, will provide the reader with an awareness of the depth of analysis and documentation required to assure programs meet user requirements.
- *Program Development:* In this section the authors of the proposal describe the process whereby program specifications are translated into source language code. If the software firm has adopted a particular methodology that it feels provides some advantage in terms of programmer productivity or code maintainability, such as structured walk-throughs and naming conventions, respectively, this point should be discussed in the management summary level portion. In the technical details area of discussion, excerpts from the firm's programming standards and naming conventions and programs developed for other clients should be included to demonstrate that the firm does possess such conventions, and programmers adhere to them. After the programs are developed, they must be tested, both individually and collectively.
- *System Testing:* This section describes the various levels of testing that are performed on the system. The management summary part of the discussion states at what levels the system will be tested, such as program self-test by the programmer, program test by the Quality Assurance group, system test by the Systems Design group, system test by the Quality Assurance group, and acceptance test by a team of client representatives and the Quality Assurance Manager. The

Figure 1. Outline of program specifications

1. Statement of System Purpose
2. System Flowchart
3. Processing Logic for Each File
4. Record Layout for Each File
5. Data Field Edits for Each Type of File Maintenance and Transaction Record
6. Report Layout for Each Report
7. Screen Layout for Each Screen Display

material provided in the technical detail level discussion will go into greater detail, describing how test transactions are developed and before-and-after file printouts are used to confirm the programs are functioning according to specifications.

- *User Training:* In the user training part of the proposal, the prospective client should be told the documentation that will be provided, the number of each classification of employee who will be trained, the total number of hours of training that will be provided, where the training will take place (i.e., the vendor's place of business, the client's place of business, or some other location), and who will conduct the training sessions. While that information is adequate for the management summary, the specifics portion is to describe in detail the estimated number of hours of training that will be provided for each specific employee. An example of user documentation should also be supplied as part of this section.
- *System Implementation:* When describing this, the last phase of the project, management readers should be informed of the recommended method of conversion from test to production status for the system. If there is currently a manual or computerized system in place that is generating output that can be correlated to the output of the new system, it should be used to verify the accuracy of the processing of the new system. This implies that a parallel operating period should be recommended, if it is feasible. In some instances the simultaneous operation of two systems is not feasible. An example would be converting a batch processing mode order entry system for a mail order outlet to real-time. The management-level readers would primarily be interested in the period of time for which parallel processing is being recommended. This is important to them, since they may have to notify vendors or customers that a change in processing is going to occur and make such organizations aware of the impact that the change will have on them, both temporarily and in the longer scheme of things. At the technical details level, individuals need to understand that the conversion process will have an impact on staffing considerations, again both in the short term and the long run.
- *Documentation Standards:* The next major area of the proposal concerns the documentation standards to be followed during the project. In the field of software development, a systems analyst has the responsibility of developing specifications that stand alone and do not require the author be present to interpret any portion of the specifications. Similarly, a programmer's code must be of such a quality that another programmer could read the program and, without difficulty, understand the program logic. Clearly, the implication is that there must be some common approach to doing things—a common approach that everyone subscribes to, albeit sometimes complainingly, for the good of the organization.

The authors of the proposal should state the items that will follow standards and provide the reader with an example of each type of standard item. The samples should be complete enough to demonstrate the implementation of the standard.

- *Change Control:* This is a critical section of any proposal. A very formal procedure must be defined for the entire system revision process. All the parties involved hope that during the requirements definition phase, every processing implication will be examined, and users will be offered every practical option. Sometimes, however, a member of the client organization or the software development team identifies either a flaw in the logic of the system or an opportunity to significantly enhance the value of the system. It is also possible that during the development of a system, some of the basic processing requirements can change. While it is in the best interests of all concerned to have an optimum system, those preparing the proposal must impress upon the client that system design changes are not to be taken lightly. A change procedure should have a standard change request form. This form should require the individual requesting the investigation of a possible system change to state, in the terms best suited to the person proposing the change, the nature of the change to be investigated for feasibility and practicality. The change control board, whose members should be specified in this section of the proposal, should be charged with investigating the impact of the change. After the implications of the change, both in terms of additional cost and/or changes in the project schedule, have been determined, the client will make the decision as to whether the change is to be implemented.

- *Project Reporting and Control:* The project manager will be holding project status meetings with his managers, as those managers will be holding status meetings with their area personnel. In the preparation of the proposal, however, only those reporting and control situations of interest to the prospective client are to be presented. Those creating the proposal will want to describe to the reader what procedures will be used to monitor the progress of the project and how frequently the status of the project will be reviewed with representatives of the client organization.

All organizations that develop software, whether the organization is a for-profit custom software firm or the management information systems department of an organization, should track the performance of its employees. There are multiple reasons for this performance reporting, which will be covered later. For the present, however, the prospective client should be assured that the members of the project team will be reporting the time devoted to each project task and the estimated percent-complete of each task on which they worked. The proposal should state that the project manager and, if required due to the specific phase of the project, the systems design manager, programming manager, and/or quality assurance manager will meet with one or more representatives of the client organization to review the project status on a weekly basis. If either the client or the project team wishes to propose the consideration of a system change, such a change request would be submitted during these meetings.

- *Deliverables List:* The most crucial point of agreement, even beyond the price of the project, is the definition of exactly what tangible items will be supplied. It would be impossible to stress this issue too much. In most cases the software development firm is familiar with what is typically provided to the client, based upon past engagements. However, there are often differences, sometimes subtle and sometimes major, from engagement to engagement. The first-time client, however, by definition has no past experiences to which the organization can refer. In order to preclude misunderstandings later, the authors of the proposal must be very careful to itemize the deliverables. Further, for each deliverable, the proposal must state the quantity that will be provided, and the form in which it will be provided and/or the medium on which it will be provided. If it is source or object code, it must also be stated whether it will be installed on hardware as part of the project. If flowcharts or structure charts are to be supplied, the proposal must contain examples so that the prospective client can determine if any changes in format, symbolism, or depth of explanation would be required in order for them to be acceptable.

In many cases both the software firm and the client organization are so anxious to get on with the project, and so sure that a mutually cooperative atmosphere exists, that they assume that vaguely defined deliverables will be acceptable and, in fact, provide some desirable degree of flexibility. This is an invitation to disaster for both parties. Without a specific set of deliverables, with descriptions and, if possible, examples of each having been agreed to by both parties, the software development firm has no way of proving it has met the conditions that indicate the project is over. In effect, they have agreed to an open-ended set of requirements for a fixed fee. This type of situation is obviously not in the vendor's interests. Similarly, however, without a clearly defined set of deliverables, the client organization has no way of refuting a software development firm's allegation that the project work has been completed.

- *Support Requirements:* In this section of the proposal, the prospective consultants state their needs in terms of client resources. The authors of the proposal must state the access to client personnel, records, system documentation, computer equipment, and even photocopying equipment that will be required to complete the project in a timely and effective manner. In the case of personnel, the specific persons to whom access is required should be identified. If the individuals are executives, the proposal should state the maximum lead time the vendor representatives can tolerate before getting access.

In the case of computer access, the proposal authors should attempt to schedule usage during the normal working hours for the client organization. If this would present a potential problem for the client, this section of the proposal would be modified during contract negotiations.

Another resource that should be requested in this section is that of workspace for the software development team. It is always preferable to perform the project tasks at the client's place of business, even though it might appear that this would be less efficient. There is an interesting phenomenon in the world of consulting regarding consultant visibility. Clients tend to perceive a strong positive correlation between the number of consultant hours observed in their place of business and the value of the work that was done. If possible, the consulting firm should obtain a lockable work area. This will allow the staff of the consulting firm the ability to install specialized equipment such as plotters or servers, and leave their desktop and laptop computers at the client location during the engagement.

- *PERT/CPM Analysis:* The key to a successful project is planning. This fact cannot be over-emphasized. There are those who would counter with a statement to the effect that one cannot plan for everything—something that was unplanned is sure to arise. While it is true that one cannot plan for every possible occurrence, that fact is not justification for not planning to the best of one's ability and knowledge.

One of the most useful techniques for planning is the Project Evaluation and Review Technique (PERT) and its allied analysis tool, the Critical Path Method (CPM). In order to use the PERT/CPM methods, those preparing the proposal must determine: (a) what tasks need to be performed; (b) what task interdependencies exist, that is, for each task, what tasks must be completed before this task can begin; and (c) what the estimated time required is to complete each individual task. The tasks that must be completed can be determined by decomposing the project into its individual component parts. In many cases there are enough similarities between the project currently under consideration and past projects to allow this portion of the PERT analysis to be performed quickly and with some accuracy. When determining the interdependencies involved, however, caution is advised. It is the area of forgotten or incorrectly defined interdependencies that can cause critical problems to arise later. When approaching the time-estimating requirement, most proposal preparers have a significant problem.

The field of data processing suffers greatly from not learning from history. If a manufacturing firm is asked to estimate the cost of producing an item that it has never made before, there is a rational methodology. The drawing of the item provided by design engineers is used to determine what materials will be required, the amount of each, and all of the processes necessary to produce the item, such as drilling holes, bending flat metal to new shapes, welding pieces together, and so forth by those known as manufacturing engineers. Since manufacturing firms have been drilling holes, bending metal, and welding pieces together for many years, and recognized that they would be doing so for several years into the future, they developed and documented time standards for these processes. By multiplying the standard time for each operation by the hourly cost associated with that operation and summing the resulting values, labor costs are easily computed. By adding the material cost, overhead, and profit percentage, one develops a price of the new item in a very straightforward manner.

Unfortunately, those involved with the information technology field have not developed their estimating skills to this level of sophistication. In fact, they have hardly developed them at all. Several techniques have been proposed, including one by this author (Chrysler, 1978). The critical component required for all methods promising any reasonable level of accuracy is historical data. Due to resistance by systems analysts and programmers and a lack of assertiveness by their managers, the requisite data has not been collected. As a consequence, project estimates have historically been little better than guesstimates. This is one of the major factors contributing to the lack of credibility of information systems departments and the MIS disasters that permeate the information systems literature.

Refer to Figure 2 for an example of a simplified project PERT chart. As shown, one of the most meaningful methods of using this model is to use the calendar time during which the project is to take place as the reference for all the activities. In this manner, the reader

Figure 2. Project PERT chart

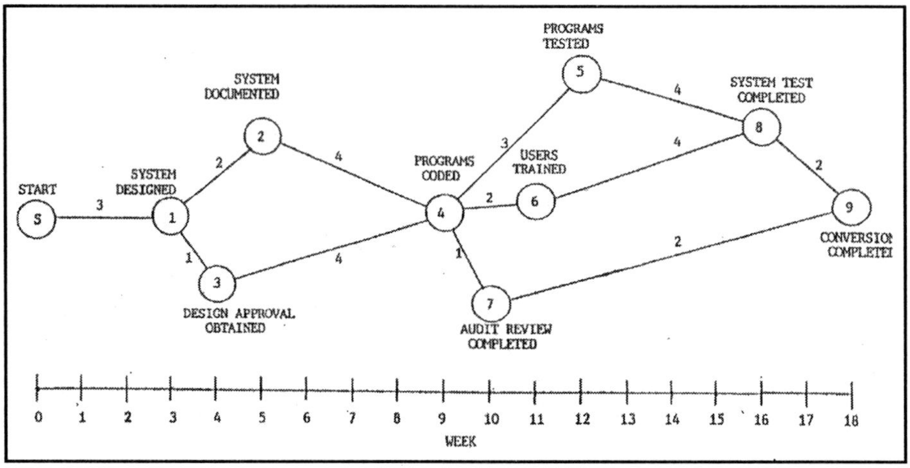

receives a visual impression as to the length of time each activity will take and the dates by which specific interdependent activities must be completed. The states associated with the nodes, their estimated times, and predecessor events are as follows:

State	Description	Time (weeks)	Predecessor Events
1	System Designed	3	None
2	System Documented	2	1
3	Customer Approved Conceptual Design	1	1
4	Programs Coded	4	2,3
5	Programs Tested	3	4
6	Users Trained	2	4
7	Code Reviewed by Audit Department	1	4
8	System Tested	4	5,6
9	Conversion to New System Completed	2	7,8

The major values of using the PERT chart are for planning and demonstrating to the prospective client that the proposers have a thorough grasp of what will be required to meet the project's objectives. An additional value is to allow the prospective client to review the proposed activities, and their sequences and interdependencies. It is much better to clear up any misunderstandings during the proposal review stage than to have to deal with such a situation midway through the project.

There are two items that can be of significant value to those who have not previously prepared a PERT chart for a software development effort. One such item is a sample list of project tasks to use as a guide. Another is a PERT/CPM planning sheet. These items are shown in Figures 3A, 3B, 3C, and 4 respectively.

For each activity, one is to number the activity, estimate the time(s) to perform the task, identify all predecessor events that must be completed before this activity can begin, and

Figures 3. Sample list of project tasks

Figure 3a

Major Task: Spec the System
- Consists of the following sub-tasks
- Determine processing requirements
- Obtain user approval of requirements
- Determine number of programs required
- Determine processing required for each program
- Obtain user approval
- Determine report layouts of reports created by each program
- Obtain user approval
- Develop program specifications for each program

Figure 3b

Major Task: Code the System
- Consists of the following sub-tasks
- Define naming conventions for all files, reports, records and fields
- Develop source statement library entries for all files and records
- Place source statement entries in files
- Develop records for all master files
- Construct dummy master files
- Develop file maintenance and transaction records to test for detection of invalid data
- Develop file maintenance and transaction records to test for proper processing of valid data
- Construct update file of dummy file maintenance and transaction records
- Design structure chart for each program
- Design processing logic for each program
- Conduct walk-through of each program
- Revise structure charts and processing logic as required
- Develop source code of each program
- Place source code of each program in a file
- Debug source code of each program until free of syntax errors
- Text each program using test files
- Debug each program until free of logic errors
- Demonstrate processing of each program to user representative and obtain user approval
- Compile each program and place object code in library for production use

Figure 3c:

Major Task: Document the System
- Execute each step necessary for successful usage of each program
- Document each step necessary for successful usage of cach program
- Obtain user approval

Major Task: Train the Users
- Executive each step necessary for successful usage of each program with user observing
- Execute each step necessary for successful usage of each program with user instructing
- Observe and assist as user executes each step necessary for successful usage of each program
- Repeat last step

Figure 4. PERT/CPM planning sheet

Task No.	Task Description	Preceding Task No.	Following Task No..	Estimated Time	Assign To

Figure 5: GANTT chart

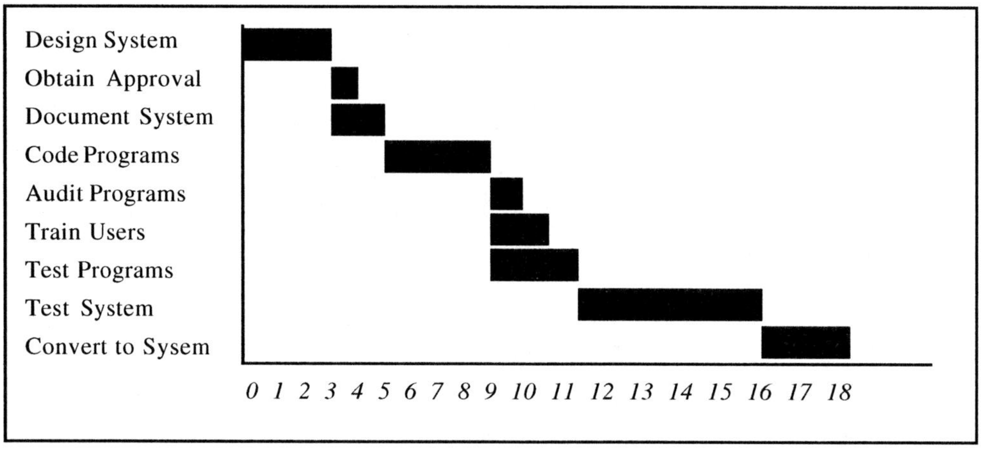

indicate the individual to whom the activity will be assigned. The last item will be used in determining the cost of the project, as will be discussed in the Project Budget section, and Gantt charts will be used for project personnel and activities.

Gantt charts are another method of visually presenting how the project will proceed, but on a more detailed level. In the Gantt chart approach, either individuals or groups of individuals with the same task are shown as longitudinal blocks of activity on a calendar-oriented chart. The starting and stopping date of each individual or group is shown, with those with the earliest start dates appearing above those with the later start dates. In this manner one can visualize the overlapping of various functions and determine when a specific project member or group will be entering the project environment and leaving the project environment. This technique can be very useful in determining when specific supervisory or quality assurance personnel will be required. It is also valuable when the proposal preparers are demonstrating to the prospective client that work space will be needed to house a given maximum number of project staff. An example of a Gantt chart for the project activities is shown in Figure 5.

Admittedly, when an estimate of the hours required must be developed based upon information that is at best vague and/or scanty, the estimation task is very difficult. However, if the proposal team either has members who have considerable experience at performing software development, or they seek the counsel of those in the organization that have the experience, the project can be decomposed into very small tasks that can be estimated with a reasonable degree of accuracy.

- *Project Milestones:* There are certain events referred to as project milestones. These are obviously the most significant points along the continuum of the life of the project. The milestones should always be indicated on the PERT chart so all concerned can be visually prompted regarding when they will occur. In this section of the proposal, however, the purpose is to set these events out as separate issues that must be prepared for. For each milestone there is typically one or more deliverables due. Examples of milestones are: (a) Completion of Documentation of System Requirements, (b) Completion of System Logic Flowchart, (c) Completion of Program Specifications, and (d) Completion of Acceptance Testing. The client should be made aware of the date when each project milestone will occur, what deliverables, if any, will need to be reviewed and approved for acceptance, and which client personnel will be required to approve each deliverable or attend each demonstration of system performance.
- *Project Staffing and Résumés:* At this point in the proposal, the authors support the project organization chart with the names and qualifications of the members of the firm who will be performing the work. There should be some introductory narrative that introduces each of the personnel in terms of their general strengths and states the special skills and/or experiences, if any, this person is bringing to the project. The actual résumés are grouped at the end of this section. In some instances, only the names and résumés of key project members are required. For example, the Project Manager, Systems Design Manager, Programming Manager, Quality Assurance Manager, Support Services Manager, and Training Manager. In other cases the narrative section would discuss only the key personnel, but the résumés of all members of the project team would be provided.

When submitting résumés for a project, most firms have the résumés of all of their staff in a standard format on word processors, sometimes in varying forms from past proposals. In the case of a student course project, students are allowed to engage in some level of creative fiction when developing their résumés.

- *Project Budget*: There are two methods of developing the project budget based upon the firm's method of developing its prices for projects. In either case, however, the non-personnel costs, such as supplies, and if required, computer time rental, travel fares or mileage charges, lodging, and meals, are estimated and charged for at cost. If the firm develops its charges for personnel based upon the estimated cost of completing the project, then the budget is developed as follows.

It will be recalled that the person to be assigned to each activity should be indicated on the PERT/CPM worksheet. The software development firm should therefore have an estimate of the total amount of time required of each staff member during the entire project. The total time for each employee should then be multiplied by the hourly cost of that employee to the firm. Those preparing the budget at this point then need to determine the cost of overhead, that is, the management personnel plus the project manager's support staff. Therefore, the number of hours that each manager will need to devote to the project must be estimated and multiplied by the cost per hour to the firm of the manager. The cost of the support staff reporting to the project manager is then to be calculated. The following personnel costs are now available: (a) production staff, (b) management personnel, (c) support staff. By summing the non-personnel costs and the personnel costs, the total estimated cost of the project is now available.

The vendor can now select from various options based upon estimated vendor cost: (a) cost-plus-fixed-fee; (b) cost-plus-a-percentage-of-costs, no adjustments; (c) cost-plus-a-percentage-of-costs, with a bonus for actual costs being less than estimated costs and, perhaps, its down-side alternative, cost-plus-a-percentage-of-costs, with a penalty for actual costs exceeding estimated costs; and the simplest of all, (d) fixed fee.

There are some organizations, most notably CPA firms and management consulting firms, that approach the software development pricing procedure from a somewhat different direction. For each employee on their staff used to service clients, a billing rate is set. The billing rate is the hourly fee charged to a client for the individual's time. The billing rate for an individual is based upon the individual's salary, the overhead of the employee's department that must be covered, and basically, what the firm believes the market will bear.

When using the pricing approach of the CPA and management consulting firms, the personnel cost component is determined quite simply. The bidding firm, using the time estimates for each type of staff member, merely multiplies the number of hours of each person who will work on the project by the person's hourly billing rate. Most firms in this arena also add an amount to the total estimated price called a "contingency factor" to protect themselves from over-optimistic time estimates.

Regardless of the type of firm preparing the proposal, the details of how the project price was derived typically do not appear in the proposal. Generally, the software development firm will list all non-personnel costs as individual line items. Then the personnel costs, including the profit allocation, are listed either as one line item or a line item for each classification of employee. In some instances the bidding firm will not even provide that amount of detail, but merely state that, based on its analysis of the project requirements, it offers to perform all tasks associated with the project as stated in the proposal for $X.

Some proposal developers set out the major project sections, such as System Requirements Definition, Computer Programming and Testing, Client Training, and Implementation Assistance. Then, within each of these areas, non-personnel costs are itemized, and the personnel cost, including profit, is listed. This approach provides the potential client with the opportunity to have some grasp of the labor intensity of some of the project phases. To many client organizations this is very educational. Many organizations, and indeed departments within firms with MIS departments, believe the major cost of a system is programming. They are relatively oblivious to the extensive front-end cost of having all of the processing requirements of the system defined down to the last detail. Likewise, many individuals are not aware of the extent to which program testing and the documentation of test results are time-consuming activities.

The student teams are encouraged to select either the cost plus fixed fee or billing rate approach to develop their project budget, but regardless of the method selected, they must show their calculations, then state the price they will charge for the project in the cover letter that accompanies their proposal to the potential client.

Figure 6. General system logic flowchart

Figure 6a

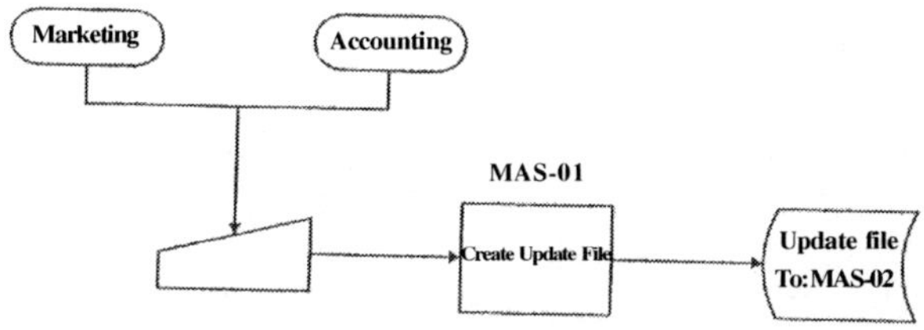

Figure 6b

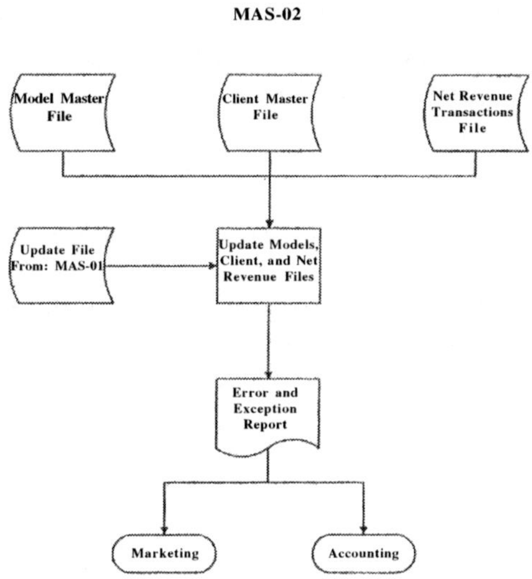

Figure 6c

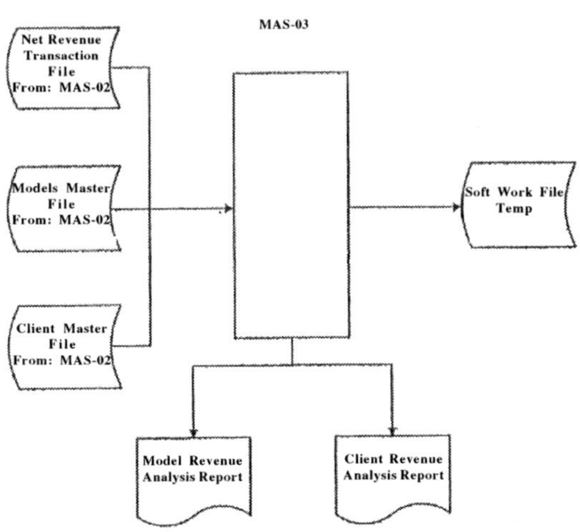

Documenting System Requirements

The most critical phase of a software project is the determination of precisely what information processing is to be performed by the system. In many cases it may also be the most difficult phase. The role of the analyst is primarily to determine the information needs of the users. This is often much more challenging than one might think. While the analyst is aware of the capabilities and limitations of hardware and software, the user typically is not. The user may therefore either ask for a feature that is impossible to provide, or neglect to ask for a feature that would be immensely valuable and easy to provide, but is not requested because the user is unaware that the required capability exists.

The first step in a project is the determination of specifically what users desire from the system. In general, the term "information processing requirements" is used to describe users' needs. These needs must be determined and documented by the systems analyst(s). In this process the analyst must initially determine the general system logic.

General System Logic

As stated previously, the operative assumption is that an organization has determined that some tasks, whether currently performed manually or with a computerized system, are to be analyzed and a new or revised computerized system put into operation. The client organization, then, does have a general idea of what the new or redesigned system should do.

By interviewing a representative of the client organization (the instructor plays this role), the general flow of the system is defined. This will typically result in the conclusion (for the purposes of the course) that three programs will be required: (a) the first program will involve the creation of a file of records used to add new records, change existing records, delete existing records, and process business transactions against the existing master files; (b) the second program that processes the file maintenance and transaction records against the master files; and (c) a program that creates a management-oriented report from data found on the master files. An example of a General System Logic Flowchart is shown as Figures 6A, 6B, and 6C.

Once the general system logic flowchart and the logic have been examined and found sound, the team must now develop a complete set of programming specifications. This means that the record layouts for all files must be designed, the edits for all input records on the update file must be documented, and the layouts of all reports must be designed and approved by the report users, including all control breaks, subtotals, and totals to be computed and printed on the report.

Defining Processing Logic

For each program, the team must clearly state each processing step that must be performed in the program and in the sequence in which the step will most likely be required. Every alternative—every option that could happen—must be stated and the required processing for that alternative clearly stated.

In the first program that creates the file of file maintenance and transaction records, the specifications provide the programmer with several screen layouts to be presented to the user. The first screen layout is one that lists the types of records that may be created and the option of ending the session of inputting record data, and asks the user to enter a selection.

The specifications should state that once the user has selected a record type to be created, the program is to present the user with a screen that lists the data fields to be entered by the user. After the user has entered all of the required data, the program is to present the data back to the user and ask the user if any corrections are to be made or if the user accepts the record data as presented. If the user selects to make a correction, the program is to repeat the above process until the user accepts the record data. Once the user has accepted the record data, the program is to enter the appropriate record code for the type of record created and write the record on the update file. The specifications should state that this process is repeated until the user opts to exit the program.

In the second program the records created in the first program are to be applied to the affected master file records. It is in this program that the specifications should refer the programmer to the edits agreed to by the user that are to be applied to the records on the update file. The specifications should state that in the event that a record is found to contain one or more errors, the record code and key field of the update record and a message(s) that describes the nature of the error(s) found are to be printed on the Error and Exception Report. In addition to the data edit errors, the specifications should include that logical errors are also to be tested for. For example, if a record contains a record code that indicates a new record is to be added to a file, the program is to assure that a record with a matching key field is not already present on the file. Similarly, if the purpose of an update record is to modify or delete a record on a master file, the program must verify that a matching record exists and, if one is not found, print an error message to this effect on the Error and Exception Report.

The purpose of the third program is to create a report. Interestingly, the records on a master file are always in a sequence that facilitates processing records against the file. Rarely does any user need or want to see data from records in the sequence in which they reside on a master file. As a consequence, the specifications for this program should refer the programmer to a record layout for a temporary or work file. The specifications should state what data items from which master files need to be extracted to create records on the work file. This is the first stage of this program. After this file is created, the specifications should state that the records on the work file are to be sorted into a sequence that the users have defined as desirable from a management viewpoint. This sorting process is the second stage of this program. The specifications should then refer the programmer to the layout(s) of the report(s) that are to be printed using the sorted records, including the number and types of control breaks and/or subtotals and grand totals to be computed and printed.

Developing the Software

The members of the team must then allocate the several remaining tasks to the team members. Some member(s) will be developing program code, while others are creating sample update records that will be used to test the correctness of the programs. Still other member(s) of the team will be writing programs that create dummy master files that must be available for the second program to process the test update records against and from which the third program will extract work record data. As members of the team are completing these support tasks, they should begin developing user instructions that will be assembled into a users' manual.

Testing the Software

When the members of the team responsible for writing the three programs are of the opinion that their programs are ready for testing, the test update records have been designed, and the programs that create the dummy master files have been completed, program testing can take place. As the testing is taking place, occasionally errors in logic will be found. The responsible programmers of the team will then make the necessary corrections. When the programs have passed all tests, before-and-after printouts of the files involved in the processing of each program will be obtained. Members of the team responsible for developing the test documentation must then prepare the evidence for each program that shows that the program executed per the program specifications.

For the first program, a sequential number should be assigned to each record on the update file printout. Then a photocopy of each type of update record layout found in the programming specifications should be made. A narrative should then relate each numbered record on the update file printout to the corresponding record layout, thus showing that the record on the update file printout corresponds to the record layout from the programming specifications.

For the second program, the sequential number of each record on the update file is to be matched by that same number on the printout of the records on the master file(s) that the update record should have affected. A narrative should then state the purpose of the update record. Additionally, if the record was in error, include the entry on the Error and Exception Report that is related to that record; if the update record was valid, describe how the reader can verify that the record was properly processed by examining the specific field(s) of the record(s) with the matching number on the related master file(s).

For the third program, the records from the master file(s) used to create the report should be highlighted on a separate printout of the records on the master file(s). A narrative should then describe how the records that appear on the report are those that should have appeared on the report, that the fields of data specified are present, that the data on the report is in the sequence described in the program specifications, and that any subtotal(s) and total(s) found on the report are indeed equal, by adding machine tape, to the check total(s).

Training the Users and System Implementation

This part of the project will not take place in the course.

Retrospective Analysis

After the teams have submitted their complete system package, which consists of their source code, test documentation, and user manual, they are required to submit a Retrospective Analysis. In this analysis, each team is required to consider the entire project as consisting of three phases: (1) developing the proposal, (2) developing the programming specifications, and (3) completing the final package, that is, source code, structure charts for the programs, test documentation, and the users' manual. For each phase, each team is to state a list of (1) what went wrong, why it went wrong, and what you would do in your next project to assure that it did not go wrong again; and (2) what went right, why it went right, and what you would do in your next project to assure that it went right again.

Summary and Conclusion

This course methodology has been used by the author for several years. Based upon feedback from alumni on a research survey questionnaire, this course content and methodology have been deemed very valuable, not only during one's first year on the job, but in one's later, non-entry-level positions (Chrysler & Van Auken, 2002). In discussions with individual students both during their undergraduate studies and after graduation, the nature of this course—that is, the integration of the material of several previous courses into a complete project—was, to them, a meaningful culminating experience. Similarly, corporate recruiters have expressed their appreciation for a course that provides students with the rigors of living through a total project and having the experience of performing as a member of a team during a semester-long project.

References

Chrysler, E. (1978). Some basic determinants of computer programming productivity. *Communications of the ACM*, (June).

Chrysler, E. & Van Auken, S. (2002). Entry-level value versus career value of MIS courses: Faculty expectations versus alumni perceptions. *Journal of Computer Information Systems,* (Summer).

Jeffrey, D. (1987). Software engineering productivity models for management information systems development. In R. Boland & R. Hirschheim (Eds.), *Critical issues in information systems research.* New York: John Wiley & Sons.

Kemerer, C. (1997). Software cost estimation models. In *Software project management: Readings and cases.* Irwin.

Mantel, S. Jr., Meredith, J., Shafer, S., & Sutton, M. (2001). Evaluating and terminating the project. In *Project management in practice.* New York: John Wiley & Sons.

Nicholas, J. (2001). Project failure, success and lessons learned. In *Project management for business and technology: Principles and practice* (2nd edition). Prentice-Hall.

Chapter XXIII

Enabling Electronic Teaching and Learning Communities with MERLOT

Gerard L. Hanley
MERLOT, USA

Sorel Reisman
MERLOT, USA

Abstract

Educational institutions have made significant progress in enabling student success in distance learning by delivering academic programs utilizing course management systems, accessing electronic library resources, and through a wealth of student services that use help desks and campus portals. Enabling instructor success in researching and designing curricula for teaching in distance learning programs is an area where institutions still face significant challenges. This chapter presents a number of these challenges and describes how MERLOT (Multimedia Educational Resource for Learning and Online Teaching), an international consortium, can facilitate successful teaching and learning with technology.

Introduction

Higher education has been undergoing a significant evolution that began in the 1990s, one that mirrors the transition corporations underwent almost 20 years earlier. That transition concerns changes of focus from information management to one of knowledge management (Frand, 2000). Bonk and Cunningham (1998), who view this transition as being technology-driven, present their perspective on these changes:

> *"Daily advances in fiber optics, multimedia, and telecommuting technology continue to force new sectors of society to grapple with information access, transmission, and collaboration issues. In the midst of this social and technological drama, vast resources at our fingertips are restructuring the way we humans work, live, learn, and generally interact regardless of 'geography, distance, resources, or disability' (US Department of Labor, 1991). Technology is becoming increasingly interactive and distributed, such that individual learners have available, at rapidly declining cost, the means to participate in incredibly complex networks of information, resources, and instruction. For instance, Internet navigation and discovery tools like the World Wide Web (WWW) have brought to many of our desktops an immense array of text, video, sound, and communication resources unthinkable even 10 years ago." (p. 26)*

This chapter describes MERLOT (Multimedia Educational Resource for Learning and Online Teaching), an international consortium organized for the purpose of facilitating through digital library technologies, successful online teaching and learning with technology in higher education. There is significant evidence of the dramatic effect of such technologies on higher education, particularly in online learning. In a recent survey of more than 3,000 degree-granting institutions of higher education in the United States, Allan and Seaman (2003) report that:

- Over 1.6 million students took at least one online course during Fall 2002; over one-third of these students took all of their courses online; 11% took at least one online course.
- Eighty-one percent of all reporting institutions offer at least one fully online or blended course, and 34% offer an online degree program; 97% of public institutions offer at least one fully online or blended course, and 49% offer an online degree program.
- When asked about the role of online education for the future of their institution, 67% answered that it is a critical long-term strategy.
- A majority of academic leaders (57%) already believe that the learning outcomes for online education are equal to or superior to those of face-to-face instruction;

> nearly 34% of these same leaders expect that learning outcomes for online education will be superior to face-to-face instruction in three years, and nearly 75% expect learning outcomes for online education to be equal to or better than face-to-face instruction.

Despite these impressive changes and also despite the forecasts of "academic leaders," practitioners who are on the front line of instructional innovation are very aware of the challenges they encounter when they undertake to develop and deliver technology-based curricula. Darling-Hammond (2000), in an extensive review of the literature concerning variables that influence student achievement, listed the following as positively correlating to instructors' success in the classroom: (1) general academic ability and intelligence, (2) teaching experience, (3) teacher behaviors and practices, (4) certification status, 5) subject matter knowledge, and 6) knowledge of teaching and learning. A close examination of her discussion of these variables reveals that there is a large degree of interconnectedness among them, and in general, instructors with greater experience and training are more likely to develop and execute successful pedagogical strategies in the classroom.

There is no reason to believe that these items are any less important in teaching in a virtual or electronic classroom. In fact, it is likely that these items are a subset of the skills and knowledge required for successful technology-based learning. The National Educational Technology Standards (NETS) Project, an ongoing initiative of the International Society for Technology in Education (ISTE), defines the fundamental concepts, knowledge, skills, and attitudes for applying technology in educational settings. The primary goal of the ISTE NETS Project[1] is to develop national standards for educational uses of technology that facilitate school improvement in the United States. The defined standards areas are:

1. *Planning and Designing Learning Environments and Experiences:* Instructors plan and design effective learning environments and experiences supported by technology.
2. *Technology Operations and Concepts*: Instructors demonstrate a sound understanding of technology operations and concepts.
3. *Teaching, Learning, and the Curriculum*: Instructors implement curriculum plans that include methods and strategies for applying technology to maximize student learning.
4. *Assessment and Evaluation*: Instructors apply technology to facilitate a variety of effective assessment and evaluation strategies.
5. *Productivity and Professional Practice*: Instructors use technology to enhance their productivity and professional practice.
6. *Social, Ethical, Legal, and Human Issues*: Instructors understand the social, ethical, legal, and human issues surrounding the use of technology in PK-12 schools, and apply those principles in practice.

A close examination of the details of each of these standards reveals significant commonality between Darling-Hammond's "factors of success" and the standards developed by ISTE. In the remainder of this chapter, we will explore some of the practices necessary to affect successful online teaching, and ways in which MERLOT can be an efficient and vital tool to produce the kinds of effective learning outcomes forecasted by academic leaders in higher education.

Preparing for Learning

This section describes closely related sets of activities that instructors must undertake to prepare curricula for traditional instruction and for distance learning.

Traditional Instruction

Two activities that instructors must perform to prepare for any kind of teaching are: (1) collecting and creating academic content, that is, conducting research for teaching; and (2) designing pedagogical strategies to deliver the collected content (Hanley, 2003). The effectiveness and efficiency of instructors in performing these activities can contribute significantly to the quality, scalability, and sustainability of the curricula, especially if they are used in distance education programs.

Research for teaching requires that instructors search for content in a variety of locations, for example, commercial publisher catalogues, libraries, and increasingly on the World Wide Web (WWW). Often, instructors must develop their own content because there does not exist any that they can easily use; such content can be incorporated to complement resources produced by others. Examples include syllabi, complete lectures, lecture notes, practice units, tests, reading lists, PowerPoint presentations, and so forth. In an online distance learning environment, such items, whether original or discovered through research, may be considered to be "learning objects" (Wiley, 2000).

Critical success factors for instructors doing research for teaching include the ability to identify relevant content within their academic discipline, the ability to customize content to satisfy local, programmatic requirements, and the ability to participate in a community of their peers wherein they can share professional knowledge. If instructors cannot effectively and efficiently determine the relevance of materials for teaching in their discipline, the process of searching, finding, evaluating, and selecting content can be overwhelming and unreliable, resulting in inferior search results. If instructors cannot effectively and efficiently customize the content, the collection of content may not meet the needs of the students within their specific academic program. Finally, if the instructor cannot participate in a community of practice for teaching, the professional development opportunities for innovation, improved effectiveness, recognition, and feedback may be insufficient to develop and sustain updated knowledge for teaching the discipline.

Designing curriculum requires instructors to organize content with particular pedagogical strategies in mind. Curriculum design also requires instructors to add a programmatic and cultural context to their collected content. This context includes defining learning objectives, understanding the prerequisite skills and knowledge of the learners, and developing learning activities and assessment methodologies, including student learning outcome success criteria. The critical success factors for instructors' composing curricula are the identification of relevant content and pedagogical strategies that are suitable for the learning objectives, as well as students' learning styles and their degree of preparedness. Instructors must customize learning and assessment activities in ways appropriate for the students, as well as for institutional academic program goals. A truly involved instructor, and one who strives for constant self- and curriculum-improvement should also participate in communities of practice for teachers.

Failure to address these matters will likely result in ineffective and inefficient curricula and teaching strategies that do not produce desired student learning outcomes, and that can lead to irrelevant and boring curricula that do not engage learners. If the instructor cannot participate in a community of practice for teaching, the professional development opportunities for innovation, improved effectiveness, professional recognition, and peer feedback will be insufficient to develop and sustain excellence in teaching skills and curriculum design

Distance Learning

Instructors face significant challenges when they collect content and design curricula for teaching in distance learning programs (Brahler, Peterson, & Johnson, 1999; Muirhead, 2001; Sheinberg, 2000). These challenges are in addition to such issues as technology infrastructure problems, student/instructor access to computing technologies, and the integration of learning systems/activities with the administrative systems necessary to collect and maintain student learning data. Traditional sources of content have not produced deep, broad, or organized collections of electronic resources for distance learning. Commercial textbook publishers have produced online and/or multimedia academic content to advance their textbook sales. Libraries are acquiring electronic index and abstract resources, and electronic versions of traditional text resources (books and journals), but have not advanced collections of digital multimedia. A large proportion of available digital multimedia content has been developed by a cottage industry of individual instructors, academic technology staff, campus technology centers, and professional organizations. Locally developed and managed digital collections of multimedia content are beginning to be developed, but they are still at early stages of reliability, sustainability, and quality. Consequently, instructors have considerable difficulty researching content and designing curricula for distance learning programs.

While these challenges are significant, distance learning programs have also created opportunities for educational communities to respond collaboratively to many of these challenges. The time and expense to develop and distribute digital content can be reduced if there are effective mechanisms for the sharing of digital content. Assuring the pedagogical quality of the content is another critical aspect of online materials, but this issue can be addressed through peer collaboration, by establishing evaluation standards and review, and sharing methodologies. Professional development programs that enable the academic community to use digital resources successfully can be delivered through the collective discovery and sharing of exemplary practices. Development and management of technology services supporting the sharing of digital resources and professional development programs are pivotal in establishing and sustaining the communities of exemplary practice in distance learning.

MERLOT is a digital library that has been designed to enable educational institutions to overcome the challenges of researching discipline-specific content and designing curricula for teaching in distance learning programs. By collaboratively designing, building, evaluating, and managing a shared digital collection of multimedia academic content, MERLOT enables instructors to perform effective and efficient research for teaching. By including capabilities for instructors to customize and contextualize the academic content, MERLOT enables instructors to design curricula effectively and efficiently. Finally, by building the MERLOT digital library on the foundation of communities of users, MERLOT enables instructors to participate in communities of practice for teaching with technology. The following sections describe the development of the MERLOT consortium, MERLOT's digital collection and services, and its strategies for facilitating the success of distance learning in higher education institutions around the world.

Background and Structure

In 1996, the California State University Center for Distributed Learning (CSU-CDL) was established as an academic technology service provider for the 23 campuses of the California State University (CSU) system. With more than 30,000 instructors and over 350,000 students in the CSU system, the CSU-CDL had to design tools and services that would be easy to use, would leverage the widespread yet uncoordinated development of academic technologies both within and outside of CSU, and would be low cost to operate. MERLOT, the online digital library, was developed and in 1997, free access was provided via the Web site, www.merlot.org. MERLOT was modeled after the National Science Foundation-funded project, "Authoring Tools and An Educational Object Economy (EOE)," hosted by Apple Computer, and other industry, university, and government collaborators. The EOE (Educational Object Economy Foundation) continues to develop and distribute tools to enable the formation of communities engaged in building shared knowledge bases of learning materials. One of the key design requirements for MERLOT was to provide a technology service that would enable users to contribute directly to a community's collection of online resources, without "human mediation." MERLOT's goal was to enable the cottage industry of campuses and individual instructor's development of academic technologies that would become scalable and sustainable.

In 1998, a State Higher Education Executives Organization/American Productivity and Quality Center (SHEEO/APQC) (Hartman, Sorg, Truman-Davis, Morris, & Marshall, 1998) benchmarking study on instructor development and instructional technology selected the CSU-CDL as one of six best practice centers in North America. Visitations to the CSU-CDL by higher education institutions who participated in the benchmarking study resulted in a number of institutions expressing interest in collaborating with CSU on the MERLOT project. As a result, the University of Georgia System, Oklahoma State Regents for Higher Education, University of North Carolina System, and the California State University system created an informal consortium representing almost 100 campuses. SHEEO was the coordinator for the cooperative of the four state systems.

In 1999, the four systems recognized the significant benefits of a cooperative initiative to expand the MERLOT collections, conduct peer reviews of the digital learning materials, and add student-learning assignments. Each system donated funds to develop the MERLOT software and contributed in-kind support to advance the peer review process. CSU maintained its leadership of and responsibilities for the operation and improvement of processes and tools.

In January, 2000, the four systems sponsored instructors from the disciplines of Biology, Physics, Business, and Teacher Education to develop evaluation standards and peer review processes for online teaching and learning material. In April, 2000, other systems and institutions of higher education were invited to join the MERLOT cooperative, and by July 2000, 23 systems and institutions of higher education had become Institutional Partners of MERLOT.

As of December 2003, the MERLOT consortium was composed of 22 higher education systems, consortia, individual institutions of higher education representing over 500 campuses and 4.8 million students, more than 20 professional academic organizations, and over 16,000 individuals—all comprising a community of participants who strive to improve teaching and learning with high-quality online resources. The MERLOT consortium is a diverse and complex mix of institutions, and there are multiple levels of participation. MERLOT's institutional partners include smaller liberal arts colleges, large state university systems, and community colleges—all focused on undergraduate teaching; participants also include research institutions focused on scholarship, research, and graduate education. Collectively, MERLOT provides services that require an approximate annual budget of $3M, but no single institution has to provide the full funding. For institutions of higher education, MERLOT has four levels of participation:

- Sustaining Partners who pay $50,000 per year and provide over $250,000 of in-kind support.
- System Partners who pay $25,000 per year and provide approximately $50,000 of in-kind support.
- Campus Partners who pay $6,500 per year and provide approximately $20,000 of in-kind support.
- Institutional Alliances who provide in-kind support for advancing the MERLOT project within their institutions.

These different levels enable institutions to participate within the constraints acceptable for their institutional culture, resources, and readiness. Participant institutions are located worldwide, including in the US, Canada, Australia, and Africa. Whether the borders are the campus property lines or the international dateline, any higher education institution can participate in MERLOT's consortium. MERLOT's responsibility is to facilitate a productive community and to engage the consortium members in shared governance and program implementation through open communications, cooperative planning, and program delivery.

Though the consortium members are very diverse, they share the commitment to MERLOT's vision to be a premier online community where people from around the world share online learning materials and pedagogy. They also share MERLOT's strategic priority to improve the effectiveness of teaching and learning by expanding the quantity and quality of peer-reviewed online learning materials that can be easily incorporated into instructor-designed courses. It is the combination of shared values, the collaborative delivery of quality services, and the public recognition of the partners' contributions to MERLOT that sustains the MERLOT consortium.

MERLOT Essentials

Without the delivery of high-quality services, the MERLOT consortium would quickly dissolve. MERLOT's services address the difficulties that institutions of higher education and their instructors experience when fulfilling the promises and challenges of technology-enhanced education. Higher education makes regular and substantial investments in the development of instructional technology amidst concerns that someone else may be "reinventing the wheel." Duplication of effort wastes time, staff resources, and funds. Instructors have difficulty reliably producing high-quality online materials, efficiently choosing online materials, receiving appropriate professional recognition for their work, and providing evidence of improvements in teaching and learning. MERLOT's community digital library and services are designed to address these issues.

MERLOT and its institutional and individual members have created a digital library which, in December 2003, contained a directory of over 16,000 members who are able provide peer-to-peer consultation. As well, there are about 10,000 online teaching/learning materials categorized by discipline (see Figure 1), and by "special interest communities." The MERLOT Web site is a cooperatively developed, free, Web-based resource where instructors, staff, administrators, and students can easily find digital learning materials together with evaluations and guidance for their use. In 2003, the Web site had more than 1.8 million hits per month and over 17,000 unique users per month. Learning materials from a wide variety of academic disciplines are indexed on the MERLOT site. Most of the learning materials found on the Web site are modular (e.g., simulations, tutorials, animations, drill and practice exercises, lecture presentations, case studies, collections, and reference materials) and are designed to be integrated into a larger course. Most of the materials run inside a Web browser, facilitating use within an online course or as Web assignments in classroom-based instruction.

MERLOT is designed for easy and effective navigation. Users may *browse* the collection or *search* for targeted learning materials. Figure 2 shows sub-areas of the Information Technology discipline, and search and browse features.

Figure 1. MERLOT homepage

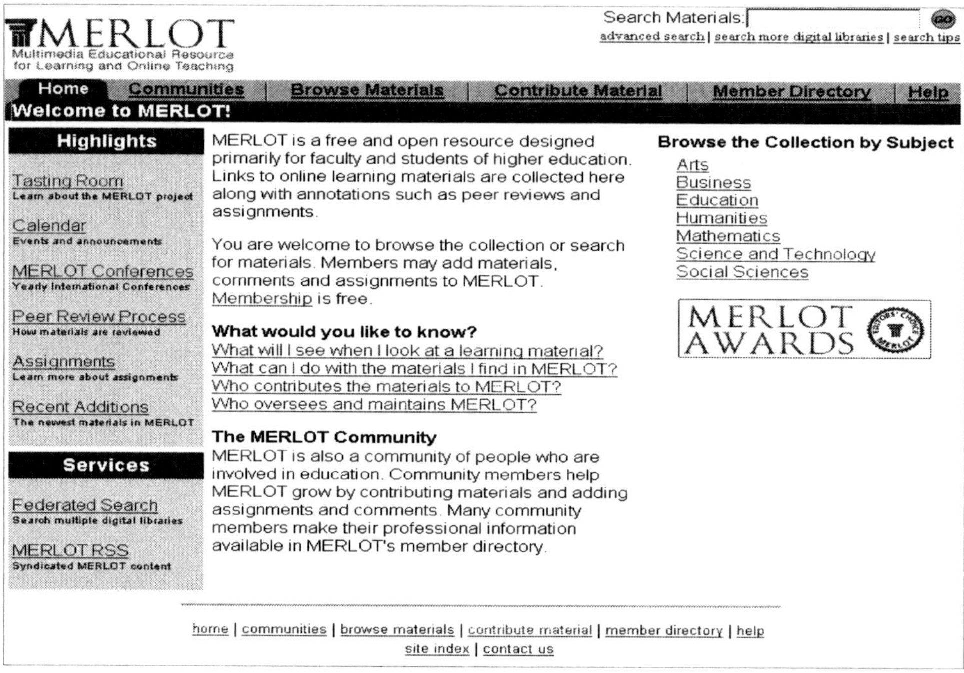

Figure 3 shows the result of browsing the Information Literacy category of the Information Technology discipline. Searching for keywords within this discipline or across the entire database would have produced a similar page, but with different contents. Users can read a preview of the items to help them decide if it is worth their time to investigate the materials more thoroughly.

MERLOT does not store the actual learning materials on its servers; it provides links and their descriptions (metadata) to materials that are stored elsewhere on the WWW. Once a link to the desired materials is found in MERLOT, users click the URL, taking them to the material's actual location where they can check for any licensing regulations or costs involved with their reuse; they can incorporate the resources into their curricula (e.g., enter a link to the material in their course Web site, or e-mail the URL to the students).

To find or use materials in the MERLOT collection, users do not need to be a member of MERLOT, nor does the user's institution need to be in the MERLOT consortium. This feature of "on-demand" access is a founding principle of MERLOT; it enables instructors to solve their research and curriculum design problems immediately.

MERLOT has recently provided a federated search service (Figure 4) that enables users to search MERLOT and other digital libraries simultaneously and provide an integrated hit list. This federated search service provides one-stop access to collections developed

Figure 2. Finding indexed materials

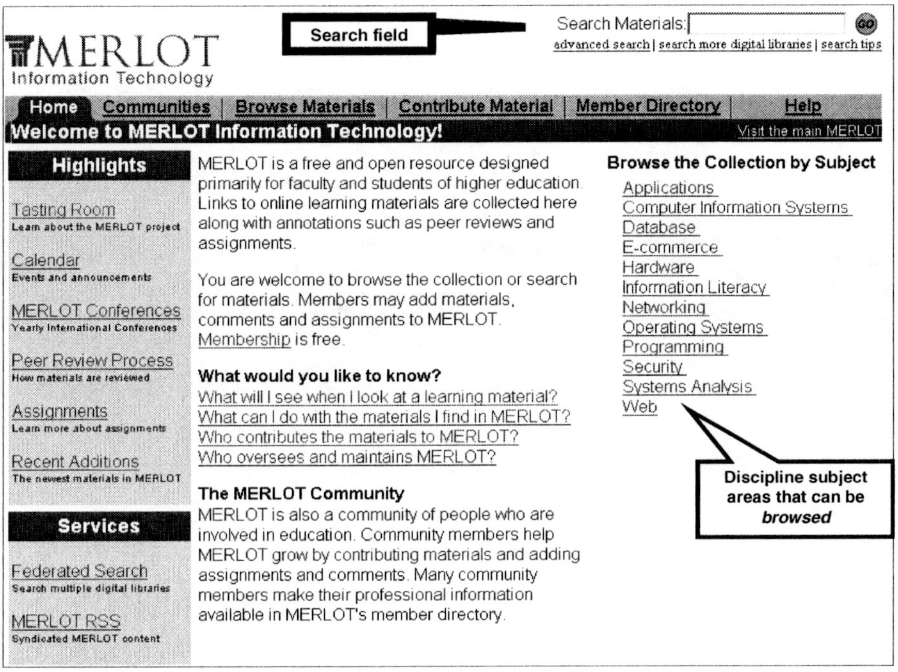

Figure 3. Search/browse results

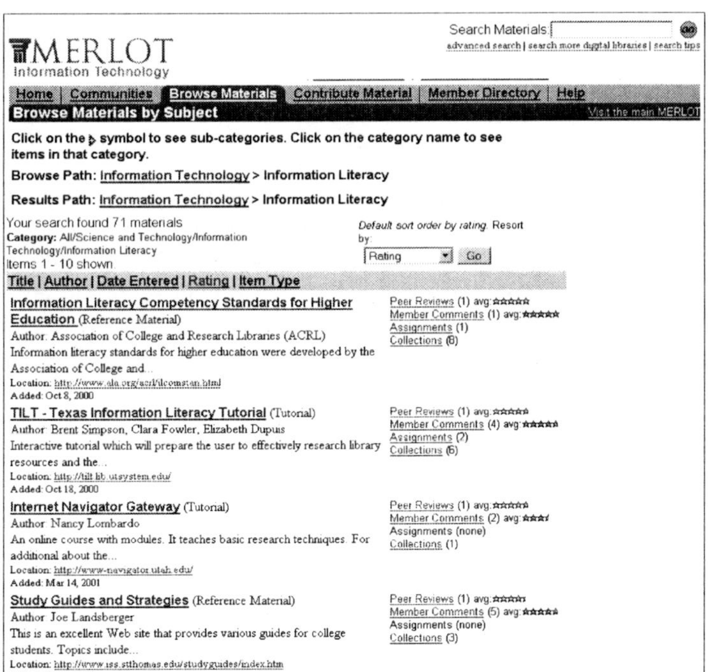

Figure 4. Federated search

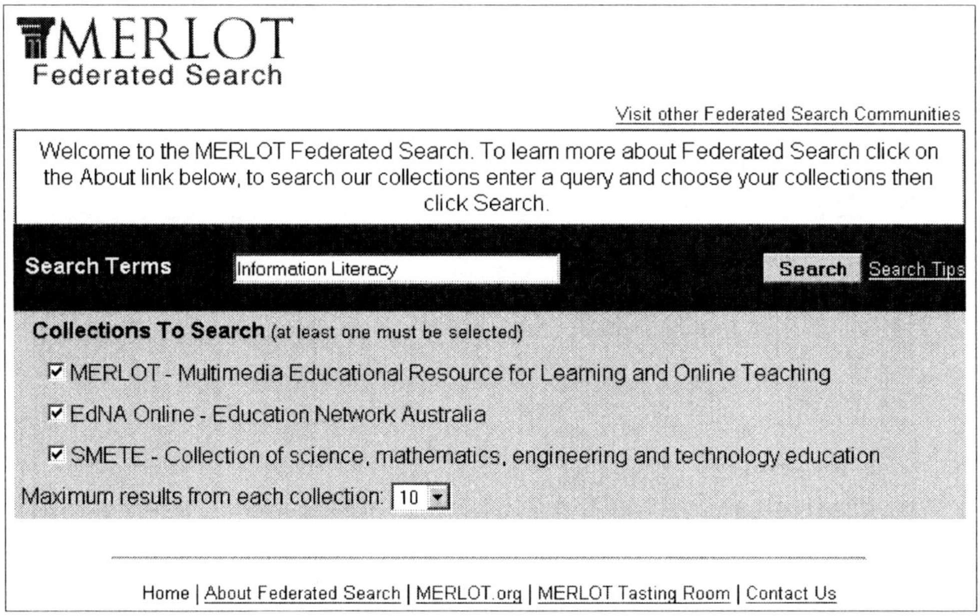

using the federated search services to leverage each other's collections for their own constituents.

A Collection of Learning Objects

A distinctive feature of MERLOT is that individual members perform the cataloguing of materials voluntarily. Once instructors register as a member of MERLOT (at no charge), they are able to create catalogue records of materials they deem worthy of sharing. Figure 5 shows some of the fields that an individual contributor must complete when adding a new item to the catalogue.

Every contributed item, comment, review, or assignment is visibly connected to the individual's MERLOT e-portfolio that is captured through the member's logon credentials; this creates some social pressures for members to apply reasonable judgment when they add new items or review existing ones. It also provides a mechanism for MERLOT to identify and discipline members for abusing their privileges. A premise underlying MERLOT's decision to open the cataloguing to the community is that if individuals are qualified enough to be hired by a higher education institution, they are qualified to identify materials that might be valuable to their peers. In addition, if users are concerned about the qualifications of the person submitting the materials, they can click on the name of the submitter and learn more about them.

Figure 5. New item input form

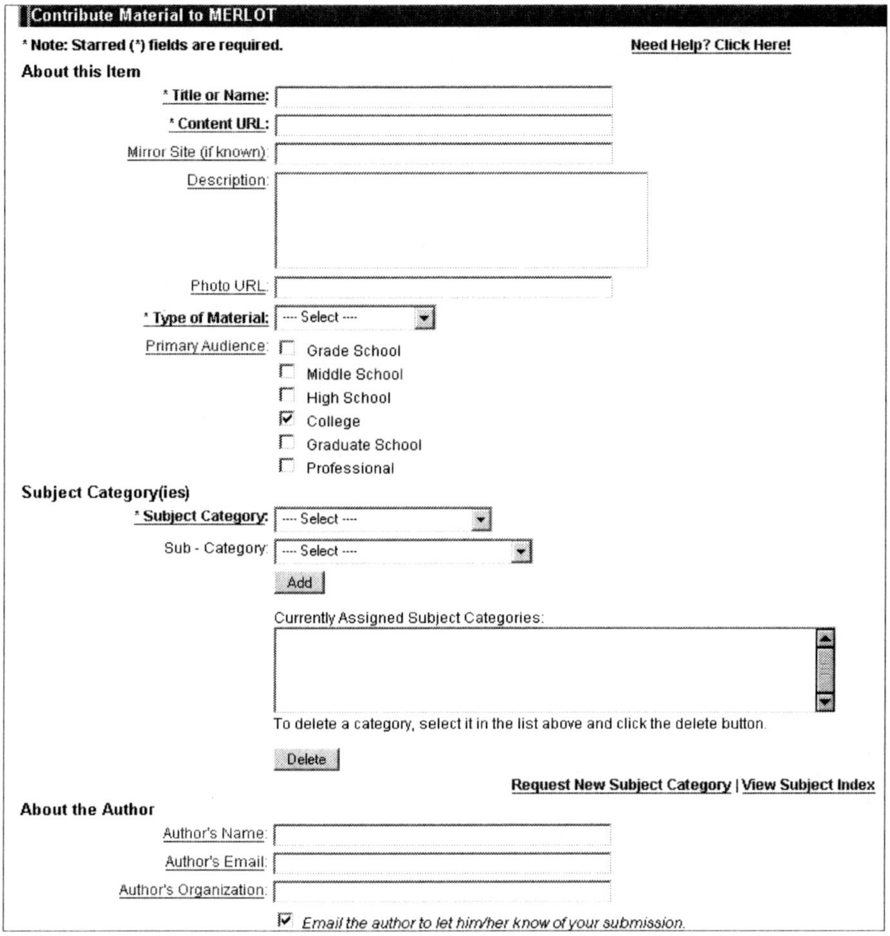

Contribute Material to MERLOT

*** Note: Starred (*) fields are required.** **Need Help? Click Here!**

About this Item

*** Title or Name:**

*** Content URL:**

Mirror Site (if known):

Description:

Photo URL:

*** Type of Material:** ---- Select ----

Primary Audience:
- Grade School
- Middle School
- High School
- ☑ College
- Graduate School
- Professional

Subject Category(ies)

*** Subject Category:** ---- Select ----

Sub - Category: ---- Select ----

Add

Currently Assigned Subject Categories:

To delete a category, select it in the list above and click the delete button.

Delete

Request New Subject Category | View Subject Index

About the Author

Author's Name:

Author's Email:

Author's Organization:

☑ *Email the author to let him/her know of your submission.*

There are a number of critical features to MERLOT that makes it more than a collection of URLs. Contributors of items write a description of the items within the context of teaching and learning. Other members can later add comments about quality and use for the materials.

MERLOT also provides the capability for members to describe specific techniques for using the materials in teaching; the Learning Assignments category includes information about the topics covered, the level of student (e.g., lower division, upper division, graduate), names of courses for which the item is appropriate, prerequisite skills and knowledge students should have before doing an assignment, learning objectives, type of learning activity (e.g., team-based vs. individual, supervised vs. unsupervised), assessment methods, time required to do assignments, and so forth. All the metadata on pedagogy enable instructors effectively and easily to choose and use online learning

Figure 6. Foreign language classification on the input form

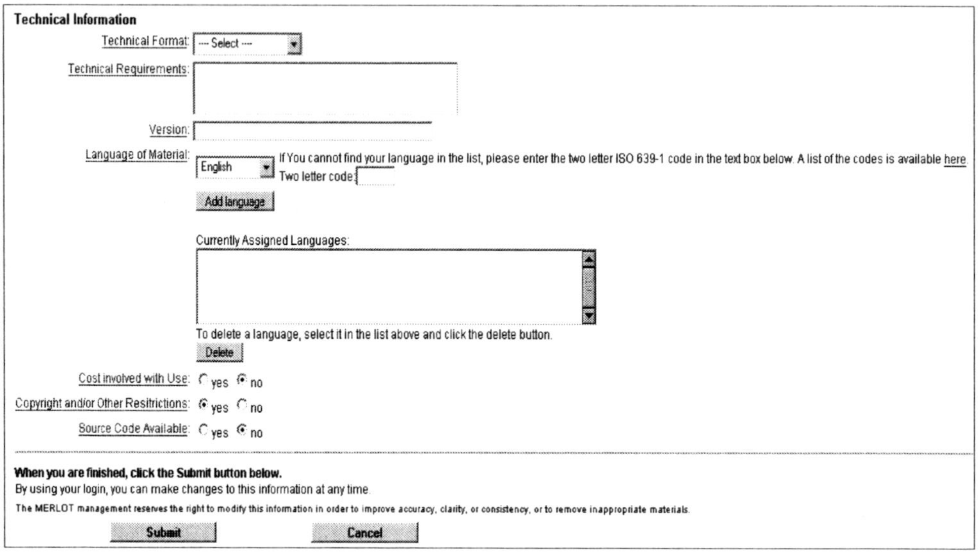

materials that are compatible with their own teaching methods and the learning goals of their academic program.

Cataloging of items by the community enables MERLOT to expand the collection in breadth and depth in ways that directly meet the needs of its members. As the community becomes more diverse in its interests, the collection can grow to satisfy members' interests. Members of different cultures and nationalities can contribute materials without having to satisfy gate-keeping requirements that could be culturally insensitive. The process for building the collection is also scalable; if every one of MERLOT's members contributed one item of material this year, the collection would grow by 16,000 without MERLOT's having to hire staff to catalogue the materials. The workload cost to catalogue one item is low compared to the benefit received by the 16,000 members. As shown in Figure 6, materials in any language can be contributed to MERLOT; using the ISO 639-1 code, the language becomes part of the catalogue record. This capability enables users to search for and contribute materials in specific languages. Both the community cataloguing process and the cataloguing by language enables cross-cultural learning communities to develop and thrive.

Personalizing the MERLOT Collection

MERLOT recognized that people can easily get overwhelmed by the volume of available materials and they can easily forget the value and relevance of materials they have found. Consequently, MERLOT implemented the capability for its members to create and

Figure 7. Adding an item to a personal collection

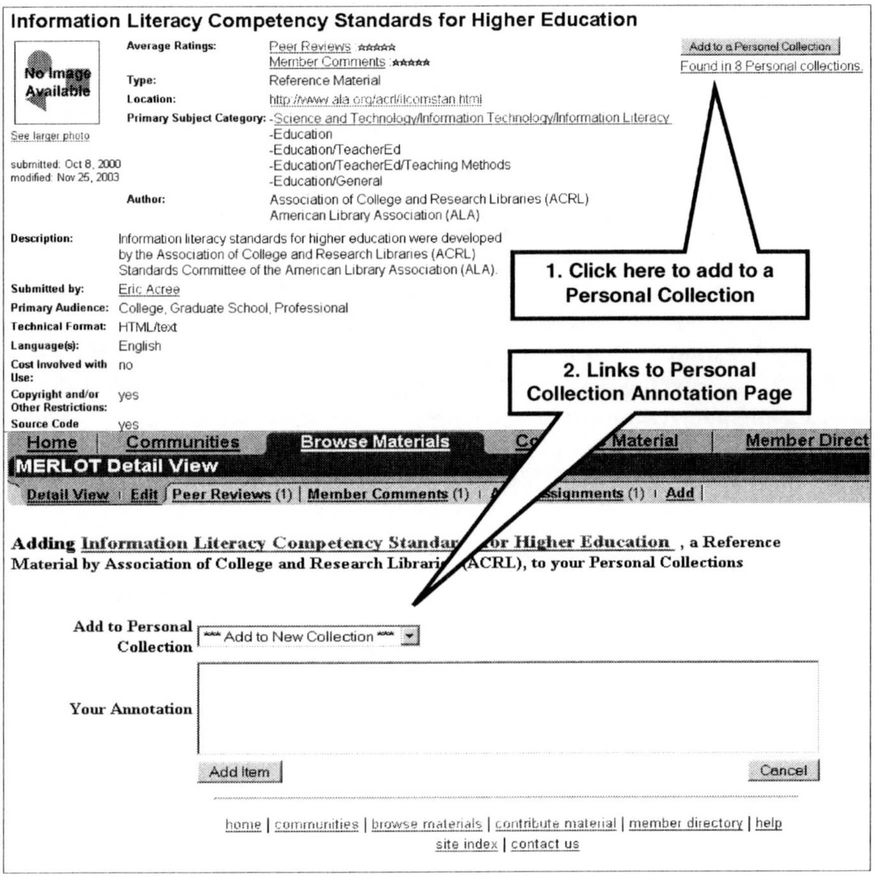

annotate *Personal Collections*. Once a member finds material that satisfies their needs, they can add it to their *Personal Collection* and describe why they found the material valuable. Figure 7 shows how an item that has been found can be added to a *Personal Collection*. Members can create multiple *Personal Collections* that can form the foundations of different course portfolios where the instructor can describe how the selected materials can be used to achieve specific learning objectives for each different course. A critical aspect of the *Personal Collections* is that members define the pedagogical and/or personal context for selecting and using the materials. The ability of users to contribute their context for the materials enables the user of any country, culture, or language to share with other members their knowledge and purpose for using the online materials.

The MERLOT Communities

Member Directory

Although the MERLOT collection of online materials facilitates the development of curricula, it is the directory of members that facilitates participation in the community of practice. The *Member Directory* contains contact information, academic areas of expertise, and an e-portfolio of the members' contributions of materials, comments, and assignments to MERLOT. As discussed earlier, the *Personal Collections* are also part of the member's e-portfolio. The *Directory* enables individuals to find and communicate with colleagues who might advise them on the effective use of digital resources. If instructors find resources that they want to use in their classes, they can contact the author of the materials, the person who contributed the description, and/or the person who wrote a member comment or assignment. The close connections between the academic content and the people who have used the content reduce the isolation of instructors and provide opportunities for dialog, feedback, collaboration, and mentoring.

Editorial Boards

The review and management of the collection is the responsibility of MERLOT's Editorial Boards. Currently, MERLOT has 13 discipline-based boards: Biology, Business, Chemistry, Engineering, Health Science, History, Information Technology, Mathematics, Music, Physics, Psychology, Teacher Education, and World Languages. MERLOT's Teaching and Technology Editorial Board mission is to build and review an interdisciplinary collection that supports the effective integration of technology in teaching and learning. Part of the commitment a MERLOT institutional partner makes is to support instructors' participation on the Editorial Boards. With each partner supporting approximately five instructors, MERLOT has a workforce of more than 100 instructors. The partnering systems and institutions use the following criteria to appoint members of the Editorial Board: (1) expertise in the discipline, (2) excellence in teaching, (3) experience in using technology in teaching and learning, and (4) connections with their disciplines' professional organizations.

The MERLOT strategy is to use the institutions of higher education to help establish the Editorial Boards and then share the responsibility for the peer review with professional discipline organizations. MERLOT provides a variety of tools and processes to ensure the integrity and manage the efficiency of the peer review process, including the training of peer reviewers, and process controls on the evaluation of the materials. MERLOT also provides conference calls, listservs, threaded discussions, and password-protected Web sites for posting documents, enabling the Editorial Boards to communicate and coordinate their work in a secure environment. Editors coordinate the workload among the instructors as they perform the reviews, add materials to the collection, and design the collection's categorization scheme.

Peer Reviews

The infrastructure of the MERLOT system was designed to manage peer review of online materials in the collection, a process that helps ensure that learning materials are contextually accurate, pedagogically sound, and technically easy to use. MERLOT has modeled its peer reviews on traditional practices of discipline-based peer review of scholarship and research. MERLOT's peer review process also provides a mechanism for professional recognition for instructors who develop and use instructional technology, independent of instructors' choices of development methodologies. The peer review process begins with the Editorial Board triaging part of the collection in their discipline to determine which materials are worthy of the intensive review process. Once identified, the material is reviewed by two trained peer reviewers who have the relevant expertise. Instructor-reviewers write individual evaluation reports; the Editor integrates them into a single report. During the peer review process, the Editorial Board members are in communication with the author of the material.

The outcome of the peer review process is a comprehensive report containing a description of the learning goals, the targeted student population(s), prerequisite knowledge and skills, the type of learning material (simulation, animation, tutorial, quiz, lecture/presentation, collection, reference material), a summary of the procedures for using the learning object, technical requirements for usage, and an evaluation of the quality, potential effectiveness for teaching and learning, and usability. Comments and recommendations for the author are also included.

Evaluation Standards

The Editorial Board members (and reviewers) must consider the following three sets of criteria when assessing the online learning materials:

1. *Quality of Content:* The learning materials must present valid (correct) concepts, models, and illustrations. Content validity is verified by the reviewers. Quality of content also means that the learning materials must present educationally significant concepts, models, and skills for the discipline. To evaluate the educational significance of the content, reviewers decide if the content is part of the core curriculum within the discipline, difficult to teach/learn, and/or is a pre-requisite for understanding more advanced material in the discipline.
2. *Potential Effectiveness for Teaching and Learning:* Determining the effectiveness of the material requires consideration of the actual use of the digital learning materials by both students and instructors, together with a systematic assessment of possible learning outcomes. Evaluation of the potential effectiveness of the material requires that reviewers judge the materials based upon their expertise as teachers. The reviews document whether or not the materials are likely to improve teaching and learning, given the ways the instructors and students might use them. Reviewers are provided with an established set of guiding principles to determine if the material is consistent with MERLOT's standards.

3. *Ease of Using the Material:* The primary feature of this standard concerns ease of use of the material for teachers and students who might use the materials for the first time. MERLOT provides a summary of appropriate usability standards to follow as a guideline. The standards are based on Nielson's (1994) heuristics for usability.

Member Comments

While MERLOT peer reviewers must be appointed and then must be trained, in fact any individual member of MERLOT can contribute Member Comments and rate MERLOT materials. This user-centered review process is very important in a number of highly used and popular Web sites such as Amazon.com, allowing individuals to submit their comments and evaluations on the learning materials within MERLOT. Members are asked first to describe how they reviewed the materials (e.g., five minutes browsing or used it in teaching a course) and then asked to evaluate the quality of the content, effectiveness for teaching and learning, and ease of use.

Figures 8, 9, and 10 illustrate the member peer review process. Figure 8 illustrates a "found" item that has been peer reviewed and that has member comments annotated with it. The item has been found useful by seven members who have added it to their personal e-portfolio collections. Figure 9 displays one (of many) comments that members have posted regarding this item. Figure 10 displays the member input form that can be completed if an individual member wishes to add additional comments regarding the item.

Figure 8. Finding a relevant item

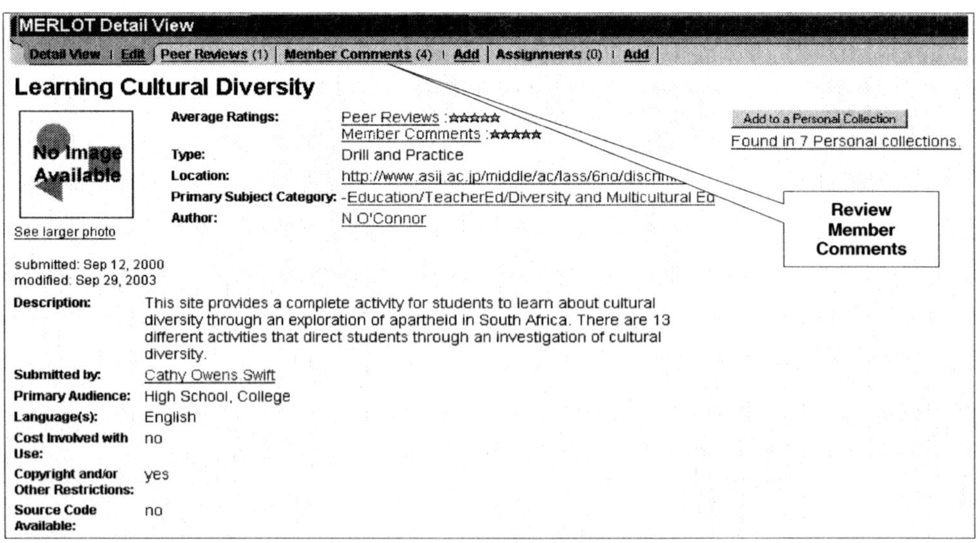

Figure 9. Reviewing member comments

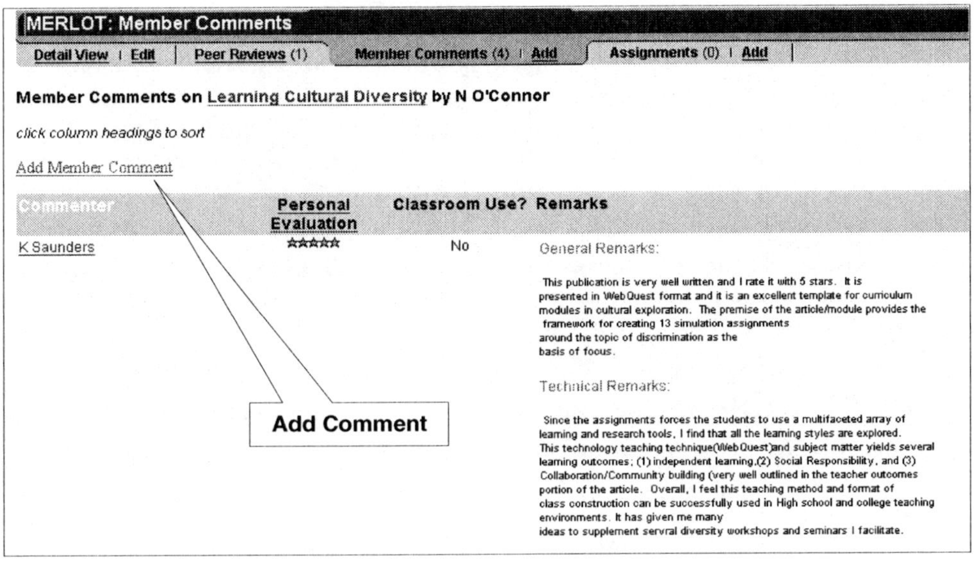

Figure 10. Adding member comments

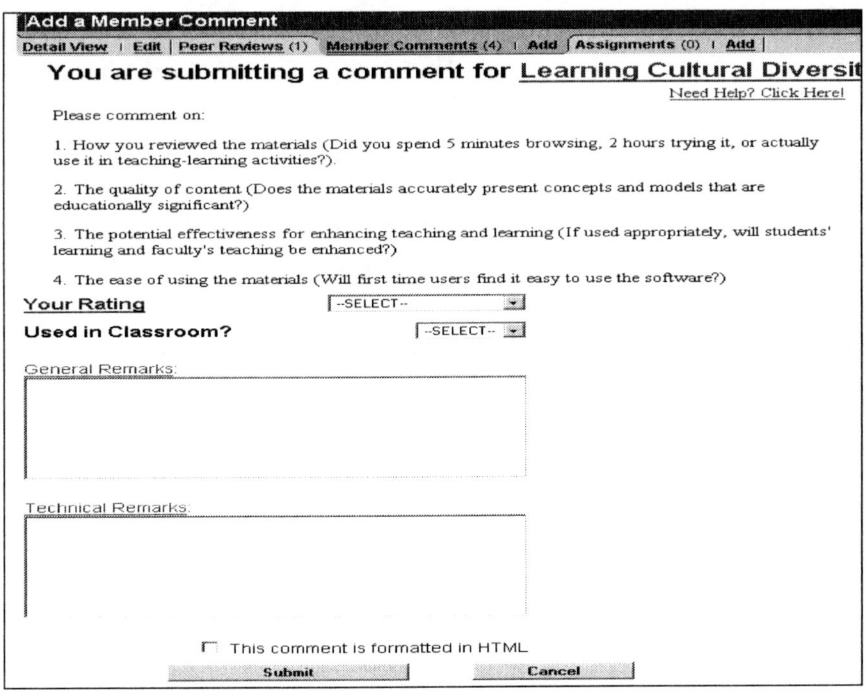

Technology, Teaching, and Tenure

One of the pervasive issues for both instructors and administration is recognition and reward for effective teaching with technology within the hiring, retention, tenure, and promotion process. The discontinuity between stated priorities for innovative uses of technology and actual policies and practices for personnel evaluation is a major barrier to effective and sustained use of technology in teaching and learning. For those institutions that are ready to align priorities with policies and practices, MERLOT provides a means to their success.

Guidelines for evaluating the quality of innovation of the use of technology in instruction have been published by a number of professional societies and institutions. Examples include:

- Conference on College Composition and Communication: www.hu.mtu.edu/~cyselfe/P&TStuff/P&TWeb/Introduction.htm
- Modern Language Association: www.mla.org/reports/ccet/ccet_frame.htm
- Duquesne University: www.tltgroup.org/resources/rduqten.html
- University of Michigan: www.personal.umich.edu/~cberger/InstructorsRecandReward.doc
- American Association for History and Computing: www.theaahc.org/tenure_guidlines.htm

An examination of these guidelines reveals a number of common principles (Somers, 2002), including:

- Peer evaluation and testimony by experts in a discipline are required to verify quality and importance of the materials to the discipline.
- An innovator's digital scholarship should be made "visible" to the professional community.
- Instructor-candidates for tenure/promotion should provide electronic portfolios of their innovations for review.
- The evaluation of the materials should be performed in the medium in which the scholarship was created.

MERLOT provides resources and tools to campus administrations, review committees, and candidates to implement these kinds of evaluation guidelines. MERLOT's peer reviews are performed by an independent panel of experts who have been trained to reliably apply a standards-based evaluation process. Administrators, committees, and candidates can use the peer reviews as external reviews validating the quality and significance of the candidate's digital scholarship. MERLOT provides an international venue to make the digital scholarship visible, and enables the professional community to evaluate, use, augment, and reference in their *Personal Collections*. Finally, MERLOT provides documentation for the quality and quantity of digital scholarship contributions instructors make through the e-portfolios and with letters of recognition.

Conclusion

The success of any program is determined in large part on its ability meet the immediate needs of the institution and individuals that comprise it. MERLOT provides services that can meet the immediate needs for curriculum research and design for distance learning programs. MERLOT continues to serve the needs and capabilities of institutions and individuals as their needs develop and mature. For those who wish simply to explore for digital content, MERLOT provides a very low entry-level threshold of effort. For those who require tutoring on how to use digital content in teaching and learning, MERLOT provides a professional development program. The annual MERLOT International Conference provides many opportunities for professional development. The MERLOT Instructors Development Workshop provides its Institutional Partners an intensive training program for their staff to learn how to implement MERLOT at their campuses. For those wishing to demonstrate leadership in academic technology, MERLOT provides opportunities, resources, and participation in the strategic directions of MERLOT. MERLOT conducts a variety of planning and training meetings for its Project Directors' Council, Editorial Council, and Advisory Board, as it continuously shapes its future.

MERLOT's own success is determined by its ability to facilitate different educational institutions' success, as measured by local variables, through shared and customized services. It is through the expanding collaborative participation in an international community that individuals and institutions will be able to more effectively and efficiently prepare their teachers to design and deliver effective, innovative, and customized distance learning programs that will grow with and sustain the educational needs of the world's population.

References

Allen, I.E. & Seaman, J. (2003). *Sizing the opportunity: The quality and extent of online education in the United States, 2002 and 2003*. Needham, MA: Sloan Center for OnLine Education (SCOLE).

Brahler, C.J., Peterson, N.S., & Johnson, E.C. (1999). Developing on-line learning materials for higher education: An overview of current issues. *Educational Technology & Society 2*(2).

Bonk, C.J. & Cunningham, D.J. (1998). Searching for learner-centered, constructivist, and sociocultural components of collaborative educational learning tools. In C.J. Bonk & K.S. King (Eds.), *Electronic collaborators learner-centered technologies for literacy, apprenticeship, and discourse.* NJ: Lawrence Erlbaum.

Darling-Hammond, L. (2000) Teacher quality and student achievement: A review of state policy evidence. *Educational Policy Analysis Archives, 8*(1). Retrieved from *epaa.asu.edu/epaa/v8n1/*

Frand, J.L. (2000). The information-age mindset. *Educause Review, 35,* 14-21.

Hanley, G.L. (2003, October 23-24). Enabling educational institutions' success in distance learning: MERLOT's facilitation strategy. *Proceedings of the National Institute for Multimedia Education Conference, Networks without Borders: Toward Cross-Cultural Learning Communities*, Japan.

Hartman, J., Sorg, S., Truman-Davis, B., Morris, J., & Marshall, R. (1998, November 19). Faculty development for teaching with technology. *Proceedings of the SHEEO-APQC Conference,* Houston, Texas, USA

ISTE. *Educational technology standards and performance indicators for all teachers.* Retrieved from *cnets.iste.org/teachers/t_stands.html*

Muirhead, B. (2001). Practical strategies for teaching computer-mediated classes. *Educational Technology & Society, 4*(2).

Nielsen, J. (1994). Heuristic evaluation. In J. Nielsen & R.L. Mack (Eds.), *Usability inspection methods.* New York: John Wiley & Sons.

Sheinberg, M. (2000). E-learning 1.0—stave off these seven pitfalls of distance learning. ASTD's online magazine, *Learning Circuits.* Retrieved December 23, 2003, from *www.learningcircuits.org/apr2000/apr2000_elearn.html*

Somers, J. (2002, August). *Tenure and promotion reviews with MERLOT. Proceedings of the Annual MERLOT International Conference,* Atlanta, Georgia, USA.

U.S. Department of Labor. (1991). *What work requires of schools: A SCANS report for America 2000.* Washington, DC: Labor Secretary's Commission on Achieving Necessary Skills.

Wiley, D.A. (2000). Connecting learning objects to instructional design theory: A definition, a metaphor, and a taxonomy. In D.A. Wiley (Ed.), *The instructional use of learning objects: Online version.* Retrieved December 23, 2003, from reusability.org/read/chapters/wiley.doc.

Endnote

[1] Although the ISTE NETS Project is specifically targeted at PreK-12 education and addresses educational technologies in general, its work also has important relevance to online teaching and learning in higher education.

Chapter XXIV

Virtual Reality, Telemedicine, and Beyond: Some Examples

Franco Orsucci
Institute of Psychiatry and Clinical Psychology,
Catholic University of Rome, Italy

Nicoletta Sala
Università della Svizzera Italiana, Switzerland

Abstract

This chapter introduces virtual reality and telemedicine as instruments inserted in a path of medicine. It argues that virtual reality, combined with communication technologies, offers potential help to doctors and psychiatrists in overcoming physical and geographic barriers, and examining patients in remote locations. The authors describe two examples for better health and therapy. They hope that understanding these technologies and their use in the field of the medicine will help doctors use them in their future work.

Introduction

The implementation and integration of new communication technologies within organizations creates complex changes in communicative practices. Advances in telecommunications and digital technology allow organizations to extend their boundaries beyond physical and geographic barriers.

Within healthcare settings, telemedicine applications allow physicians to examine patients at remote locations via various types of telecommunications technologies. These telecommunications connections allow psychiatrists and patients to be present in a new way. This chapter explores implications of this presence in the context of a psychiatric exchange.

Background

The concept of presence is defined as: "...the fact or condition of being at the specified or understood place" (Kim & Biocca, 1997). Kim and Biocca (1997) suggest that the experience of presence oscillates around three senses of place: the physical environment, the virtual environment, and the 'imaginal' environment (for example, daydreaming). In a traditional face-to-face environment, the physical environment is relatively transparent to the interaction. Many information cues present in the physical environment can be incorporated into a communication exchange without the conscious awareness of the individuals involved. For example, a physician may notice that a patient seems to walk into an examining room in a reticent way. These nonverbal cues may aid the physician in formulating a diagnosis. When videoconferencing technology is used to bridge remote locations, a virtual environment is created. Many information cues present in the physical environment are not available in the virtual environment. This virtual environment can create a sense of telepresence. Telepresence describes the subjective sensation of being in a remote or artificial environment, but not the surrounding physical environment (Kim & Biocca, 1997). Lombard and Ditton (1997) suggest that telepresence creates an "illusion of nonmediation" where a person "fails to perceive or acknowledge the existence of a medium in his/her communication environment and responds as he/she would if the medium were not there." This illusion of the absence of mediation may suggest to the anticipants that they are receiving all information cues relevant to interaction, when in fact they are not.

Focus Upon the Doctor and Patient Dyad

Telepsychiatry has been explored for over 40 years through a wide range of technologies. Research has compared the telepsychiatry interview to the traditional face-to-face interview across various diagnoses and conditions. Though technology has evolved dramatically, many conclusions regarding the viability of telepsychiatry over the years have remained very similar.

The first implementation of telepsychiatry was conducted by Wittson in the early 1950s at the Nebraska Psychiatric Institute (NPI), where he investigated the potential of closed-circuit television as a teaching aid (Wheeler, 1994; Wittson & Benschoter, 1972). Ten years later, the first telepsychiatry consultations were performed at NPI. The researchers involved in the trial determined that "the isolation of the therapist from the patients had almost no effect on group sessions" (Wheeler, 1994, p. 2). Additionally, researchers found patients and relatives were very receptive to this form of communication (Wittson & Benschoter, 1972).

Similar results were found in New Hampshire, where researchers explored the use of two-way-video consultations between community family physicians and psychiatrists located at Dartmouth Medical School. Dartmouth researchers argued: "...television has presented almost no difficulties as a medium for psychiatric consultation. It has not proved to be a significant barrier in establishing rapport with the patient or in perceiving emotional nuances" (Solow, Weiss, Bergen, & Sanborn, 1971, p. 1686). Telepsychiatry presented an additional benefit in that local physicians became educated in the treatment of their patients through observations of the interviews with remote psychiatrists. Local physicians reported notable changes in their use and knowledge of psychotropic drugs.

A telepsychiatry program for children that linked a medical school and an inner-city, child-health station received similar support from users, while also providing the additional benefits of improved access and decreased travel time (Straker, Mostyn, & Marshall, 1976). Findings from programs developed in the 1960s and 1970s suggest that both patients and therapists "do not feel that televised sessions interfere with the quality of therapeutic relationships" (Maxmen, 1978, p. 452).

Another study, conducted in the 1980s, directly examined telepsychiatry, in comparison to traditional face-to-face interviews, and found no significant difference in patient and physician perceptions of the two (Dongier, Tempier, Lalinec-Michaud, & Meunier, 1986). These initial explorations suggest the technology may be adequate for diagnosis of some conditions.

A pilot study of telemedicine used for patients with obsessive-compulsive disorder showed that telemedicine resulted in near-perfect inter-rater agreement on scores on semi-structured rating scales for obsessive-compulsive, depressive, and anxiety disorders (Baer, Jenike, Leahy, O'Laughlen, & Coyle, 1995).

Virtual Reality in Medicine

What is virtual reality? Virtual reality (VR) is the technology that allows its users to immerse into a computer-generated virtual world. Virtual reality includes the technology for three dimensional (3-D) displays, methods for generating virtual images including 3-D modeling, and techniques for orienting the user in the virtual world. Medicine is one of the major application areas for virtual reality, along with games and scientific visualization (Orsucci & Sala, 2003). VR is a set of computer technologies which, when combined, provide an interface to a computer-generated world, and in particular, provide such a convincing interface that the user believes he is actually in a three-dimensional computer-generated world. This computer-generated world may be a model of a real-world object, such as a house; it might be an abstract world that does not exist in a real sense but is understood by humans, such as a chemical molecule or a representation of a set of data; or it might be in a completely imaginary science fiction world. A key feature is that the user believes that he is actually in this different world. A second key feature of virtual reality is that if the human moves his head, arms, or legs, the shift of visual cues must be those he would expect in a real world. In other words, besides immersion, there must be navigation and interaction.

VR is applied to a wide range of medical areas, for example remote and local surgery, surgery planning, medical education and training, treatment of phobias and other causes of psychological distress, skill training, preoperative planning and pain reduction. It is also used for the visualization of large-scale medical records, and in the architectural planning of medical facilities (Waterworth, 1999).

According to an assessment on current diffusion of VR in the medical sector, gathered by the Gartner Group, the forecast of VR's future in this area is quite promising. Within the medical application its strategic relevance will increase and gain importance. It is envisaged that very early in the twenty-first century, despite possible technological barriers, virtual reality techniques will be integrated in endoscopic surgical procedures. VR will also affect the medical educational strategy for students as well as experienced practitioners, who will increasingly be involved in immersive simulated techniques. It is expected that these educational routines can become routine by 2005.

VR has been, until now, widely underused, probably because of prohibitive hardware costs; nevertheless, this technology is pushing forward new challenges and advances that will materialize any day now. The medical use of VR will take place mainly in four domains:

1) *Teaching*: VR will reproduce environments or special conditions that will enable the education of medical personnel.
2) *Simulation*: VR will mix video and scanner images to represent and plan surgical intervention, effects of therapy.
3) *Diagnostics*: It will be possible to forecast the effects of complex combinations of healing treatments.
4) *Therapy*: A valuable exploitation of VR in the medical sector is seen with interest in the therapy of psychiatric/psychological disorders such as acrophobia, claustrophobia, nyctophobia, agoraphobia, eating disorders, and so forth. Therapeutic techniques will include practices that will allow patients to reproduce and master problem environments.

VR provides an important resource for education about anatomical structure. One of the main problems for medical education in general is to provide a realistic sense of the interrelation of anatomical structures in 3D space. New computer graphics techniques can help to solve these problems. With VR, the learner can explore the structures of interest, take them apart, put them together, and view them using different perspectives. This is obviously impossible with a live patient, and is really infeasible with cadavers, which have already lost many of the important characteristics of live tissue (Waterworth, 1999).

Two Examples for Better Health and Therapy

The Angelo Project

Angelo (EU IST 11696) aims to provide a new approach to what is becoming an important social and business issue, namely quality of work for call center employees. Market research shows that it costs roughly 10 times more to acquire a new customer than to maintain an existing one. Levels of customer satisfaction depend partly on technology, but largely on the operator's behavior. It follows that happy call center operators are likely to translate into better business performance. Angelo is based on the assumption that operators' quality of work depends on the quality of the working environment. A high-quality working environment will take into account differing individual needs, strategies, and preferences, thus allowing operators a significant degree of control over key environmental parameters. At the same time, it will provide operators with rapid access to quality information and an ergonomic human-machine interface.

Angelo creates such an environment by integrating research results and technologies from a number of different disciplines. In particular the project will use advanced techniques in knowledge engineering and linguistic analysis to analyze customer-operator interactions and provide operators with immediate access to relevant information resources. The project will apply advanced sensor technology for measuring environmental and physiological variables, adaptive computing techniques to model and anticipate operator needs and requests, as well as augmented reality tools to enhance the human-machine interface. This way, Angelo will introduce important innovations in workplace design, allowing an unprecedented degree of individual control over the working environment.

The project evaluates industry requirements and functional specifications; develops appropriate measurement system, communication equipment, and human interface components; develops information management and network components; integrates, networks, and operates through volunteers from a user group. At the same time, it disseminates the results in a user-friendly form.

Figure 1. Angelo project's scheme

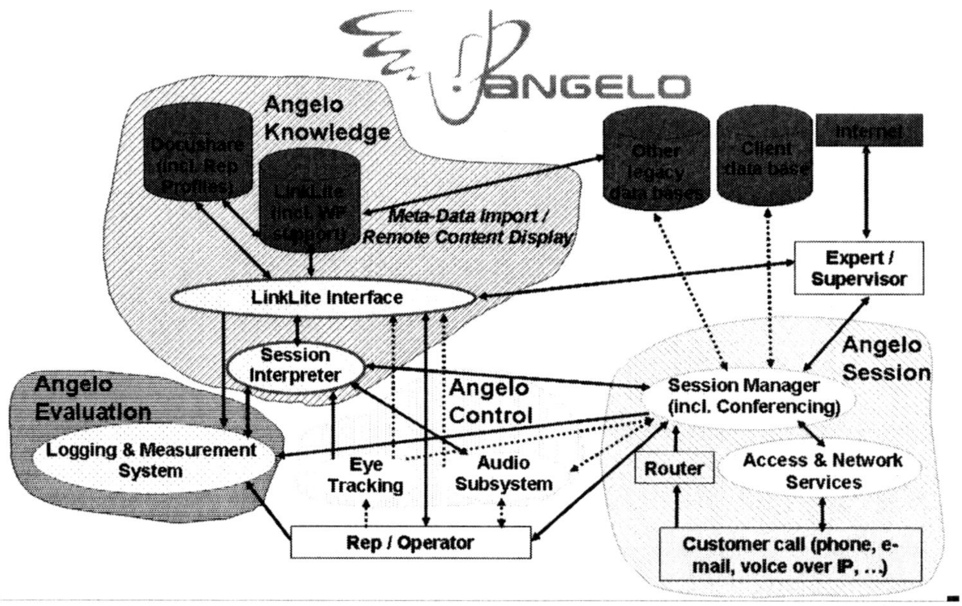

Airone Project

The Airone VR-based learning environment will:

- provide a therapeutic environment that highlights the consequences of patients' actions to allow them to identify the (changed) characteristics of their system (Movement Principle: Forward Modeling—Cognition of Planning Strategies);
- provide a setting where they can try and test adaptive movement strategies (Movement Principle: Inverse Modeling);
- present the patients with functionally related tasks that have clear goals, rather than prescribe movement sequences or patterns of contraction (Action Principle 1); and
- allow the patient to explore the environment and arrive at a solution to his/her specific movement and cognitive problems, rather than guide them through constrained routines (Action Principle 2).

Airone components include:

- a human interface set (glasses for augmented reality, head and hand trackers, odor generator);
- augmented shared reality environment (sand-box play, virtual house, virtual library, etc.);
- bio-feedback (EEG, thermal, EMG, etc.);
- VR, giving added value to therapy;
- a stimulus not available in the natural therapy setting;
- odor generation, which enables aromatherapy and enlarges the sensory spectrum in VR;
- augmentation or amplification of sensory feedback to a perceptual system that may have lost some degree of its natural sensitivity;
- enhancement of the therapeutic setting, providing the patient with a virtual body;
- a repeatable process that uses random variations to keep patients' attention;
- broadband Internet;
- the "thin client" approach for shared VR which empowers a runtime client-server platform for using interactive 3D environments with all the power of component-oriented programming; and
- a service provider strongly involved under a business development focus.

Figure 2. Airone project's scheme

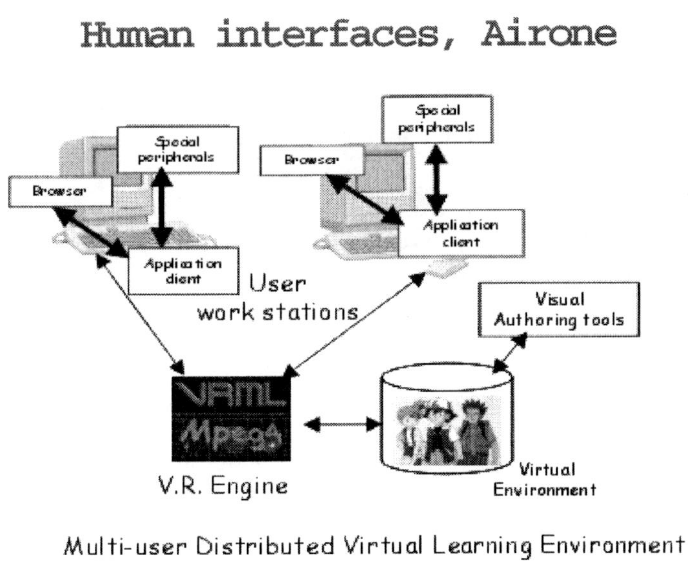

Conclusion

There is a great deal of research and development going on around the world in the application of virtual reality to medicine. Many implications and differences between virtual reality VR, augmented reality AR and the ecological psychology of everyday reality ER still need to be explored. Promises in this new area of interface between man, machines and world are undoubtedly rich.

References

Baer, L., C, P. (1997). Telepsychiatry at forty: What have we learned? *Harvard Review of Psychiatry, 5*(1), 7-17.

Dongier, M., Tempier, R., Lalinec-Michaud, M., & Meunier, D. (1986). Telepsychiatry: Psychiatric consultation through two-way television. A controlled study. *Canadian Journal of Psychiatry, 31,* 32-34.

Kim, T. & Biocca, F. (1997). Telepresence via television: Two dimensions of telepresence may have different connections to memory and persuasion. *Journal of Computer Mediated Communication, 3*(2).

Lombard, M. & Ditton, T. (1997). At the heart of it all: The concept of presence. *Journal of Computer Mediated Communication, 3*(2).

Maxmen, J. (1978). Telecommunications in psychiatry. *American Journal of Psychotherapy, 32,* 450-456.

Orsucci, F. (2002). *Changing mind. Transitions in natural and artificial environments.* Singapore: World Scientific.

Orsucci, F. & Sala, N. (2003). Virtual reality, telemedicine and beyond. In *Information technology & organizations: Trends, issues, challenges, & solutions* (pp. 755-757). Hershey, PA: Idea Group Publishing.

Riva, G. (Ed.). (1997-1998). *Virtual reality in neuro-psycho-physiology.* Amsterdam: Ios Press.

Solow, C., Weiss, R., Bergen, B., & Sanborn, C. (1971). 24-hour psychiatric consultation via TV. *American Journal of Psychiatry, 127*(12), 1684-1686.

Straker, N., Mostyn, P., & Marshall, C. (1976). The use of two-way TV in bringing mental health services to the inner city. *American Journal of Psychiatry, 133*(10), 1202-1205.

Warisse Turner, J. (2001). Telepsychiatry as a case study of presence: Do you know what you are missing? *JCMC, 6*(4).

Waterworth, J. (1999). *3 medical VR: The main application areas and what has been done.* Retrieved December 2, 2003, from *www.informatik.umu.se/_jwworth/3ApplicationAreas.html*

Wheeler, T. (1994). In the beginning...telemedicine and telepsychiatry. *Telemedicine Today, 2*(2), 2-4.

Wittson, C. & Benschoter, R. (1972). Two-way television: Helping the medical center reach out. *American Journal of Psychiatry, 129*(5), 624-627.

Endnote

The Angelo Project is research funded by the European Union (EU IST 11696).

Chapter XXV

Virtual Reality in Education

Nicoletta Sala
Università della Svizzera Italiana, Switzerland

Massimo Sala
Università della Svizzera Italiana, Switzerland

Abstract

This chapter introduces the technology of virtual reality as an educational tool. It argues that virtual reality, combined with multimedia technologies and in support of different learning styles, offers potential help in teaching environments. The authors describe different examples of applications of virtual reality in different kinds of schools (primary schools, high schools, and universities) and in different countries (USA, Italy, Morocco, Romania, and Switzerland). They hope that by understanding the characteristics of this technology and its use in the education field, teachers will be able to use virtual reality in future teaching endeavors.

Introduction

Virtual reality (VR) is a modern technology that gives to its users the illusion of being immersed in a computer-generated virtual world with the ability to interact with it. A virtual reality system has the following three primary requirements (Rosemblum & Cross, 1997):

1) immersion (which requires physically involving the user, both by capturing exclusive visual attention and by transparently responding to three-dimensional input);
2) interaction (through the three-dimensional control device to investigate and control the virtual environment);
3) visual realism (that is an accurate representation of the virtual world using computer graphics techniques).

The interface hardware components consist of a visual display apparatus, some sort of input device, and a position sensor. Input devices can comprise a keyboard, a mouse (2-D or 3-D), a head-mounted display (HMD), and motion-sensing data gloves. The purpose of the input device is to permit the human participant to give electrical signals to the computer which can be transformed as specific commands. Of virtual reality, Derrick de Kerckhove states:

> *"Like any interactive medium with a cursor present inside the spectrum of the screen, virtual reality is a 'total surround' effect, an actual replacement of reality, its substitution, foundation for the values of the new environments. We are no longer operating with only two spaces, physical space and mental space, but have added a third zone of exploration: digital space, cyberspace, virtual space, call it what you like." (Barzon, 2003, pp. 38-39)*

The types of VR are usually classified according to their method of display; there is immersive VR and non-immersive VR. In particular, low-cost non-immersive VR is used in the educational field. Several research institutes around the world have demonstrated the potential of virtual reality systems as a visualization tool, and as technology continues to improve, VR systems will become pervasive instrumentation for research in education. This work describes some examples of virtual reality in educational fields and intends to answer to the following question: "Is an active use of virtual reality possible in schools?"

The chapter presents some applications of this technology in different kinds of schools, for example, in primary schools to create a collaborative learning environment, in high schools, in universities, and in different countries. All experiences emphasize VR's strong impact in educational environments.

Background

The potential of VR in education is recognized and supported by interesting results (Winn, 1993; Pantelidis, 1995; Byrne, 1996; Youngblut, 1998; Gerval, Popovici, & Tisseau, 2003). Many researchers believe that virtual reality offers benefits that can support education. For some, VR's ability to facilitate constructivist learning activities is the key issue (Jonassen, 1991). Constructivism is learning that takes place when learners actively construct their own reality and/or knowledge, or at least interpret it based upon their perceptions of experience. Using the constructivist theory, Byrne (1996) created a virtual environment to stimulate students to learn by exploring and interacting with information from the world of chemistry. Instead of staying in a classroom and passively viewing images of atomic structures, the students can place electrons in the atoms and they can see the atomic orbital appear as the electron buzzes (Byrne, 1996). VR is also a good medium for making abstract concepts concrete; for example, to emphasize the laws of physics or the principles of chemistry (Zoller, 1990; Johnstone, 1991). Hedberg and Alexander (1994) furnished a list of 12 questions they felt should be asked when contemplating the use of VR in education:

- To what extent is collaboration with peers possible and useful in the VR experience?
- What use does the learner make of conversations, stories, and multiple points of view?
- What and how does the learner learn in a 'virtual' community of practice?
- Is there a complex combination of physical and cognitive skills?
- Are the motivation and the context important?
- Does the learner need to combine information from different forms of representation (visual, temporal, etc.), and is a context required to limit the cognitive load of the task?
- Does the learner need to experiment with a scenario which might have dangerous consequences if actually experienced?
- Does the learned concept require links to objects that behave with a defined set of attributes and relationships?
- Are the learner's explorations independent of size of the world being explored (microscopic or macroscopic)?
- Are physical and improbable phenomena, related to the creation of micro-worlds, independent of time explorations with beings real, or historical, within their context?
- Is the learned concept a relationship in space independent of physical laws?
- Does the learner have to work with abstract relationships, and manipulate data structures and mathematical functions?

Youngblut (1998) wrote about the educational curriculum available for use by VR: "The range of educational subjects covered is quite broad, showing a fairly equal split between the arts and sciences." In addition, she says that VR "applications are fairly equally split between those designed for elementary and middle school levels, those for high school students, and those for college students (undergraduate and graduate)" (Youngblut, 1998, p. 29).

An other important question is where to use VR in education. Pantelidis (1997) proposed a model based on the work of Gagnè and Briggs (1979). The model comprises the following 11 phases:

1) Define the objectives for specific course.
2) Mark the objectives that could use a simulation as a measurement or means.
3) Each of the marked objectives is examined: first determine if it could use a computer-generated simulation for attainment or measurement, then determine if it could use a three-dimensional (3-D), interactive simulation.
4) Choose for each selected objective the level of realism required, on a scale from very symbolic to very real.
5) Decide the type of interaction needed, on a scale from no immersion into the 3-D environment (for example, desktop VR) to full immersion (for example, using head-mounted display, and data gloves).
6) Establish the type of sensory output from the virtual world or environment desired (for example, 3-D sound, or visual only).
7) Choose VR software and hardware/equipment.
8) Design and build the virtual environment (VE). The virtual environment may be built by the teacher, the students, or both.
9) Evaluate the resulting virtual environment using a pilot or experimental group of students.
10) Modify the virtual environment using the results of the evaluation.
11) The modification continues until the VE is shown to successfully measure or aid in attainment of the objective.

Applying this model, different research laboratories studied VR's applications in different kinds of schools. For example, students in Trenton, North Carolina, realized some virtual environments in a class on technical mathematics (Basal, 1995). Students at the Virtual Reality Lab (VRlab), Swiss Federal Institute of Technology (Lausanne, Switzerland, vrlab.epfl.ch/), are exploring modeling and animation of 3-D inhabited virtual worlds. One of their projects developed in these years was VPARK (Virtual Amusement Park), which includes a virtual environment that allowed two distant users to share the same virtual world for a lesson of aerobic dancing.

Gerval, Popovici, and Tisseau (2003) are examining VR's potential in the multicultural integration in the primary schools; the project, named EVE (Environment Virtuels pour Enfants), involves nine primary schools of three different countries (France, Morocco, and Romania). The EVE application has been developed in order to help primary school children learn French and especially reading. The project's goals are to create a new cooperative environment for learning which involves the young students from three different countries, and to find a new kind of software tool for primary school children. From a pedagogical point of view, the main goal of the EVE project is teamwork. In fact, children from different countries are involved in cooperative work. They have to achieve a common task together, hoping that this will encourage the respect in a multicultural framework. From a technical point of view, this project implements distributed virtual reality technologies. From both perspectives, it is like NICE (narrative, immersive, constructionist, and collaborative) environment.

Antonietti, Imperio, Rasi, and Sacco (2001) proposed a prototypal system for machine tools teaching in a virtual reality environment integrated with hypermedia. The goal is to lead students not only to understand the structure and functioning of the lathe, but also to use such a machine. To reach this, the prototype tries to foster conceptual changes in students' mental models and to increase students' control over the learning process. A series of experimental tests have been carried out to assess the educational validity of the instructional tool that has been devised. The aim of the first phase of the project was to assess whether students could easily use the virtual lathe and to verify what they learn about such a machine. The purpose of the second phase was to focus on some critical aspects of the learning process activated by using the virtual lathe in order to realize which are the instructional procedures that give the best learning outcomes. These educational experiences emphasize that one problem at the moment is the cost to realize immersive virtual reality environments. The price may drop if the market grows, but in terms of products for education, we have to pay much for modest quality hardware and software.

Another problem is connected to the simulation of some effects that are familiar to the human body. For example, haptic feedback is not like the real tactile sensation. Figures 1 and 2 show two examples of virtual objects created using two different kinds of VR: immersive VR, with data gloves, and non-immersive VR, with two different degrees of interaction and different costs.

To realize VR's low-cost applications, some schools use the Virtual Reality Modeling Language (VRML), which is a language that specifies the parameters to create virtual

Figure 1. A virtual object manipulated using the data gloves

Figure 2. Non-immersive VR: A virtual object

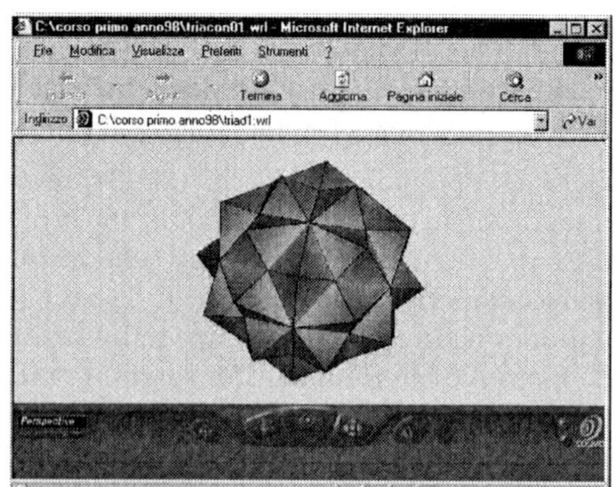

worlds networked together via the Internet and accessed via the Web's hyperlinks. A VRML file is an ASCII file (with the suffix.wrl), which is interpreted by the browser, for example Cosmoplayer®, and converted into a 3-D display of the described world.

Virtual Reality in the Educational Environment: A Case Study

It is interesting to analyze the contribution of new media and virtual reality in university courses of mathematics. The investigations follow these three questions:

1) Is it possible to organize some courses of mathematics conceived for a faculty of architecture?
2) Can virtual reality help the teaching process in mathematics courses in a faculty of architecture?
3) How does one integrate VR's technologies in a specific curriculum of architectural studies?

To answer the first question, the mathematicians at the Academy of Architecture (Università della Svizzera Italiana, Switzerland) have decided to organize four courses of mathematics specifically conceived for a Faculty of Architecture, with interdisciplinary connections between philosophy, arts, architecture, and urban design (Sala, 2003).

To answer the second question relating to including new media as a teaching strategy, the authors have integrated traditional lectures using new media, because 60% of students today are visual learners (McKay & Garner, 1999). This category of learners may benefit most from multimedia presentations, which combine words with pictures and audio to help redefine teaching methods (McKay, 2002). In this educational approach the term 'virtual reality' is used to cover both immersive and non-immersive VR. This technology has been used firstly to help architecture students to visualize in three dimensions, since this is arguably the most difficult part of understanding architecture. In the course of Mathematics 1 (named Mathematical thought), VR is a good medium for making abstract concepts concrete; for example:

- to observe and to rotate the polyhedra from different points of view (outside and inside the virtual objects);
- to create some virtual objects using VRML in the laboratory activities; and
- to observe and manipulate the geodesic domes.

To answer the third question, the authors integrated VR's technology into a training path to visualize the projects connected to the territory and to determine some 'virtual buildings' that students can visit. For example, in the course of Mathematics and territory (fourth year), VR has been analyzed as a medium to visualize the design in 3-D using computer-generated animations. Traditional CAAD (computer-aided architectural design) tools have as limits the 'believability' (related mainly to display techniques and power requirements) that VR attempts to overcome. Improved visualization through the use of VR in architectural practice clearly benefits the architects (De Francesco & Nardini, 2002). Other educational goals were to create 'virtual tours' using hypermedia presentations of the project, and to emphasize the virtual communities with their sociological implications (Rheingold, 2000). In the future, architects will themselves design virtual environments instead of real buildings (Prestinenza Puglisi, 1999). This will require people who understand the psychological effects of the spaces generated by the computer on people inside them; further, the architects must prepare themselves for this new work opportunity. Architects as designers of virtual worlds will be required to make these environments interesting, rich, and engaging places. Therefore, it is important to prepare proper training on the use of VR in the faculties of architecture.

What happens to the relationships between teachers and students during this educational approach? There are two ways to answer this question. The first is instrumental and strictly connected to assessment in the traditional sense, and the answer it provides is to use VR as another medium in the classroom. Thus, VR becomes a technology transmission. It may more efficiently help to impart knowledge, but this is not its potential. The second answer is found by thinking of VR as a place in which students can create knowledge and get to know places by exploration. They may walk around, meet people and avatars, and talk with them. Therefore, virtual reality technologies have to be persistent, easily accessible, and navigable; but it is also necessary to think about the educational value, and consider more than efficiency scheduling for learning.

Future Trends

The combination of the Internet, the World Wide Web, and virtual reality will have great potential for educational environments. A revolution is already underway outside of education, with the Web for primary information, and retrieval tools and virtual reality as a medium to reconstruct and interact with virtual objects. One of the main aims of VR is to create virtual worlds and virtual environments in which humans can interact together; however, the problem of interaction with other users is sure to rise in the future.

How does on create virtual worlds? Some virtual worlds will certainly be oriented to education, and others for business, work, or fun. Architects will potentially help to make the virtual world a pleasant and stimulating place to work and live in, with a good quality of life. For architectural education, virtual reality will become the place to go to do things that you could not normally do in architect-designed buildings. Spaces created with Fractal and non-Euclidean geometry will exist and could be modified using algorithms (Galofaro, 1999). As famous architect Peter Eisenman says:

> *"These new complexities have always existed, hidden within the pre-existing conventions. At the same time, the present potentialities furnished [to] us by the computer simultaneously also repress and hide other operative possibilities. It becomes the job of we architects to construct the new tools and new algorithms able to produce the environmental complexes necessary for our present condition." (Barzon, 2003, p. 37)*

Virtual reality could revolutionize the process of design, not only for its potential value as a communication and visualization tool, but because it offers a 'trial run' in designing architecture. All architects, regardless of their visualization ability, innate or developed through years of practice, will have a better opportunity to visualize and to create a correct 'way of thinking' using virtual reality technologies.

Conclusion

The use of VR in education represents another phase in the evolution of teaching methods; it starts with a teacher who used only books, films, and audio to bring people into the classroom, and ends with computers, bringing students outside the classroom. The wireless networks now blur the distinction between inside and outside the classroom, and in some sense there are rooms within rooms and spaces within spaces, like Russian dolls, using VR technologies. Virtual reality, connected to the Internet and the World Wide Web, can create virtual spaces that contribute to helping an active learning process. Future evolutions in computer technologies will bring ever more powerful graphics to students' desktops, which will relieve some of the current simulation restrictions. The construction of virtual environments should be seen as a design problem in the broadest sense. VR projects with an educational remit should recall at all times the criteria of educational effectiveness. The aspects of the educational project that involves VR technologies should be evaluated, including the effects of concretizing information, of appropriateness of spatial metaphors, and of the interface.

References

Antonietti, A., Imperio, E., Rasi, C., & Sacco, M. (2001). Virtual reality and hypermedia in learning to use a turning lathe. *Journal of Computer Assisted Learning, 17,* 142-155.

Barzon, F. (2003). *The charter of Zurich. Eisenman, De Kerckhove, Saggio.* Basel: Birkhäuser.

Basal, F. (1995). Virtual reality and schools project report. *VR in the Schools, 1*(1). Retrieved February 15, 2004, from *eastnet.educ.ecu.edu/vr/vr1n1a.txt*

Byrne, C.M. (1996). *Water on tap: The use of virtual reality as an educational tool.* PhD Dissertation, University of Washington, USA.

De Francesco, L. & Nardini, M. (2002). *Behind the scene avant-garde techniques in contemporary design.* Basel: Birkhäuser.

Gagnè, R.M. & Briggs, L.J. (1979). *Principles of instructional design* (2nd edition). New York: Holt, Rinehart and Winston.

Galofaro, L. (1999). *Digital Eisenman: An office of the electronic era.* Basel: Birkhäuser.

Gerval, J.P., Popovici, M., & Tisseau, J. (2003). Virtual stories authoring tools for pedagogical purposes. *Proceedings of the IASTED International Conference on Computer and Advanced in Education* (pp. 642-646), Rhodes, Greece.

Hedberg, J. & Alexander, S. (1994). Virtual reality in education: Defining researchable issues. *Educational Media International, 31*(4), 214-220.

Johnstone, A.H. (1991). Why is science difficult to learn? Things are seldom what they seem. *Journal of Computer Assisted Learning, 7,* 75-83.

Jonassen, D.H. (1991). Evaluating constructivistic learning. *Educational Technology,* (September), 28-33.

McKay, E. (2002). Human-computer interaction: Effective multi-media presentations. *Computer Education, 101,* 2-10.

McKay, E. & Garner, B. (1999). The complexities of visual learning: Measuring cognitive skills performance. In G. Cumming, T. Okamoto, & L. Gomez (Eds.), *Proceedings of the 7th International Conference on Computers in Education—Advanced Research in Computers and Communications in Education: New Human Abilities for the Networked Society (ICCE'99)* (Volume 1, pp. 208-215).

Pantelidas, V.S. (1995). Reasons to use virtual reality in education. *VR in the Schools, 1*(1). Retrieved February 15, 2004, from *eastnet.educ.ecu.edu/vr/vr1n1a.txt*

Pantelidis, V.S. (1997). *Virtual reality (VR) as an instructional aid: A model for determining when to use VR.* Retrieved February 15, 2004, from *www.coe.ecu.edu/vr/vredmod.html*

Prestinenza Puglisi, L. (1999). *HyperArchitecture spaces in the electronic age.* Basel: Birkhäuser.

Rheingold, H. (2000). *The virtual community.* Boston: MIT Press.

Rosemblum, L.J. & Cross, R.A (1997). The challenge of virtual reality. In W.R. Earnshaw, J. Vince, & H. Jones (Eds.), *Visualization & modeling* (pp. 325-399). San Diego: Academic Press.

Sala, N. (2003). The role of new technologies to support the teaching and the learning of mathematics. *International Journal of Continuing Engineering Education and Lifelong Learning, 13*(3/4), 303-317.

Winn, W. (1996). *A conceptual basis for educational applications of virtual reality.* HITL Technical Report No. TR-93-9. Seattle, WA: Human Interface Technology Laboratory. Retrieved March 10, 2001, from *www.hitl.washington.edu/publications/r-93-9*

Youngblut, C. (1998). *Educational uses of virtual reality technology*. Institute for Defense Analyses, IDA Document D-2128. Retrieved June 5, 2001, from *www.hitl.washington.edu/scivw/youngblut-edvr/D2128.pdf*

Zoller, U. (1990). Students' misunderstandings and misconceptions in college freshman chemistry (general and organic). *Journal of Research in Science Teaching, 27*(10), 1053-1065.

About the Editor

David D. Carbonara is a teacher-researcher at Duquesne University, in Pittsburgh, Pennsylvania (USA). His field is instructional technology, in the School of Education. He teaches doctoral classes in Instructional Technology Leadership and Management. These classes conduct research in the visual representation of knowledge and the theoretical constructs of curriculum management, total cost of ownership and return on investment. Master's classes involve the integration of technology into the curriculum using instructional system design. Other master's classes construct technology integration plans that include curriculum alignment with ISTE standards along with curriculum management concepts. Undergraduate classes begin with information and computer literacy skills and expand into the instructional system design concepts and include applications in which technology can enhance the development and implementation of teaching materials and student learning environments. Dr. Carbonara's research interests begin with the identification of the basic skills, knowledge and disposition of pre-service and in-service educators. The second set of questions ask about the efficacy of these concepts on the teaching/learning process. One also has to ask the same set of questions of the schools, colleges, and departments of education (SCDE's). The impact of college professors on pre-service and in-service teachers is profound. Finally, due to the graphical nature of online learning, Dr. Carbonara is interested in the impact on cognition of the visual representation of knowledge.

About the Authors

For the past decade, **Palmer W. Agnew** has taught contact and online graduate courses in various aspects of multimedia, co-authored three books on related subjects, and published and consulted in this and related areas. Prior to this, for 31 years, he designed a wide variety of hardware, microcode, and software products and systems for the IBM Corporation. Before retiring from IBM, he was a senior technical staff member for seven years. At a development and manufacturing site that included 14,000 employees, he was one of six people who held the highest technical rank. He was one of the original evangelists and developers for hand-held and laptop computers and other mobile devices starting in the early 1980s. He ended his IBM career on the headquarters staff of the Multimedia and Education Division and Multimedia Business Unit, where both he and his co-author helped set the corresponding strategies for all of IBM and much of the industry. During this and several prior assignments, he enjoyed and benefited from traveling throughout the United States and most of the world from Austria to China, learning about and consulting on important aspects of multimedia, particularly in education. He holds six patents, three IBM Patent Achievement Awards, two Publication Achievement awards, and five Outstanding Contribution Awards.

Sandra Barker is a lecturer in the School of Accounting and Information Systems of the University of South Australia (Australia), where she has been based since 1999. She teaches internal and external students in Australia and Hong Kong. Her current subject areas are end-user development and desktop publishing for business at the undergraduate level and end-user development at the master's level. She previously owned her own business developing small-scale databases and designing business documents for the mining and fitness industries. She has an ongoing research interest in the area of end-user development of small-scale databases, as well as distance education, information literacy, and the implementation and development of graduate qualities.

Stefan L. Biancaniello has been a practicing educator for 35 years, serving students as a classroom teacher, building and central office administrator, and staff developer. As a member of the National Staff Development Council and the NSDC Academy X, he has worked with professional staff implementing standards for professional development and organizational leadership. Experience as a district fellow to the University of Pittsburgh Institute for Learning has provided him the opportunity to work with cognitive psychologists and instructional specialists on strategies and practices of standards-based instruction for all children. Twenty years of curriculum design and delivery has focused on the curriculum and cognition connection. He holds a PhD degree.

Daniel Brandon is a professor and the chairperson of the Information Technology Management Department at Christian Brothers University (CBU) in Memphis, Tennessee (USA). His education includes a BS and MS in engineering, and a PhD in engineering computation. He also holds the PMP (Project Management Professional) certification. His research interest is focused on software development and project management. In addition to his academic work at CBU, Dr. Brandon has more than 20 years of experience in the information systems industry, and he continues that commercial work today as an independent consultant and software developer.

D. Scott Brandt is professor of library science, and technology training librarian at Purdue University Libraries (USA). He oversees a technology training program for a combined staff and faculty of 175, and develops and implements 40-60 library information technology training courses yearly. His latest book, *Teaching Technology* (2002), applies principles of educational technology and instructional design to library-oriented environments. His research interests include investigating mental models of technology use and applying ISD to IT training. He is on the conference program committee for *Internet Librarian*, and an editorial reviewer for the international journal Online Information Review.

Kemal Cakici is a lead systems architect in the US Government and an adjunct instructor in the School of Business and Public Management at George Washington University. Prior to his current position, he worked at George Washington as a technology expert and advisor. He specializes in new technologies and applications of these technologies to health care, government, and higher education. He also consults and provides solutions in identifying information technology strategies for companies. Kemal holds a BS and MSc in Mechanical Engineering, and is pursuing a PhD in Information and Decision Systems at George Washington University.

Antonio Cartelli is a researcher in didactics and special pedagogy in the Faculty of Humanities at the University of Cassino (Italy). He earned his degree in Mathematics in 1976 at "La Sapienza" University in Rome, and after the degree received the special school diploma in Physics in 1983 at the same university. He teaches education, learning technologies, and ICT literacy in the science education course of his faculty and also manages the faculty center for ICT and online teaching. His main fields of interest are: conceptualization, misconceptions and mental schemes, the use of Web technologies in education, and e-learning.

Klarissa Ting-Ting Chang is a doctoral candidate in the Tepper School of Business at Carnegie Mellon University (USA). She holds a First Class Honors degree in computer and information sciences, an MSc in information systems from the National University of Singapore, and an MSIA in organizational behavior from the Carnegie Mellon University. Her research interests include social networks in distributed teams, psychological contracts of knowledge sharing, organizational learning, and educational application of collaborative technology.

Earl Chrysler has been associated with the MIS field for more than 30 years. During that time he has been a systems analyst for Ford Motor Company, a systems consultant for Laventhol and Horwath, CPAs, an independent consultant serving national and international clients, chair of the Computer Information Systems Department at Quinnipiac University, and professor of MIS at California State University, Chico, where he designed the initial MIS program, as well as at Quinnipiac University and Black Hills State University (USA). He has published or presented more than 40 papers in the MIS area and written chapters for two computer-related books.

Robert J. Colon is an associate professor of educational administration at Purdue University Calumet (USA). In addition to his work in administration, Dr. Colon serves as chair of the Graduate School in the School of Education. He has written several articles on school leadership and is a co-director of the Center for Educational Leadership.

Leighann S. Forbes is an instructor in the Secondary Education/Foundations of Education Department in the College of Education, Slippery Rock University (USA). She earned her MEd in School Administration from Edinboro University of Pennsylvania, an Instructional Technology Specialist certificate from Gannon University, and is currently enrolled in EdDIT, the instructional technology doctoral program, at Duquesne University. Forbes also has 15 years of experience teaching in Pennsylvania public and charter K-12 schools. She is experienced as both a new teacher mentor and technology mentor teacher. Her research interests focus on mentoring and the use of Internet content in K-12 education.

Pamela M. Frampton is an associate professor at Purdue University Calumet in Hammond, Indiana. Prior to her university work, she served as a teacher and principal in the Lafayette, Indiana (USA), public schools. In addition to her work as executive director of the Center for Educational Leadership, and the director of the Purdue Calumet and Northwest Indiana Schools Professional Development Partnership, she serves as the state university representative on the Indiana Professional Standards Board Committee for administrative licensure. She is published in several journals concerning school reform and leadership.

Jerry P. Galloway is an associate professor of education at Indiana University Northwest (USA) and the coordinator of computer education. Dr. Galloway has been involved in computer education for teachers for over two decades, beginning at the University of

Houston in the 1970s. With almost 50 published articles in educational computing and several books, Dr. Galloway has also published two electronic textbooks on CD-ROM, the latest of which is titled, *Educational Computing in the Electronic Age*. Dr. Galloway consults with Gary School Corporation, local businesses, and school districts. He is also the astronomy lecturer for the Royal Caribbean Cruise Lines.

Gerard L. Hanley is the executive director of MERLOT (USA) and senior director for academic technology services for the California State University. At MERLOT, he directs the development, delivery, and sustainability of MERLOT's organization and services to enhance teaching and learning with academic technologies. At CSU, Dr. Hanley oversees the development and implementation of integrated electronic library resources and academic technology initiatives supporting CSU's 23 campuses. He is also the director of the Center for Usability in Design and Assessment (CUDA) at the California State University, Long Beach. Previously held positions in the CSU include professor of psychology, director of faculty development and, director of strategic planning. He received his degrees from SUNY at Stony Brook in Psychology and has published in a variety of areas including cognition, learning, memory, neuroscience, clinical and community psychology, educational processes & assessment, critical thinking, industrial & organizational psychology, human factors, knowledge engineering, and technology in higher education.

June K. Hilton has taught all levels of secondary and postsecondary science and mathematics. She has served as Mathematics and Science Department chair in three secondary schools. She holds teaching credentials in Rhode Island, New Jersey, and California, and has National Board Certification in Adolescent/Young Adult Science–Physics. She received her PhD in Education from Claremont Graduate University in December 2003. Her research centers on the use of technology to increase student achievement.

Kim Johnson Hyatt is the graduate program coordinator for elementary education at Duquesne University (USA). As an assistant professor, she specializes in teacher education, gifted education, literacy education, and team teaching. She also works as an educational consultant and in-service program instructor. Dr. Hyatt has spent more than 10 years in K-12 schools, working in diverse capacities as an instructional leader, teacher, and sign language interpreter. She belongs to many professional organizations that support educational research, technology integration, and student-centered approaches to learning.

For the past decade, **Anne S. Kellerman** has taught contact and online graduate courses in various aspects of multimedia, co-authored three books on related subjects, and published and consulted in this area and in related areas. Before retiring from IBM, she managed and contributed to strategic, innovative projects involving many areas of the computer business. She also managed large joint projects with major universities, including UCLA (for networking initiatives), University of Michigan (the Institutional File System), and MIT (the Media

Lab), and represented IBM in a national kindergarten-through-twelfth-grade education initiative. Her last positions at IBM involved setting company-wide strategies for consumer products and multimedia. She holds five patents. She especially enjoys helping interesting groups of people use technology effectively, meaningfully, and enjoyably. She has a special interest in constructing educational multimedia content that documents the histories of people. She edits an educational multimedia site on Suite101 and is a frequent reviewer of scholarly publications for Computing Reviews of the ACM. She has been online for a large fraction of her waking hours since 1984, when she pioneered IBM's Home Terminal Program.

Barbara E. Kemmerer is associate professor of management at Eastern Illinois University (USA). She received her PhD in Business Administration from the University of Nebraska-Lincoln. Her research interests include management history, group dynamics, and academic assessment.

Jaroslav Král graduated in 1959 at from the Faculty of Mathematics and Physics of Charles University, Prague (Czech Republic). Since 1959 he has been working in Computer Science at the Czech Academy of Sciences, Czech Technical University, Masaryk University Brno, and Charles University Prague. His research interests were random number generators and simulations, hash methods, combinatorial problems connected with the problem of optimal program segmentation, formal language theory, parsing and compiler construction, and the development of process control systems. His present interests are the development of large information systems, software confederations, education of software experts, and computational linguists. Professor Král published more than 100 publications in international journals and at international conferences, and took part (mainly as the project leader) in several successful projects focused on macroprocessors, compilers, flexible manufacturing systems, and automated warehouse systems. He is now a full professor at the Faculty of Mathematical Physics of Charles University and a visiting professor at the Faculty of Informatics of Masaryk University Brno.

John Lim is associate professor of computing at the National University of Singapore (Singapore). He currently heads the Information Systems Research Lab. He graduated with First Class Honors in Electrical Engineering and an MSc in MIS from the National University of Singapore, and a PhD from the University of British Columbia. His current research interests include IT and education, e-commerce, collaborative technology, negotiation support, and IS implementation. He has published in MIS and related journals, including the *Journal of Management Information Systems, Journal of Global Information Management, Decision Support Systems, International Journal of Human Computer Studies, Organizational Behavior and Human Decision Processes, Behavior and Information Technology, Journal of Database Management,* and *Small Group Research.*

Mara Linaberger is currently serving as writing and technology specialist at Dilworth Traditional Academy for the Arts and Humanities in the Pittsburgh Public School District

(USA). In that capacity, she mentors and teaches collaboratively with colleagues, serving students in grades K-5. She has conducted a number of technology integration workshops for teachers in the school district. Linaberger received her Master's of Arts in Teaching from the University of Pittsburgh and is currently enrolled in Duquesne University's doctoral program in Instructional Technology. Her research interests include teacher attitudes towards technology use and training, as well as technology mentoring.

Glenn Lowry is professor of management information systems in the College of Business and Economics of the United Arab Emirates University (UAE), where he was foundation executive director of MBA. He holds a PhD from Rutgers University. A charter member of the Association for Information Systems (AIS), Dr. Lowry has held a number of senior academic posts in Australia and the US. His research and teaching interests include software engineering, systems development, organizational technology uptake and change management, diffusion of innovation, and research methods. An editor of the *Journal of Information Technology Education* and member of the editorial board of the *Journal for Information Technology Theory and Application,* Dr. Lowry has authored or edited six books and more than 75 refereed papers in the discipline.

Rose Mary Mautino is an assistant professor at Duquesne University's School of Education (USA). Dr. Mautino is the Duquesne University Reading Clinic director, coordinator of Graduate Reading and Language Arts program, and a member of the design team for the undergraduate "Literacy Block," which is part of the Leading Teacher Program at Duquesne University. She also is a committee member of the Professional Development Schools and has presented several times at national PDS conferences. Her educational experiences include classroom teaching, reading specialist, supervisor, administrative curriculum coordinator, and professor in higher education. Currently she is involved in the redesign of the Graduate Reading and Language Arts program at Duquesne University which uses International Reading Association standards as its framework.

Ann Monday is a lecturer in the School of Accounting and Information Systems of the University of South Australia (Australia), where she has been based since 1997. She teaches internal and external students in Australia and Hong Kong. Her current subject areas are decision support and end-user development at the undergraduate level, and information and systems for competitive advantage at master's level. She previously worked in the UK tertiary sector for 17 years teaching a range of information systems subjects at undergraduate and masters' levels. She has also taught in Singapore. Previous research was in the area of quality monitoring in the manufacturing sector and more recently in education, supply chain management in the wine industry, e-mail policy, and end-user development and decision support.

Michael S. Mott is an assistant professor of literacy and early childhood education at Purdue University Calumet (USA). Dr. Mott has conducted, presented, and published research findings in literacy, technology, and writing assessment. Prior to working at Purdue, he taught elementary school in the New York City Public Schools and at the Lowell School in Washington, DC, for a total of nine years. Current interests and projects address literacy improvement for children in school districts in Northwest Indiana and the South Suburban Chicago metropolitan area, and adult learning in professional teacher education through teaching, service, and scholarship.

Karen S. Nantz is a professor of computer information systems at Eastern Illinois University (USA), where she teaches database, management of information systems, and computer concepts and applications. She serves as an associate editor of the *Journal of Information Technology Education* and is on the editorial review boards of several information systems journals. She is certified to administer and evaluate the Myers-Briggs Type Inventory. Her research interests include information ethics, the role of personality in information systems professions, and the appropriate uses of technology for enterprise communications.

Franco Orsucci received his first degree in Medicine and second degree in Psychiatry at La Sapienza University in Rome (Italy). He has been a researcher at the Italian National Research Council. Now he is professor of clinical psychology and psychiatry at the Catholic University and Gemelli University Hospital in Rome. He is also a research fellow at the London University College, and editor-in-chief of *Chaos and Complexity Letters—International Journal of Dynamical System Research* (Nova Science, New York). His last published books are *Changing Mind, Transitions in Natural and Artificial Environments* (World Scientific, Singapore, 2003) and *Bioethics in Complexity* (Imperial College Press, London, 2004). He has also published about 80 scientific articles on neuroscience and cognitive science.

Marco Palma is professor of Latin palaeography in the Faculty of Humanities of the University of Cassino (Italy). His main research interests are the morphology and development of different scripts of books and charters in the Western Middle Ages. He is also working on the material aspects of manuscripts, as well the transmission of classic and medieval texts before the invention of printing. He is particularly interested in the theoretical and practical problems of the description of medieval manuscripts, and the diffusion of scientific information and didactic contents through the Internet.

Katia Passerini is assistant professor of MIS at the School of Management of the New Jersey Institute of Technology (USA), where she teaches graduate and undergraduate courses in MIS, e-commerce, and IT strategy. Dr. Passerini has published in a number of refereed journals and proceedings, particularly in the area of computer-mediated learning, IT productivity, and knowledge management. Her professional IT experience includes multi-industry work at Booz Allen Hamilton and the World Bank. She holds a PhD in information systems and an MBA from George Washington University.

Jonathan D. Pemberton is a senior lecturer and senior researcher in organizational and individual performance at Newcastle Business School, Northumbria University (UK). He lectures in a range of subjects, including quantitative business research, forecasting, and strategic knowledge management. His research interests and publications cover socio-technical issues of knowledge management, knowledge management and competitive advantage, organizational and individual learning, technology initiatives, and knowledge management in general practice.

Sorel Reisman is professor of information systems in the College of Business at California State University, Fullerton (CSUF); academic technology coordinator at CSUF; and special consultant on academic technology to the California State University Office of the Chancellor. His teaching, research, publications, and presentation concern multimedia, information systems development, the management of information technology, e-commerce, electronic communities, and Internet-based distance learning. Dr. Reisman is a member of the IEEE Computer Society's Publications Board, as well as the Electronic Products and Services Board, where he is responsible for initiatives related to print publications, digital libraries, distance learning, online books, and electronic communities. He serves as an editorial board member on a number of information and academic technology online and print journals. His books include *Multimedia Computing: Preparing for the 21st Century* (1996) and *Electronic Learning Communities—Issues and Practices* (2003).

Massimo Sala received his engineering degree from Politecnico of Milan (Italy). He is a high school professor of technology and mechanics, as well as in the Laboratory of Mathematics in Italy. He is assistant professor at the Accademia di Architettura, Mendrisio (Switzerland), and chair of computer graphics and new media. He studies the multimedia and new technologies in education, and in particular the use of virtual reality in architecture, engineering, and design.

Nicoletta Sala received her degree in physics and applied cybernetics from the State University of Milan, Italy, and her PhD in communication science from the Università della Svizzera Italiana of Lugano (Switzerland). She completed an additional four years of postgraduate work on the topics of didactics of the communication and multimedia technologies and journalism and mass media. She currently is professor of mathematics, teaching Mathematics Thought, and Computer Graphics and New Media at the Academy of Architecture of Mendrisio, Università della Svizzera Italiana, Switzerland. She is co-editor of the *Chaos and Complexity Letters International Journal of Dynamical System Research* (Nova Science, New York). He research now focuses on the new media in education, and in particular the use of virtual reality in architecture and design. She has written 14 mathematics and information technology textbooks, and several scientific papers dedicated to new media in education.

Silvia L. Sapone is the graduate program coordinator for secondary education and graduate mathematics advisor in the Department of Instruction and Leadership at

Duquesne University in Pittsburgh, Pennsylvania. As an assistant professor, her research interests include teacher preparation, coaching/mentoring of teachers and principals, differentiated instruction, and team teaching. Prior to joining the university, Dr. Sapone was an elementary principal, assistant middle school principal, and teacher in the Mt. Lebanon School District. She also works as an educational consultant and in-service program instructor.

Maureen Diana Sasso is director of the Information Services Division of the Gumberg Library at Duquesne University (USA). She earned her master's degree and advanced certificate in library science from the University of Pittsburgh's School of Information Sciences. She joined the Reference Department in 1986 and was appointed director of the Information Services Division in 1991. She has been a leader in Duquesne's information literacy efforts, coordinating the team that designed and implemented a mandatory freshman course, and co-chairing the Provost's Information Literacy Steering Committee. Her accreditation experience includes serving as an evaluator on Middle States visiting teams and participating in Duquesne's most recent self-studies. In 2003 she served on Duquesne's Periodic Review Committee, chairing the Institutional Resources Taskforce.

Jennifer Sharkey is assistant professor of library science and information integration librarian at Purdue University Libraries (USA). She oversees the Digital Learning Collaboratory, a student-focused collaborative/active learning facility where technology and information literacy are merged into course projects and curriculum. She partners with faculty to help them incorporate information literacy into their courses and enhance their course projects with multimedia components. She lectures for numerous courses focusing on the research process, credible electronic resources, and selected multimedia applications. Her research interests include the application of graphic design, instructional design, and Web design principles for course development, as well as creative incorporation of information literacy and technology into curricula.

George Stonehouse is associate dean for postgraduate programs at Newcastle Business School, Northumbria University (UK), and specializes in strategic management, global and transnational business, and organizational learning. He is a visiting professor at a number of institutions in Russia and China. As well as publishing a number of texts in strategic management and global business, he has written several journal articles on organizational learning, knowledge management, strategic management, and competitive advantage.

Lawrence A. Tomei is an assistant professor at Duquesne University's School of Education (USA) and director of its program in international technology. Born in Akron, Ohio, he earned a BSBA from the University of Akron (1972) and entered the U.S. Air Force, serving until his retirement as a Lt. Colonel in 1994. Dr. Tomei completed his MPA and MEd at the University of Oklahoma (1975, 1978) and his EdD at USC (1983). His articles and books on instructional technology include: *Professional Portfolios for*

Teachers (1999), *Teaching Digitally: Integrating Technology into the Classroom* (2001), *Technology Façade* (2002), *Challenges of Teaching with Technology Across the Curriculum* (2003), and *Taxonomy for the Technology Domain* (2004).

Anastasia M. Trekles is the coordinator of education media and technology for the School of Education at Purdue University Calumet (USA). Additionally, she is an instructor for undergraduate courses in instructional technology, and she serves as the technical director for the Center for Educational Leadership. Ms. Trekles obtained her undergraduate degree in English from Purdue University Calumet, and is currently working toward a Master's in Instructional Technology.

Rodney Turner is a lecturer in the School of Information Systems at Victoria University, Melbourne (Australia). Previously he worked in industry and was a teacher for 12 years. He is a graduate of Monash University, RMIT, and Melbourne CAE with qualifications in science, mathematics education, computer education, and information technology. He is currently engaged in research leading towards a PhD. His main research interests are in IS education and the skills required in a changing IS environment. He has consulted for government aid projects in the Philippines and China, and has authored more than 20 papers in refereed journals and conferences in the discipline.

Ellen Whybrow has had a long career dealing with marginalized groups and projects that reside outside the mainstream. She completed an interdisciplinary master's degree in Instructional Technology and Adult Education in 2000, and is currently an instructional designer in the Faculty of Extension at the University of Alberta (Canada), where she works in the design, project management, and delivery of both blended and online environments and programs. Her contribution to this text builds on research interests she has in the lives of disadvantaged students who are pursuing post-secondary education.

Junko Yamamoto teaches Japanese at Mt. Lebanon High School in Pittsburgh, Pennsylvania (USA). She has also taught at the University of Pittsburgh and at Shady Side Academy Junior School, also in Pittsburgh. She has assisted elementary, secondary, and higher education faculties with integrating technology into their classroom through workshops and mentoring. Her special interests are faculty training and Computer-Assisted Language Learning (CALL). Ms. Yamamoto is currently working towards an EdD in Instructional Technologies at Duquesne University. She holds a master's degree in Public and International Affairs from the University of Pittsburgh and a bachelor's degree in Business Administration from Ritsumeikan University, Kyoto, Japan.

Michal Žemlička an assistant professor on the Faculty of Mathematics and Physics of Charles University, Prague (Czech Republic). He graduated in 1996. His current research interests are extensible compilers, parsing theory, design of large software systems, data structures, and computational linguistics.

Index

D

E

K

L

M

N

O

P

Q

R

U

V

W

ENCYCLOPEDIA OF
DATA WAREHOUSING AND MINING

ENCYCLOPEDIA OF
DATABASE
TECHNOLOGIES
AND APPLICATIONS

ENCYCLOPEDIA OF
Multimedia Technology and Networking